For Her Own Good

150 Years of the Experts' Advice to Women

Barbara Ehrenreich
Deirdre English

ANCHOR PRESS/DOUBLEDAY
GARDEN CITY, NEW YORK
1978

ISBN: 0-385-12650-6
Library of Congress Catalog Card Number 77-76234
Copyright © 1978 by Barbara Ehrenreich and Deirdre English
All Rights Reserved
Printed in the United States of America
First Edition

To our mothers,
Fanita English and Isabelle Isely

Contents

THE FALL OF THE EXPERTS

Authors' Note

The first glimmerings of the ideas which were to lead to this book came in 1972, when we were co-teaching a course on "Women and Health" at the College at Old Westbury (State University of New York). Preparation for the course led us along a surprising trail which stretched from the persecution of witches in medieval Europe to the suppression of midwives in America, from the nineteenth-century epidemic of hysteria to the mid-twentieth century epidemic of "frigidity." Perhaps because we are not professional historians (or social scientists of any kind), we approached this material in a spirit of fresh discovery. We had the feeling that we were uncovering a long-suppressed story, one which had the power to explain many things about our own present-day experience as women. Our students —almost all "older" women who had raised families and held down jobs for many years—not only encouraged our research but contributed their own experiences as nurses, nurses' aides, housewives, mothers, healers, and would-be healers of all varieties.

At the same time, in 1972, a women's health movement—composed of women health workers, community activists, and dissatisfied health care consumers—was taking form as a distinct feminist force. In the midst of heated discussions about the direction of the new movement, we decided to try to write out some of our research and ideas from the course. The first result was a booklet *Witches, Midwives and Nurses: A History of Women Healers*. We filled the text with illustrations, paid to have it printed, and for over a year mailed it to people who wrote for copies, working from a kitchen-table office. To our surprise, demand for this pamphlet quickly outgrew our capacity to distribute it. Fortunately The Feminist Press, in Old Westbury, New York, offered to take over publication and distribution, and later to publish a second, companion booklet, *Complaints and Disorders: The Sexual Politics of Sickness.**

The response to the two booklets (which were never advertised) was both overwhelming and unexpectedly diverse. They served as discussion material for dissident grassroots health organizations and they found their way onto the required reading lists of some of the most elite nursing schools. They were adopted in university women's studies programs and, we were told, were passed from hand to hand among women hospital workers. They were discussed, excerpted or reviewed in publications as different from each other as professional journals, underground newspapers and the "Scenes" column of *The Village Voice*. Friends and acquaintances told us that they discovered the booklets in such places as feminist bookstores, medical libraries, and in the waiting rooms of community health centers. Best of all, we heard from hundreds of readers—ranging from an illegal midwife in Texas to a Catholic nursing sister in New Jersey, from suburban housewives to participants in the growing feminist counterculture, from well-known professors to lower-rank hospital workers. Some offered us bits of information or pieces from their own life experiences, or sent books or articles they thought we should see. In every way they encouraged us to keep on working.

So in 1974 we began work on this book. At first we intended simply to expand the material in the pamphlets and bring the historical themes up to the present. But the project soon outgrew this modest goal. For one thing, the amount of available material (ranging from academic articles to the dozens of unpublished papers people sent us) on the original themes of the pamphlets had expanded severalfold since our first researches in 1972. Just to incorporate all the new information we had to expand our conceptual framework greatly. For another thing, we took an open-ended approach to our work—following out-of-the-way trails as the spirit moved us and willingly straying into areas and ideas quite remote from our original theme of women and medicine. If at times we had a hard time explaining what we were doing to anyone, we had the satisfaction of seeing an unexpected pat-

* *Witches, Midwives, and Nurses,* 48 pp. illus., $1.95. *Complaints and Disorders,* 96 pp. illus., $2.50, both available by mail from The Feminist Press, Box 334, Old Westbury, New York 11568.

tern fall into place, something much more sweeping than anything we had originally intended.

These were good years to be working in. Feminist scholarship began its explosive growth in the colleges and women's studies programs. The women's health movement expanded, and took daring steps toward self-help and lay midwifery. Networks of activists were set up, nationally and internationally. We were fortunate to be able to visit dozens of women's projects around the country. One of us (B.E.) worked with HealthRight, a New York-based women's health project, and we both made inspiring contact with the organizers of the Feminist Women's Health Centers. We took part in innumerable meetings, study groups, pot-luck dinners, conferences, etc., with women who were willing to share their ideas and help us develop ours. We debated, we corresponded, we participated—and what we have written reflects not just our solitary research, but a whole milieu we have been lucky enough to inhabit.

It would be impossible then to acknowledge by name every person to whom we are indebted for information, ideas, criticism, and encouragement. But we would like to single out those people who made the special effort to read and discuss drafts with us: Diane Alexander, Rick Brown, Beth Cagan, Anne Farrar (and other editors of *Socialist Review*), Rachel Fruchter, Diane Horwitz, and Barbara Waterman. Others who read various chapters and gave us their comments include Ros Baxandall, Claudia Carr, Betts Collett, Barbara Easton, Candace Falk, Steve Karakashian, Carol Lopate, Joy Marcus, Gail Pellett, Susan Reverby, Gary Stevenson, Steve Talbot and Shirley Whitney.

Many people contributed their skills and support in the writing and production of this book—Verne Moberg, Margery Cuyler, and Brian English—who gave us brotherly encouragement along with practical advice. Loretta Barrett, our editor at Anchor Press, and Kathy O'Donnell, her assistant, not only made the publication of this book possible but also worked hard to make it lively and readable. Iris Jones typed the final draft and managed to correct thousands of errors. In addition, we thank the many librarians who helped us with our frequently farfetched requests.

We also thank Maurice English for his support as a father and fellow writer and Elena Ottolenghi for her generous encouragement. Rosa and Benjy Ehrenreich provided us with affection, comic relief, and sometimes even concrete help.

There are two people to whom we owe a special intellectual debt: Liz Ewen, whose combination of blunt criticism and intellectual insight was a constant stimulus, and John Ehrenreich—loving friend, ruthless editor, and an irrepressible source of ideas.

ONE

Introduction:
The Romantic Solution

"If you would get up and do something you would feel better," said my mother. I rose drearily, and essayed to brush up the floor a little, with a dustpan and small whiskbroom, but soon dropped those implements exhausted, and wept again in helpless shame.

I, the ceaselessly industrious, could do no work of any kind. I was so weak that the knife and fork sank from my hands—too tired to eat. I could not read nor write nor paint nor sew nor talk nor listen to talking, nor anything. I lay on the lounge and wept all day. The tears ran down into my ears on either side. I went to bed crying, woke in the night crying, sat on the edge of the bed in the morning and cried —from sheer continuous pain. Not physical, the doctors examined me and found nothing the matter.[1]

It was 1885 and Charlotte Perkins Stetson had just given birth to a daughter, Katherine. "Of all angelic babies that darling was the best, a heavenly baby." And yet young Mrs. Stetson wept and wept, and when she nursed her baby "the tears ran down on my breast. . . ."

The doctors told her she had "nervous prostration." To her it felt like "a sort of gray fog [had] drifted across my mind, a cloud that grew and darkened." The fog never entirely lifted from the life of Charlotte Perkins Stetson (later Gilman). Years later, in the midst of an active career as a feminist writer and lecturer, she would find herself overcome by the same lassitude, incapable of making the smallest decision, mentally numb.

Depression struck Charlotte Perkins Gilman when she was only twenty-five years old, energetic and intelligent, a woman who seemed to have her life open before her. It hit young Jane Addams—the famous social reformer—at the same time of life. Addams was affluent, well-educated for a girl, ambitious to study medicine. Then, in 1881, at the age of twenty-one, she fell into a "nervous depression" which paralyzed her for seven years and haunted her long after she began her work at Hull-House in the Chicago slums. She was gripped by "a sense of futility, of misdirected energy" and was conscious of her estrangement from "the active, emotional life" within the family which had automatically embraced earlier generations of women. "It was doubtless true," she later wrote of her depression, "that I was

> 'Weary of myself and sick of asking
> What I am and what I ought to be.' "

Margaret Sanger—the birth control crusader—was another case. She was twenty years old, happily married, and, physically at least, seemed to be making a good recovery from tuberculosis. Suddenly she stopped getting out of bed, refused to talk. In the outside world, Theodore Roosevelt was running for President on the theme of the "strenuous life." But when relatives asked Margaret Sanger what she would like to do, she could only say, "Nothing." "Where would you like to go?" they persisted: "Nowhere."

Ellen Swallow (later Ellen Richards—founder of the early-twentieth-century domestic science movement) succumbed when she was twenty-four. She was an energetic, even compulsive, young woman; and, like Addams, felt estranged from the intensely domestic life her mother had led. Returning home from a brief period of independence, she fell into a depression which left her almost too weak to do household chores. "Lay down sick . . ." she entered in her diary, "Oh so tired . . ." and on another day, "Wretched," and again, "tired."

It was as if they had come to the brink of adult life and then refused to go on. They stopped in their tracks, paralyzed. The problem wasn't a lack of things to do. Charlotte Perkins Gilman, like Jane Addams, felt "intense shame" that she was not up and about. All of them had family responsibilities to meet; all but Jane Addams had houses to run. They were women with other interests too—science, or art, or philosophy—and all of them were passionately idealistic. And yet, for a while, they could not go on.

For, in the new world of the nineteenth century, what was a woman to do? Did she build a life, like her aunts and her mother, in the warmth of the family—or did she throw herself into the nervous activism of a world which was already presuming to call itself "modern"? Either way, wouldn't she be ridiculous, a kind of a misfit? Certainly out of place if she tried to fit into the "men's world" of business, politics, science. But in a historical sense, perhaps even more out of place if she remained in the home, isolated from the grand march of industry and progress. "She was intelligent and generous;" Henry James wrote of the heroine in *Portrait of a Lady,* "it was a fine free nature; but what was she going to do with herself?"

Certainly the question had been asked before Charlotte Perkins Gilman's and Jane Addams' generation, and certainly other women had collapsed because they did not have the answers. But only in the last one hundred years or so in the Western world does this private dilemma surface as a gripping public issue—the Woman Question or "the woman problem." The misery of a Charlotte Gilman or Jane Addams, the crippling indecisiveness, is amplified in the nineteenth and twentieth centuries among tens of thousands of women. A minority transform their numbness into anger and become activists in reform movements; many—the ones whose names we don't know—remained permanently depressed, bewildered, sick.

Men, men of the "establishment"—physicians, philosophers, scientists—addressed themselves to the Woman Question in a constant stream of books and articles. For while women were discovering new questions and doubts, men were discovering that women were themselves a question, an anomaly when viewed from the busy world of industry. They couldn't be included in the men's world, yet they no longer seemed to fit in their traditional place. "Have you any notion how many books are written about women in the course of one year?" Virginia Woolf asked an audience of women. "Have you any notion how many are written by men? Are you aware that you are, perhaps, the most discussed animal in the universe?" From a masculine point of view the Woman Question was a problem of control: Woman had become an issue, a social problem—something to be investigated, analyzed, and solved.

This book is about the scientific answer to the Woman Question, as elaborated over the last hundred years by a new class of experts—physicians, psychologists, domestic scientists, child-raising experts. These men—and, more rarely, women—presented themselves as authorities on the painful dilemma confronted by Charlotte Perkins Gilman, Jane Addams, and so many others: What is woman's true nature? And what, in an industrial world which no longer honored women's traditional skills, was she to *do?* Physicians were the first of the new experts. With claims to knowledge encompassing all of human biological existence, they were the first to pass judgment on the social consequences of female anatomy and to prescribe the "natural" life plan for women. They were followed by a horde of more specialized experts, each group claiming dominion over some area of women's lives, and all claiming that their authority flowed directly from biological science. In the first part of this book we will trace the rise of the psychomedical experts, focusing on medicine as a paradigm of professional authority. In the second part of the book we will see how the experts used their authority to define women's domestic activities down to the smallest details of housework and child raising. With each subject area we will move ahead in time until we reach the present and the period of the *decline* of the experts—our own time, when the Woman Question has at last been reopened for new answers.

The relationship between women and the experts was not unlike conventional relationships between women and men. The experts wooed their female constituency, promising the "right" and scientific way to live, and women responded—most eagerly in the upper and middle classes, more slowly among the poor—with dependency and trust. It was never an equal relationship, for the experts' authority rested on the denial or destruction of women's autonomous sources of knowledge: the old networks of skill-sharing, the accumulated lore of generations of mothers. But it was a relationship that lasted right up to our own time, when women began to discover that the experts' answer to the Woman Question was not science after all, but only the ideology of a masculinist society, dressed up as objective truth. The reason why women would seek the "scientific" answer in the first place, and the reason why that answer would betray them in the end, are locked together in history. In the section which follows we go back to the origins of the Woman Question, when science was a fresh and liberating force, when women began to push out into an unknown world, and the romance between women and the experts began.

The Woman Question

The Woman Question arose in the course of a historic transformation whose scale later generations have still barely grasped. It was the "industrial revolution," and even "revolution" is too pallid a word. From the Scottish highlands to the Appalachian hills, from the Rhineland to the Mississippi Valley, whole villages were emptied to feed the factory system with human labor. People were wrested from the land suddenly, by force; or more subtly, by the pressure of hunger and debt—uprooted from the ancient security of family, clan, parish. A settled, agrarian life which had persisted more or less for centuries was destroyed in one tenth the time it had taken for the Roman Empire to fall, and the old ways of thinking, the old myths and old rules, began to lift like the morning fog.

Marx and Engels—usually thought of as the instigators of disorder rather than the chroniclers of it—were the first to grasp the cataclysmic nature of these changes. An old world was dying and a new one was being born:

> All fixed, fast-frozen relations, with their train of ancient and venerable prejudices and opinions, are swept away, all new-formed ones become antiquated before they can ossify. All that is solid melts into air, all that is holy is profaned, and man is at last compelled to face with sober senses his real conditions of life and his relations with his kind.[2]

Incredible, once unthinkable, possibilities opened up as all the "fixed, fast-frozen relations"—between man and woman, between parents and children, between the rich and the poor—were thrown into question. Over one hundred and fifty years later, the dust has still not settled.

On the far side of the industrial revolution is what we will call, for our purposes, the Old Order. Historians will mark off many "eras" within these centuries of agrarian life: royal lines, national boundaries, military technology, fashions, art and architecture—all evolve and change throughout the Old Order. History is made: there are conquests, explorations, new lines of trade. Nevertheless, for all the visible drama of history, the lives of ordinary people, doing ordinary things, change very little—and that only slowly.

Routine predominates at the level of everyday life: corn is sown as it
was always sown, maize planted, rice fields levelled, ships sail the
Red Sea as they have always sailed it.[3]

Only here, at the level of everyday life, do we find the patterns that
make this an "order." If these patterns are monotonous and repetitive compared to the spectacle of conventional history—with its brilliant personalities, military adventures and court intrigues—that is because these patterns are shaped by natural events which are also
monotonous and repetitive—seasons, plantings, the cycle of human
reproduction.

Three patterns of social life in the Old Order stand out and give it
consistency: the Old Order is *unitary*. There is of course always a minority of people whose lives—acted out on a plane above dull necessity and the routines of labor—are complex and surprising. But life,
for the great majority of people, has a unity and simplicity which will
never cease to fascinate the "industrial man" who comes later. This
life is not marked off into different "spheres" or "realms" of experience: "work" and "home," "public" and "private," "sacred" and
"secular." Production (of food, clothing, tools) takes place in the
same rooms or outdoor spaces where children grow up, babies are
born, couples come together. The family relation is not secluded in
the realm of emotion; it is a working relation. Biological life—sexual
desire, childbirth, sickness, the progressive infirmity of age—impinges
directly on the group activities of production and play. Ritual and superstition affirm the unity of body and earth, biology and labor: menstruating women must not bake bread; conception is most favored at
the time of the spring planting; sexual transgressions will bring blight
and ruin to the crops, and so on.

The human relations of family and village, knit by common labor
as well as sex and affection, are paramount. There is not yet an external "economy" connecting the fortunes of the peasant with the decisions of a merchant in a remote city. If people go hungry, it is not because the price of their crops fell, but because the rain did not. There
are marketplaces, but there is not yet *a market* to dictate the opportunities and activities of ordinary people.

The Old Order is *patriarchal:* authority over the family is vested in
the elder males, or male. He, the father, makes the decisions which
control the family's work, purchases, marriages. Under the rule of the
father, women have no complex choices to make, no questions as to

their nature or destiny: the rule is simply obedience. An early-nineteenth-century American minister counseled brides:

> Bear always in mind your true situation and have the words of the apostle perpetually engraven on your heart. Your duty is submission —"Submission and obedience are the lessons of your life and peace and happiness will be your reward." Your husband is, by the laws of God and of man, your superior; do not ever give him cause to remind you of it.[4]

The patriarchal order of the household is magnified in the governance of village, church, nation. At home was the father, in church was the priest or minister, at the top were the "town fathers," the local nobility, or, as they put it in Puritan society "the nursing fathers of the Commonwealth," and above all was "God the Father."

Thus the patriarchy of the Old Order was reinforced at every level of social organization and belief. For women, it was total, inescapable. Rebellious women might be beaten privately (with official approval) or punished publicly by the village "fathers," and any woman who tried to survive on her own would be at the mercy of random male violence.

But the rule of the fathers is not based on mere coercion. Patriarchal authority seeks to justify itself in the minds of each of its children, and this justification takes the form of a father-centered religion. Religion projects the rule of the father into the firmament where it becomes the supreme law of nature—and then reflects this majesty back on each earthly father in his household.

> He was her superior, the head of the family, and she owed him an obedience founded on reverence. He stood before her in the place of God: he exercised the authority of God over her, and he furnished her with the fruits of the earth that God had provided.[5]

And yet, to a degree that is almost unimaginable from our vantage point within industrial society, the Old Order is *gynocentric:* the skills and work of women are indispensable to survival. Woman is always subordinate, but she is far from being a helpless dependent. Women of the industrial world would later look back enviously on the full, productive lives of their foremothers. Consider the work of a woman in colonial America:

> It was the wife's duty, with the assistance of daughters and women servants, to plant the vegetable garden, breed the poultry, and care for

the dairy cattle. She transformed milk into cream, butter and cheese, and butchered livestock as well as cooked the meals. Along with her daily chores the husbandwoman slated, pickled, preserved, and manufactured enough beer and cider to see the family through the winter. Still, the woman's work was hardly done. To clothe the colonial population, women not only plied the needle, but operated wool carders and spinning wheels—participated in the manufacture of thread, yarn and cloth as well as apparel. Her handwrought candles lit the house; medicines of her manufacture restored the family to health; her homemade soap cleansed her home and family. . . .[6]

It was not only women's productive skills which gave her importance in the Old Order. She knew the herbs that healed, the songs to soothe a feverish child, the precautions to be taken during pregnancy. If she was exceptionally skilled, she became a midwife, herbal healer or "wise woman," whose fame might spread from house to house and village to village. And all women were expected to have learned, from their mothers and grandmothers, the skills of raising children, healing common illnesses, nursing the sick.

So there could be no Woman Question in the Old Order. Woman's work was cut out for her; the lines of authority that she was to follow were clear. She could hardly think of herself as a "misfit" in a world which depended so heavily on her skills and her work. Nor could she imagine making painful decisions about the direction of her life, for, within the patriarchal order, all decisions of consequence would be made *for* her by father or husband, if they were not already determined by tradition. The Woman Question awaits the arrival of the industrial epoch which, in the space of a few generations, will overthrow all the "fixed, fast-frozen relations" of the Old Order. The unity of biological and economic, private and public, life will be shattered; the old patriarchs will be shaken from their thrones; and—at the same time—the ancient powers of women will be expropriated.

The fundamental social transformation, of which even industrialization was a correlate and not a cause, was the triumph of the Market economy. In the Old Order production had been governed by natural factors—human needs for food and shelter, and the limits of the labor and resources available. Only the occasional surplus would be sold or bartered. But in the Market economy the laws of commercial exchange would dictate the employment of human labor and resources. The parochialism of household production would break down to make way for a vast network of economic interdependencies linking the livelihood of the farmer to the townsman, the Northerner to the Southerner. This network of dependencies—the Market—had been gaining ground inch by inch throughout the late Middle Ages. But it was for a long time a creature of the cities, this infant capitalism. Most people—over ninety-five per cent—still lived on the land, in the "natural economy" of the Old Order. Only in the nineteenth century, with industrialization and the development of modern capitalism, did the Market come to replace nature as the controlling force in the lives of ordinary people: prices regulate existence as surely as rainfall and temperature once did—and seem just as arbitrary. Depressions are calamities on the scale of famines or epidemics, spilling over national boundaries and seeking out the most innocent, the most insignificant, victim.

With the triumph of the Market, the settled patterns of life which defined the Old Order were shattered irrevocably. The old unity of work and home, production and family life, was necessarily and decisively ruptured. Henceforth the household would no longer be a more or less self-contained unit, binding its members together in common work. When production entered the factory, the household was left with only the most personal biological activities—eating, sex, sleeping, the care of small children, and (until the rise of institutional medicine) birth and dying and the care of the sick and aged. Life would now be experienced as divided into two distinct spheres: a "public" sphere of endeavor governed ultimately by the Market; and a "private" sphere of intimate relationships and individual biological existence.

This new ordering of the world is not to be imagined as a mere compartmentalization, along some neutral dividing line. The two spheres stand, in respect to their basic values, *opposed* to each other, and the line between them is charged with moral tension. In its most fundamental operations the Market defies centuries of religious morality which (in principle, at least) exalted altruism and selflessness while it condemned covetousness and greed. In the Old Order commerce was tainted with dishonor, and lending money at interest was denounced as usury. But the Market which dominates the new order dismisses all moral categories with cold indifference. Profits can only be won by some at the price of poverty for others and there is no room for human affection, generosity, or loyalty. The greatest dramas of the marketplace—profits, losses, bankruptcies, investments, sales— can be recounted quite adequately as a series of numbers; the most brilliant moments are recorded in double-entry ledger books; and the human costs make no difference on the "bottom line."

In the face of the Market, all that is "human" about people must crowd into the sphere of private life, and attach itself, as best it can, to the personal and biological activities which remain there. Only in the home, or private life generally, can one expect to find the love, spontaneity, nurturance or playfulness which are denied in the marketplace. Sentiment may exaggerate the emotional nobility of the home, and gloss over its biological realities. But private life does, almost necessarily, invert the values of the Market: here what is produced, like the daily meals, is made for no other purpose than to meet immediate human needs; people are indeed valued "for themselves" rather than for their marketable qualities; services and affection are given freely, or at least given. For men, who must cross between the two spheres daily, private life now takes on a sentimental appeal in proportion to the coldness and impersonality of the "outside" world. They look to the home to fulfill both the bodily needs denied at the workplace, and the human solidarity forbidden in the Market.

At the same time, the forces which divide life into "public" and "private" spheres throw into question the place and the function of women. The iron rule of patriarchy has been shaken, opening up undreamed of possibilities. But at the same time the womanly skills which the economy of the Old Order had depended on have been torn away—removing what had been the source of woman's dignity in even the most oppressive circumstances. Consider these changes, with their contradictory implications for women's status:

It was the end of the gynocentric order. The traditional productive skills of women—textile manufacture, garment manufacture, food processing—passed into the factory system. Women of the working class might follow their old labor into the new industrial world, but they would no longer command the productive process. They would forget the old skills. In time, as we shall see, even the quintessentially feminine activity of healing would be transformed into a commodity and swept into the Market. The homemade herbal tonic is replaced by the chemical products of multinational drug firms; midwives are replaced by surgeons.

But, at the same time, it was the end of the rule of the father. Patriarchal privilege, of course, allows men to claim the new public world of industry and commerce as their own. But the ancient network of patriarchal social relations had been irreversibly undermined by the new economy. As the production of necessary goods goes out of the home, the organic bonds holding together the family hierarchy are loosened. The father no longer commands the productive processes of the home; he is now a wage-earner, as might be his son, daughter, or even wife. He may demand submission, may tyrannize his wife and children, may invoke the still-potent sanctions of patriarchal religion, but no matter how he blusters, now it is the corporation which brings in "the fruits of the earth" and dictates the productive labor of the family. In the early twentieth century, historian Arthur Calhoun noted the rising rates of divorce (and desertion), the increased male absence from the home, the greater independence of wives and children, and concluded that "only in out-of-the-way places can the archaic patriarchism maintain itself." The decline of patriarchal authority within the family was a constant theme of early-twentieth-century sociological writing.[7]

These changes—the division of life into public and private spheres, the decline of gynocentricity and patriarchy*—should not be thought of merely as results of the industrial revolution. They were, as much as smokestacks and steam power, railways and assembly lines, the *definition* of the cataclysmic reorganization of life which took place in northern Europe and North America in the nineteenth century. This was a total and revolutionary reorganization. To go from a society organized around household production to one organized around large-scale factory production, from a society ruled by seasons and climate to one ruled by the Market, is to reach into the heart of human social life and uproot the deepest assumptions. Everything that was "natural" is overturned. What had unquestionably been "human nature" suddenly appears archaic; what had been accepted for centuries as human destiny is no longer acceptable, and in most cases, is not even possible.

The lives of women—always much more confined by nature and social expectation than those of men—were thrown into confusion. In the Old Order, women had won their survival through participation

---

* The reader should be reminded that, unlike some feminist writers, we do not use the word "patriarchy" to mean male dominance in general. We use "patriarchy" to refer to a specific historical organization of family and social life (see p. 7). So when we talk about the "decline of patriarchy" we are by no means suggesting that *male dominance* has declined—only that it has taken a different historical form.

in the shared labor of the household. Outside of the household there was simply no way to earn a livelihood and no life for a woman. Women could be, at different ages or in different classes, wives, mothers, daughters, servants, or "spinster" aunts, but these are only gradations of the domestic hierarchy. Women were born, grew up, and aged within the dense human enclosure of the family.

But with the collapse of the Old Order, there appeared a glimmer, however remote to most women, of something like a choice. It was now possible for a woman to enter the Market herself and exchange her labor for the means of survival (although at a lower rate than a man would). In Europe, in Russia, in America, wherever industry demanded more workers, there arose a new wave of "single women," like those honored by Bolshevik leader Alexandra Kollontai:

> They are girls and women who ceaselessly wage the grim struggle for existence, who spend their days sitting on the office chair, who bang away at telegraph apparatuses, who stand behind counters. Single women: they are the girls with fresh hearts and minds, full of bold fantasies and plans who pack the temples of science and art, who crowd the sidewalks, searching with vigorous and virile steps for cheap lessons and casual clerical jobs.[8]

Entering the Market as a working woman might mean low wages and miserable working conditions, loneliness and insecurity, but it also meant the possibility—unimaginable in the Old Order—of independence from the grip of the family.

But this atomized and independent existence hardly seemed "natural" to women whose own mothers had lived and died in the intimacy of the family. There was still the household of course, a life centered on husband and children. But the household had been much diminished by the removal of productive labor. Women like Charlotte Perkins Gilman questioned whether there could be any dignity in a domestic life which no longer centered on women's distinctive skills, but on mere biological existence. The logic of the Market led a few outspoken feminist analysts of the nineteenth century to a cynical answer: that the relation between the unemployed wife and the breadwinning husband was not very different from prostitution. Could such a mode of existence, despite its superficial resemblance to women's traditional way of life, be "natural"?

These were the ambiguous options which began to open up to

women in the late eighteenth and early nineteenth centuries. In most cases, of course, the "choice" was immediately foreclosed by circumstances: some women were forced to seek paid work no matter how much their working disrupted the family, others were inescapably tied to family responsibilities no matter how much they needed or wanted to work outside. But the collapse of the Old Order had broken the pattern which had tied every woman to a single and unquestionable fate. The impact of the change was double-edged. It cannot simply be judged either as a step forward or a step backward for women (even assuming that that judgment could be made in such a way as to cover all women—the black domestic, the manufacturer's wife, the factory girl, etc.). The changes were, by their nature, contradictory. Industrial capitalism freed women from the endless round of household productive labor, and in one and the same gesture tore away the skills which had been the source of women's unique dignity. It loosened the bonds of patriarchy, and at once imposed the chains of wage labor. It "freed" some women for a self-supporting spinsterhood, and conscripted others into sexual peonage. And so on.

It was these changes—the backward steps as well as the forward ones—which provided the material ground for the emergence of the Woman Question. For women generally, from the hard-working women of the poorer classes to the cushioned daughters of the upper classes, the Woman Question was a matter of immediate personal experience: the consciousness of possibilities counterpoised against prohibitions, opportunities against ancient obligations, instincts against external necessities. The Woman Question was nothing less than the question of how women would survive, and what would become of them, in the modern world. The women who lost years of their youth to nervous depression, the women who first tasted the "liberation" of grinding jobs and exploitative sex, the women who poured their hearts into diaries while their strength drained into childbearing and rearing—our great- and great-great-grandmothers—lived out the Woman Question with their lives.

The New Masculinism

At the same time that it arose as a subjective dilemma among women, the Woman Question entered the realm of public life as an "issue" subject to the deliberations of scholars, statesmen and scien-

tists. There can be no clearer acknowledgment of the problem than
Freud's:

> Throughout history people have knocked their heads against the rid-
> dle of the nature of femininity. . . . Nor will *you* have escaped wor-
> rying over this problem—those of you who are men; to those of
> you who are women this will not apply—you are yourselves the
> problem.[9]

Patronizing as this statement may sound, it is not an example of
patriarchal thought. Freud projects his own age's obsession with the
Woman Question to a universal and timeless status. Yet the old patriarchs would never have raised such a question themselves. To them,
the nature and purpose of women posed no riddle. But the old ways
of thinking about things—which posited a static, hierarchical social
order presided over by the Heavenly Father—were already losing
their credibility when Freud wrote. The "miracles" of technology had
outdone the feats of the saints several times over; the smokestacks of
industrial towns had outgrown the church steeples. The new age
needed a new way of explaining human society and human nature.
That way, as it developed in the last three centuries, was not accepting but questioning; not religious but scientific. Freud's riddle does
not represent a tradition running back to patriarchal times. The mentality which framed the Woman Question and later drafted the
significant answers to it, was born with the rise of the new order in
the struggle *against* patriarchal authority.

If the history of the West from sixteen hundred to the eighteen
hundreds was condensed down to a single simple allegory, it would
be the drama of the overthrow of the once all-powerful father.† In
politics, in science, in philosophy, there was one dominant theme:
the struggle against the old structures of patriarchal authority, represented by the king, the feudal lords, the Pope, and often, the father
in the family. To put it another way, the Old Order did not simply
collapse under the weight of impersonal forces, it was defeated in
actual human confrontations. The Market itself was not an abstract
"system" expanding as a result of mysterious internal pressures. It

---

† In this light Freud's theory of the Oedipus Complex takes on historical
meaning. Freud lived in a time when the "sons" of the triumphant bourgeoisie
were in the ascendency and the "fathers"—the traditional authorities of society
—were in the decline. Freud could discern the marks of the struggle—envy,
guilt, and the effort to become like the father—in the psychological makeup of
the sons. Intellectually, Freud himself was among the most daring of the "sons."

consisted, at any particular time, of real men, acting through a network of economic relationships. The expansion of this network required, at every step of the way, hostile confrontations over the constraints imposed by patriarchal authority—feudal restrictions on trade, guild restrictions on manufacturing, religious prohibitions against usury and profit-making. It was a time, remote from this age of corporate domination, when the members of the rising middle class —the "bourgeoisie"—were not yet "the establishment," but the rebels. In the English, American, and French revolutions, they took up arms and led large numbers of ordinary people against the forces which would restrict trade and individual profit-making ("the pursuit of happiness"). The French Revolution featured the ultimate collective act of patricide: the murder of the king (and less dramatically, but no less significantly, the closing of the churches). The triumphant revolutionaries cast off the yoke of the father and declared themselves a *fraternity* of free citizens.

While revolutionaries of the rising middle class slashed out against Old Order restrictions on business, letting crowned and tonsured heads fall where they might, thinkers and churchmen were working to develop systems of thought which would be congenial to the new age. Philosophy (especially in Britain and the United States) abandoned its search for the Good and the True and made a pragmatic peace with the materialism and individualism of the Market economy. Religion learned to turn an ethical blind spot toward the Market and confine itself to matters of private life. But the way of thinking which best suited the conditions of the Market and the inclinations of the men who dominated it did not come from philosophy or religion; it came from science.

Science had led the intellectual assault on patriarchal ideology. Ever since Galileo, at the beginning of the seventeenth century, had faced the Inquisition over the issue of whether the earth was the center of the universe, science had set itself up as antagonistic, or at least, disdainful toward religious doctrine and traditional authority in all fields. Galileo, and the scientists who followed him, claimed the entire observable world—stars, tides, rocks, animals and "man" himself—as an area for unfettered investigation, just as businessmen were laying stake to the marketplace as a secular zone, free of religious or feudal interference. Newton's physics, Lavoisier's chemistry, and later, Darwin's biology, had no need of gods or other incomprehensible forces to explain nature. (Except, perhaps, to get things started in the first

place.) Science grew with the Market. It took the most revolutionary aspects of the business mentality—its loyalty to empirical fact, its hard-headed pragmatism, its penchant for numerical abstraction—and hammered them into a precision tool for the understanding and mastery of the material world.

Science mocked the old patriarchal ideology, ripped through its pretensions, and left it as we know it today—a legacy of rituals, legends and bedtime stories retold to children. Science in the eighteenth and nineteenth centuries was the sworn enemy of ghosts and mystery and mumbo jumbo—the traditional trappings of patriarchy—and an old friend to revolutionaries. Socialists like Karl Marx and feminists like Charlotte Perkins Gilman were devotees of science as a liberating force against injustice and domination. "Let us never forget that long before we did," proclaimed a participant in the Paris Commune, "the sciences and philosophy fought against the tyrants."[10]

We are indebted, then, to the critical and scientific spirit which arose with the Market, for defeating the patriarchal ideology which had for centuries upheld the tyrants. But to be opposed to patriarchal structures of authority is not necessarily to be *feminist* in intent or sensibility. The emerging world view of the new age was, in fact, distinctly *masculinist*. It was a world view which proceeded from the Market, from the realm of economic, or "public" life. It was by its nature external to women, capable of seeing them only as "others" or aliens.

Patriarchal ideology subordinated women too, of course. But it was not formed in some other realm than that inhabited by women, for life in the Old Order had not been fractured into separate realms. Masculinist opinion, however, is cast in a realm apart from women. It proceeds from the male half of what has become a sexually segregated world. It reflects not some innate male bias but the logic and assumptions of that realm, which are the logic and assumptions of the capitalist market.

The masculinist view of human nature almost automatically excludes woman and her nature. Whether expressed in popular opinion or learned science, it is not only biased toward biological man and his nature, but specifically toward capitalist man, the "economic man" described by Adam Smith. Economic man leads a profoundly lonely existence. Like the hard little atoms of eighteenth-century physics, he courses through space on his own trajectory, only incidentally interacting with the swarm of other atomized men, each bound

to his own path. He is propelled by an urgent sense of self-interest, and guided by a purely rational and calculative intellect.

To economic man, the inanimate things of the marketplace—money and the commodities which represent money—are alive and possessed of almost sacred significance. Conversely, things truly alive are, from a strictly "rational" point of view, worthless except as they impinge on the Market and affect one's economic self-interest: employees are "production factors"; a good wife is an "asset," etc. The successful economic man, the capitalist, ceaselessly transforms life—human labor and effort—into lifeless capital, an activity which is to him eminently rational, sane and "human." Ultimately the laws of the Market come to appear as the laws of human nature.

From this vantage point, woman inevitably appears alien, mysterious. She inhabits (or is supposed to inhabit) the "other" realm, the realm of private life, which looks from the Market like a pre-industrial backwater, or a looking-glass land that inverts all that is normal in the "real" world of men. The limited functions now reserved for that realm attach to woman's person and make her too appear to be an anachronism, or a curious inversion of normality. Biologically and psychologically, she seems to contradict the basic principles of the Market. The Market transforms human activities and needs into dead things—commodities—woman can, and does, create life. Economic man is an individual, a monad, connected to others only through a network of impersonal economic relationships; woman is embedded in the family, permitted no individual identity apart from her biological relationships to others. Economic man acts in perfect self-interest; a woman cannot base her relationships within the family on the principle of *quid pro quo:* she gives.

It appears, from a masculinist perspective, that woman might be a more primitive version of man—not because there is *prima facie* evidence of her lower intelligence, but because of her loving and giving nature, which is itself taken as evidence of lower intelligence. Rousseau's "noble savage" like his ideal woman was compassionate and nurturing. And Darwin found that:

> Woman seems to differ from man in mental disposition, chiefly in her greater tenderness and less selfishness. . . .
> It is generally admitted that with woman the powers of intuition, of rapid perception, and perhaps of imitation, are more strongly marked than in man; but some, at least, of these faculties are charac-

teristic of the lower races, and therefore of a past and lower state of civilization.[11]

Everything that seems uniquely female becomes a challenge to the rational scientific intellect. Woman's body, with its autonomous rhythms and generative possibilities, appears to the masculinist vision as a "frontier," another part of the natural world to be explored and mined. A new science—gynecology—arose in the nineteenth century to study this strange territory and concluded that the female body is not only primitive, but deeply pathological. (See Chapter 4.) Woman's psyche, of course, becomes an acknowledged scientific enigma, like the inner substance of matter, or the shape of the universe. The American psychologist G. Stanley Hall calls it "terra incognita," and when Freud wrote of the "riddle of the nature of femininity" he spoke for generations of scientists who puzzled over the strange asymmetry of nature which had made only one sex fully normal.

The discovery of woman as an anomaly—a "question"—this was the essential masculinist perception. Patriarchal ideology had seen women as *inferior,* but always as organically linked to the entire hierarchy which extended from the household to the heavens. Now those links had been broken; patriarchal ideology, which had been the organizing principle of human society for centuries, lay tattered and demoralized, and yet woman had not been freed by its downfall, but had become a curiosity, a social issue which would somehow have to be resolved.

Rationalist and Romantic Answers

Within the framework of the new masculinist ideology there are only two possible answers to the Woman Question. We will call them "rationalist" and "romantic." Many people would call them, after a quick glance, "feminist" and "male chauvinist." But it is not that simple. They *are* opposed to each other, but they emerge from the same ground and they grow together, back to back, in the development of masculinist culture. At any moment, each "solution" would have its proponents, and neither could be completely put to rest. But ultimately one would come to dominate Anglo-American and Western culture in general from the early nineteenth century until the rise of the women's liberation movement in our own day. That choice would

be overwhelmingly for the romantic solution—and it would be en-
forced in real life with all the weight of the economy and the persuasion of scientific authority.

The *rationalist* answer is, very simply, to admit women into modern society on an equal footing with men. If the problem is that
women are in some sense "out," then it can be solved by letting them
"in." Sexual rationalism shares the critical spirit of science: it mocks
the patriarchal myths of female inferiority, denounces modern "sex
roles" as arbitrary social inventions, and dreams of a social order in
which women and men will be not only equal, but, insofar as possible, functionally interchangeable. Born in the exuberantly clear-
headed days of the French Revolution and nurtured by every suc-
ceeding wave of social movement, sexual rationalism is a radical ideology. It takes the ideals of middle-class liberalism—individual freedom and political equality—to a conclusion which even the French
and American revolutionaries of the eighteenth century would have
found, on the whole, dangerously extremist.

But, being radical, the sexual rationalist position is no less masculinist. It looks out from the Market *at* the world of women, critical of
that world but largely uncritical of the Market, except insofar as it
has excluded women. Charlotte Perkins Gilman, perhaps the most
brilliant American proponent of the sexual rationalist position, held
that the home was "primitive" and that women, as a result of their
confinement to it, suffered from "arrested development" to the
point where they had become almost a separate species. Betty
Friedan, the best-known sexual rationalist of our period, found the
home a "trap" and housewives stunted in mind and spirit. But in re-
coiling, justifiably, from "woman's sphere" (and not so justifiably,
from the women in it), sexual rationalism rushes too eagerly into the
public sphere as men have defined it. "We demand," wrote South African feminist Olive Schreiner, a sexual rationalist in the spirit of Charlotte Perkins Gilman, that:

> . . . we also shall have our share of honored and socially useful
> human toil, our full half of the labor of the Children of Woman. We
> demand nothing more than this, and we will take nothing less. This
> is our "WOMAN'S RIGHT!"[12]

The rationalist feminist seldom questions the nature of that "toil"
and whom it serves. Gilman, and to an even greater degree, Friedan,
saw women entering "fulfilling" careers, presumably in business and

the professions, with no evident concern about the availability of such jobs to all women, much less about the larger social purpose of the available occupations. The sexual rationalist program is one of *assimilation,* with ancillary changes (day care, for example) as necessary to promote women's rapid integration into what has been the world of men.

If the ideological assault on patriarchal authority had made sexual rationalist ideas thinkable, the industrial revolution made the rationalist program seem achievable, even inevitable. The bulk of women's old labor had been removed into the factories; why shouldn't the remaining domestic activities follow suit? Gilman urged that restaurants, kindergartens, housecleaners be set up "on a business basis" to take over women's chores. Freed of this "clumsy tangle of rudimentary industries," the family would become a voluntary association of individuals. Women would no longer be identified by a mere sexual or biological connection to other people, but by their independent endeavors in the public world. From a nineteenth-century vantage point, these developments seemed likely to happen by themselves. The machine was eliminating the importance of the muscular difference between the sexes; and the factory was proving itself far more efficient than the home. The Market had taken over so many of women's activities, from clothesmaking to food processing—what was to stop it from swallowing up the home and family and spitting out autonomous, genderless individuals?

It was, in large part, the horror of such a prospect that inspired the other answer to the Woman Question: sexual romanticism. In keeping with the masculinist spirit, sexual romanticism sees women as anomalous, half outside the world of men. The rationalist rebelled against this situation; the romantic finds comfort in it. Sexual romanticism cherishes the mystery that is woman and proposes to *keep* her mysterious, by keeping her outside.

Just as sexual rationalism is linked historically to a larger stream of rationalist thinking, sexual romanticism emerged with the "romantic movement" of the eighteenth and nineteenth centuries. Rationalism welcomed the new age of industrial capitalism; romanticism shrank back from it in revulsion. The industrial revolution, as a walk through any major city reminds us, was an aesthetic tragedy. Green pastures gave way overnight to the "dark, satanic mills" which tormented Blake's vision; rustic villages, forests, streams vanished with the onslaught of industrial "progress." Within the world of the industrial capitalist Market, human relationships never achieved the impersonal benevolence which Adam Smith had predicted. The "invisible hand" which Smith had invoked to keep the social order running smoothly and fairly did not reach down to soothe the bankrupt businessman, the starving worker, or the farmer driven from his land. It was a brutal world, not even tempered by the charitable paternalism and *noblesse oblige* of feudal times. Where middle-class revolutions had made men free, their freedom consisted in the solitary right to sink or swim, to "make it" or be crushed by those who were making it. The romantic spirit reached with nostalgia for the Old Order, or for imaginary versions of it: a society not yet atomized, but linked organically in trust and mutual need; enlivened by the warmth of "irrational" passions, and enriched by the beauty of an untouched nature.

Nothing could be more abhorrent from a romantic standpoint than the sexual rationalist program. To dissolve the home (by removing the last domestic chores and letting women out to work) would be to remove the last refuge from the horrors of industrial society. Communal dining halls, child care services, and housekeeping services would turn out to be outposts of the hated factory—or factories themselves, imposing their cold and regimented operations on the most intimate and personal details of life. And to liberate woman would be to take away the only thing which cushioned man from psychic destruction in the rough world of the Market. If she became a female version of "economic man," an individual pursuing her own trajectory, then indeed it would be a world without love, without human warmth. The lonely prospect which stretched before economic man—". . . a forbidding and frostbound wilderness to be subdued with aching limbs beneath solitary stars"[13]—would have to be accepted as inescapable reality.

But this, of course, is what the romantic could not do. Man must have a refuge from the savage scramble of the Market, he must have consolation for his lonely quest as "economic man." Sexual romanticism asserts that the home will be that refuge, woman will be that consolation. The English critic and author John Ruskin laid out exactly what the sexual romanticist seeks in "women's sphere":

> This is the true nature of home—it is the place of peace; the shelter, not only from all injury, but from all terror, doubt and division. In so far as it is not this, it is not home; so far as the anxieties of the outer life penetrate into it, and the inconsistently minded, unknown, unloved or hostile society of the outer world is allowed by either

husband or wife to cross the threshold it ceases to be a home; it is
then only a part of the outer world which you have roofed over and
lighted fire in. But so far as it is a sacred place, a vestal temple, a
temple of the hearth watched over by household gods. . . . so far it
vindicates the name and fulfills the praise of home.[14]

Here the world of private life and biological existence has become
suffused with a holy radiance. Not a whisper from the marketplace
must be allowed to penetrate this "temple," where a woman lives out
her days in innocence.‡ Here will be preserved a quaint and domesticated version of patriarchy, as if nothing had ever happened in the
world outside. There is in the romantic spirit a passionate and humanistic rejection of the Market, but it settles for only this furtive and half-
hearted rebellion: not to overthrow the Market, but to escape from it
—into the arms of woman. The deity who makes Ruskin's ideal home
sacred is no vengeful patriarch, capable of driving out money-lenders
and idolators, but a mere "household god."

The romantic imagination feverishly set out to construct a woman
worthy of occupying Ruskin's "vestal temple." The guidelines were
simple: Woman should be, in every feature, a counterpoint to the
Market; she should be the antithesis of economic man. Now, from
our perspective, there is a real basis to this romantic construction:
There is a strength in women's nurturance which does contradict the
rules and assumptions of the Market, and which is potentially opposed to the Market. But the romantics have no interest in discovering the authentic strengths and impulses of women—any more than
they had, in most cases, in an authentic attack on the inhumanity of

‡ The romantic nostalgia of the nineteenth century was not reserved for
women. The primitive peoples uncovered by expanding Euro-American capitalism, lived, like women of the industrial countries, in the shadowy realm outside the Market. To the romantic imagination, they shared with women generally
the human qualities denied by the Market, and gladdened the world with their
pastoral simplicity. In the words of psychologist G. Stanley Hall: "Nearly all
savages are in many respects children or youth of adult size. . . . They are
naturally amiable, peaceful among themselves, affectionate, light-hearted, thoroughly goodnatured, and the faults we see are those we have made. They live
a life of feeling, emotion, and impulse, and scores of testimonials from those
who know them intimately and who have no predilection for Rousseau-like
views are to the effect that to know a typical savage is to love him."[15]
Hall castigated imperialist attempts to "commercialize them and overwork
them." They must be allowed to remain outside the Market, "to linger in the
paradise of childhood," for without their refreshing charm "our earthly home
would be left desolate indeed."

the Market. The romantic construction of woman is as artificial as
the sixteen-inch waists and three-foot-wide hooped skirts popular in
mid-nineteenth century. Economic man is rational; therefore romantic woman is intuitive, emotional, and incapable of quantitative reasoning. Economic man is competitive; she is tender and submissive.
Economic man is self-interested; she is self-effacing, even masochistic. A popular Victorian poem depicts the result of all these nega-
tions: a creature who was supposed to be all that is "human" (as opposed to "economic") and ends up being subhuman, more like a
puppy than a priestess:

> Her soul, that once with pleasure shook
> Did any eyes her beauty own,
> Now wonders how they dare to look
> On what belongs to him alone;
> The indignity of taking gifts
> Exhilarates her loving breast;
> A rapture of submission lifts
> Her life into celestial rest;
> There's nothing left of what she was;
> Back to the babe the woman dies,
> And all the wisdom that she has
> Is to love him for being wise.*[16]

The sexual rationalist who does not gag on the foregoing lines can
respond with a certain cynical impatience: the lovely wife of romantic yearnings is in fact her husband's financial dependent and ward.
Charlotte Perkins Gilman argued that she was a kind of combined
housemaid-prostitute, earning her keep. And Olive Schreiner's heroine Lyndall defiantly declares:

> . . . a woman who has sold herself, even for a ring and a new name,
> need hold her skirt aside for no creature in the street. They both
> earn their bread in one way.[17]

* It has become common today to confuse this kind of romanticist goo with
patriarchal ideology. But the two views of women are fundamentally incompatible. Patriarchy's women were not gushing, limp-wristed creatures; they were
hard workers and stout partners. And patriarchal ideology never for a moment
dreamed of ascribing to women moral superiority, as the romantics did in making women the custodians of the Sacred. Patriarchal ideology rested on the
assumption of women's moral *inferiority* and their utter dependency on males
to mediate and interpret scripture. Sexual romanticism draws heavily on archaic
imagery, but this is only nostalgia—a product of the new epoch, not a continua-
tion of the Old Order.

To cover with "rapture" and "exhilaration" the acknowledged "in-dignity of taking gifts" is from a rationalist point of view a perverse denial of economic reality. Sexual rationalism may suffer from being overly cynical about family relationships and overly accepting of the "free" interactions of the Market, but it has the courage to acknowl-edge the social world the Market has created; it does not turn coyly away from facts which happen to be unpleasant.

Sexual romanticism, on the other hand, is by its nature committed to lies and evasion. The glorified home allows the sexual romantic to escape from the Market, and his intense need for that home—precisely as an escape—forces him to lie about the realities of the human rela-tionships within it. Marx and Engels had rejoiced prematurely that the triumph of capitalism "at last compelled [man] to face with sober senses his real conditions of life and his relations with his kind." Sex-ual romanticism befogs the senses, draws lace curtains against the industrial landscape outside, and offers a cozy dream in which men are men and women are—mercifully—not men.

Science and the Triumph of Sexual Romanticism

Yet it was sexual romanticism which triumphed—from the Vic-torian ideal of the nineteenth century to the feminist mystique of the mid-twentieth century. When the cataclysmic transition from the Old Order ended in the United States and Europe, when society began to re-form itself into something which could be once again called an "order," a settled and reproducible way of life, that new "order" rested heavily on the romantic conception of woman and the home. Sexual rationalism, which at one time had seemed to be as inevitable as technological progress, remained a dissident stream, associated with bohemianism, radicalism and feminism.† The dominant ideology

† Feminism has oscillated between romantic and rationalist ideas: the first generation of American feminists (Susan B. Anthony, Elizabeth Cady Stanton, etc.) were unswerving sexual rationalists, but the second generation, which came to maturity in the eighteen eighties and nineties, unhesitatingly embraced sexual romanticism, arguing that women should have the vote, not because it was their *right*, but because they were mothers, "the guardians of the race." Contemporary feminism is overwhelmingly rationalist, but it is not without un-dercurrents of romanticism: feminists who reject "integration" and aspire to resurrect a pretechnological matriarchy, or rule by women. Women have pinned their hopes on technological "progress," or they have sought vindica-tion in a remote and imagined past—all in the name of feminism.

defined woman as a perpetual alien, and the home as an idyllic refuge from the unpleasant but "real" world of men. Sexual romanticism triumphed not only because it was psychologically comforting to a majority of men (and many, many women) but also for a pragmatic reason which the sexual rationalists of the early industrial period could never have foreseen. Sexual romanticism, it turned out, meshed ideally with the needs of the maturing economy, which would increasingly depend on the economic pattern of individual domestic consumption to fuel its growth. And, once shaped by the ideology of sexual romanticism, woman makes a more convenient worker when she is needed by industry: the "romanticized" woman is supposed to work for low wages, typically in work which requires submissiveness and/or nurturance, and quickly goes back where she "belongs" when the jobs run out.

But the legitimacy of this new sexual/economic order has only been secured through great effort. The romantic solution, by its very nature, cannot be justified by direct application of the laws and assumptions of the Market. There is nothing in the logic of the Market which can distinguish between male and female (or black and white) workers, consumers, owners, or investors. From a hard-headed capitalist point of view, the only distinctions which matter ultimately are those which can be measured in hard currency: variations in human anatomy or color make no difference in the ledger book. And the revolutionary new ideas of "rights" and "liberty" which the rising middle class had once hurled in the face of monarchs were implicitly oblivious to gender, as feminists have always been quick to point out. In fact, the tenets of the business world, and the political ideals of the class who dominated that world, had opened the ground for sexual rationalism. Sexual romanticism was forced to seek legitimacy outside the normal, workaday world of men—from some authority higher than either economic realism or political idealism.

That authority was science. For over a hundred years, the romantic answer to the Woman Question would be articulated not in political, or aesthetic or moral terms but in the language of science. And herein lies a painful irony. Science had been a revolutionary force— opposed to prejudice, folly, and obfuscation wherever they arose. But as the Old Order faded into the past, and the "rising middle class" became the new ruling class, science made its peace with the social order. The science which arose to the defense of sexual romanticism was a pale, and not wholly legitimate, descendant of the science which had once challenged the authority of kings and popes.

The scientific experts, who committed themselves to the defense of sexual romanticism—professional physicians, psychologists, domestic scientists, parent educators, etc.—each claimed a specialized body of scientific knowledge. Their careers rested on this claim. Without a connection to science, they have no legitimacy, no audience for their ideas or market for their skills. But science, in their hands, is weirdly distorted and finally debased beyond recognition—as this book will illustrate.

Science had once attacked entrenched authority, but the new scientific expert himself became an authority himself. His business was not to seek out what is *true,* but to pronounce on what is *appropriate.*

The experts' rise to power over the lives of women was neither swift nor easy. The old networks through which women had learned from each other had to be destroyed, or discredited. The power of great wealth had to be invoked against competing sources of information and skill. The authority of science had to be promoted as if science were not a critical method, but a new religion. Many women resisted, clinging to the old wisdom and customs, or, more radically, organizing new networks of mutual support and study.

But the experts could not have triumphed had not so many women welcomed them, sought them out, and even (in the early twentieth century) organized to promote their influence. It was not only gullible women, or conservative women, who embraced the experts, but independent-minded and progressive women, even feminists. The experts were "scientific" and it seemed that only science could vanquish ignorance and injustice. Had not science opposed the patriarchal authorities of the Old Order, and, by implication, the entire web of constraints which had bound women for centuries? This was the basis of the "romance" between women and the new experts: science had been on the side of progress and freedom. To ignore the dictates of science was surely to remain in the "dark ages"; to follow them was to join the forward rush of history. Charlotte Perkins Gilman, Ellen Richards, Margaret Sanger, and, it could be argued, Jane Addams, were all, in their different ways, firm believers in the progressiveness of science and its representative experts. It would take another two generations for the "romance" to unravel itself, and for women to discover that the experts had, in fact, betrayed science, and betrayed them.

The Rise of the Experts

TWO

Witches, Healers, and Gentleman Doctors

The story of the rise of the psychomedical experts—the doctors, the psychologists, and sundry related professionals—might be told as an allegory of science versus superstition: on the one side, the clear-headed, masculine spirit of science; on the other side, a dark morass of female superstition, old wives' tales, rumors preserved as fact. In this allegorical version, the triumph of science was as inevitable as human progress or natural evolution: the experts triumphed because they were *right*.

But the real story is not so simple, and the outcome not so clearly "progressive." It is true that the experts represented a less parochial vision than that of the individual woman, submerged in her family and household routines: the experts had studied; they were in a position to draw on a wider range of human experience than any one woman could know. But too often the experts' theories were grossly unscientific, while the traditional lore of the women contained wisdom based on centuries of observation and experience. The rise of the experts was not the inevitable triumph of right over wrong, fact over myth; it began with a bitter conflict which set women against men, class against class. Women did not learn to look to an external "science" for guidance until after their old skills had been ripped away, and the "wise women" who preserved them had been silenced, or killed.

The conflict between women's traditional wisdom and male expertise centered on the right to heal. For all but the very rich, healing had traditionally been the prerogative of women. The art of healing was linked to the tasks and the spirit of motherhood; it combined wisdom and nurturance, tenderness and skill. All but the most privileged women were expected to be at least literate in the language of herbs and healing techniques; the most learned women traveled widely to share their skills. The women who distinguished themselves as healers were not only midwives caring for other women, but "general practitioners," herbalists, and counselors serving men and women alike.

The historical antagonist of the female lay healer was the male medical professional. The notion of medicine as a *profession* was in some ways an advance over the unexamined tradition of female healing: A profession requires systematic training, and, at least in principle, some formal mechanisms of accountability. But a profession is also defined by its *exclusiveness,* and has been since the professions of medicine and law first took form in medieval Europe. While the female lay healer operated within a network of information-sharing and mutual support, the male professional hoarded up his knowledge as a kind of property, to be dispensed to wealthy patrons or sold on the market as a commodity. His goal was not to spread the skills of healing, but to concentrate them within the elite interest group which the profession came to represent. Thus the triumph of the male medical profession is of crucial significance for our story: it involved the destruction of women's networks of mutual help —leaving women in a position of isolation and dependency—and it established a model of expertism as the prerogative of a social elite.

The conflict over healing in nineteenth-century America had its roots in the darkest ages of European history. The American female lay healer, like Anne Hutchinson, who was renowned as a midwife as well as a religious leader, represented a tradition which stretched back across the ocean and through countless generations of women. And the earliest American medical professionals, like the energetic Dr. Benjamin Rush, drew their aristocratic ideal for the profession from a tradition which went back to the medieval universities.

In Europe the conflict between female lay healing and the medical profession had taken a particularly savage form: the centuries-long witch hunts which scar the history of England, Germany, France, and Italy. The witch hunts themselves were linked to many broad historical developments: the reformation, the beginnings of commerce, and a period of peasant uprisings against the feudal aristocracy. But for our purposes the important point is that the targets of the witch hunts were, almost exclusively, peasant women, and among them female lay healers were singled out for persecution. It is to this aspect of the witch hunts that we now turn briefly.

The Witch Hunts

The extent of the witch craze is startling: in the late fifteenth and early sixteenth centuries there were thousands upon thousands of executions—usually live burnings at the stake—in Germany, Italy, and other countries. In the mid-sixteenth century the terror spread to France, and finally to England. One writer has estimated the number of executions at an average of six hundred a year for certain German cities—or two a day, "leaving out Sundays." Nine hundred witches were destroyed in a single year in the Würzburg area, and a thousand in and around Como. At Toulouse, four hundred were put to death in a day. In the Bishopric of Trier, in 1585, two villages were left with only one female inhabitant each. Many writers have estimated the total number killed to have been in the millions. Women made up some 85 per cent of those executed—old women, young women, and children.[1]

The charges leveled against the "witches" included every misogynist fantasy harbored by the monks and priests who officiated over the witch hunts: witches copulated with the devil, rendered men impotent (generally by removing their penises—which the witches then imprisoned in nests or baskets), devoured newborn babies, poisoned livestock, etc. But again and again the "crimes" included what would now be recognized as legitimate medical acts—providing contraceptive measures, performing abortions, offering drugs to ease the pain of labor. In fact, in the peculiar legal theology of the witch hunters, healing, on the part of a woman, was itself a crime. As a leading English witch hunter put it:

> For this must always be remembered, as a conclusion, that by Witches we understand not only those which kill and torment, but all Diviners, Charmers, Jugglers, all Wizards, commonly called wise men and wise women . . . and in the same number we reckon all good Witches, which do no hurt but good, which do not spoil and destroy, but save and deliver . . . It were a thousand times better for

the land if all Witches, but especially the blessing Witch, might suffer death.[2]

The German monks Kramer and Sprenger, whose book *Malleus Maleficarum,* or *The Hammer of Witches,* was the Catholic Church's official text on witch-hunting for three centuries, denounced those "notoriously bad" witches, "such as use witch's medicines and cure the bewitched by superstitious means."[3] They classed witches in "three degrees": "For some both heal and harm; some harm, but cannot heal; and some seem only able to heal, that is, to take away injuries."[4] Kramer and Sprenger showed no sympathy for those who consulted the witch-healers:

> For they who resort to such witches are thinking more of their bodily health than of God, and besides that, God cuts short their lives to punish them for taking into their own hands the vengeance for their wrongs.[5]

The inquisitors reserved their greatest wrath for the midwife, asserting:

> The greatest injuries to the Faith as regards the heresy of witches are done by midwives; and this is made clearer than daylight itself by the confessions of some who were afterwards burned.[6]

In fact, the wise woman, or witch, as the authorities labeled her, did possess a host of remedies which had been tested in years of use. *Liber Simplicis Medicinae,* the compendium of natural healing methods written by St. Hildegarde of Bingen (A.D. 1098–1178) gives some idea of the scope of women healers' knowledge in the early middle ages. Her book lists the healing properties of 213 varieties of plants and 55 trees, in addition to dozens of mineral and animal derivatives.[7] Undoubtedly many of the witch-healers' remedies were purely magical, such as the use of amulets and charms, but others meet the test of modern scientific medicine. They had effective pain-killers, digestive aids, and anti-inflammatory agents. They used ergot for the pain of labor at a time when the Church held that pain in labor was the Lord's just punishment for Eve's original sin. Ergot derivatives are still used today to hasten labor and aid in the recovery from childbirth. Belladonna—still used today as an anti-spasmodic—was used by the witch-healers to inhibit uterine contractions when miscarriage threatened. Digitalis, still an important drug in treating heart ailments, is said to have been discovered by an English witch.

Meanwhile, the male, university-trained physicians, who practiced with the approval of the Church, had little to go on but guesswork and myth. Among wealthier people, medicine had achieved the status of a gentlemanly occupation well before it had any connection to science, or to empirical study of any kind. Medical students spent years studying Plato, Aristotle, and Christian theology. Their medical theory was largely restricted to the works of Galen, the ancient Roman physician who stressed the theory of "complexions" or "temperaments" of men, "wherefore the choleric are wrathful, the sanguine are kindly, the melancholy are envious," and so on. Medical students rarely saw any patients at all, and no experimentation of any kind was taught. Medicine was sharply differentiated from surgery, which was almost everywhere considered a degrading, menial craft, and the dissection of bodies was almost unheard of.

Medical theories were often grounded more in "logic" than in observation: "Some foods brought on good humours, and others, evil humours. For example, nasturtium, mustard, and garlic produced reddish bile; lentils, cabbage and the meat of old goats and beeves begot black bile." Bleeding was a common practice, even in the case of wounds. Leeches were applied according to the time, the hour, the air, and other similar considerations. Incantations and quasi-religious rituals mingled with the more "scientific" treatments inherited from ancient Greece and Rome. For example, the physician to Edward II, who held a bachelor's degree in theology and a doctorate in medicine from Oxford, prescribed for toothache writing on the jaws of the patient, "In the name of the Father, the Son, and the Holy Ghost, Amen," or touching a needle to a caterpillar and then to the tooth. A frequent treatment for leprosy was a broth made of the flesh of a black snake caught in a dry land among stones.

Such was the state of medical "science" at the time when witch-healers were persecuted for being practitioners of satanic magic. It was witches who developed an extensive understanding of bones and muscles, herbs and drugs, while physicians were still deriving their prognoses from astrology and alchemists were trying to turn lead into gold. So great was the witches' knowledge that in 1527, Paracelsus, considered the "father of modern medicine," burned his text on pharmaceuticals, confessing that he "had learned from the Sorceress all he knew."[8]

Well before the witch hunts began, the male medical profession had attempted to eliminate the female healer. The object of these early conflicts was not the peasant healer but the better-off, literate woman healer who competed for the same urban clientele as that of the university-trained doctors. Take, for example, the case of Jacoba Felicie, brought to trial in 1322 by the Faculty of Medicine at the University of Paris, on charges of illegal practice. She was a literate woman and had received some unspecified "special training" in medicine. That her patients were well off is evident from the fact that (as they testified in court) they had consulted well-known university-trained physicians before turning to her. The primary accusations brought against her were that

> . . . she would cure her patient of internal illness and wounds or of external abscesses. She would visit the sick assiduously and continue to examine the urine in the manner of physicians, feel the pulse, and touch the body and limbs.[9]

Six witnesses affirmed that Jacoba had cured them, even after numerous doctors had given up, and one patient declared that she was wiser in the art of surgery and medicine than any master physician or surgeon in Paris. But these testimonials were used against her, for the charge was not that she was incompetent, but that—as a woman—she dared to cure at all.

Along the same lines, English physicians sent a petition to Parliament bewailing the "worthless and presumptuous women who usurped the profession" and asking the imposition of fines and "long imprisonment" on any woman who attempted to "use the practyse of Fisyk." By the fourteenth century, the medical profession's campaign against urban, educated women healers was virtually complete throughout Europe. Male doctors had won a clear monopoly over the practice of medicine among the upper classes (except for obstetrics, which remained the province of female midwives even among the upper classes for another three centuries). They were ready to take on an important role in the campaign against the great mass of female healers—the "witches."

Physicians were asked to distinguish between those afflictions which had been caused by witchcraft and those caused by "some natural physical defect." They were also asked to judge whether certain women were witches. Often the accused would be stripped and shaved and examined by doctors for "devil's marks." Through the witch hunts, the Church lent its authority to the doctor's professionalism, denouncing non-professional healing as equivalent to heresy: "If a woman dare to cure *without having studied* she is a witch and must die." (Of course, there wasn't any way for a woman to attend a university and go through the appropriate study.)

The witch trials established the male physician on a moral and intellectual plane vastly above the female healer. It placed him on the side of God and Law, a professional on par with lawyers and theologians, while it placed her on the side of darkness, evil and magic. The witch hunts prefigured—with dramatic intensity—the clash between male doctors and female healers in nineteenth-century America.

The Conflict over Healing Comes to America

The European model of medicine as an elite occupation was not easy to transplant to the new world. University trained physicians did not emigrate to the colonies, and domestic medical education—or higher education of any kind—caught on only slowly. In general, medical practice was open to anyone who could demonstrate healing skills, regardless of formal training, race, or sex. The medical historian Joseph Kett reports that "one of the most respected medical men in late-eighteenth-century Windsor, Connecticut, for example, was a freed Negro called "Dr. Primus." In New Jersey, medical practice, except in extraordinary cases, was mainly in the hands of women as late as 1818 . . ."[10] Medical care in rural areas was dominated by lay healers: "root and herb" doctors who relied on Indian remedies, "bonesetters," and midwives.

The tradition of female lay healing flourished in colonial America and the early republic. Colonial women brought centuries' worth of healing lore with them from the old countries, knowledge which they carefully revised and adapted to meet the conditions of the new land. For their knowledge of the available herbs, they depended ultimately on the Indians, who alone knew the healing powers of the native plants. The mixing of Indian, African and European lore produced a rich new tradition of female healing—complex in its knowledge of the plants and the seasons, involving not only how to find or grow healing herbs, but how to pick and dry them, how to administer and mix them, or combine them with the use of steam, exercise, massage. Golden seal powder or tea, and pennyroyal, still considered to be among the most potent herbal remedies, are otherwise known, respectively, as yellow Indian paint or Indian plant and "squaw mint." Cayenne pepper, another legendary cure, is described by a fairly contemporary herbalist as originating among the "negroes of the West Indies."[11]

The writer Sarah Orne Jewett sketched the female lay healer in the late nineteenth century, in a story that even then rang with nostalgia. "This is most too dry a head," says the aging healer Mrs. Goodsoe, rejecting a particular herb, and goes on:

> There! I can tell you there's win'rows o' young doctors, bilin' over with book-larnin', that is truly ignorant of what to do for the sick, or how to p'int out those paths that well people foller toward sickness. Book-fools I call 'em, them young men, an' some on 'em never'll live to know much better, if they git to be Methuselahs. In my time every middle-aged woman who had brought up a family had some proper ideas of dealin' with complaints. I won't say but there was some fools amongst *them*, but I'd rather take my chances, unless they'd forsook herbs and gone to dealin' with patent stuff. Now my mother really did sense the use of herbs and roots. I never see anybody that come up to her . . .[12]

The North American female healer, unlike the European witch-healer, was not eliminated by violence. No Grand Inquisitors pursued her; flames did not destroy her stock of herbs or the knowledge of them.* The female healer in North America was defeated in a struggle which was, at bottom, economic. Medicine in the nineteenth century was being drawn into the marketplace, becoming—as were needles, or ribbons, or salt already—a thing to be bought and sold. Healing was female when it was a neighborly service, based in stable communities, where skills could be passed on for generations and where the healer knew her patients and their families. When the attempt to heal is detached from personal relationships to become a commodity and a source of wealth in itself—then does the business of healing become a male enterprise.

None of this took place automatically, though. In North America, the ouster of female healers took place over a century-long struggle

---

* There were witch hunts in colonial New England, and the reader may be wondering whether they involved the persecution of female healers. As far as we know, the answer is no. The Salem witch trials, which occurred well after the peak of witch hunting in Europe seem to have reflected commercial and status rivalries among the townspeople. It is interesting, though, that witchcraft entered Governor Winthrop's charges against Anne Hutchinson, and her assistance at the birth of a deformed baby was cited as proof of God's displeasure with her heresies.

which ebbed and flowed with the deeper social changes of the times. If the methods were not torture and execution, but repression and slander, they were, in the end, just as effective.

The chief opponents of the female healer, the men who were drawn, from the late seventeen hundreds on, by the possibility of medicine as a lucrative career, were hardly "professionals" in the genteel, European sense, but they were no less exclusive. The great majority of these "regular" doctors, as they called themselves, had been trained by apprenticeship to an older physician, who had probably been trained the same way himself. Others had taken a two- or three-year course of lectures at a medical school; still others mixed apprenticeship and classroom training. There were no formal standards to meet; one became a "regular" doctor essentially by meeting the approval of one's preceptors (or preceptor, one was enough) among the existing "regular" doctors. The regulars were, then, a kind of club. Women could not join because no physician would take a woman as an apprentice and no school would admit one as a student.

Among the regulars was a small elite who had capped off their education with a few years of medical study in Great Britain and a "grand tour" of the Continent. There they had a tantalizing glimpse of medicine as an established and gentlemanly profession, an ideal that American medicine would aspire to for the rest of the century. This ideal, as it took form in the late eighteenth century, was based on the successful British physician. Not yet a man of science, he was however, beyond question, a gentleman. As with the medieval physicians before him, his classical education had not been sullied by too much practical training (though he had spent some years "reading" medicine, usually in Latin): he mingled only with the best people and he would perform no task which was unworthy of his rank,[13] such as surgery or the concoction of drugs. To underline their gentlemanly status, London physicians sported enormous wigs and gold-headed canes, and "often bore themselves in a ridiculously stately manner, and spoke with absurd solemnity."[14]

All this made an awesome impression on American students like young Benjamin Rush, who found that his status as a medical graduate gave him access to the cream of London and Parisian salon society.[15] Men like Rush (who later distinguished himself as a physician in the revolutionary army) and his older contemporary, John Morgan, attempted to transplant the genteel model of the profession to Philadelphia. They urged that the British system of ranking physicians above surgeons and druggists be adopted in this country; Morgan hoped to restrict the title of physician to men who had had a full classical education before embarking on their medical training. The idea was that the physician should "soar above the sordid views of vulgar minds."[16]

But at the heart of professional medicine there still lay a frightful theoretical void. Air and water were blamed by the medical men as bringers of disease, and people lived in dread of getting wet or being surprised by a breeze, thereby "catching cold." Consequently bathing was considered a risky activity, and houses were unventilated and close, hung with heavy draperies to keep out sun and air, while women protected themselves with parasols and veils. Doctors considered water, air, and light especially injurious in disease, to the extent of keeping drinking water away from the ill.

Even the finest British or French medical education could tell an American doctor little that was useful or even accurate. It was known that the blood circulated, for example, but it was not known why or how.[17] Medical theory still consisted largely of efforts to classify all known diseases—according to their symptoms—in order to discover "the Disease" which underlay all human ills. In Rush's time, approximately two thousand diseases had been classified and Rush was able to announce in a lecture:

> I have formerly said there was but one fever in the world. Be not startled, Gentlemen, follow me and I will say there is one disease in the world. The proximate cause of disease is irregular convulsive or wrong action in the system affected. This, Gentlemen, is a concise view of my theory of disease . . .[18]

Rush, now considered the most outstanding physician of late-eighteenth-century America, was a man of boundless theoretical imagination. He once happened to observe a Negro whose skin had turned white in the course of some disease. Rush nimbly concluded that all Negroes were suffering from a disease which had turned them black, and that he had just witnessed a spontaneous "cure"!

Female lay healers did not have a rational theory of disease causation and therapy either, but then they did not make any claims to "book larnin'." What they had was experience—experience which had been discussed and revised for generations. To all accounts, a patient would have done better with an illiterate lay healer than with an ex-

pensive regular doctor who could write out prescriptions in Latin
Healers who had not studied at least knew enough to trust nature:

The existing situation was well stated by E. M'Dowell of Utica,
Michigan. "In 1840, under a popular allopath [regular doctor], I
was fast sinking under a fever. On a feather bed, windows and door
closed on a hot summer day, pulse and breath nearly gone, I lay
roasting. Friends stood around, 'looking at me to die'.

"At this critical moment a woman called in to see me. She ordered both doors and windows thrown open, and with a pail of cold
water and towel, she began to wash me. As the cold water towel
went over me, I could feel the fever roll off and in less than five
minutes I lay comfortable, pulse and breath regular, but weak, and
soon got well."[19]

The herbal brews the female healer might prescribe were, for the
most part, gentle, and she knew when to draw back and wait out a
difficult delivery or an obstinate fever. Knowing her patients as neighbors, she knew also the disappointments, the anxieties, and the overwork which could mimic illness or induce it. If she could not always
cure, neither could she do much harm, and very often she *was* able to
soothe. Apparently with her in mind, a Dr. Douglass observed ruefully in the mid-eighteenth century:

Frequently there is *more Danger* from the Physician, than from the
Distemper . . . but sometimes notwithstanding the Male *Practice*,
Nature gets the better of the Doctor, and the Patient recovers.[20]

Healing as a Commodity

The dangers of the "Male Practice" lay not so much in the gender
of its practitioners as in the economics of their situation. The early
American regular doctors were not, in most cases, men of wealth and
status like the British physicians they took as models. Their survival
depended on their ability to convince large numbers of people that
healing was a commodity—and that it was well worth paying for. This
required that the act of healing become, first of all, tangible and
discrete—so you could see what it was you were paying for—and, second of all, quantifiable, so you could be convinced to pay various
amounts of money for various "amounts" of healing.

Herein lies a contradiction that haunts regular medicine to this
day: healing is not something that can easily be bent into such a

form. The medical care which we all recognize without question as a commodity today—something produced by an "industry," bargained for by unions, and paid for by "consumers" (increasingly, with the same credit cards that buy airplane tickets, restaurant meals, and shoes)—is a far cry from the more ancient and holistic notion of healing. *Healing* cannot be made discrete and tangible; it involves too many little kindnesses, encouragements, and stored-up data about the patients' fears and strengths (all the things trivialized today as "bedside manner"). It cannot be quantified: the midwife does not count the number of times she wiped the parturient woman's forehead or squeezed her hand. Above all, it cannot be plucked out—as a thing apart—from the web of human relationships which connect the healer and those she helps.

So the problem faced by the early regular doctors (which we might call the congenital defect of commercial medicine) was not merely to convince people that they had something beneficial to sell, but to convince people that they had some *thing* at all to sell. John Morgan discovered this in his campaign to bring the British distinction between physicians and druggists to colonial America. He tried to persuade his own clients to pay for his services separately from the drugs he prescribed (it was customary at the time for one bill to cover both). But the patients balked: Drugs were one thing, but what were his "services"? Why pay for advice, or for visits from a man who should be concerned about you anyway? Unable to sell himself, Morgan had to be content with selling drugs.

The late-eighteenth-century regular doctors' solution to this quandary was a system of therapeutics which came to be known as "heroic" medicine—in reference to the drastic measures employed by the doctor (though it might as well have referred to the heroism required of the patients). The point was to produce the strongest possible effect on the patient, of any kind, as if the physician were competing with the disease to see which—the disease or the physician—could produce the most outrageous symptoms. Thus there could be no question but that the doctor was doing something: something visible, tangible, and roughly measurable.

Unfortunately for the health of the young republic, the heroic approach contained an inherent drift toward homicide. Since the point was to prove that the treatment was more powerful than the disease, it followed that the more dangerous a drug or procedure, the more powerful a remedy it was presumed by most doctors to be. For example, blisters (induced by mustard plaster, etc.) were a common treatment for many diseases. In an 1847 paper a physician observed that extensive blistering frequently had a disastrous effect on children, sometimes causing convulsions, gangrene, or even death. He concluded from this that blisters "ought to hold a high rank" in the treatment of diseases of childhood![21]

The most common regular remedies were bloodletting and purges which consisted of "cleansing" through vomiting, laxatives, and enemas. Bloodletting, which was still favored by many physicians well into the twentieth century, was used for every possible ailment, including accidental injuries, malaria, puerperal fever, discomfort in pregnancy, and anemia. It was not a matter of a finger-prick. Many physicians in the early nineteenth century bled until the patient fainted or pulse ceased, whichever came first. During the great yellow fever epidemic of 1793, Dr. Rush achieved Transylvanian excesses. According to his biographer:

> Toward the end of the epidemic Rush drew from seventy to eighty ounces from a patient in five days, and in some cases much more. Mr. Gribble, a cedar-cooper on Front Street, lost 100 ounces in ten bleedings; Mr. George, a carter, was bled the same quantity in five days; and Mr. Peter Mierken, 114 ounces in five days.[22]

Historian Rothstein cites the following anecdote:

> I remember that a horse kicked me once as Dr. Colby was passing the house. I was not injured much, yet mother called in the doctor, and he at once proceeded to bleed me—I presume on general principles. I had seen my mother bled a great many times. The doctor would always bleed her sitting up in bed, and when she would faint and fall over in the bed he loosened the bandages. The doctor had me sitting upon the bed, and when a small quantity of blood escaped, I shut my eyes and fell over on the bed. I remember he told mother that he never saw any one so speedily affected by bleeding. This was the only time I ever was bled.[23]

Laxative purges were usually accomplished by the administration of calomel, a mercury salt. Like bloodletting, calomel was considered an all-purpose remedy, something which no conscientious doctor would omit, no matter what the patient's problem. It was used in large doses for acute problems like fevers and in small daily doses for chronic diseases; it was used for diarrhea, for teething pains—anything. It was, however, poisonous—probably no less poisonous than the arsenic "tonics" then in vogue. Long term use caused the gums, the teeth and eventually the tongue and entire jaw to erode and fall off. According to Rothstein, physicians knew of these side effects, but they did not let the knowledge inhibit them. During a cholera epidemic in St. Louis, physicians ran around with the calomel loose in their pockets and simply dosed it out by the teaspoonful.[24]

It is impossible to calculate the harm done by late-eighteenth- and early-nineteenth-century regular doctors. William Cobbett, who witnessed the rise of heroic medicine under Rush's leadership, described the new therapeutics as "one of those great discoveries which are made from time to time for the depopulation of the earth."[25] But heroic medicine did accomplish something: It gave the regular doctors something to do, something activist, masculine, and imminently more salable than the herbal teas and sympathy served up by rural female healers. Some of the regular doctors achieved considerable wealth and came, like Rush, to hobnob with statesmen and merchants and gentlemen farmers. The patrician dream—that healing would be restricted to the regulars and that their ranks, in turn, would be restricted to "gentlemen"—gleamed bright in the early decades of the new century. Between 1800 and 1820, the organized forces of regular medicine were able to get seventeen states to pass licensing laws restricting the practice of medicine. In most cases local and state regular medical societies were given the power to grant licenses; in ten states the unlicensed practice of medicine was made punishable by fine or imprisonment.[26]

It was a premature move on the part of the regular doctors. There was no mass support for the idea of medical professionalism, much less for the particular set of healers who claimed it. Furthermore, there was simply no way to enforce the new licensing laws: The ubiquitous lay healers could not be just legislated out of practice. Worse still, for the "regulars," this early grab for medical monopoly inspired a radical health movement which aimed not only at foreclosing the patrician ideal, but at reclaiming healing from the marketplace.

The Popular Health Movement

Whether out of respect for the regular doctor's presumed education or for his sex, many thousands of ordinary Americans had had some exposure to regular (heroic) medicine by the early eighteen hundreds. In the thirties, things had gone so far that calomel was said to have replaced butter on the bread of frontier families.[27] Some kind of public reaction to the hazards—and the pretensions—of regular medicine was inevitable. In the twentieth century, such a reaction would probably take the form of consumer organizations lobbying, through familiar channels, for stiffer regulation, "quality control," etc. But in the early nineteenth century, there were no channels to contain the reaction. Outrage against regular medicine mounted into a mass movement against medical professionalism and expertism in all forms—the "Popular Health Movement."

Small farmers and shopkeepers, independent artisans, and, in all cases, their hard-working wives provided the constituency for the Popular Health Movement. These were people who had a tradition of self-reliance and independence that went back to the first rock-filled farms in Plymouth Colony. It was to secure this tradition that their fathers and grandfathers had fought in the Revolutionary War. But now, in the early eighteen hundreds the forces of the Market were grinding free citizens down to a condition of dependency and in some cases servitude. In the cities, the factory system was sweeping up skilled artisans and reducing them to the status of mere "wage-slaves." Meanwhile, depressions and financial manipulations by the banks were proving to small farmers and storekeepers that hard work was no longer a sufficient guarantee against ruin. Everywhere, class divisions were deepening. The urban upper class flaunted the latest fashions from London—as if there had never been a war of independence. The ideals of "liberty, equality and fraternity" were still in the air, but that air was now polluted with the unfamiliar smells of factory smoke and foreign perfumes.

Out of these changes and upsets came the two movements—the "workingmen's movement," composed of small farmers, artisans, and workers in the early factories, and the women's movement—which converged in the Popular Health Movement of the eighteen thirties. These movements were as American as Davy Crockett or Betsy Ross, respectively, but each was in its own way profoundly subversive. Without any help from Karl Marx (who was only about twelve at the time) the workingmen's movement came to the conclusion that all their problems stemmed from the capitalist system. Society, in their analysis, was divided into a working class, which produced all real wealth, and the "parasitical" upper class which lived off the labor of others. It was this latter class, the propertied class, which now seemed to control the courts, the legislatures, and other institutions of society; and this, in the minds of these early American radicals, was a violation of the principles of the Declaration of Independence, if nothing else. "What distinguishes the present from every struggle in which the human race has been engaged" declared workingmen's (and women's) leader Fanny Wright, "is that the present is, evidently and openly and acknowledgedly, a war of class, and that this war is universal . . ."[28]

It was easy to guess which side doctors would be on in the coming class war. The regular doctors' claims to educational superiority were particularly irksome to working-class people. Men who worked fourteen-hour days complained that they had no time left over for reading or discussion, and no money to finance their children's education. The absence of free public schooling meant that working-class children grew up semiliterate, unprepared for anything but manual labor, while sons of the propertied class enjoyed the kind of classical education which led to gentlemanly professions. Members of the workingmen's parties sensed the emergence of a European-style aristocracy composed of the big property owners and the "nonproducing thinkers." With equal fervor, they denounced "King-craft, Priest-craft, Lawyer-craft and Doctor-craft."

The women's movement (and by this we mean something broader than the suffrage movement—suffrage did not become the central issue of feminism until mid-century) came to the problem of medicine from a different direction. With the rise of the Market, women began to find themselves in a monosexual world cut off from that of men, and frequently confined to home and church. Even working women found themselves by and large segregated into an all-women's world, like that of the early New England mill towns. Left to themselves, activist women of the early nineteenth century drew on each other's energy and inspiration to organize hundreds of benevolent associations, charitable institutions, and mutual-support groups. This "feverish congregation of women in extra-familial groups," as historian Mary Ryan describes it, provided a setting for the later emergence of the suffrage movement and the abolition movement.[29]

Within the developing female subculture, women inevitably discovered their common aversion to heroic medicine and began to grope for alternatives. Elizabeth Cady Stanton tells in her autobiography, for example, how an early encounter with male medicine reinforced her feminist consciousness. Her four-day-old infant (one of seven children) was found to have a bent collarbone.

> The physician, wishing to get a pressure on the shoulder, braced the bandage round the wrist, "leave that," he said, "ten days, and then it will be all right." Soon after he left I noticed that the child's hand was blue, showing that the circulation was impeded.[30]

Stanton removed the bandage and tried a second doctor, who bandaged the infant in a slightly different way. Soon after he left, she noticed that the baby's fingers had turned purple, so she tore off his bandages and sat down to devise her own method of bandaging the bent collarbone.

> At the end of ten days the two sons of Aesculapius appeared and made the examination, and said all was right, whereupon I told them how badly their bandages worked, and what I had done myself. They smiled at each other, and one said, "Well, after all, a mother's instinct is better than a man's reason." "Thank you, gentlemen, there was no instinct about it. I did some hard thinking before I saw how I could get pressure on the shoulder without impeding the circulation, as you did." . . . I trusted neither men nor books absolutely after this, either in regard to the heavens above or the earth beneath, but continued to use my "mother's instinct", if "reason" is too dignified a term to apply to a woman's thoughts . . .[31]

From swapping medical horror stories, women's circles moved on to swapping their own home remedies and from there to seeking more systematic ways to build their knowledge and skills. There were "Ladies' Physiological Societies," where women gathered in privacy to learn about female anatomy and functioning—something like the "know-your-body" courses offered by the women's movement today. There were popular lecturers, like Mrs. A. Nicholson, who gave presentations of female hygiene. Masses of women, many of whose husbands were involved in the workingmen's parties, were drawn into these nascent feminist health activities at a time when the demand for female suffrage had scarcely been raised. At this time in history, according to medical historian Richard Shryock, the health and feminist movements were "indistinguishable."[32]

Feminism, class struggle and the general social ferment of the twenties and thirties all came together in one figure, Fanny Wright. Fanny Wright was an outstanding intellectual leader of the workingmen's movement; she was also a woman and a feminist. Her revolutionary vision was relentlessly and, for the time, shockingly, rationalist: not only must the "parasitic classes" be overthrown, but the family must be abolished if human beings were to be liberated. Child raising must be lifted out of the private family and collectivized so that all children would receive the finest education from infancy on. Sex must be freed from the inhibiting clutches of economic and familial dependency to make way for free love. To the establishment newspapers, she was "the Great Red Harlot," perhaps as much for her unconcealed affair with socialist Robert Owen as for her political ideas. Yet, according to historian Arthur Schlesinger, "Her followers adored her. Hard-handed mechanics and workers crowded the halls when she lectured, and pored over copies of the *Free Enquirer* [the newspaper she edited] in flickering light late into the evening."[33] Five years before the Grimke sisters flaunted patriarchal rule by speaking out on abolition, Fanny Wright was thrilling audiences with the news of imminent cataclysm:

> . . . The priest trembles for his craft, the rich man for his hoard, the politician for his influence . . . From the people—ay! from the people, arise the hum and stir of awakening intelligence, enquiry and preparation.[34]

Fanny Wright helped focus the workingmen's movement on the subject of education and the control of knowledge. The problem, as she saw it, was not just to make education more available but to free it of class prejudice. What Americans now had was "a false system of education, stolen from aristocratic Europe."[35] If the working class was to achieve its goals, it would need to create a new kind of education, in fact, a new *culture,* of its own—one which was not handed down to the people by the "professional aristocrats." As an example, Fanny Wright established a people's "Hall of Science" in the Bowery district of New York which offered, among many other services, public instruction in physiology.[36]

While Fanny Wright was inciting people to think for themselves, and while mutterings against sex and class injustice were gaining volume in parlors and factories and public places, a poor New Hampshire farmer was piecing together the healing system which would become the main basis of the working class and feminist alternative to regular medicine. Samuel Thomson had watched his wife suffer and his mother die in the hands of regular doctors. Outraged by the violent effects of regular medicine, he began to reconstruct the folk med-

icine he had learned as a boy from a female lay healer and midwife
named Mrs. Benton:

> The whole of her practice was with roots and herbs, applied to the
> patient, or given in hot drinks, to produce sweating which always
> answered the purpose . . . By her attention to the family, and the
> benefits they received from her skill, we became very much attached
> to her; and when she used to go out to collect roots and herbs, she
> would take me with her, and learn me their names, with what they
> were good for. . . .[37]

Thomson's system was little more than a systematization of Mrs.
Benton's combination of herbs and steam, which in turn was derived
from Native American healing lore. But it was a great success with
the people Thomson visited, perhaps because by this time so many
people had had a brush with regular medicine. Thomson could, at
this point, have settled down to become a respected local healer, but
his medical philosophy involved much more than a set of techniques.
His goal was to remove healing from the Market and utterly democ-
ratize it; every person should be his or her own healer. To this end
he set out to spread his healing system as widely as possible among
the American people. In 1822 he first published his entire system as
the *New Guide to Health,* which sold 100,000 copies by 1839[38] and
in the decades that followed he set up hundreds of "Friendly Botanical Societies" in which people met to share information and study the
Thomsonian system.

At its height the Thomsonian movement claimed four million adherents out of a total United States population of 17 million.[39] The
movement was strongest among farmers in the Midwest and South
(the governor of Mississippi claimed in 1835 that one half of the
state's population were Thomsonians)[40] and among working-class
people in the cities. Five Thomsonian journals were published, and,
at a time when hardly anybody traveled much beyond the nearest
town, the Friendly Botanical Societies attracted large numbers of
members to their annual national conferences. Although other healing systems arose in the eighteen thirties, such as Sylvester Graham's
system based on whole grain cereal, none rivaled Thomsonianism in
popularity. Thomsonianism was, for all practical purposes, the core
of the Popular Health Movement.

Thomsonianism, at least at first, was concerned with much more
than health. The Thomsonian journals included discussions of

women's rights and attacks on such affronts to female health as tight-lacing and "heroic" obstetrical practice. Thomson himself strongly disapproved of male, regular obstetrical practice. The doctors were less experienced than midwives, he argued (at this time most regular physicians received their degrees without having witnessed a delivery), and too prone to try to rush things with the forceps, a practice which often resulted in crushed or deformed babies. Women were "natural" healers, according to the Thomsonians. John Thomson (Samuel's son) wrote:

> We cannot deny that women possess superior capacities for the science of medicine, and although men should reserve for themselves the exclusive right to mend broken limbs and fractured skulls, and to prescribe in all cares for their own sex, they should give up to women the office of attending upon women.[41]

Women were attracted to Thomsonianism in large enough proportions for regular doctors to be able to claim that the success of the movement was all due to the gullibility of the female sex. In Thomsonianism women could find a dignified and neighborly system of care for themselves, plus public validation for their traditional role as healers for their families and friends.

Thomsonianism identified itself with the workingmen's movement to the extent that one historian could write, in a negative vein, that it ". . . appealed to a class bias and a class consciousness in a way unacceptable to many Americans."[42] Echoing the philosophy of the workingmen's movement, the Thomsonian literature attacked the parasitical nonproducing classes and glorified manual labor. The universities which trained the experts of various sorts only bred snobbery:

> They [university students] learn to look upon labor as servile and demeaning, and seek their living in what they consider the higher classes of society.[43]

Other healing systems grew in the radical climate of the eighteen thirties which were equally opposed to the regular practice. Sylvester Graham (ignominiously remembered today only in the "graham cracker") founded a movement for "physiological reform"—the Hygienic movement—which rejected even the botanical remedies of the Thomsonians as well as drugs of any kind. Graham called for a vegetarian diet with plenty of raw fruits and vegetables and whole-grain

breads and cereals (far-fetched ideas in his day, when the medical
profession often counseled that uncooked produce was injurious, and
white bread was considered a mark of status). The Grahamian movement was popular and influential. Grahamian restaurants, boarding-
houses and "health food stores" opened; a Grahamian table was set
at utopian Brook Farm and at Oberlin College.

The Grahamians were as radical as the Thomsonians, equating
natural living habits with liberty and classlessness. A latter-day leader
of the hygienic movement, Dr. Herbert Shelton, expressed this vision
of a world in which people had not surrendered their autonomy to
experts:

> Any system that, of itself, creates a privileged class who can by law,
> or otherwise, lord it over their fellow nen, destroys true freedom
> and personal autonomy. Any system that teaches the sick that they
> can get well only through the exercise of the skill of someone else,
> and that they remain alive only through the tender mercies of the
> privileged class, has no place in nature's scheme of things, and the
> sooner it is abolished, the better will mankind be.[44]

Both Thomsonians and Grahamians were incensed by the regulars'
drive to gain a monopoly over healing; monopoly in medicine, like
monopoly in any area of endeavor, was undemocratic and oppressive
to the common people. All of this meshed exactly with what the
workingmen's movement was saying in general; in fact, early Thomsonianism was little more than the health wing of a general movement. Working-class activists rallied to the Thomsonian assault on
medical licensing laws. In New York, which had the most punitive
law against irregular medicine, the legislative battle was led by Job
Haskell, of the Workingman's Party of New York.

It was a disastrous rout for the regular doctors—one which contemporary medical historians often prefer to forget. In state after state
the popular health movement forces triumphed over the "medical
monopolists." Every state which had had a restrictive licensing law
softened it or repealed it in the eighteen thirties. Some, like Alabama
and Delaware, simply changed their laws to exempt Thomsonian and
other popular kinds of irregular healers from persecution.[45] This was
an enormous victory for the "people's medicine." At least one of the
movement's principles—antimonopolism—had been driven home.

But, at the same time, ironically, the life was going out of the Popular Health Movement. By the late eighteen thirties, the Thomsonian

movement was becoming a cult. A sizable faction within Thomsonianism began to hanker for respectability and something very much like
professionalism—even though this meant reversing the original tenets
of the movement. If Thomsonianism was going to fit with the personal
ambitions of these upwardly mobile healers, it would have to break
with the old "do it yourself" philosophy and ragtag collection of radical causes which had kept company with the early movement.

Thus Alva Curtis, a Thomsonian healer in Virginia, publicly denounced some fellow Thomsonians who were implicated in a slave insurrection in Mississippi in 1835:

> We greatly fear a number of botanic practitioners of Mississippi,
> have been led by blind fatuity to embark with other misguided citi-
> zens in a scheme of folly and madness, that has not only called
> down the vengeance of an exasperated community upon their
> head, but will justly cover their names and memories with execra-
> tions and infamy.[46]

Next, the would-be professionals within the movement maneuvered
to take Thomsonianism out of the hands of the masses and concentrate in a few approved healers. John Thomson (Samuel's son)
founded the New York Thomsonian Medical Society in 1835 on the
basis of two grades of membership: one for lay people and one for
society-licensed practitioners. Alva Curtis went further, splitting from
the 1838 annual Thomsonian convention to set up the Independent
Thomsonian Botanic Society for professionally minded Thomsonian
practitioners. When Curtis founded the first Thomsonian medical
school (the Literary and Botanico-Medical Institute of Ohio), old
Samuel Thomson sputtered:

> We had heard a great deal about Dr. Curtis and his school . . . but
> we never dreamed that it was his intention to make the healing art
> an odious monopoly and imitate the regular medical profession by
> conferring a sheepskin diploma.[47]

Thomson protested vigorously that his discoveries were being "taken
from the people generally, and like all other crafts monopolized by a
few learned individuals." But the trend was irresistible. Post-Thom-
sonian botanical medical colleges were mushrooming into existence;
groups which had campaigned against all licensing laws were now demanding accreditation for their own schools.

The Popular Health Movement had always ridden along on a

much deeper current of social unrest. Now that current had slowed, or turned off in new directions. Feminism, as it grew into a more articulate and organized force, was turning away from health and "body issues" and concentrating on the struggle for women's rights in the public world controlled by men. By the mid-thirties the workingmen's movement no longer existed as a distinct thrust in American politics. Its radical analysis trailed off in the end, towards Andrew Jackson's Democratic Party rather than toward socialist revolution.* Without being pushed from below by a mass constituency, the Thomsonians easily succumbed to the very forces they had set out to challenge. Where once they had denounced the transformation of healing into a commodity, now they sought to package their own alternative into a new commodity. Where once they had denounced medical elitism, they now aimed for a patrician exclusiveness of their own.

The Hygienic movement also suffered eclipse. Its very principles were incompatible with commercial success. Dr. Russell Trall, once a regular doctor who had crossed over to druglessness and then had systematized the Grahamian principles into a distinct school, had said:

> We cannot practice our system without educating the people in its principles. No sooner do they comprehend them, than they find themselves capable of managing themselves, except in rare, and extraordinary cases, without our assistance. Not only this, but our patrons learn from our teachings, examples, and prescriptions, how to live so as to avoid, to a great extent, sickness of any kind. When you become physicians, you will be continually teaching the people how to do without you.[48]

The business and professional ethics of the Hygienic movement, then, had once amounted to a plea for no business and no profession. Some Hygienists did open schools which offered the degree "Doctor of Medicine," and began to describe themselves as "physicians" and practitioners of "hygienic medication." But these feeble attempts to

* Labor historian Philip Foner explains this outcome in terms of the limited class the workingmen's movement represented: they were the "old" working class who had been free artisans and journeymen, as opposed to the new industrial proletariat drawn from southern and eastern Europe. Compared to these people, the adherents of the workingmen's movement were an elite themselves. In the decades to come, the sons of artisans would increasingly have a chance to get an education of some sort, and some would even find their way, ironically, into the expanding ranks of the regular medical profession.

imitate the medical profession were short-lived and later lamented even within the movement as a "very unfortunate mistake."

In the meantime, regular medicine "adopted enough Hygiene to save itself."[49] The Hygienic movement credits itself with these accomplishments, incorporated into regular medicine:

> People learned to bathe, to eat more fruits and vegetables, to ventilate their homes, to get daily exercise, to avail themselves of the benefits of sunshine, to cast off their fears of night air, damp air, cold air and draughts, to eat less flesh and to adopt better modes of food preparation.

> It has now been forgotten who promulgated these reforms; the record has been lost of the tremendous opposition to these reforms that the medical profession raised; it is believed that the medical profession was responsible for the decline of disease and death, the decline of the infant death rate, the inauguration of sanitation, and the increased life-span.[50]

Lady Doctors Join the Competition

The assaults of the Popular Health Movement left the regular doctors—who were still aspiring to become *the* medical profession—as debilitated as if they had been forced to undergo their own heroic treatments. But the worst was yet to come. Between the eighteen forties and seventies, the banner of professionalism, already tattered by populist attacks, fell into the mud of crude commercial competition. The regulars' drive for a medical monopoly became a defensive holding operation.

First there was the problem of "irregular" competition. Where there had once been a health movement, there was now a bevy of organized medical sects—eclectics, botanicists, homeopaths, hydropaths —each with its own schools, journals, and claims to scientific superiority. Trained botanical healers and eclectics (so-named because they aimed to combine the best of both regular and Thomsonian-type approaches) inherited the loyalty Thomsonianism had won earlier among small farmers and the urban working class. A far worse threat to the regulars was homeopathy: first, because it was popular among upper-class consumers. And, in these days before Medicaid and Medicare, when gentlemanly physicians still liked to think of their fees coyly as "honoraria" paid out of sheer gratitude, it was the upper-class consumer who counted in the struggle for occupational survival.

The second challenging feature of homeopathy was that it did not hurt people. (The botanical healing practices of the Popular Health Movement had been harmless too, but they were unacceptable to upper-class consumers because of their radical associations.)

Homeopathic therapy was, in a sense, heroic therapy inverted. While the regular physician recklessly escalated doses and mixed medications in order to produce a maximal affront to human physiology, the homeopath's maxim was—the less the better. The homeopathic physician began by diluting the basic medicine (usually a plant extract of some kind) to 1/100 of its original strength; the second dilution brought it to 1/10,000 of its original strength; the third to 1/1,000,000 of its original strength. According to Hahnemann, the founder of homeopathy, one should then proceed to the *thirtieth* dilution.[51] A *drop* of this could then be administered to the patient in a sugar cube. As any chemistry student could tell you, the chances of such a drop containing even a single molecule of the original medicine would be infinitesimal. But the homeopaths claimed to have discovered a new physical principle: that substances gained in curative power as they were diluted.

They had, in fact, discovered something extremely valuable: they had found a way to make a commodity out of doing nothing at all. The regular doctor feverishly dosed, probed, and (increasingly as the century went on) cut his patient. This produced a commendable and altogether marketable display of effort—but only at the risk of mortal injury to the patient. An honest and intelligent doctor might have admitted his helplessness in most cases and refrained from doing anything, but this would hardly have merited a fee. Thus the homeopathic compromise: to expend a great deal of effort and time without doing a bit of harm. To the patient who had known the bitterness of calomel, there must have been balm indeed in the homeopath's moistened sugar cube.

Then, quite aside from the competing sects, there was a mounting problem of competition within the ranks of the regular doctors themselves. To open a medical school, a group of doctors had to do little more than rent a building, collect a skeleton, a preserved fetus, and perhaps a few other visual aids, and then advertise to the public. Students paid the professors by the course, and were virtually guaranteed a degree in two years or so, so long as they kept up their payments. Thanks in large part to these medical degree mills, the number of regular doctors in the United States increased from a few thousand in 1800 to over 40,000 by mid-century.[52] And, of course, the stiffer the competition for paying patients, the more doctors were tempted into the business of occupational reproduction—medical teaching—to supplement their incomes. So the cycle went: poverty and "overpopulation," as the doctors saw it, going hand in hand as the profession marched toward ruin.

In the second half of the nineteenth century, occupational prestige sank so low that the days when Benjamin Rush could confer with statesmen and take tea with countesses began to look like a lost paradise of professionalism. The regular doctors banded together in 1847 to form their first national organization, pretentiously entitled *the American Medical Association*, and one of the AMA's first tasks was to survey the competition—the 40,000 regulars plus a "long list of irregular practitioners who swarm like locusts in every part of the country." The report concluded, "No wonder the profession of medicine has measurably ceased to occupy the elevated position which once it did; no wonder that the merest pittance in the way of remuneration is scantily doled out even to the most industrious of our ranks."[53]

The regular doctors were caught in a contradiction of their own making. Medicine had once been embedded in a network of community and family relationships. Now, it had been uprooted, transformed into a commodity which potentially anyone could claim as merchandise, a calling which anyone could profess to follow. So long as medical education was cheap, and medical fees were *not* too cheap, there was no limit to the numbers of regular doctors. Thus the patrician ideal of the gentleman doctor could never be realized. And of course, the deeper the doctors sank into commercialism, and the more they spawned in this fertile muck—producing new doctors simply for profit—the less likely they were to achieve the status and authority of their collective dreams. Ahead lay nothing but humiliation. Dr. C. H. Reed of Toledo wrote poignantly in the *Journal of the American Medical Association* about "a doctor who was found crying because he was hungry."[54]

A great deal—it is impossible to say exactly how much—of the competition which was reducing male regular doctors to tears was coming from *women*. By mid-century there were not only female lay healers to contend with, there was a new breed of middle-class women who aspired to enter the Market as regular, professional physicians. Like the women who had become involved in the Popular

Health Movement earlier, they were motivated by a spirit of reform:
they were opposed to the excesses of heroic medicine and—equally
important—they were outraged at the implicit indecency of the male
doctor-female patient relationship. The extreme division between
"men's sphere" and "women's sphere" had put the male doctor in a
decidedly awkward position. How could a woman, especially a lady,
expose her most private parts to his peerings and pokings? Doctors
were fond of citing female patients who died in quiet agony rather
than submit to male medical care. "If I could have been treated by a
lady doctor my worst sufferings would have been spared me,"[55] a
friend confided to the young Dr. Elizabeth Blackwell.

By mid-century the private horrors of mixed-sex medical encounters had become a public issue. Samuel Gregory, an "irregular" physician argued in 1850 that male obstetricians, by their very presence,
created enough anxiety in their patients to lengthen the process of
labor.[56] Gregory's book *Man-midwifery Exposed and Corrected; or
the Employment of Men to attend women in childbirth, shown to be
a modern innovation, unnecessary, unnatural and injurious to the
physical welfare of the community, and pernicious in its influence on
Professional and Public Morality* was a great success, and in 1852 "a
few ladies of Philadelphia" organized around their belief that "the
BIBLE recognizes and approves *only women* in the sacred office of
midwife."[57] And Catherine Beecher raised the charge of seduction
and sexual abuse, taking place in the practices of the most apparently
benevolent, honorable, and pious doctors:

> . . . A terrific feature of these developments has been the *entire
> helplessness* of my sex, amidst present customs and feelings, as to any
> redress for such wrongs, and the reckless and conscious impunity
> felt by the wrong-doers on this account. What can a refined, delicate,
> sensitive woman do when thus insulted? The dreadful fear of *public-
> ity* shuts her lips and restrains every friend. . . . *When such as these*
> have been thus assailed, who can hope to be safe?[58]

The popular magazine *Godey's Lady's Book* waged an all-out campaign for female physicians:

> Talk about this being the appropriate sphere of man, and his
> alone! With tenfold more plausibility and reason might we say, it is
> the appropriate sphere of woman, and hers alone.
> Female physicians will produce an era in the history of women
> . . . We would, in all deference, suggest that, first of all, there will

be candor in the patient to the female physician, which could not be expected when a sense of native delicacy and modesty existed to the extent of preferring to suffer rather than divulge the symptoms.[59]

Given the tensions and moral compromise associated with male medical care, the mid-nineteenth-century movement of women into medical training took on the aspects of a *crusade*—for female health, for morality, for decency.

It was this sense of being involved in a moral crusade which accounts for the determination of our early female doctors. For example, Elizabeth Blackwell applied to over sixteen schools before she found one which would accept her, but, as she said, "The idea of winning a doctor's degree gradually assumed the aspect of a great moral struggle, and the moral fight possessed attraction for me."[60] In the same year that Blackwell gained admission, Harriet Hunt was admitted to Harvard Medical College—only to have the decision reversed because the students threatened to riot if she came. (Harvard had admitted three black male students the year before and that, according to the white male majority, was enough!) Undaunted, Hunt went to seek a medical education at an "irregular" school.† Through the efforts of women like Blackwell, Hunt, Marie Zakrzewska, Lucy Sewall, Sarah Adamson, Ann Preston, Helen Morton, and Mary Putnam Jacobi—to mention only a few—there were, by 1900, approximately five thousand trained women doctors in the land,[61] fifteen hundred female medical students[62] and seven medical schools exclusively for women.

Male doctors recognized that women in the profession posed a threat which was far out of proportion to their numbers. The woman patient who considered herself socially superior to female lay healers, yet was repelled by male medicine, would naturally welcome a woman professional. Faced with this threat to their practice, the male doctors responded with every argument they could think of: How could a lady who was too refined for male medical care travel at night to a medical emergency? Operate when indisposed (e.g., menstruating)? If women were too modest for mixed-sex medical care, how could they expect to survive the realities of medical training—the

---

† An extreme example, from Cuba, of female determination to practice medicine in the nineteenth century: Henrietta Faber practiced medicine in Havana for years—disguised as a man. In 1820 she made the mistake of "coming out" —to marry a man—and was sentenced at once to ten years imprisonment for having practiced medicine.[63]

vulgar revelations of anatomy class, the shocking truths about human reproduction, and so on?‡ (Elizabeth Blackwell admitted that she first found the idea of medical training "disgusting.")[64]

The incongruity of a lady practicing medicine was a frequent inspiration to cartoonists. One in the English magazine *Punch* in 1872 shows a fashionable and feminine "Dr. Evangeline" looking up at the tall and manly "Mr. Sawyer" (British surgeons are not addressed as "doctor"):

> Doctor Evangeline: "By the bye, Mr. Sawyer, are you engaged to-morrow afternoon? I have rather a ticklish operation to perform—an amputation, you know."
> Mr. Sawyer: "I shall be very happy to do it for you."
> Doctor Evangeline: "O, no, not *that!* But will you kindly come and administer the chloroform for me?"[65]

(The full humor is of course lost in an age which has forgotten about smelling salts, seventeen-inch waists, and graceful swoons.)

Dr. Augustus Gardner, a leading American gynecologist summarized the paternalistic view of women's unfitness for medicine in 1872:

> More especially is medicine disgusting to women, accustomed to softnesses and the downy side of life. They are sedulously screened from the observation of the horrors and disgusts of life. Fightings, and tumults, the blood and mire, bad smells and bad words, and foul men and more intolerable women she but rarely encounters, and then, as a part of the privileges of womanhood, is permitted, and till now, compelled, to avoid them by a not, to her, disgraceful flight.[66]

There were contradictions in this nineteenth-century romanticist argument against women in medicine. Even the most sheltered Victorian lady—never mind the working-class mother struggling to raise her family in a one- or two-room tenement apartment—knew something of "blood and mire." A woman necessarily encounters blood more often than a man, not counting surgeons and soldiers. Mothers

‡ Nor is this perception of the incompatibility of women and medicine dead among American gynecologists today. One who was recently interviewed in the January 1977 *Ms.* magazine explained, "You have to be kind of crazy to go into the field, because it's a difficult, physically demanding residency. I had to be extremely obsessive-compulsive to get through it. This kind of behavior doesn't look good on a woman. And I'm so attuned to ob/gyn as a male speciality that I find it hard to accept women in it. I just don't see them as very feminine. I only know a couple of them who are feminine and good doctors too."

know much more about mire and bad smells, even if they are cushioned by servants, than businessmen and professors. The romantic
argument against women in medicine seemed to say that even the
sphere which women were expected to inhabit was too rough for
them—as if menstruation, childbirth, defecation, etc. were too un-
dignified for a lady to experience. Male doctors would have to take
over the female body for women's own protection. The vagina,
which had for too long sullied "woman's sphere," would have to be
removed to the province of medical professionalism.

Not too far under the romanticist arguments against women in
medicine lay a nasty streak of misogyny. If women were inherently too
delicate to desire medical training and certainly too modest to survive
it, then it followed that any female who did succeed at medicine must
be not a lady at all, but some kind of a freak. In his 1871 presidential
address to the AMA, Dr. Alfred Stillé made this observation on the
subject of women in medicine:

> Certain women seek to rival men in manly sports . . . and the
> strong-minded ape them in all things, even in dress. In doing so, they
> may command a sort of admiration such as all monstrous produc-
> tions inspire, especially when they tend towards a higher type than
> their own.[67]

He left it unclear which was more repulsive: the "strong-minded,"
though "monstrous" female medical aspirant, or her sisters who were
content with their genetically inferior condition. An editor of the
Buffalo Medical Journal took a less ambiguous stand:

> If I were to plan with malicious hate the greatest curse I could con-
> ceive for women, if I would estrange them from the protection of
> men, and make them as far as possible loathsome and disgusting to
> man, I would favor the so-called reform which proposed to make
> doctors of them.[68]

The regular doctors did not rely on persuasion alone to discourage
women from medical education. The would-be woman doctor faced
some very solid road blocks at every step of her career. First it was
difficult to gain admission to a "regular" school (the "irregular"
sects, descended from the Popular Health Movement, maintained
their feminist sympathies and openness to female students). Once inside, female students faced harassment from the male students ranging from "insolent and offensive language" to "missiles of paper, tin-

foil [and] tobacco quids."[69] There were professors who wouldn't discuss anatomy with a lady present and textbooks such as the 1848 obstetrics text which declared, "She [woman] has a head almost too small for intellect but just big enough for love."[70]

Having completed her academic work the would-be woman doctor often found the next steps blocked. Hospitals were usually closed to women doctors, and even if they weren't, the internships were not open to women. When she did finally make it into practice, she found her brother regulars unwilling to refer patients to her and absolutely opposed to her membership in their medical societies. It was not until 1915 that the AMA itself admitted female physicians.

If the male regulars seem to have been overreacting, recall the historical circumstances. In the United States, middle-class women began to knock on the doors of the medical schools at a time when the profession, such as it was, was suffering from what its members saw as extreme overcrowding.* The male doctors were afraid of the competition, and given the popular mistrust of them, not without reason. Irregular physician Augusta Fairchild, M.D., boasted in the *Water Cure Journal,* October 1861:

> Comets were once looked upon as omens of war. Female doctors may be viewed in very much the same light, for wherever they have made their appearance, a general uprising of the people to welcome them, and the most vigorous attempt of the *regular* masculine dignitaries of the 'profession' to quell the 'insurrection' have been the result.[71]

The movement of women into medical training had a whole train of unpleasant associations for the regular male physicians. Feminism, "irregular" medicine, and the populist assault on medical professionalism had all been indissolubly linked together in the decade of the Popular Health Movement. Throughout the century, botanic and eclectic schools continued to welcome women, so for that reason alone the feminine cause was always tainted with "irregularity," or the "irregular" cause tainted with feminism, whichever way you cared to look at it.† Irregulars such as Mary Gove Nichols, Harriet

---

* By contrast, medical historian Shryock argues, women began entering medical training in Russia at a time of physician *shortage;* in the Soviet Union today over 70 per cent of physicians are female.

† Similarly, in the mid-twentieth century, the anti-Semitism of most regular medical schools forced many Jewish students into schools of osteopathy.

Austin, M.D., Susannah W. Dodds, M.D., and others completed the
association by their activity in such reform movements as temper-
ance, sex education of the young, and, especially, dress reform. Drs.
Austin and Dodds wore pants, and Mary Gove Nichols wore
bloomers, about which experience she reminisced in 1853:

> I acknowledge that I have been mobbed on account of my dress.
> Fourteen years ago several persons determined to tar and feather me
> if I dared to lecture in a certain small city. . . . Years have greatly
> mended the manner of the mobs, but more than one scamp has felt
> the weight of my husband's cane in this city.[72]

Finally, the feminist/moralist argument against male doctors for
female patients had exposed the doctors' most vulnerable spot. There
was simply no public confidence that doctors were "gentlemen." A
doctor complained in the *Journal of the American Medical Association* that:

> the truth is patent that very many of its members are persons of in-
> ferior ability, questionable character and coarse and common fiber.

And in his presidential address to the American Medical Association
in 1903, Dr. Billings stated his concern that commercial night schools
were enabling "the clerk, the street-car conductor, the janitor and
others employed during the day to earn a degree."[73] The patrician
dream had been dashed against the commercial reality. Yet at the
very same time, Victorian sexual anxieties made it all the more urgent that a synthesis be found. If it was almost prohibitively difficult
for a lady to be examined by a gentlemanly doctor, how could she
possibly put herself in the care of an ex-janitor or street-car conductor? The very words—"lady" and "gentleman"—have moral as well
as class connotations, suggesting an ability to rise above sex in a way
that could not be expected of the "lower" classes. If regular medicine
drew too heavily from the "lower" types, it not only would lost status,
it would lose business. Achievement of the patrician ideal was becoming, in the late nineteenth century, a commercial necessity.

The AMA Code of Ethics, adopted in 1847, had enjoined doctors
"to unite *tenderness* with *firmness,* and *condescension* with *authority,*
[so] as to inspire the minds of their patients with gratitude, respect
and confidence."[74] (Emphasis in original.) But this would require
more than a skillful bedside manner. The longed-for *authority* would
have to come from somewhere. Keeping women out was a step in the

right direction (in a male-dominated society, women are inherently less authoritative than men). But, by the late nineteenth century, patriarchal tradition was no longer in and of itself, a firm enough basis for professional power. The average regular doctor (and there were more and more average doctors as the century wore on) may have been male, white, and Anglo-Saxon, but he was no more imposing a public figure than a druggist or real estate agent. If medicine was to become an authority in the lives of women, it would finally have to find a way to "soar above the sordid views of vulgar minds"—to float above cheap commercialism and sex itself.

THREE

Science and the Ascent of the Experts

By the late nineteenth century, the solution was near at hand. According to Sir William Osler, America's only titled physician, "the spirit of science was brooding on the waters."[1] Science was the transcendent force to which the doctors looked to lift medicine out of the mire of commercialism and gird it against its foes.

It was not only doctors who were eying science with professional self-interest. Science was well on its way to becoming a sacred national value, and any group which hoped to establish itself as the "experts" in a certain area would have to prove that they were rigorously scientific. Social work, before the eighteen eighties, had been a voluntary activity, left largely to the charitable impulses of upper-class women. As career-oriented, middle-class women began to enter the field, insisting that social work be regarded as a profession, more and more talk of "science" crept into the social work literature. The sentimental Lady Bountiful approach would have to make way for "scientific charity" based on systematic investigation in each case and carefully calculated professional intervention. Even law, in its anxiety about professional overpopulation and public distrust, began to search for a "scientific" basis. In all areas, making something "scientific" became synonymous with reform. Between roughly 1880 and 1920 progressive Americans campaigned not only for scientific medicine, but for scientific management, scientific public administration, scientific housekeeping, scientific child raising, scientific social work. The United States was, according to the *Atlantic Monthly,* a "nation of science."

The zeal to "reform" old professions and carve out new ones was coming from a specific group of people—a "new middle class," according to some historians.[2] These were the sons and daughters of the old-time gentry (small-to-medium-size businessmen, successful professionals, and the like) which had been on top of the social hierarchy in the early republic. But since the Civil War, rapid industrialization and the ferocious growth of monopolies had created a new polarization of American society: the "robber barons" were mowing down hundreds of small- and medium-size businessmen as they built up their monopolies and cartels. Immigration was swelling the ranks of the poor. The sons of the old gentry found themselves thrust into a hostile world, often with little more collateral than their college degrees and "good breeding." Education and background made them feel superior, but hardly secure. Above, they saw a "plutocracy" gorging itself on the wealth drained from small businessmen; below, an untamed, menacing proletariat:

> Two enemies, unknown before, have risen like spirits of darkness on our social and political horizon—an ignorant proletariat and a half-taught plutocracy.[3]

The trouble with these two classes from the point of view of the new middle class was not only that they were boorish, but that they were engaged in a war which seemed likely to destroy the entire social order. During the eighteen seventies and eighties, strikes, riots, and armed insurrections filled the newspapers and the nightmares of the middle class. Anyone could see, they argued, that there was an urgent need for scientific experts and administrators to

> . . . disinterestedly and intelligently mediate between [the] contending interests. When the word "capitalist classes" and "the proletariate" [sic] can be used and understood in America, it is surely time to develop such men, with the ideal of service to the State, who may help to break the force of these collisions.[4]

"Experts" could solve society's problems because they were, as scientific men, by definition totally objective and above special interests of any kind. In the process, the problems of the new middle class itself could be solved too. Specialized "expert" occupations, accessible only after lengthy training, would provide them a secure occupational niche and a share of power far out of proportion to their numbers. Far-seeing spokesmen of their class even prophesied a future society in which—not the "half-taught plutocracy," not the "ignorant proletariat"—but the experts themselves would rule. This, it was felt, would be the utopian summit of human civilization, since the experts would of course manage things scientifically, i.e., for the good of all.* As a leading engineer explained it, "the golden rule will be put into practice through the slide rule of the engineer."[5]

To this new middle class, science was not just a method or a discipline, but a kind of religion. Asking what "creed" best suited Americans, social commentator Thaddeus Wakeman wrote in 1890:

> The answer is, that which he knows to be true,—and that, in one word is *Science.* The majority of the American people are already *practically secularists*—people of this world. . . . Our people are unconsciously welcoming the incoming sway of Science and Man; and this is proved by their absence from the Churches.[7]

The Moral Salvation of Medicine

If the transformation of regular medicine into "scientific medicine" were retold as a story of religious conversion, Sinclair Lewis's *Arrowsmith* would be its *Pilgrim's Progress*. Lewis's novel was based on the real-life experiences of a young medical researcher, and it captures in fiction the moral fervor of the scientific reformers as no historical study has done. At the University of Winnemac medical school, young Martin Arrowsmith encounters the extremes of scientific purity and medical commercialism, personified in his professors. There is, at one extreme, Dr. Roscoe Geake, newly resigned from the chair of otolaryngology to the vice-presidency of the New Idea Medical Instrument and Furniture Company of Jersey City, who exhorts the medical students to "put pep in their salesmanship":

> . . . Have your potted palms and handsome pictures—to the practical physician they are as necessary a part of his working equipment

---

* Even at the time, this plan smacked too overtly of middle-class self-interest to gain much support. Edward A. Ross, the founder of American sociology and a leading advocate of an expanded role for experts, was forced to retreat in 1920 with the defensive rejoinder that, "There is of course no such thing as 'government by experts.' The malicious phrase is but a sneer flung by the scheming self-seekers who find in the relentless veracity of modestly-paid investigators a barrier across their path."[6]

as a sterilizer or a Baumanometer. But so far as possible have every-thing in sanitary-looking white—and think of the color-schemes you can evolve, or the good wife for you, if she be blessed with artistic tastes! Rich golden or red cushions, in a Morris chair enameled the purest white! A floorcovering of white enamel, with just a border of delicate roses! Recent and unspotted numbers of expensive maga-zines, with art covers, lying on a white table! Gentlemen, there is the idea of imaginative salesmanship which I wish to leave with you . . .[8]

And there is at the other extreme Dr. Max Gottlieb—"the mystery of the University" because he is a Jew, a foreigner, and a scientist obsessed by his work:

He was unconscious of the world. He looked at Martin and through him; he moved away, muttering to himself, his shoulders stooped, his long hands clasped behind him. He was lost in the shadows, him-self a shadow.

He had worn the threadbare top-coat of a poor professor, yet Martin remembered him as wrapped in a black velvet cape with a sil-ver star arrogant on his breast.[9]

Martin and his friend Clif swear drunkenly to follow the lonely path of science:

". . . I'm jus' sick o' c'mmercialism an' bunk as you are," confides Clif.

"Sure. You bet," Martin agreed with alcoholic fondness. "You're jus' like me. . . . Ideal of research! Never bein' content with what *seems* true! Alone, not carin' a damn, square-toed as a captain on the bridge, working all night, getting to the bottom of things!"[10]

But the path is more arduous than the young men can see. Distrac-tions beckon from all sides—quick money, worldly power, venal women, even the quagmire of sentimental humanitarianism. Arrow-smith is only human, he falls again and again. But each time he real-izes he has lost his soul (his work) and picks himself up once again to pursue the austere ideal of science. In the end he must set aside all worldly things—wealth, position, a rich and gorgeous wife—and retire to a laboratory built in the remote wilderness.

Biological science had not always had the mystic and holy power with which it pulled at Martin Arrowsmith. In the eighteen seventies and eighties, when the ideas of the new biology began to circulate in the American middle class, they were greeted with a suspicion which often bordered on moral revulsion. Darwin's theory of evolution—

the most brilliant synthetic breakthrough of nineteenth- and perhaps twentieth-century biological science—"shattered the Christian cosmos." It was not only that the theory violated the letter of the Old Testament; Darwinism went further and asserted that the world of living creatures could have gotten the way it is without the intervention of God, in fact, without conscious effort on anybody's part. What was left, in the view of leading American Christians, was a godless universe, a moral desert—

> Life without meaning; death without meaning; the universe without meaning. A race tortured to no purpose, and with no hope but annihilation. The dead only blessed; the living standing like beasts at bay, and shrieking half in defiance and half in fright.[11]

The spiritual implications of the new biological truth were, as one minister put it, "brutalizing."

In a lesser way, biology's second great contribution to popular culture—the Germ Theory of Disease—further undercut the religious foundations of morality. Traditional religion saw individual disease as the price of moral failings, epidemics as acts of a vengeful God. In the mid-nineteenth century, Albert Barnes, a leading Presbyterian minister, declared cholera to be a punishment for the "vanities of natural science," especially Darwinism. But, through the lenses of the new high power microscopes available in the mid-eighteen hundreds, disease began to look like a natural event which depended less on God than on the growth rates of what appeared to be fairly amoral species of microbes. If diseases were dispensed in some sort of microbial lottery, rather than by moral plan, then indeed this was a "race tortured to no purpose."

In order to become a moral force in society, biological science had had to undergo a kind of moral transformation itself. For example, Darwin's popularizers managed to identify "evolution" with "progress," as if natural history were a long uphill moral pilgrimage. This stratagem excused some of the more savage aspects of natural selection and—even more important—it left room for a divine Plan. The laws which science was uncovering would turn out to be the expression of the will of God—revelations of the divine Plan. Thus science could provide moral guidelines for living: for example, that one had an "evolutionary duty" to "advance the race" through proper selection of a mate, good health habits, etc. By the eighteen eighties it is difficult to find a popular tract or article on any subject—education, suffrage, immigration, foreign relations—which is not embellished with Darwinian metaphors. Charlotte Perkins Gilman's classic *Women and Economics, the* theoretical breakthrough for a whole generation of feminists, appealed not to right or morality but to evolutionary theory. Women's confinement to domestic activities had made them more "primitive" and undeveloped than men. If women were not emancipated, the whole race would be dragged down, she argued (with the naïve racism which was typical of her time):

> In keeping her on this primitive basis of economic life, we have kept half humanity tied to the starting-post, while the other half ran. We have trained and bred one kind of qualities into one-half the species, and another kind into the other half. And then we wonder at the contradictions of human nature! . . . We have bred a race of psychic hybrids, and the moral qualities of hybrids are well known.[12]

Germ Theory went through a similar moral transformation. If it was germs and not sin that were the immediate cause of disease, then sin could be still retained as an ultimate cause. Germ Theory was transformed into a doctrine of individual guilt not at all out of tune with old-fashioned Protestantism. Anyone who transgressed "the laws of hygiene" deserved to get sick, and anyone who got sick had probably broken those laws. The English physician Elizabeth Chesser, in her book *Perfect Health for Women and Children,* warned that "the time has nearly arrived when we shall not be permitted to be unhealthy."[13]

If, to the middle-class public, science was a source of moral precepts, a kind of secularized religion, then the scientist was its prophet. In him, progressive-minded Americans found a culture hero for the new century. General Francis A. Walker, the president of MIT, announced in 1893 that America's scientists outdistanced all other occupational groups in their "sincerity, simplicity, fidelity, and generosity of character, in nobility of aims and earnestness of effort."[14]

The experimental scientist was a fitting moral paragon for the modern age. He was an intellectual of sorts; that is, he did "brain work," but he had none of the effete otherworldliness which Americans found so distasteful in philosophy professors, poets and other impractical types. In fact, the lab man was as ruthlessly hardheaded, materialistic and pragmatic as any capitalist entrepreneur—"a real man." Yet, at the same time, he was an altruist whose unselfishness reached superhuman heights: Metchnikoff drank cholera vibrios by the tumblerful to test their effects; later "microbe hunters" cheerfully exposed themselves to the carriers of yellow fever, malaria, tuberculosis.

With his selflessness, his obsessive drive, his apparent scorn for material reward, the scientist assumed some of the qualities of the Christian Redeemer: taking on his shoulders (bent from too many hours over the microscope) the sins—and diseases—of the multitude. "Within these walls," says the inscription on New York's Sloan-Kettering Institute for cancer research, "a few labor unceasingly that many may live." And it was to the altar of biological science that America's first billionaires, Rockefeller and Carnegie, went to expiate their guilt through philanthropy—as if in the ascetic atmosphere of the biological laboratory the wages of sinful accumulation could be turned into *life*.

What happened to elevate biological science and science in general from the status of a godless rebel to such a state of grace? "Good works" were part of the answer. The "miracles" of modern science outdid anything that the nineteenth-century Christian God deigned to effect. Sir William Osler pictured science pouring from a cornucopia, down onto man's head, "blessings which cannot be enumerated . . ." After the late nineteenth century, an evangelist would be as foolish to denounce science as the devil's work as he would be to forego microphones, electric lights, and all vehicles based on the principle of internal combustion. But science did not triumph through works alone. In fact, it sometimes went the other way: the prestige of science was so great that science took credit, in the public mind, for innovations from other sources. An instrument maker, not a scientist, invented the steam engine; two bicycle mechanics designed the first airplane; a rising standard of living, not vaccines and antitoxins, eventually brought down the rate of infant mortality. So the "scientism"— science worship—of the nineteenth and twentieth centuries was not just a matter of pragmatic appreciation. Science was able to become a neo-religion because of its special qualities as an ideology. It was tough and yet transcendent—hardheaded and masculine, yet at the same time able to "soar above" commercial reality.

No one could question the masculinity, the aggressiveness, of the new experimental biology. Earlier generations of biologists had been content to observe nature—to catalog it, describe it, label its parts. The new scientist pursued nature, trapped it in his laboratory, encircled it with experimental conditions representing different possible truths, and tightened the circle until the answers came out. Oliver Wendell Holmes, Sr., a regular doctor and early champion of scientific medicine, described his attitude toward scientific investigation in the language of undisguised sexual sadism. "I liked to follow the workings of another mind through these minute, teasing investigations," he confided to his friend and fellow physician S. Weir Mitchell, "to see a relentless observer get hold of Nature and squeeze her until the sweat broke out all over her and Sphincters loosened . . ."[15]

But the aggressiveness of science—true science—is very different from the commercial aggressiveness of the Market. The only value known to the marketplace is self-interest; and if the Market encourages the qualities of rationalism and quantitative thinking, it does so only to put them at the service of profit. Science, on the other hand, is the embodiment of disinterestedness (or perhaps we could say, the disembodiment of the self-interestedness of the Market). It is rational and calculative, but only in the interests of *truth*. Ideally, neither whimsy nor wishful thinking nor the desire for fame can becloud the scientist's deliberations: The judgment of the "results"—the graphs, columns of figures, comparative measurements—is final. It is this image of uncompromising disinterestedness and objectivity which gives science its great moral force in the mind of the public. Science is supposed to serve no special interests, no class or privileged group. It rises above all that is narrow, mundane, greedy, just as the "McGurk Institute" for medical research in *Arrowsmith* perches majestically on top of twenty-eight floors of commercial offices:

> The McGurk Institute is probably the only organization for scientific research in the world which is housed in an office building. It has the twenty-ninth and thirtieth stories of the McGurk Building, and the roof is devoted to its animal house and to tiled walks along which (above a world of stenographers and bookkeepers and earnest gentlemen who desire to sell Better-bilt Garments to the golden dons of the Argentine) saunter rapt scientists dreaming of osmosis in Spirogyra.[16]

With the moral transformation of science, the laboratory took on a sacred quality. The laboratory was the temple of objectivity from which science could survey the world of man and nature—a kind of "germ-free zone" separated off from the filth, commercialism, and cheap sentiment of the world. Martin Arrowsmith's first few moments in his new lab at the "McGurk Institute" are as refreshing to his spirit as a cathedral to a pilgrim:

> . . . When he had closed the door and let his spirit flow out and fill that minute apartment with his own essence, he felt secure.
>
> No Pickerbaugh or Rouncefield could burst in here and drag him away to be explanatory and plausible and public; he would be free to work, instead of being summoned to the package-wrapping and dictation of breezy letters which men call work. . . .
>
> Suddenly he loved humanity as he loved the decent, clean rows of test-tubes, and he prayed then the prayer of the scientist . . .[17]

The Laboratory Mystique

While young Dr. Arrowsmith was struggling along on his pilgrimage in quest of scientific purity, other regular doctors—the leaders of their occupation—were beginning to appraise the laboratory as a possible solution to medicine's troubles.

The men who were to reform medicine, that is, transform it from regular medicine into "scientific" medicine, came from the new middle class and shared its visions and anxieties. If they were science-minded, that was not so much because they were doctors as because they were members of a class which had staked its future on science and expertism. They were not graduates of commercial medical schools; they were college-educated men who had studied medicine at Harvard, Johns Hopkins, or Penn and had finished off their studies with a year or two in Berlin or Heidelberg (Germany had replaced England as the mecca for young doctors). There they had listened reverently to the great European fathers of experimental biology, drunk beer in rathskellers with the scions of European nobility, and perhaps had a chance to dabble in a laboratory. They returned to the United States, perhaps not with a thorough education in experimental science, but at least with "the idea of experiment," as Dr. S. Weir Mitchell put it, and a passion to stamp this idea on the murky form of regular medicine.

The scientific reform of medicine was not as easy a project as one might expect from the vantage point of the late twentieth century, with our supertechnological, instrument-dominated medicine. The average regular doctor, as opposed to the scientific elite, still had the mentality of a small businessman, worrying more about the day-to-day competition than the long-range future of the profession. He was respectful, as were most native-born middle-class Americans, toward science, though not through any firsthand acquaintance. Few practicing physicians had ever seen a microscope or used a thermometer, nor is it likely that they had much interest in such "advanced" technology. As one regular doctor remarked cynically upon the invention of the ophthalmoscope, "what the ophthalmoscope discloses are morbid conditions which are not for the most part more curable by being seen."[18]

"Heroic" bleeding and purging had subsided somewhat in the late nineteenth century, but regular therapy was still dominated by the need to produce some sort of a tangible commodity. Surgery had been added to the doctors' repertoire, thanks to the introduction of ether and chloroform in the eighteen forties, and it was performed for all sorts of excuses on a variety of organs (see Chapter 4). In terms of drugs, opium and quinine were edging calomel out of the doctor's little black bag by the eighteen sixties. Quinine—which is useful for controlling malaria, if prescribed properly—was handed out in erratic doses for fevers in general. With opium, however, and alcohol, the doctors had at last found something which really worked. Opium, alcohol, and cocaine did indeed "cure" pain, and the pragmatic physician used them liberally for everything from pneumonia to "nerves."

Much as they might have liked to, the scientific reformers of medicine could not simply denounce their regular colleagues and insist that they be outlawed along with midwives, lay healers and irregular doctors. For one thing, the handful of scientific doctors knew that no reform could be made against the will of the now 120,000-strong rank and file. For another, there were still no "scientific" therapies with which to replace the fumbling therapies of the average doctor. European bacteriology had produced diphtheria antitoxin, but little more of therapeutic value.

The general reform strategy, then, had to be to ignore the sea of incompetence that was turn-of-the-century regular medical practice, and to focus on medical education. Attacking the schools had the advantages of not offending the bulk of the rank and file while circumventing the whole issue of effective therapy. In education the issue was not what doctors *did,* but who they were and what they knew. The specific reform strategy was of course to add *science* to medical education. The Johns Hopkins medical school—the first American medical school to meet German standards—provided the model. There were solid courses in bacteriology, chemistry, pathology, physiology, clinical courses featuring live patients; full-time professors who were also experimental scientists; and, above all, laboratories. After all, what the public meant by science was something that had to do with laboratories, and by a "scientific fact" they meant a piece of information whose lineage could be traced to a neat (preferably quantitative) entry in a dog-eared, chemical-stained lab notebook. To be "scientific," in the fullest evangelical sense, medicine needed laboratories.

The rationale for scientizing medicine was provided by the Germ Theory of Disease. If all diseases had a single, known cause, as Benjamin Rush had argued, or if they were caused by "bad air" or "unbalanced humors," as most prescientific doctors believed, there would be no good reason for putting medical students through the trials of a scientific education. If, on the other hand, they were caused by actual physical particles—"germs"—as Pasteur and Koch and the other great figures of European biology claimed, then science was indispensable. Germs, as everyone knew, were invisible to ordinary people. They could be seen only by scientists skilled in microscopy, handled only by the most meticulous laboratory man. If germs caused disease, and if germs could only be ambushed in a well-stocked laboratory, then medicine without laboratories was like law without courts or theology without churches.

So the reasoning went, though there was no evidence that anyone would be a better doctor for having once confronted a purple-stained bacillus at the end of a microscope barrel. From a scientific point of view, there were other problems. Germ Theory did not forge quite as firm a link between medicine and bacteriology as the scientific doctors liked to think. It is true that by 1900 specific germs had been associated with typhoid, leprosy, tuberculosis, cholera, diphtheria and tetanus—but in what sense the germs *caused* these diseases was not so clear.

Koch demonstrated that tubercle bacilli could be found in the tissues of all experimental animals which had the disease, but he could not explain the fact that disease-causing germs could also be found in the tissues of healthy animals. Nor could he have explained why Metchnikoff and his colleagues could gulp cholera germs without any more serious effect than mild intestinal discomfort—or why in general one person contracted a disease and another did not, despite exposure to the same germs. As a result, George Bernard Shaw had no trouble demolishing bacteriology as a "superstition" in his play *The Doctor's Dilemma:*

B.B. [Sir Ralph Bloomfield Bonington, a scientific doctor]: . . . If youre not well, you have a disease. It may be a slight one; but it's a disease. And what is a disease? A lodgement in the system of a pathogenic germ, and the multiplication of that germ. What is the remedy? A very simple. Find the germ and kill it.

SIR PATRICK: Suppose there's no germ?

B.B.: Impossible, Sir Patrick: there must be a germ: else how could the patient be ill?

SIR PATRICK: Can you show me the germ of overwork?

B.B.: No; but why? Why? Because, my dear Sir Patrick, though the germ is there, it's invisible. Nature has given it no danger signal for us. These germs—these bacilli—are translucent bodies, like glass, like water. To make them visible you must stain them. Well, my dear Paddy, do what you will, some of them wont stain. They wont take cochineal: they wont take any methylene blue: they wont take gentian violet: they wont take any coloring matter. Consequently, though we know, as scientific men, that they exist, we cannot see them. But can you disprove their existence? Can you conceive the disease existing without them? Can you, for instance, shew me a case of diphtheria without the bacillus?

SIR PATRICK: No; but I'll shew you the same bacillus, without the disease, in your own throat.

B.B.: No, not the same, Sir Patrick. It is an entirely different bacillus; only the two are, unfortunately, so exactly alike that you cannot see the difference. . . . There is the genuine diphtheria bacillus discovered by Loeffler; and there is the pseudo-bacillus, exactly like it, which you could find, as you say, in my own throat.

SIR PATRICK: And how do you tell one from the other?

B.B.: Well, obviously, if the bacillus is the genuine Loeffler, you have diphtheria; and if it's the pseudo-bacillus, youre quite well. Nothing Simpler. Science is always simple and always profound.[19]

Without question, bacteriology had cast a bright light on medicine, but the beam was all too narrow. Germ Theory led to some spectacular victories: effective methods of immunization, antitoxins, and, later, antibiotics—to give a few examples. But at the same time Germ Theory (and the general effort of scientific medicine to search for a single cellular or molecular "cause" for each disease) helped distract medicine from the environmental and social factors in human health —poor nutrition, stress, pollution, etc. The result is a kind of medicine which, for example, is obsessed with finding the cellular "cause" of cancer, even though an estimated 80 per cent or more of cancer cases are environmentally induced.[20]

But none of these reflections deterred the scientific doctors of the turn of the century. Germ Theory seemed to provide a solid scientific basis for medicine, and if there were still a few loopholes which could not be filled up with "pseudo-bacilli" or similar theoretical cosmetics, that was only because there were not enough well-trained men doing full-time research. The important thing was to get science into the medical schools, and that in itself was a problem sufficient to challenge the best scientific minds.

First there was the problem of money. The old two-hundred-dollar-a-year fees would not pay for laboratory equipment and German-trained professors. So, for a start, tuition would have to rise dramatically. That, of course, had some advantages. John S. Billings, one of the leaders of the reform of medical education, pointed out that the new, scientific schooling would be so expensive that poor boys should not even try to become physicians.[21] But in fact, middle-class boys wouldn't be able to either. So unless scientific medical education was to be restricted to young Vanderbilts and Morgans, tuition increases would never cover the costs. Vast sources of outside subsidization would have to be found.

Medicine and the Big Money

The medieval medical profession had depended, directly and indirectly, on the sponsorship of the landed nobility. In colonial America and the early republic, there were no equivalent concentrations of wealth—hence little support for universities, elite professions, or "culture" generally. But by 1900 the money was there. The period of hectic industrialization following the Civil War had produced concentrations of wealth that would have been unimaginable a generation before. Among America's new plutocrats, no one outweighed John D. Rockefeller and Andrew Carnegie. Through a combination of luck, shrewdness, and sheer plunder, Rockefeller (Standard Oil) and Carnegie (U. S. Steel) had put together fortunes that ran into nine figures. It was this money, extracted from the labor of thousands of American working people and the wreckage of hundreds of smaller businesses, which financed the triumph of scientific (previously known as "regular") medicine in the early twentieth century.

It would be easy enough to find a capitalist conspiracy here. Both Rockefeller and Carnegie subscribed to the "gospel of wealth"—the idea that they had been appointed by some higher power to shape society through the instrument of philanthropy. (Rockefeller, a Baptist, believed he was appointed by God; Carnegie, a devout social Darwinist, believed he had risen through evolutionary natural selection.) Medicine was a traditional outlet for philanthropy; and, within medicine, the two robber-barons-turned-philanthropists would be expected to favor the gentleman-scientist breed of doctor over the sundry competition—"irregulars," low-class regulars, lady doctors, midwives, etc.

But it was not that simple. Rockefeller, for example, placed his personal trust in homeopathy, that archrival of regular medicine. Moreover, as one otherwise uncritical biographer points out, Rockefeller "had sharp limitations of education and outlook; he was not well read, not much interested in literature, science, or art. . . ."[22] Carnegie presented another kind of problem: he had a profound distrust of "experts" and had made it clear that they were the "last men" he wanted on the board of the Carnegic Institute in Pittsburgh.[23] Business entrepreneurs, he believed, were the most progressive force in society and should exert direct control over philanthropic and educational institutions:

Americans do not trust their money to a lot of professors and principals [college presidents] who are bound in set ways, and have a class feeling about them which makes it impossible to make reforms.[24]

But two things drove Rockefeller and Carnegie, and their money, into the arms of medicine's scientific reformers. First there was the philanthropists' own insistence on absolute impartiality and objectivity in their giving. Recall that these two men were about as widely hated by their fellow country-people as any American could be and expect to ride the streets without a police escort. Their charity had to be as seemingly impartial and detached as their money-making had been ruthless. Rockefeller, for example, refused to endow a medical school at the University of Chicago because the university's president insisted that the school had to be "regular" and Rockefeller was opposed to supporting any particular medical sect—even the "regular" one. Carnegie, on his part, excluded from his college faculty pension plan any school which showed the slightest trace of denominational leanings. Of course such a determined impartiality contained an inevitable bias toward any cause which could represent itself as purely "scientific."

Secondly, Rockefeller and Carnegie simply could not spend their money all by themselves. Despite the "gospel of wealth" which upheld the plutocrat's unique and personal ability to dispense charity, both men were forced to delegate more and more of the responsibility for managing their philanthropic enterprises. In time philanthropy became institutionalized in corporate-style foundations, but initially there was no one to turn to except, of course, experts—experts in philanthropy. Such men identified with the scientific approach to medicine because it mirrored their own approach to philanthropy. If philanthropy was a matter of sentiment, then rich men could handle it themselves, but if it was a matter of science, then experts would have to do it for them.

The first of the philanthropic experts was Frederick T. Gates, an ex-teacher, ex-farmer, ex-bank clerk, ex-salesman, ex-minister and, as far as one can tell, general hustler from Minneapolis. When John D. found him in 1891, Gates was heading up something called the American Baptist Education Society and saw himself principally as a minister. But, once established with an office and secretary by Rockefeller, Gates took a more secular turn of mind. To paraphrase one historian, Gates found himself converted from Baptism to Scientism. He came to the conclusion that "the whole Baptist fabric was built upon texts which had no authority. . . ."[25] In his work for Rockefeller, he developed what he called "scientific giving," which chiefly meant funneling money through relatively large centralized agencies rather than handing it out piecemeal to small agencies.

Then, in 1897, Gates read Johns Hopkins Professor Osler's *Principles and Practice of Medicine* and was converted overnight to scientific medicine. There was not much to the "practise," as Gates wrote, but the "principles" were first rate. Gates immediately dashed off a memo to John D. Rockefeller urging the support of medical research and the development of scientifically based medicine.

The bait was set, and medicine's gentleman-scientists began to close in on the money. The story goes that Dr. L. Emmett Holt, pediatrician to the family of John D. Rockefeller, Jr., and a member of the Fifth Avenue Baptist Church attended by the Rockefeller family, converted John D. Rockefeller Jr. to scientific medicine during a train ride between Cleveland and New York. John Jr. was sufficiently impressed to offer Holt and six of his friends—including the dean of Johns Hopkins medical school and several well-known biological scientists and professors—the money to open a new research institute. These seven men, all united by ties of friendship and common academic interests, accepted twenty thousand dollars from

Rockefeller and became the first board of directors of the Rockefeller Institute for Medical Research. The money had begun to come together with the men.

The Rockefeller Institute brought all the glamour and mystery of European laboratory research to America. Here at last was a place where medicine's pure scientists could labor undistracted by patients or financial worries. But to Gates, it was much more—it was a "theological seminary, presided over by the Rev. Simon Flexner, D.D."[26] It was a model not only of medical science, but of the gentility to which medicine aspired. The main building featured an enormous paneled dining hall in which the researchers, in obligatory jackets and ties, were served by uniformed waiters. The fictional description of the McGurk Institute in *Arrowsmith* recreates the effect of the Rockefeller Institute and many of its actual features:

> The real wonder of the Institute had nothing visible to do with science. It was the Hall, in which lunched the staff, and in which occasional scientific dinners were given, with Mrs. McGurk as hostess. Martin gasped and his head went back as his glance ran from glistening floor to black and gold ceiling. The Hall rose the full height of the two floors of the Institute. Against the oak paneling of the walls were portraits of the pontiffs of science, in crimson robes, with a vast mural by Maxfield Parrish, and above all was an electrolier of a hundred globes.
>
> "Gosh—*Jove!*" said Martin, "I never knew there was such a room!"[27]

By the mid-nineteen sixties, the Rockefeller Institute, with an endowment of close to $200 million and a staff of over fifteen hundred, remained committed to the patrician ideal. There were chamber music concerts every other week in Caspary Hall; Calders and Klines hanging in the Abby Aldrich Rockefeller dining hall; sherry parties with David Rockefeller. The aim, according to then-president Detlev Bronk, who had been a student and friend of the Institute's founders, was to produce "*gentleman* scientists."

The Rockefeller Institute and Johns Hopkins (the first American medical school with labs and full-time professors) stood out as citadels of scientific medicine and within a few years they were to produce a stream of important discoveries in bacteriology and immunology. But these two institutions could not, by sheer force of example, produce all the desired "reforms" in medicine. The next step was to weed out the "irregular," non-scientific and generally

low-class medical schools and see that philanthropic funds were channeled into the few institutions which could hope to meet scientific
standards. To this end the AMA's Council on Medical Education, an
elite committee composed of research-oriented doctors, approached
the Carnegie Foundation in 1907. The Council on Medical Education had already done a nationwide survey of medical schools, rated
them, and decided which ones should be purged and which provided
for. What they needed from the Carnegie Foundation at this point
was not its money, but its imprimatur. The AMA could easily be accused of sectarianism and self-interest, but the Carnegie Foundation,
with its board composed of an impeccable roster of university presidents, had a reputation for expertise and impartiality. The foundation's president "at once grasped the possibilities" in the AMA pro-
posal and agreed to finance a new, completely "objective" study of
medical education.

To make sure that the Carnegie study would not be tarnished with
medical sectarianism of any variety, a layman was hired to do the job
—one Abraham Flexner, who happened to be the brother of Simon
Flexner, M.D., director of the Rockefeller Institute, and was himself
a graduate of Johns Hopkins University. The resulting Flexner Report, which has been hailed by most medical historians as the most
decisive turning point in American medical history, was about as un-
biased as, say, a television commercial for a cold remedy. There were,
according to Flexner, "too many" doctors in the United States and
they were too low-class—any "crude boy or jaded clerk" was able to
get medical training. Some black doctors would be needed, if only to
check the spread of disease from black to white neighborhoods: "ten
millions of them live in close contact with sixty million whites,"
Flexner pointed out. Few women doctors were needed, though, he
observed. The evidence? The lack of "any strong demand for women
physicians or any strong ungratified desire on the part of women to
enter the profession." (!) As for the different sectarian approaches to
medicine, the issue was not which of the existing sects should prevail,
he insisted, but whether scientific medicine (i.e., the regular sect suitably reformed) should prevail over all of them.[28]

What Abraham Flexner *did* in 1909 was probably every bit as important as what he wrote. He traveled to every medical school in the
country, and there were about 160 at the time. Being from Carnegie,
he smelled of money. Being a Flexner, he sounded like Science. His
message was simple: conform to the Johns Hopkins model, complete

with laboratories in all sciences, salaried professors, etc. or close. For the smaller, poorer schools, this could only mean one thing: close. For the bigger and better schools (i.e., those which like Harvard already had enough money to begin to institute the prescribed reforms), it meant the promise of fat foundation grants for further reforms. In fact, the published report was to serve as a convenient guidebook for medical philanthropists. It found that only about 15 per cent of the nation's medical schools began to meet "scientific" standards, and identified as salvageable those which were already big, rich, and prestigious. In the twenty years following the publication of the Flexner Report, the nine largest foundations poured over $150 million—one half of what they gave for all purposes—into medical education, adhering strictly to the standards set by Flexner.[29]

The effects of the crusade to "reform" medical education which had begun in the late nineteenth century and culminated, symbolically, with the Flexner Report, were already visible in the teens. Between 1904 and 1915, ninety-two medical schools closed down or merged.[30] The "irregular" schools descended from the Popular Health Movement (which had been a haven for women students) closed in droves; and seven out of ten exclusively female medical colleges shut down. Between 1909 and 1912, the proportion of medical graduates who were women dropped from 4.3 per cent to 3.2 per cent.[31] Blacks fared even worse, losing all but two (Meharry and Howard) of the original seven black medical schools.

When it came to the social-class composition of medicine, the "reforms" were equally decisive. The regular schools offering low-cost medical training to working- and lower-middle-class youths went the way of the schools for women and black people. Beyond that, Flexner had set a minimum of two years of college education as a requirement for entrance to medical school. At a time when less than 5 per cent of the college age population was enrolled in a college or university, this requirement alone closed the medical schools to all but the upper and upper middle class.

It could be argued that these measures were necessary. A majority of the schools closed by the medical reformers undoubtedly were too small and poorly equipped to offer an adequate medical education. But there could have been an alternative strategy for reform—to spread out the wealth so that many more schools could be improved. This would have left medical education open to large numbers of people. But that, of course, was exactly what the doctors were trying to avoid. With the strategy the foundations chose, medicine became ever more the property of an elite—white, male, and overwhelmingly upper-middle class. Beyond that, the scientific reformers never questioned the real medical value of the professional requirements they sought to impose. The requirement of lengthy scientific training, for example, guaranteed that doctors would be largely from privileged backgrounds, but it did not guarantee that they would have any more practical experience and human empathy than the uneducated healers they replaced.

The rank-and-file regular doctor watched the reforms with mixed feelings. By and large the rank-and-file distrusted scientific medicine and the elite doctors who crusaded for it. New York doctors used to walk out on medical papers dealing with the Germ Theory of Disease because "They wanted to express their contemptuous scorn for such theories and refused to listen to them."[32] Why blame disease on a hypothetical entity, germs, which no honest practitioner had ever seen? More generally, a prominent medical writer warned physicians in 1902:

> Do not allow yourself to be biased too quickly or too strongly in favor of new theories based on physiological, microscopical, chemical, or other experiments, especially when offered by the unbalanced to establish their abstract conclusions or preconceived notions. . . .[33]

Only under pressure from public health authorities and the public would the doctors agree to try diphtheria antitoxin or report TB cases. Those who did subscribe to the Germ Theory of Disease often used it to justify the glad-handed prescribing of alcohol—it killed germs, didn't it? Then too, it must have been painful to watch one's alma mater branded as "third rate" by a mere layman like Flexner who had never driven out to an emergency in a blizzard or held a dying person's hand. (Even the elite felt this change. Hopkins professor William Osler quipped to his colleague William Welch, "We are lucky to get in as professors, for I am sure that neither you nor I could ever get in as students.")[34]

But despite all this, the rank-and-file were not about to buck the reform movement. Medicine's scientific elite was achieving through a precise and methodical campaign what the rank-and-file could never have achieved through bluster and politicking. The competition was falling, and the regulars had all but captured the field. In the eighteen hundreds licensing laws which had been thrown out or emasculated in the thirties and forties had been reinstated, but the laws did not exclude "irregular" doctors, so long as they were trained. Now, as part of the scientific reforms, licensing examinations were brought into line with the standards of the most scientific, regular schools. And, at the same time, most states ruled that practicing medicine *without* a license was a crime punishable not by a fine, or a reprimand, but a prison sentence. The regular sect had gained, at long last, a legal monopoly over the practice of medicine.

And, probably to the great relief of many a practitioner, all this was achieved without ever having to purge the ranks of the existing regulars. The purifying reign of terror which the reformers brought to the schools was never visited on the practitioners themselves. The average practitioner was still free to go around bleeding consumptives, mumbling about "humors," and hooking housewives on opium. To this day, when the profession has become so exclusive that it is easier for even a rich man to enter heaven than medical school, the profession views its most unscientific and outright murderous members with a spirit of gentle forebearance. The standards erected to exclude the "crude boys"—and the girls in general—have never been applied to those who have already entered the brotherhood.

A truly scientific medicine would, of course, have to be self-critical, would have to subject its practitioners to continual evaluation and review. But that could hardly be done without putting a few cracks in the patrician image which regular medicine had fought for so long to achieve. "I warn all of you not to uncover the mistakes of a fellow practitioner," J. E. Stubbs, M.D., wrote in an 1899 issue of the *Journal of the American Medical Association:*

> . . . because, if you do, it will come back like a boomerang, and it will sting to the bitter end. . . . We do wrong when we do not try to cover up the mistakes of our brethren. There are many cases that require extreme surgical dexterity and a large amount of knowledge in order to operate successfully; yet those who are operating all the time make mistakes. We have to do a great many things empirically, and if we tell people . . . this or that physician has made a great blunder, it hurts him; it hurts the community, because the opinion of the physician in society is considered authority, and particuarly in the community in which he lives, among his associates and friends. They consult him as they do no other man; they consult him more confidentially and give up their secrets to him more unreservedly than they do to their priest or minister.[35]

Stubbs, clearly, was not tortured by a nagging loyalty to science. The doctor who aspired to the patriarchal authority once held by the "priest or minister" could not be bothered with picayune technical criticisms.

The aspirations—and achievements—of nineteenth-century regular medicine can all be summarized in the figure of one man: Sir William Osler. He not only played a role in the medical-reform movement; to thousands of admirers, he was the *goal* of it. He was a professor at Johns Hopkins medical school, author of the textbook that turned Frederick Gates on to scientific medicine, and, although he never did any original research in his life, he could expound on the scientific renaissance of medicine in hundred-word-long Victorian sentences gracefully adorned with references to the Greek and Latin classics. The rank-and-file regulars loved him. From "the Atlantic to the Pacific . . . [a visitor] . . . will find a picture of Osler hanging on the wall in almost every doctor's house."[36] The Osler portraits reminded doctors that medicine was about something more than money, more, even, than science—a mystical kind of power that flowed not just from what the doctor *did,* but from *who he was*.

He himself was, by any standards, an aristocrat among physicians. The son of a clergyman (like a surprisingly large number of the scientists of his generation), he studied medicine at McGill and then made the pilgrimage to the great German university laboratories. His combination of good breeding and scientific education quickly brought him to the attention of America's medical elite. According to Osler's memoirs, S. Weir Mitchell traveled to Leipzig for the University of Pennsylvania:

> . . . "to look me over," particularly with reference to personal habits. Dr. Mitchell said there was only one way in which the breeding of a man suitable for such a position [professor of clinical medicine], in such a city as Philadelphia, could be tested—give him cherry-pie and see how he disposed of the stones. I had read of the trick before, and disposed of them genteely in my spoon—and got the Chair.[37]

Mitchell was so impressed that he wrote back, "Osler is socially a man for the Biological Club [an elite Philadelphia dining club] if by any good luck we can get him."[38] Osler's subsequent career as a professor, author, lecturer, and physician to the social elite of Europe and North America (he treated the Prince of Wales) culminated in his receiving a baronetcy—hence the "Sir"—from Queen Victoria in 1911. He saw himself as one link in a genteel tradition which stretched back to Hippocrates, whom he credited with the first "conception and realization of medicine as a profession of a cultivated gentleman."[39] "The way is clear," he told students, as if regular medicine had never known a moment of self-doubt, "blazed for you by generations of strong men. . . ."[40]

To a generation of doctors who were still anxious about evolution and skeptical about germs, Osler provided much-needed reassurance. The patriarchal authority of the doctor, he argued, rests on something more ancient and venerable than science. Science itself was not something integral to medicine; it was a kind of extra, "an incalculable gift," a "leaven" to the hard-working practitioner. Science, in fact, was just one part of the general "culture" the physician needed if he was to serve a wealthy clientele. As part of the doctor's general "culture," science could also serve as a kind of disinfectant to protect him in "the most debasing surroundings," such as those inhabited by the poor. "Culture" became all the more important, of course, with a wealthy patient clientele:

> The wider and freer a men's [sic] general education the better practitioner he is likely to be, particularly among the higher classes to whom the reassurance and sympathy of a cultivated gentleman of the type of Eryximachus [an aristocratic ancient Greek doctor], may mean much more than pills and potions.[41]

So if science was culture, and culture was really class, then, in the end, it was class that healed. Or rather, it was the combination of upper class and male superiority that gave medicine its essential authority. With a patriarchal self-confidence that had almost no further need for instruments, techniques, medications, Osler wrote:

> If a poor lass, paralyzed apparently, helpless, bed-ridden for years, comes to me, having worn out in mind, body, and estate a devoted family; if she in a few weeks or less by faith in me, and faith alone, takes up her bed and walks, the saints of old could not have done more . . .[42]

Now at last the medical profession had arrived at a method of faith-healing potent enough to compare with woman's traditional healing—but one which was decisively masculine. It did not require a nurturant attitude, nor long hours by the patient's bedside. In fact, with the new style of healing, the less time a doctor spends with a patient, and the fewer questions he permits, the greater his powers would seem to be.

Exorcising the Midwives

There was one last matter to clean up before the triumph of (male) scientific medicine would be complete, and that was the "midwife problem." In 1900, 50 per cent of the babies born were still being delivered by midwives. Middle- and upper-class women had long since accepted the medical idea of childbirth as a pathological event requiring the intervention and supervision of a (preferably regular) physician. It was the "lower" half of society which clung to the midwife and her services: the rural poor and the immigrant working class in the cities. What made the midwives into a "problem" was then not so much the matter of direct competition; the regular doctors were not interested in taking the midwife's place in a Mississippi sharecropper's shack or a sixth-story walk-up apartment in one of New York's slums. (Although one exceptionally venal physician went to the trouble of calculating all the fees "lost" to doctors on account of midwifery):[43] It only makes sense to speak of "competition" between people in the same line of business; and this was not the case with the midwives and the doctors.

The work of a midwife cannot be contained in a phrase like "practicing medicine." The early-twentieth-century midwife was an integral part of her community and culture. She spoke the mother's language, which might be Italian, Yiddish, Polish, Russian. She was familiar not only with obstetrical techniques, but with the prayers and herbs that sometimes helped. She knew the correct ritual for disposing of the afterbirth, greeting the newborn or, if necessary, laying to rest the dead. She was prepared to live with the family from the onset of labor until the mother was fully recovered. If she was a southern black midwife, she often regarded the service as a religious calling:

> "Mary Carter," she [an older midwife] told me, "I'm getting old and I done been on this journey for 45 years. I am tired. I won't give up until the Lord replace me with someone. When I asked the Lord, he showed me you."
> The [young] midwife responded, "Uh, uh, Aunt Minnie, the Lord didn't show you me." She say, "Yes Sir, you got to serve. You can't get from under it."

She did serve because, repeatedly, "Something come to me, within me, say, 'Go ahead and do the best you can.' "[44]

All of this was highly "unscientific," not to mention unbusinesslike. But the problem, from the point of view of medical leaders, was that the midwife was in the way of the development of modern institutional medicine. One of the reforms advanced by medicine's scientific elite was that students should be exposed somewhere along the line not only to laboratories and lectures but to live patients. But which live patients? Given the choice, most people would want to avoid being an object of practice for inexperienced medical students. Certainly no decent woman in 1900 would want her delivery witnessed by any unnecessary young males. The only choice was the people who had the least choice—the poor. And so the medical schools, the most "advanced" ones anyway, began to attach themselves parasitically to the nearest "charity" hospital. In an arrangement which has flourished ever since, the medical school offered its medical trainees as staff for the hospital; the hospital in turn provided the raw "material" for medical education—the bodies of the sick poor. The moral ambiguities in this situation were easily rationalized away by the leaders of scientific medicine. As a doctor on the staff of Cornell Medical College put it:

There are heroes of war, who give up their lives on the field of battle for country and for principle, and medical heroes of peace, who brave the dangers and horrors of pestilence to save life; but the homeless, friendless, degraded and possibly criminal sick poor in the wards of a charity hospital, receiving aid and comfort in their extremity and contributing each one his modest share to the advancement of medical science, render even greater service to humanity.[45]

Medical science now called on poor women to make their contribution to that "most beneficent and disinterested of professions." Obstetrics-gynecology was America's most rapidly developing specialty, and midwives would just have to get out of the way. Training and licensing midwives was out of the question, for, as one doctor argued, these measures would

decrease the number of cases in which the stethoscope, pelvimeter, and other newly developed techniques could be used to increase obstetrical knowledge.[46]

A Dr. Charles E. Zeigler was equally blunt in an article addressed to his colleagues in the *Journal of the American Medical Association:*

> It is at present impossible to secure cases sufficient for the proper training in obstetrics, since 75% of the material otherwise available for clinical purposes is utilized in providing a livelihood for midwives.[47]

Note the curious construction here: "the material . . . is utilized . . ." The woman who was seen by her midwife as a neighbor, possibly a friend, was, in the eyes of the developing medical industry, not even a customer: she has become inert "material."

The public campaign against midwives was, of course, couched in terms of the most benevolent concern for the midwives' clientele. Midwives were "hopelessly dirty, ignorant and incompetent, relics of a barbaric past."[48]

> They may wash their hands, but oh, what myriads of dirt lurk under the fingernails. Numerous instances could be cited and we might well add to other causes of pyosalpinx "dirty midwives." She is the most virulent bacteria of them all, and she is truly a micrococcus of the most poisonous kind.[49]

Furthermore the midwife and, as we shall see, dirtiness in general, were un-American. Overturning almost three hundred years of American history, obstetricians A. B. Emmons and J. L. Huntington argued in 1912 that midwives are

> not a product of America. They have always been here, but only incidentally and only because America has always been receiving generous importations of immigrants from the continent of Europe. We have never adopted in any State a system of obstetrics with the midwife as the working unit. It has almost been a rule that the more immigrants arriving in a locality, the more midwives will flourish there, but as soon as the immigrant is assimilated, and becomes part of our civilization, then the midwife is no longer a factor in his home.[50]

In the rhetoric of the medical profession, the midwife was no more human than her clientele. She was a foreign "micrococcus" brought over, as was supposedly the case with other germs, in the holds of ships bearing immigrant workers. The elimination of the midwife was presented as a necessary part of the general campaign to uplift and Americanize the immigrants—a mere sanitary measure, beyond debate.

Certainly the midwives were "ignorant" according to the escalating standards of medical education; possibly some also deserved the charge of being "dirty" and "incompetent." The obvious remedy for these shortcomings was education and some system of accountability, or supervision. England had solved its "midwife problem" without rancor by simply offering training and licensing to the midwives. Even the least literate midwife could be trained to administer silver nitrate eye drops (to prevent blindness in babies whose mothers have gonorrhea) and to achieve certain standards of cleanliness. But the American medical profession would settle for nothing less than the final solution to the midwife question: they would have to be eliminated—outlawed. The medical journals urged their constituencies to join the campaign:

> surely we have enough influence and friends to procure the needed legislation. Make yourselves heard in the land; and the ignorant meddlesome midwife will soon be a thing of the past.[51]

In fact, the doctors were not prepared, in any sense of the word, to take over once the midwives were eliminated. For one thing, there were simply not enough obstetricians in the United States to serve the masses of poor and working-class women, even if the obstetricians were inclined to do so. According to historian Ben Barker-Benfield, "even a hostile obstetrician admitted in 1915 that 25 percent of births in New York State outside New York City would be deprived *entirely* of assistance when the midwife was eliminated."[52]

Then too, obstetricians introduced new dangers into the process of childbirth. Unlike a midwife, a doctor was not about to sit around for hours, as one doctor put it, "watching a hole"; if the labor was going too slow for his schedule he intervened with knife or forceps, often to the detriment of the mother or child. Teaching hospitals had an additional bias toward surgical intervention since the students did have to practice something more challenging than normal deliveries. The day of the totally medicalized childbirth—hazardously overdrugged and overtreated—was on its way.[53] By the early twentieth century it was already clear even to some members of the medical profession that the doctors' takeover was a somewhat dubious episode in the history of public health. A 1912 study by a Johns Hopkins professor found that most American doctors at the time were *less* competent than the midwives they were replacing.[54] The physicians were usually less experienced than midwives, less observant, and less likely to even be *present* at a critical moment.

But, between 1900 and 1930, midwives were almost totally eliminated from the land—outlawed in many states, harassed by local medical authorities in other places. There was no feminist constituency to resist the trend. In the eighteen thirties, women in the Popular Health Movement had denounced the impropriety—and dangers—of male assistance at births. But this time, when *female* assistance at births was in effect being turned into a crime, there was no outcry. Middle-class feminists had no sisterly feelings for the "dirty" immigrant midwife. They had long since decided to play by the rules laid down by the medical profession and channel their feminist energies into getting more women into (regular) medical schools. Elizabeth Blackwell, for example, believed that no one should assist in childbirth without a complete medical education.

There may have been some resistance to the male takeover within the immigrant communities, but we have no evidence of this. Most women no doubt accepted male, institutional care in the interests of their children. With the elimination of midwifery, all women—not just those of the upper class—fell under the biological hegemony of the medical profession. In the same stroke, women lost their last autonomous role as healers. The only roles left for women in the medical system were as employees, customers, or "material."

The Reign of the Experts

FOUR

The Sexual Politics of Sickness

When Charlotte Perkins Gilman collapsed with a "nervous disorder," the physician she sought out for help was Dr. S. Weir Mitchell, "the greatest nerve specialist in the country." It was Dr. Mitchell—female specialist, part-time novelist, and member of Philadelphia's high society—who had once screened Osler for a faculty position, and, finding him appropriately discreet in the disposal of cherry-pie pits, admitted the young doctor to medicine's inner circles. When Gilman met him, in the eighteen eighties, he was at the height of his career, earning over $60,000 per year (the equivalent of over $300,000 in today's dollars). His reknown for the treatment of female nervous disorders had by this time led to a marked alteration of character. According to an otherwise fond biographer, his vanity "had become colossal. It was fed by torrents of adulation, incessant and exaggerated, every day, almost every hour. . . ."¹

Gilman approached the great man with "utmost confidence." A friend of her mother's lent her one hundred dollars for the trip to Philadelphia and Mitchell's treatment. In preparation, Gilman methodically wrote out a complete history of her case. She had observed, for example, that her sickness vanished when she was away from her home, her husband, and her child, and returned as soon as she came back to them. But Dr. Mitchell dismissed her prepared history as evidence of "self-conceit." He did not want information from his patients; he wanted "complete obedience." Gilman quotes his prescription for her:

> "Live as domestic a life as possible. Have your child with you all the time." (Be it remarked that if I did but dress the baby it left me shaking and crying—certainly far from a healthy companionship for her, to say nothing of the effect on me.) "Lie down an hour after each meal. Have but two hours intellectual life a day. And never touch pen, brush or pencil as long as you live."[2]

Gilman dutifully returned home and for some months attempted to follow Dr. Mitchell's orders to the letter. The result, in her words, was—

> . . . [I] came perilously close to losing my mind. The mental agony grew so unbearable that I would sit blankly moving my head from side to side . . . I would crawl into remote closets and under beds —to hide from the 'grinding pressure of that distress. . . .[3]

Finally, in a "moment of clear vision" Gilman understood the source of her illness: she did not want to be a *wife;* she wanted to be a writer and an activist. So, discarding S. Weir Mitchell's prescription and divorcing her husband, she took off for California with her baby, her pen, her brush and pencil. But she never forgot Mitchell and his near-lethal "cure." Three years after her recovery she wrote *The Yellow Wallpaper*[4] a fictionalized account of her own illness and descent into madness. If that story had any influence on S. Weir Mitchell's method of treatment, she wrote after a long life of accomplishments, "I have not lived in vain."[5]

Charlotte Perkins Gilman was fortunate enough to have had a "moment of clear vision" in which she understood what was happening to her. Thousands of other women, like Gilman, were finding themselves in a new position of dependency on the male medical profession—and with no alternative sources of information or counsel. The medical profession was consolidating its monopoly over healing, and now the woman who felt sick, or tired or simply depressed would no longer seek help from a friend or female healer, but from a male physician. The general theory which guided the doctors' practice as well as their public pronouncements was that women were, by nature, weak, dependent, and diseased. Thus would the doctors attempt to secure their victory over the female healer: with the "scientific" evidence that woman's essential nature was not to be a strong, competent help-giver, but to be a *patient.*

A Mysterious Epidemic

In fact at the time there were reasons to think that the doctors' theory was not so farfetched. Women were decidedly sickly, though not for the reasons the doctors advanced. In the mid- and late nineteenth century a curious epidemic seemed to be sweeping through the middle- and upper-class female population both in the United States and England. Diaries and journals from the time give us hundreds of examples of women slipping into hopeless invalidism. For example, when Catherine Beecher, the educator, finished a tour in 1871 which included visits to dozens of relatives, friends and former students, she reported "a terrible decay of female health all over the land," which was "increasing in a most alarming ratio." The notes from her travels go like this:

> Milwaukee, Wis. Mrs. A. frequent sick headaches. Mrs. B. very feeble. Mrs. S. well, except chills. Mrs. L. poor health constantly. Mrs. D. subject to frequent headaches. Mrs. B. very poor health . . .
> Mrs. H. pelvic disorders and a cough. Mrs. B. always sick. Do not know one perfectly healthy woman in the place. . . .[6]

Doctors found a variety of diagnostic labels for the wave of invalidism gripping the female population: "neurasthenia," "nervous prostration," "hyperesthesia," "cardiac inadequacy," "dyspepsia," "rheumatism," and "hysteria." The symptoms included headache, muscular aches, weakness, depression, menstrual difficulties, indigestion, etc., and usually a general debility requiring constant rest. S. Weir Mitchell described it as follows:

> The woman grows pale and thin, eats little, or if she eats does not profit by it. Everything wearies her,—to sew, to write, to read, to walk,—and by and by the sofa or the bed is her only comfort. Every effort is paid for dearly, and she describes herself as aching and sore, as sleeping ill, and as needing constant stimulus and endless tonics. . . . If such a person is emotional she does not fail to become more so, and even the firmest women lose self-control at last under incessant feebleness.[7]

The syndrome was never fatal, but neither was it curable in most cases, the victims sometimes patiently outliving both husbands and physicians.

Women who recovered to lead full and active lives—like Charlotte

Perkins Gilman and Jane Addams—were the exceptions. Ann Greene
Phillips—a feminist and abolitionist in the eighteen thirties—first took
ill during her courtship. Five years after her marriage, she retired to
bed, more or less permanently. S. Weir Mitchell's unmarried sister
fell prey to an unspecified "great pain" shortly after taking over
housekeeping for her brother (whose first wife had just died), and
embarked on a life of invalidism. Alice James began her career of
invalidism at the age of nineteen, always amazing her older brothers,
Henry (the novelist) and William (the psychologist), with the stub-
born intractability of her condition: "Oh, woe, woe is me!" she wrote
in her diary:

> . . . all hopes of peace and rest are vanishing—nothing but the
> dreary snail-like climb up a little way, so as to be able to run down
> again! And then these doctors tell you that you will die or *recover!*
> But you *don't* recover. I have been at these alterations since I was
> nineteen and I am neither dead nor recovered. As I am now forty-
> two, there has surely been time for either process.[8]

The sufferings of these women were real enough. Ann Phillips
wrote, ". . . life is a burden to me, I do not know what to do. I am
tired of suffering. I have no faith in anything."[9] Some thought that if
the illness wouldn't kill them, they would do the job themselves.
Alice James discussed suicide with her father, and rejoiced, at the age
of forty-three, when informed she had developed breast cancer and
would die within months: "I count it the greatest good fortune to
have these few months so full of interest and instruction in the
knowledge of my approaching death."[10] Mary Galloway shot herself
in the head while being attended in her apartment by a physician and
a nurse. She was thirty-one years old, the daughter of a bank and
utility company president. According to the New York *Times* account (April 10, 1905), "She had been a chronic dyspeptic since
1895, and that is the only reason known for her suicide."[11]

Marriage: The Sexual Economic Relation

In the second half of the nineteenth century the vague syndrome
gripping middle- and upper-class women had become so widespread
as to represent not so much a disease in the medical sense as a way of
life. More precisely, the way this type of woman was expected to live
predisposed her to sickness, and sickness in turn predisposed her to

continue to live as she was expected to. The delicate, affluent lady, who was completely dependent on her husband, set the sexual romanticist ideal of femininity for women of all classes.

Clear-headed feminists like Charlotte Perkins Gilman and Olive Schreiner saw a link between female invalidism and the economic situation of women in the upper classes. As they observed, poor women did not suffer from the syndrome. The problem in the middle to upper classes was that marriage had become a "sexuo-economic relation" in which women performed sexual and reproductive duties for financial support. It was a relationship which Olive Schreiner bluntly called "female parasitism."

To Gilman's pragmatic mind, the affluent wife appeared to be a sort of tragic evolutionary anomaly, something like the dodo. She did not work: that is, there was no serious, productive work to do in the home, and the tasks which were left—keeping house, cooking and minding the children—she left as much as possible to the domestic help. She was, biologically speaking, specialized for one function and one alone—sex. Hence the elaborate costume—bustles, false fronts, wasp waists—which caricatured the natural female form. Her job was to bear the heirs of the businessman, lawyer, or professor she had married, which is what gave her a claim to any share of his income. When Gilman, in her depression, turned away from her own baby, it was because she already understood, in a half-conscious way, that the baby was living proof of her economic dependence—and as it seemed to her, sexual degradation.

A "lady" had one other important function, as Veblen pointed out with acerbity in the *Theory of the Leisure Class*. And that was to do precisely nothing, that is nothing of any economic or social consequence.[12] A successful man could have no better social ornament than an idle wife. Her delicacy, her culture, her childlike ignorance of the male world gave a man the "class" which money alone could not buy. A virtuous wife spent a hushed and peaceful life indoors, sewing, sketching, planning menus, and supervising the servants and children. The more adventurous might fill their leisure with shopping excursions, luncheons, balls, and novels. A "lady" could be charming, but never brilliant; interested, but not intense. Dr. Mitchell's second wife, Mary Cadwalader, was perhaps a model of her type: she "made no pretense at brilliancy; her first thought was to be a foil to her husband. . . ."[13] By no means was such a lady to concern herself with politics, business, international affairs, or the aching injustices of the industrial work world.

But not even the most sheltered woman lived on an island detached from the "real" world of men. Schreiner described the larger context:

> Behind the phenomenon of female parasitism has always lain another and yet larger social phenomenon . . . the subjugation of large bodies of other human creatures, either as slaves, subject races, or classes; and as a result of the excessive labors of those classes there has always been an accumulation of unearned wealth in the hands of the dominant class or race. *It has invariably been by feeding on this wealth, the result of forced or ill-paid labor,* that the female of the dominant race or class has in the past lost her activity and has come to exist purely through the passive performance of her sexual functions.[14] [Emphasis in original]

The leisured lady, whether she knew it or not and whether she cared or not, inhabited the same social universe as dirt-poor black sharecroppers, six-year-old children working fourteen-hour days for subsubsistence wages, young men mutilated by unsafe machinery or mine explosions, girls forced into prostitution by the threat of starvation. At no time in American history was the contradiction between ostentatious wealth and unrelenting poverty, between idleness and exhaustion, starker than it was then in the second half of the nineteenth century. There were riots in the cities, insurrections in the mines, rumors of subversion and assassination. Even the secure business or professional man could not be sure that he too would not be struck down by an economic downturn, a wily competitor, or (as seemed likely at times) a social revolution.

The genteel lady of leisure was as much a part of the industrial social order as her husband or his employees. As Schreiner pointed out, it was ultimately the wealth extracted in the world of work that enabled a man to afford a more or less ornamental wife. And it was the very harshness of that outside world that led men to see the home as a refuge—"a sacred place, a vestal temple," a "tent pitch'd in a world not right," presided over by a gentle, ethereal wife. A popular home health guide advised that

> . . . [man's] feelings are frequently lacerated to the utmost point of endurance, by collisions, irritations, and disappointments. To recover his equanimity and composure, home must be a place of repose, of

peace, of cheerfulness, of comfort; then his soul renews its strength, and will go forth, with fresh vigor, to encounter the labor and troubles of the world.[15]

No doubt the suffocating atmosphere of sexual romanticism bred a kind of nervous hypochondria. We will never know, for example, if Alice James's lifelong illness had a "real" organic basis. But we know that, unlike her brothers, she was never encouraged to go to college or to develop her gift for writing. She was high-strung and imaginative, but *she* could not be brilliant or productive. Illness was perhaps the only honorable retreat from a world of achievement which (it seemed at the time) nature had not equipped her to enter.

For many other women, to various degrees, sickness became a part of life, even a way of filling time. The sexuo-economic relation confined women to the life of the body, so it was to the body that they directed their energies and intellect. Rich women frequented resortlike health spas and the offices of elegant specialists like S. Weir Mitchell. A magazine cartoon from the eighteen seventies shows two "ladies of fashion" meeting in an ornately appointed waiting room. "What, *you* here, Lizzie? Why, ain't you well?" asks the first patient. "Perfectly thanks!" answers the second. "But what's the matter with *you*, dear?" "Oh, nothing whatever! I'm as right as possible dear."[16] For less well-off women there were patent medicines, family doctors, and, starting in the eighteen fifties, a steady stream of popular advice books, written by doctors, on the subject of female health. It was acceptable, even stylish, to retire to bed with "sick headaches," "nerves" and various unmentionable "female troubles," and that indefinable nervous disorder "neurasthenia" was considered, in some circles, to be a mark of intellect and sensitivity. Dr. Mary Putnam Jacobi, a female regular physician, observed impatiently in 1895:

> . . . it is considered natural and almost laudable to break down under all conceivable varieties of strain—a winter dissipation, a houseful of servants, a quarrel with a female friend, not to speak of more legitimate reasons. . . . Women who expect to go to bed every menstrual period expect to collapse if by chance they find themselves on their feet for a few hours during such a crisis. Constantly considering their nerves, urged to consider them by well-intentioned but short-sighted advisors, they pretty soon become nothing but a bundle of nerves.[17]

But if sickness was a reaction, on women's part, to a difficult situation, it was not a way out. If you have to be idle, you might as well be sick, and sickness, in turn, legitimates idleness. From the romantic perspective, the sick woman was not that far off from the ideal woman anyway. A morbid aesthetic developed, in which sickness was seen as a source of female beauty, and, beauty—in the high-fashion sense—was in fact a source of sickness. Over and over, nineteenth-century romantic paintings feature the beautiful invalid, sensuously drooping on her cushions, eyes fixed tremulously at her husband or physician, or already gazing into the Beyond. Literature aimed at female readers lingered on the romantic pathos of illness and death; popular women's magazines featured such stories as "The Grave of My Friend" and "Song of Dying." Society ladies cultivated a sickly countenance by drinking vinegar in quantity or, more effectively, arsenic.[18] The loveliest heroines were those who died young, like Beth in *Little Women,* too good and too pure for life in this world.

Meanwhile, the requirements of fashion insured that the well-dressed woman would actually be as frail and ornamental as she looked. The style of wearing tight-laced corsets, which was *de rigeur* throughout the last half of the century, has to be ranked somewhere close to the old Chinese practice of foot-binding for its crippling effects on the female body. A fashionable woman's corsets exerted, on the average, twenty-one pounds of pressure on her internal organs, and extremes of up to eighty-eight pounds had been measured.[19] (Add to this the fact that a well-dressed woman wore an average of thirty-seven pounds of street clothing in the winter months, of which nineteen pounds were suspended from her tortured waist.[20]) Some of the short-term results of tight-lacing were shortness of breath, constipation, weakness, and a tendency to violent indigestion. Among the long-term effects were bent or fractured ribs, displacement of the liver, and uterine prolapse (in some cases, the uterus would be gradually forced, by the pressure of the corset, out through the vagina).

The morbidity of nineteenth-century tastes in female beauty reveals the hostility which never lies too far below the surface of sexual romanticism. To be sure, the romantic spirit puts woman on a pedestal and ascribes to her every tender virtue absent from the Market. But carried to an extreme the demand that woman be a *negation* of man's world left almost nothing for women to actually *be:* if men are busy, she is idle; if men are rough, she is gentle; if men are strong, she is frail; if men are rational, she is irrational; and so on. The logic which insists that femininity is negative masculinity necessarily ro-

manticizes the moribund woman and encourages a kind of paternalistic necrophilia. In the nineteenth century this tendency becomes
overt, and the romantic spirit holds up as its ideal—the *sick* woman,
the invald who lives at the edge of death.

Femininity as a Disease

The medical profession threw itself with gusto on the languid
figure of the female invalid. In the home of an invalid lady, "the
house physician like a house fly is in chronic attention"[21] and the
doctors fairly swarmed after wealthy patients. Few were so successful
as S. Weir Mitchell in establishing himself as *the* doctor for hundreds
of loyal clients. Yet the doctors' constant ministrations and interven-
tions—surgical, electrical, hydropathic, mesmeric, chemical—seemed
to be of little use. In fact, it would have been difficult, in many cases,
to distinguish the *cure* from the *disease*. Charlotte Perkins Gilman of
course saw the connection. The ailing heroine of *The Yellow Wallpaper,* who is being treated by her physician-husband, hints at the fearful truth:

> John is a physician, and *perhaps*—(I would not say it to a living
> soul, of course, but this is dead paper and a great relief to my mind)
> —*perhaps* that is one reason I do not get well faster.[22]

In fact, the theories which guided the doctor's practice from the
late nineteenth century to the early twentieth century held that
woman's *normal* state was to be sick. This was not advanced as an
empirical observation, but as physiological fact. Medicine had "discovered" that female functions were inherently pathological. Menstruation, that perennial source of alarm to the male imagination,
provided both the evidence and the explanation. Menstruation was a
serious threat throughout life—so was the lack of it. According to Dr.
Engelmann, president of the American Gynecology Society in 1900:

> Many a young life is battered and forever crippled on the breakers
> of puberty; if it crosses these unharmed and is not dashed to pieces
> on the rock of childbirth, it may still ground on the ever-recurring
> shallows of menstruation, and lastly upon the final bar of the meno-
> pause ere protection is found in the unruffled waters of the harbor
> beyond reach of sexual storms.[23]

Popular advice books written by physicians took on a somber tone as they entered into "the female functions" or "the diseases of women."

> It is impossible to form a correct opinion of the mental and physical suffering frequently endured from her sexual condition, caused by her monthly periods, which it has pleased her Heavenly Father to attach to woman. . . .[24]

Ignoring the existence of thousands of working women, the doctors assumed that every woman was prepared to set aside a week or five days every month as a period of invalidism. Dr. W. C. Taylor, in his book *A Physician's Counsels to Woman in Health and Disease,* gave a warning typical of those found in popular health books of the time:

> We cannot too emphatically urge the importance of regarding these monthly returns as periods of ill health, as days when the ordinary occupations are to be suspended or modified. . . . Long walks, dancing, shopping, riding and parties should be avoided at this time of month invariably and under all circumstances. . . .[25]

As late as 1916, Dr. Winfield Scott Hall was advising:

> All heavy exercise should be omitted during the menstrual week . . . a girl should not only retire earlier at this time, but ought to stay out of school from one to three days as the case may be, resting the mind and taking extra hours of rest and sleep.[26]

Similarly, a pregnant woman was "indisposed," throughout the full nine months. The medical theory of "prenatal impressions" required her to avoid all "shocking, painful or unbeautiful sights," intellectual stimulation, angry or lustful thoughts, and even her husband's alcohol and tobacco-laden breath—lest the baby be deformed or stunted in the womb. Doctors stressed the pathological nature of childbirth itself—an argument which also was essential to their campaign against midwives. After delivery, they insisted on a protracted period of convalescence mirroring the "confinement" which preceded birth. (Childbirth, in the hands of the medical men, no doubt was "pathological," and doctors had far less concern about prenatal nutrition than they did about prenatal "impressions.") Finally after all this, a woman could only look forward to menopause, portrayed in the medical literature as a terminal illness—the "death of the woman in the woman."

Now it must be said in the doctors' defense that women of a hundred years ago *were,* in some ways, sicker than the women of today.

Quite apart from tight-lacing, arsenic-nipping, and fashionable cases of neurasthenia, women faced certain bodily risks which men did not share. In 1915 (the first year for which national figures are available) 61 women died for every 10,000 live babies born, compared to 2 per 10,000 today, and the maternal mortality rates were doubtless higher in the nineteenth century.[27] Without adequate, and usually without any, means of contraception, a married woman could expect to face the risk of childbirth repeatedly through her fertile years. After each childbirth a woman might suffer any number of gynecological complications, such as prolapsed (slipped) uterus or irreparable pelvic tear, which would be with her for the rest of her life.

Another special risk to women came from tuberculosis, the "white plague." In the mid-nineteenth century, TB raged at epidemic proportions, and it continued to be a major threat until well into the twentieth century. Everyone was affected, but women, especially young women, were particularly vulnerable, often dying at rates twice as high as those of men of their age group. For every hundred women aged twenty in 1865, more than five would be dead from TB by the age of thirty, and more than eight would be dead by the age of fifty.[28]

So, from a statistical point of view, there was some justification for the doctors' theory of innate female frailty. But there was also, from the doctors' point of view, a strong commercial justification for regarding women as sick. This was the period of the profession's most severe "population crisis." (See Chapter 3.) The theory of female frailty obviously disqualified women as healers. "One shudders to think of the conclusions arrived at by female bacteriologists or histologists," wrote one doctor, "at the period when their entire system, both physical and mental, is, so to speak, 'unstrung,' to say nothing of the terrible mistakes which a lady surgeon might make under similar conditions."[29] At the same time the theory made women highly qualified as patients. The sickly, nervous women of the upper or middle class with their unending, but fortunately non-fatal, ills, became a natural "client caste" to the developing medical profession.

Meanwhile, the health of women who were *not* potential patients—poor women—received next to no attention from the medical profession. Poor women must have been at least as susceptible as wealthy women to the "sexual storms" doctors saw in menstruation, pregnancy, etc.; and they were definitely much more susceptible to the hazards of childbearing, tuberculosis, and, of course, industrial diseases. From all that we know, sickness, exhaustion, and injury were

routine in the life of the working-class woman. Contagious diseases
always hit the homes of the poor first and hardest. Pregnancy, in a
fifth- or sixth-floor walk-up flat, really was debilitating, and childbirth, in a crowded tenement room, was often a frantic ordeal. Emma
Goldman, who was a trained midwife as well as an anarchist leader,
described "the fierce, blind struggle of the women of the poor against
frequent pregnancies" and told of the agony of seeing children grow
up "sickly and undernourished"—if they survived infancy at all.[30] For
the woman who labored outside her home, working conditions took
an enormous toll. An 1884 report of an investigation of "The Working Girls of Boston," by the Massachusetts Bureau of Statistics of
Labor, stated:

> . . . the health of many girls is so poor as to necessitate long rests,
> one girl being out a year on this account. Another girl in poor health
> was obliged to leave her work, while one reports that it is not possi-
> ble for her to work the year round, as she could not stand the strain,
> not being at all strong.[31]

Still, however sick or tired working-class women might have been,
they certainly did not have the time or money to support a cult of
invalidism. Employers gave no time off for pregnancy or recovery
from childbirth, much less for menstrual periods, though the wives of
these same employers often retired to bed on all these occasions. A
day's absence from work could cost a woman her job, and at home
there was no comfortable chaise longue to collapse on while servants
managed the household and doctors managed the illness. An 1889
study from Massachusetts described one working woman's life:

> Constant application to work, often until 12 at night and sometimes
> on Sundays (equivalent to nine ordinary working days a week),
> affected her health and injured her eyesight. She . . . was ordered
> by the doctor to suspend work . . . but she must earn money, and
> so she has kept on working. Her eyes weep constantly, she cannot
> see across the room and "the air seems always in a whirl" before her
> . . . [she] owed when seen three months' board for self and chil-
> dren . . . She hopes something may be done for working girls and
> women, for, however strong they may be in the beginning, "they
> cannot stand white slavery for ever."[32]

But the medical profession as a whole—and no doubt there were
many honorable exceptions—sturdily maintained that it was affluent
women who were most delicate and most in need of medical atten-

tion. "Civilization" had made the middle-class woman sickly; her physical frailty went hand-in-white-gloved-hand with her superior modesty, refinement, and sensitivity. Working-class women were robust, just as they were supposedly "coarse" and immodest. Dr. Lucien Warner, a popular medical authority, wrote in 1874, "It is not then hard work and privation which make the women of our country invalids, but circumstances and habits intimately connected with the so-called blessings of wealth and refinement."

Someone had to be well enough to do the work, though, and working-class women, Dr. Warner noted with relief, were *not* invalids: "The African negress, who toils beside her husband in the fields of the south, and Bridget, who washes, and scrubs and toils in our homes at the north, enjoy for the most part good health, with comparative immunity from uterine disease."[33] And a Dr. Sylvanus Stall observed:

> At war, at work, or at play, the white man is superior to the savage, and his culture has continually improved his condition. But with woman the rule is reversed. Her squaw sister will endure effort, exposure and hardship which would kill the white woman. Education which has resulted in developing and strengthening the physical nature of man has been perverted through folly and fashion to render woman weaker and weaker.[34]

In practice, the same doctors who zealously indulged the ills of wealthy patients had no time to spare for the poor. When Emma Goldman asked the doctors she knew whether they had any contraceptive information she could offer the poor, their answers included, "The poor have only themselves to blame; they indulge their appetites too much," and "When she [the poor woman] uses her brains more, her procreative organs will function less."[35] A Dr. Palmer Dudley ruled out poor women as subjects for gynecological surgery on the simple ground that they lacked the leisure required for successful treatment:

> . . . the hardworking, daily-toiling woman is not as fit a subject for [gynecological surgery] as the woman so situated in life as to be able to conserve her strength and if necessary, to take a long rest, in order to secure the best results.[36]

So the logic was complete: better-off women were sickly because of their refined and civilized lifestyle. Fortunately, however, this same lifestyle made them amenable to lengthy medical treatment. Poor and working-class women were inherently stronger, and this was also fortunate, since their lifestyle disqualified them from lengthy medical treatment anyway. The theory of innate female sickness, skewed so as to account for class differences in ability to pay for medical care, meshed conveniently with the doctors' commercial self-interest.

The feminists of the late nineteenth century, themselves deeply concerned about female invalidism, were quick to place at least part of the blame on the doctors' interests. Elizabeth Garrett Anderson, an American woman doctor, argued that the extent of female invalidism was much exaggerated by male doctors and that women's natural functions were not really all that debilitating. In the working classes, she observed, work went on during menstruation "without intermission, and, as a rule, without ill effects."[37] Mary Livermore, a women's suffrage worker, spoke against "the monstrous assumption that woman is a natural invalid," and denounced "the unclean army of 'gynecologists' who seem desirous to convince women that they possess but one set of organs—and that these are always diseased."[38] And Dr. Mary Putnam Jacobi put the matter most forcefully when she wrote in 1895, "I think, finally, it is in the increased attention paid to women, and especially in their new function as lucrative patients, scarcely imagined a hundred years ago, that we find explanation for much of the ill-health among women, freshly discovered today. . . ."[39]

Men Evolve, Women Devolve

But it would be overly cynical to see the doctors as mere businessmen, weighing theories of female physiology against cash receipts. The doctors of the late nineteenth century were also men of science, and this meant, in the cultural framework which equated science with goodness and morality, that doctors saw themselves almost as moral reformers. They (and members of the new field of psychology) saw it as their mission to bring the clear light of scientific objectivity to the Woman Question, even when all others were gripped by passionate commitments to one answer or another. "The most devoted patron of woman's political and educational advancement," wrote psychologist George T. Patrick:

> would hardly deny that the success and permanency of the reform
> will depend in the end upon the fact that there shall be no inherent

contradiction between her duties and her natural physical and mental constitution.[40]

It was the self-assigned duty of the medical profession to define "her natural physical and mental constitution," no matter how galling the facts might be to any interest groups or vocal minorities. In 1896, one physician asserted peevishly that the feminist influence had become so powerful that "the true differences between men and women have never been pointed out, except in medical publications."[41] But with great determination—and we might add—imagination, the doctors set out to elaborate the true nature of woman, the sources of her frailty, and the biological limits of her social role.

The groundwork had already been laid in the natural sciences. Nineteenth-century scientists had no hesitation in applying the results of biological studies to human society: All social hierarchies, they believed, could be explained in terms of natural law. Nothing was more helpful in this intellectual endeavor than the Theory of Evolution. Darwin's theory proposes that man had evolved from "lower," i.e., less complex, forms of life to his present condition. Nineteenth-century biologists and social commentators, observing that not all men were the same and that not all were in fact men, hastened to conclude that the variations represented different stages of evolution which happened to be jostling each other within the same instant of natural history. Some went so far as to declare that rich men must be in the evolutionary vanguard, since they were obviously so well adapted to the (capitalist) environment. (Andrew Carnegie was an ardent subscriber to this theory.)

Almost all agreed that the existing human races represented different evolutionary stages. A vast body of research—consisting chiefly in measurements of brain weights, head sizes, and facial proportions—"proved"—to no one's great surprise—that if the ethnic groups were ordered in terms of their distance up the ladder of evolution, WASPs would be in the lead, followed by Northern Europeans, Slavs, Jews, Italians, etc., with Negroes trailing in the far rear.

This was the intellectual framework with which nineteenth-century biologists approached the Woman Question: everyone must have an assigned place in the natural scheme of things. Attempts to get out of this place are unnatural and in fact diseased. By the eighteen sixties, natural scientists could pinpoint woman's place on the evolutionary ladder with some precision—she was at the level of the Negro. For example, Carl Vogt, a leading European professor of natural history, placed the Negro (male) as follows:

> . . . the grown-up Negro partakes, as regards his intellectual faculties, of the nature of the child, the female, and the senile White.[42]

(Where this left the Negro female one shudders to think, not to mention the "senile" female of either race.)

But it was not sufficient to rank women on a static evolutionary scale. A full response to the Woman Question required a dynamic view, including not only where woman was now, but where her evolutionary destiny was taking her. Darwin's theory postulates a drift toward ever greater biological variation and differentiation among the species. Where once there were a few formless protozoa, now there were porcupines, platypuses, peacocks, etc.—each one specialized to survive in a particular environmental niche. Nineteenth-century medical men read this loosely to mean that everything is getting more "specialized," and that "specialization" was the goal of evolution—an interpretation which was no doubt influenced by the ongoing formation of the academic disciplines (and within medicine, the medical specialties and subspecialties).

The next step in the logic was to interpret sexual differentiation within a species as a kind of "specialization" and mark of evolutionary advance. As G. Stanley Hall, a founder of psychology and leading child-raising expert of the early twentieth century put it in his famous book *Adolescence:*

"In unicellular organisms the conjugating [mating] cells are alike, but forms become more and more dimorphic. As we go higher [up the evolutionary ladder] sexes diverge not only in primary and secondary sex characteristics, but in functions not associated with sex."[43] Thus the difference between the sexes could be expected to widen ever further as "man" evolved, and since evolution was commonly equated with progress, this must be a good thing. As natural history professor Vogt saw it, "the inequality of the sexes increases with the progress of civilization."[44] ·

What was this difference between the sexes which was widening with every evolutionary leap? The answer rested on a certain masculinist assumption about the process of evolution itself. Evolutionary change occurs as environmental conditions "select" for certain variants in the species. For example, in an arctic environment the fox which is accidentally born with white fur has a survival advantage over its red sisters and brothers, so white foxes tend to displace red ones over time. We know now that the variations which allow for change occur through the random and unpredictable process of genetic mutation. But to nineteenth-century scientists, who knew nothing whatsoever about genes, heredity, mutations, etc., the ability to vary in potentially successful ways (as the white fox had done) seemed to require a degree of cleverness and daring. It must, therefore, be a male trait. So in the grand chain of evolution, males were the innovators, constantly testing themselves against the harsh environment while females dumbly passed on whatever hereditary material they had been given. Males produced the variations; females merely reproduced them.

From there it was only a hop, skip, and jump to a theory of contemporary human sexual differences. Males were made to "vary," that is, to fill a variety of functions in the social division of labor. Females, being more primitive, were non-varying and identical in evolutionary function, and that function was to reproduce. Woman represented the ancient essence of the species; man represented its boundless evolutionary possibilities. (G. Stanley Hall leaped quickly to the implications for the professions: "The male in all the orders of life is the agent of variation and tends by nature to *expertness and specialization,* without which his individuality is incomplete.")[45] [Emphasis added.] Suddenly the professional differences among middle-class men represented the "variations" required for evolution, as if natural selection would be picking between psychologists and mathematicians, gynecologists and ophthalmalogists! It followed in his line of reasoning that women could not be experts because they represented a more primitive, undifferentiated state of the species and were incapable of "specialization": "She is by nature more typical and a better representative of the race and less prone to specialization."[46]

But of course in the post-Darwinian scientific value system, "specialization" was good ("advanced"); despecialization was bad ("primitive"). Now put this together with the fact that the species as a whole was getting ever more "specialized" sexually as part of its general evolutionary advance: it followed that men would become ever more differentiated, while women would become progressively *de*-differentiated, and ever more concentrated on the ancient animal function of reproduction. Taken to its extreme conclusion, this logic could only mean that for every rung of the evolutionary ladder man ascended, woman would fall back a rung, as if, in some Elysian future, a superman would stand at the top of the ladder, a blob of reproductive protoplasm at the bottom.

Hall backed off from this conclusion with a diversionary outburst of romanticism, calling for

> . . . a new philosophy of sex which places the wife and mother at the heart of a new world and makes her the object of a new religion and almost of a new worship, that will give her reverent exemption from sex competition [i.e., competition with men] and reconsecrate her to the higher responsibilities of the human race, into the past and future of which the roots of her being penetrate; where the blind worship of mere mental illumination has no place. . . .[47]

The fact was, as Charlotte Perkins Gilman observed too, but with a very different set of emotions, that society was channeling women (or at least the more affluent of them) into the "sex function." If the natural scientists were right, she would evolve to become ever more exclusively consecrated to sex, shedding "mere mental illumination" and other artifices, as she strode—or, more likely, crawled, toward her evolutionary destiny.

The Dictatorship of the Ovaries

It was medicine's task to translate the evolutionary theory of women into the language of flesh and blood, tissues and organs. The result was a theory which put woman's mind, body and soul in the thrall of her all-powerful reproductive organs. "The Uterus, it must be remembered," Dr. F. Hollick wrote, "is the *controlling* organ in the female body, being the most excitable of all, and so intimately connected, by the ramifications of its numerous nerves, with every other part."[48] Professor M. L. Holbrook, addressing a medical society in 1870, observed that it seemed "as if the Almighty, in creating the female sex, *had taken the uterus and built up a woman around it.*"[49] [Emphasis in original.]

To other medical theorists, it was the ovaries which occupied center stage. Dr. G. L. Austin's 1883 book of advice for "maiden, wife and mother" asserts that the ovaries "give woman all her characteristics of body and mind."[50] This passage written in 1870 by Dr. W. W. Bliss, is, if somewhat overwrought, nonetheless typical:

Accepting, then, these views of the gigantic power and influence of the ovaries over the whole animal economy of woman,—that they are the most powerful agents in all the commotions of her system; that on them rest her intellectual standing in society, her physical perfection, and all that lends beauty to those fine and delicate contours which are constant objects of admiration, all that is great, noble and beautiful, all that is voluptuous, tender, and endearing; that her fidelity, her devotedness, her perpetual vigilance, forecast, and all those qualities of mind and disposition which inspire respect and love and fit her as the safest counsellor and friend of man, spring from the ovaries,—*what must be their influence and power over the great vocation of woman and the august purposes of her existence when these organs have become compromised through disease!*[51][Emphasis in original.]

According to this "psychology of the ovary" woman's entire personality was directed by the ovaries, and any abnormalities, from irritability to insanity, could be traced to some ovarian disease. Dr. Bliss added, with unbecoming spitefulness, that "the influence of the ovaries over the mind is displayed in woman's artfulness and dissimulation."

It should be emphasized, before we follow the workings of the uterus and ovaries any further, that woman's total submission to the "sex function" did not make her a *sexual* being. The medical model of female nature, embodied in the "psychology of the ovary," drew a rigid distinction between reproductivity and sexuality. Women were urged by the health books and the doctors to indulge in deep preoccupation with themselves as "The Sex"; they were to devote themselves to developing their reproductive powers and their maternal instincts. Yet doctors said they had no predilection for the sex act itself. Even a woman physician, Dr. Mary Wood-Allen wrote (perhaps from experience), that women embrace their husbands "without a particle of sex desire."[52] Hygiene manuals stated that the more cultured the woman, "the more is the sensual refined away from her nature," and warned against "any spasmodic convulsion" on a woman's part during intercourse lest it interfere with conception. Female sexuality was seen as unwomanly and possibly even detrimental to the supreme function of reproduction.

The doctors themselves never seemed entirely convinced, though, that the uterus and ovaries had successfully stamped out female sexuality. Underneath the complacent denials of female sexual feelings, there lurked the age-old male fascination with woman's "insatiable lust," which, once awakened, might turn out to be uncontrollable. Doctors dwelt on cases in which women were destroyed by their cravings; one doctor claimed to have discovered a case of "virgin nymphomania." The twenty-five-year-old British physician Robert Brudenell Carter leaves us with this tantalizing observation on his female patients:

> . . . no one who has realized the amount of moral evil wrought in girls . . . whose prurient desires have been increased by Indian hemp and partially gratified by medical manipulations, can deny that remedy is worse than disease. I have . . . seen young unmarried women, of the middle class of society, reduced by the constant use of the speculum to the mental and moral condition of prostitutes; seeking to give themselves the same indulgence by the practice of solitary vice; and asking every medical practitioner . . . to institute an examination of the sexual organs.[53]

But if the uterus and ovaries could not be counted on to suppress all sexual strivings, they were still sufficiently in control to be blamed for all possible female disorders, from headaches to sore throats and indigestion. Dr. M. E. Dirix wrote in 1869:

> Thus, women are treated for diseases of the stomach, liver, kidneys, heart, lungs, etc.; yet, in most instances, these diseases will be found on due investigation, to be, in reality, no diseases at all, but merely the sympathetic reactions or the symptoms of one disease, namely, a disease of the womb.[54]

Even tuberculosis could be traced to the capricious ovaries. When men were consumptive, doctors sought some environmental factor, such as overexposure, to explain the disease. But for women it was a result of reproductive malfunction. Dr. Azell Ames wrote in 1875:

> It being beyond doubt that consumption . . . is itself produced by the failure of the [menstrual] function in the forming girls . . . one has been the parent of the other with interchangeable priority. [Actually, as we know today, it is true that consumption may *result* in suspension of the menses.][55]

Since the reproductive organs were the source of disease, they were the obvious target in the treatment of disease. Any symptom—backaches, irritability, indigestion, etc.—could provoke a medical assault on the sexual organs. Historian Ann Douglas Wood describes the "local treatments" used in the mid-nineteenth century for almost any female complaint:

This [local] treatment had four stages, although not every case went through all four: a manual investigation, "leeching," "injections," and "cauterization." Dewees [an American medical professor] and Bennet, a famous English gynecologist widely read in America, both advocated placing the leeches right on the vulva or the neck of the uterus, although Bennet cautioned the doctor to count them as they dropped off when satiated, lest he "lose" some. Bennet had known adventurous leeches to advance into the cervical cavity of the uterus itself, and he noted, "I think I have scarcely ever seen more acute pain than that experienced by several of my patients under these circumstances." Less distressing to a 20th century mind, but perhaps even more senseless, were the "injections" into the uterus advocated by these doctors. The uterus became a kind of catch-all, or what one exasperated doctor referred to as a "Chinese toy shop": Water, milk and water, linseed tea, and "decoction of marshmellow . . . tepid or cold" found their way inside nervous women patients. The final step, performed at this time, one must remember, with no anesthetic but a little opium or alcohol, was cauterization, either through the application of nitrate of silver, or, in cases of more severe infection, through the use of much stronger hydrate of potassa, or even the "actual cautery," a "white-hot iron" instrument.[56]

In the second half of the century, these fumbling experiments with the female interior gave way to the more decisive technique of surgery—aimed increasingly at the control of female personality disorders. There had been a brief fad of clitoridectomy (removal of the clitoris) in the sixties, following the introduction of the operation by the English physician Isaac Baker Brown. Although most doctors frowned on the practice of removing the clitoris, they tended to agree that it might be necessary in cases of nymphomania, intractable masturbation, or "unnatural growth" of that organ. (The last clitoridectomy we know of in the United States was performed in 1948 on a child of five, as a cure for masturbation.)

The most common form of surgical intervention in the female personality was ovariotomy, removal of the ovaries—or "female castration." In 1906 a leading gynecological surgeon estimated that there were 150,000 women in the United States who had lost their ovaries under the knife. Some doctors boasted that they had removed from fifteen hundred to two thousand ovaries apiece.[57] According to historian G. J. Barker-Benfield:

Among the indications were troublesomeness, eating like a ploughman, masturbation, attempted suicide, erotic tendencies, persecution mania, simple "cussedness," and dysmenorrhea [painful menstruation]. Most apparent in the enormous variety of symptoms doctors took to indicate castration was a strong current of sexual appetitiveness on the part of women.[58]

The rationale for the operation flowed directly from the theory of the "psychology of the ovary": since the ovaries controlled the personality, they must be responsible for any psychological disorders; conversely, psychological disorders were a sure sign of ovarian disease. Ergo, the organs must be removed.

One might think, given the all-powerful role of the ovaries, that an ovaryless woman would be like a rudderless ship—desexed and directionless. But on the contrary, the proponents of ovariotomy argued, a woman who was relieved of a diseased ovary would be a *better* woman. One 1893 advocate of the operation claimed that "patients are improved, some of them cured; . . . the moral sense of the patient is elevated . . . she becomes tractable, orderly, industrious, and cleanly."*[59] Patients were often brought in by their husbands, who complained of their unruly behavior. Doctors also claimed that women—troublesome but still sane enough to recognize their problem —often "came to us pleading to have their ovaries removed."[60] The operation was judged successful if the woman was restored to a placid contentment with her domestic functions.

The overwhelming majority of women who had leeches or hot steel applied to their cervices, or who had their clitorises or ovaries removed, were women of the middle to upper classes, for after all, these procedures cost money. But it should not be imagined that poor women were spared the gynecologist's exotic catalog of tortures simply because they couldn't pay. The pioneering work in gynecological surgery had been performed by Marion Sims on black female slaves he kept for the sole purpose of surgical experimentation. He operated on one of them thirty times in four years, being foiled over and over by postoperative infections.[61] After moving to New York, Sims continued his experimentation on indigent Irish women in the wards of the New York Women's Hospital. So, though middle-class women suffered most from the doctors' actual practice, it was poor and black women who had suffered through the brutal period of experimentation.

* It is unlikely that the operation had this effect on a woman's personality. It would have produced the symptoms of menopause, which do not include any established personality changes.

The Uterus vs. the Brain

The reign of the uterus (and ovaries) was never entirely as tranquil and secure as the doctors might have wished. There was the constant threat of subversion by sexual feelings, arising from God knows what disorders of the brain or genitals. Doctors warned that vice in any form could derange the entire woman, flesh and spirit. Nothing alarmed them more than masturbation—known at the time as self-abuse or simply "the vice"—which could lead to menstrual dysfunction, uterine disease, lesions on the genitals, tuberculosis, dementia, and general decay.

With the fervor of public health officials battling plague germs, the doctors pursued "the vice" into its dark and solitary hideouts. Parents were urged to watch their children for the first symptoms (pallor, languor, peevishness) and if necessary to strap their hands to their sides at night. Patients of both sexes were urged to "confess." In women even amorous thoughts inspired by reading, parties, flirtations, or "hot drinks" could upset the entire physiology. Doctors acknowledged a stern duty to oppose the reading of romantic novels "as one of the greatest causes of uterine disease in young women."[62]

As the century wore on, the hegemony of the uterus appeared to grow ever shakier. More and more women were rejecting the doctor's passive, sickly model of femininity and carving out activist roles for themselves. The suffrage movement had grown to nationwide proportions and was waging highly organized campaigns state by state. More and more middle-class women were seeking college educations either in the burgeoning women's colleges, like Smith (opened in 1875), Wellesley (1875), Bryn Mawr (1885), and Mills (1885), or in all-male institutions like Cornell, Williams, and Harvard.[63] To the doctors it seemed as if a new organ had entered the scene to contest for power—the female brain. Nineteenth-century gynecology became absorbed in the combat between the brain and the uterus for dominion over the female persona. It was as if the Woman Question were being fought out on the dissecting table: on the one hand, the brain—aggressive, calculating—bearing the standard of sexual rationalism; on the other hand, the uterus, bearing the standard of sexual romanticism—moistly receptive, nurturing, still governed by the ancient tempo of the moon and tides.

The possibility of peaceful coexistence between the two organs was ruled out by the basic laws of physiology. Medical men saw the body as a miniature economic system, with the various parts—like classes or interest groups—competing for a limited supply of resources. Each body contained a set quantity of energy which could be directed variously from one function to another. Thus there was inevitably a tension between the different functions, or organs—one could be developed only at the expense of the others. Strangely enough, doctors saw no reason to worry about conflicts between the lungs and the spleen, or the liver and the kidneys, or other possible pairs of combatants. The central drama, in bodies male or female, was that great duel between the *brain* and the *reproductive organs*.

Needless to say, the desirable outcome of this struggle was quite different for the two sexes. Men were urged to back the brain, and to fight the debilitating effects of sexual indulgence. Since the mission of the male (the middle-class male, anyway) was to be a businessman, professor, lawyer, or gynecologist—he had to be careful to conserve all his energy for the "higher functions." Doctors warned men not to "spend their seed" (the material essence of their energy) recklessly in marital relations, and of course not to let it dribble away in secret vice or prurient dreams. Historian Barker-Benfield suggests that the doctors' fanatical dread of female sexuality reflected the constant, uphill struggle to preserve the male fluids for male endeavors. The "oversexed" woman was seen as a sperm-draining vampire who would leave men weak, spent, and effeminate.

In reverse but almost parallel terms, women were urged to throw their weight behind the uterus and resist the temptations of the brain. Because reproduction was woman's grand purpose in life, doctors agreed that women had to concentrate all their energy downward toward the womb. All other activity should be slowed down or stopped during the peak periods of uterine energy demand. At puberty, girls were advised to take a great deal of bed rest in order to help focus their strength on regulating their periods—though this might take years. Too much reading or intellectual stimulation in the fragile stage of adolescence could result in permanent damage to the reproductive organs, and sickly, irritable babies.

Pregnancy was another period requiring intense mental vacuity. One theory had the brain and the pregnant uterus competing not only for energy, but for a material substance—phosphates.[64] Every mental effort of the mother-to-be could deprive the unborn child of some of this vital nutrient, or would so overtax the woman's own system that she would be driven to insanity and require "prolonged administration of phosphates." Menopause brought no relief from the imperious demands of the uterus. Doctors described it as a "Pandora's box of ills," requiring, once again, a period of bovine placidity.

But it was not enough to urge women in the privacy of the office or sickroom to side with the beleaguered uterus. The brain was a powerful opponent, as the advance of the women's movement and the growing number of educated women showed. It must have seemed to the doctors that only they had the wisdom and courage to champion the poor uterus, who was, by her nature, not so nimble and clever as her opponent. So the doctors were led, beginning in the eighteen seventies, into the ongoing public debate over female education.

Dr. Edward H. Clarke's book *Sex in Education, or a Fair Chance for the Girls* was the great uterine manifeso of the nineteenth century.[65] It appeared at the height of the pressure for co-education at Harvard, where Clarke was a professor, and went through seventeen editions in the space of a few years. Clarke reviewed the medical theories of female nature—the innate frailty of women, the brain-uterus competition—and concluded, with startling but unassailable logic, that higher education would cause women's uteruses to atrophy!

Armed with Clarke's arguments, doctors agitated vociferously against the dangers of female education. R. R. Coleman, M.D., of Birmingham, Alabama, thundered this warning:

> Women beware. You are on the brink of destruction: You have hitherto been engaged in crushing your waists; now you are attempting to cultivate your mind: You have been merely dancing all night in the foul air of the ball-room; now you are beginning to spend your mornings in study. You have been incessantly stimulating your emotions with concerts and operas, with French plays, and French novels; now you are exerting your understanding to learn Greek, and solve propositions in Euclid. Beware!! Science pronounces that the woman who studies is lost.[66]

Dozens of medical researchers rushed in to plant the banner of science on the territory opened up by Clarke's book. Female students, their studies showed, were pale, in delicate health, and prey to monstrous deviations from menstrual regularity. (Menstrual irregularity upset the doctor's sensibilities as much as female sexuality. Both were evidences of spontaneous, ungovernable forces at work in the female flesh.) A 1902 study showed that 42 per cent of the women admitted to insane asylums were well educated compared to only 16 per cent of the men—"proving," obviously, that higher education was driving women crazy.[67] But the consummate evidence was the college woman's dismal contribution to the birth rate. An 1895 study found that 28 per cent of female college graduates married, compared to 80 per cent of women in general.[68] The birth rate was falling among white middle-class people in general, and most precipitously among the college educated. G. Stanley Hall, whose chapter on "Adolescent Girls and their Education" reviewed thirty years of medical arguments against female education, concluded with uncharacteristic sarcasm that the colleges were doing fine if their aim was to train "those who do not marry or if they are to educate for celibacy." "These institutions may perhaps come to be training stations of a new-old type, the agamic or agenic [i.e., sterile] woman, be she aunt, maid—old or young—nun, school-teacher, or bachelor woman."[69]

The doctors and psychologists (for we should acknowledge Hall's influential contribution to the debate) conceded that it was possible for a woman, if she were sufficiently determined, to dodge the destiny prepared for her by untold eons of evolutionary struggle, and throw in her lot with the *brain*. But the resulting "mental woman," if we may so term this counterpart to the natural, "uterine woman," could only hope to be a freak, morally and medically. "She has taken up and utilized in her own life all that was meant for her descendants," Hall complained. "This is the very apotheosis of selfishness from the standpoint of every biological ethics." Physically, the results were predictable: "First, she loses her mammary function. . . ." Hall wrote,[70] since lactation seemed to represent woman's natural unselfishness.

Some medical writings suggested that the loss of the mammary function would be accompanied by an actual loss of the breasts. "In her evening gown she shows evidence of joints which had been adroitly hidden beneath tissues of soft flesh," wrote Arabella Kenealy, M.D., of the "mental woman," "and already her modesty has been put to the necessity of puffing and pleating, where Nature had planned the tenderest and most dainty of devices," i.e., the breast. Doctors agreed that the brain-dominated woman would be muscular, angular, abrupt in her motions. Dr. Kenealy, who directed many of her writings as polemics against Olive Schreiner, described the new woman thus:

Where before her beauty was suggestive and elusive, now it is defined. . . . The haze, the elusiveness, the subtle suggestion of the face are gone. . . . the mechanism of movement is no longer veiled by a certain mystery of motion. . . . Her voice is louder, her tones are assertive. She says everything—leaves nothing to the imagination.[71]

Uterine woman had been indistinct, mysterious, like a veil over the harsh face of industrial society. The real horror of the brain-dominated woman was that she left man with no illusions.

Even the woman who opted for the sexless, mental life could not expect the brain to have an easy victory. The struggle between the brain, with its die-hard intellectual pretensions, and the primitive, but tenacious uterus could tear a woman apart—perhaps destroying both organs in the process. So in the end all that awaited the brain-oriented woman was in most cases sickness, which of course is precisely what awaited her if she remained a "good," uterine woman. S. Weir Mitchell smugly expressed to a graduating class at Radcliffe his hope "that no wreck from these shores will be drifted into my dock-yard"—but, really, what hope was there?[72]

The medical warnings against higher education did not go un-heeded. Martha Carey Thomas, president of Bryn Mawr College, confessed that as a young woman she had been "terror-struck" after reading the chapters relating to women in Hall's *Adolescence,* lest she "and every other woman . . . were doomed to live as patho-logical invalids . . ." as a result of their education.[73] Martha Carey Thomas survived her education and pursued a full and demanding career (no doubt serving to the doctors as a repulsive example of muscular, brain-dominated woman), but there were also casualties. Margaret Cleaves, M.D. of Des Moines ended by confessing the futil-ity of her own attempts at a career. In her own description she had been a "mannish Maiden" from the start and had let her masculine ambition draw her into a medical education. But no sooner had she achieved her goal than she developed a galloping case of neuras-thenia, or "sprained brain" as she diagnosed it. "It may be true," she admitted in her book *The Autobiography of a Neurasthene:*

as emphasized by [S. Weir] Mitchell and others, that girls and women are unfit to bear the continued labor of mind because of the disqualifications existing in their physiological life.[74]

Similarly, Antoinette Brown, America's first female minister, dropped out of the ministry after being converted to the "scientific" theory of woman's nature.[75]

As the century wore on, fewer and fewer women were willing to take the doctor's advice seriously, though. Feminists vigorously attacked the idea that women did not have the stamina for higher education, and even satirized the medical injunctions, as in this poem, "The Maiden's Vow":

> I will avoid equations
> And shun the naughty surd
> I must beware the perfect square
> Through it young girls have erred
> And when men mention Rule of Three
> Pretend I have not heard.[76]

The Rest Cure

The notion of the female body as the battleground of the uterus and the brain led to two possible therapeutic approaches: one was to intervene in the reproductive area—removing "diseased" organs or strengthening the uterus with bracing doses of silver nitrate, injections, cauterizations, bleedings, etc. The other approach was to go straight for the brain and attempt to force its surrender directly. The doctors could hardly use the same kind of surgical techniques on the brain as they had on the ovaries and uterus, but they discovered more subtle methods. The most important of these was the rest cure—the world-famous invention of Dr. S. Weir Mitchell.

The rest cure depended on the now-familiar techniques of twentieth-century brainwashing—total isolation and sensory deprivation. For approximately six weeks the patient was to lie on her back in a dimly lit room. She was not permitted to read. If her case was particularly severe, she was not even permitted to rise to urinate. She was to have no visitors and to see no one but a nurse and the doctor. Meanwhile, while the unwary brain presumably drifted off into a twilight state, the body would be fortified with feedings and massages. The feedings consisted of soft, bland foods and were supposed to result in a daily weight gain. The massages lasted for one hour a day, covering the entire body, and increasing in vigor as the cure wore on.

The cure became immensely popular—largely because, unlike other gynecological treatments, this one was painless. As a result of the rest cure, Philadelphia (where Mitchell practiced) was soon "the mecca for patients from all over the world."[77] Jane Addams underwent the rest cure, but it was apparently unsuccessful since it had to be followed with six more months of rest during which Addams was "literally bound to a bed" in her sister's house.[78] Charlotte Perkins Gilman underwent the cure before being discharged to "live as domestic a life as possible"—the results of which we have already recounted. But the majority of the patients seem to have come out of the cure filled, if not with health, with a sycophantic worship of Dr. Mitchell. Ex-patients and would-be patients plied him with small gifts and admiring letters, such as this one, which contrasts the writer's continued invalidism with the virile strength of the physician:

> Whilst laid by the heels in a country-house with an attack of grippe, also an invalid from gastric affection, the weary eyes of a sick woman fall upon your face in the *Century* [magazine] of this month—a thrill passed through me—at last I saw the true physician![79]

The secret of the rest cure lay not in the soft foods, the massages, or even, ultimately, in the intellectual deprivation, but in the doctor himself. S. Weir Mitchell must be counted as one of the great pioneers, perhaps the greatest, in the development of the twentieth-century doctor-patient relationship, or more generally, the expert-woman relationship. His personal friend and colleague Sir William Osler came to represent for posterity the masculinist ideal of the healer. But it was Mitchell, blessed with an endless supply of female invalids and neurasthenics, who perfected the technique of healing by *command*.

Mitchell was, by his own description, a "despot" in the sickroom. Patients were to ask no questions (or, like poor Gilman, attempt to volunteer information). His manner would be gentle and sympathetic one moment, abrupt and commanding the next. Now magnify Dr. Mitchell's authoritarianism by the conditions of the rest cure: the patient has been lying in semidarkness all day. She has not seen any other man, and no person but the nurse, for weeks. She is weak and languid from lying still for so long. Perhaps the long massage has left her with inadmissible sensations which she hesitates to localize even in imagination. Enter Dr. Mitchell. His lack of physical stature makes no difference to a prostrate woman. He is confident, commanding, scientific. He chides the patient for her lack of progress, or predicts exactly how she will feel tomorrow, in one week, in a month. The patient can only feel a deep gratitude for this particle of attention, this strange substitute for human companionship. She resolves that she *will* get better, as he has said she must, which means she will try to be a better woman, more completely centered on her reproductive functions.

It is as if Dr. Mitchell recognized that in the battle between the uterus and the brain, a third organ would have to be called into play —the phallus. The "local treatments" of earlier decades had already recognized the need for direct male penetration to set errant females straight. Nineteenth-century doctors universally expected sick (or cantankerous) women to spread their legs and admit leeches, "decoctions," the scalpel—whatever the physician chose to insert. But these were mere adolescent pokings compared to the mature phallic healing introduced by S. Weir Mitchell. He deplored "local treatments," foreswearing physical penetration altogether (unless you count the constant oral ingestion of soft foods). The physician, according to Mitchell, could heal by the force of his masculinity alone. This was, of course, the ultimate argument against female doctors: they could not "obtain the needed control over those of their own sex."[80] Only a male could command the total submissiveness which constituted the "cure."

If the patient did not yield to Mitchell's erect figure at the bedside, he would threaten to bring out his own, literal phallus. For example, according to a popular anecdote, when one patient failed to recover at the end of her rest cure:

> Dr. Mitchell had run the gamut of argument and persuasion and finally announced, "If you are not out of bed in five minutes—I'll get into it with you!" He thereupon started to remove his coat, the patient still obstinately prone—he removed his vest, but when he started to take off his trousers—she was out of bed in a fury![81]

Subverting the Sick Role: Hysteria

The romance of the doctor and the female invalid comes to full bloom (and almost to consummation) in the practice of S. Weir Mitchell. But as the anecdote just cited reveals, there is a nastier side to this affair. An angry, punitive tone has come into his voice; the possibility of physical force has been raised. As time goes on and the invalids pile up in the boudoirs of American cities and recirculate through the health spas and consulting rooms, the punitive tone grows louder. Medicine is caught in a contradiction of its own making, and begins to turn against the patient.

Doctors had established that women are sick, that this sickness is innate, and stems from the very possession of a uterus and ovaries. They had thus eliminated the duality of "sickness" and "health" for the female sex; there was only a drawn-out half-life, tossed steadily by the "storms" of reproductivity toward a more total kind of rest. But at the same time, doctors *were* expected to cure. The development of commercial medicine, with its aggressive, instrumental approach to healing, required some public faith that doctors could *do something,* that they could fix things. Certainly Charlotte Perkins Gilman had expected to be cured. The husbands, fathers, sisters, etc. of thousands of female invalids expected doctors to provide cures. A medical strategy of disease by decree, followed by "cures" which either mimicked the symptoms or caused new ones, might be successful for a few decades. But it had no long-term commercial viability.

The problem went deeper, though, than the issue of the doctors' commercial credibility. There was a contradiction in the romantic ideal of femininity which medicine had worked so hard to construct. Medicine had insisted that woman was sick *and* that her life centered on the reproductive function. But these are contradictory propositions. If you are sick enough, you cannot reproduce. The female role in reproduction requires stamina, and if you count in all the activities of child raising and running a house, it requires full-blown, energetic *health.* Sickness and reproductivity, the twin pillars of nineteenth-century femininity, could not stand together.

In fact, toward the end of the century, it seemed that sickness had been winning out over reproductivity. The birth rate for whites shrank by a half between 1800 and 1900, and the drop was most precipitous among white Anglo-Saxon Protestants—the "better" class of people. Meanwhile blacks and European immigrants appeared to be breeding prolifically, and despite their much higher death rates, the fear arose that they might actually replace the "native stock." Professor Edwin Conklin of Princeton wrote:

> The cause for alarm is the declining birth rate among the best elements of a population, while it continues to increase among the poorer elements. The descendants of the Puritans and the Cavaliers . . . are already disappearing, and in a few centuries at most, v have given place to more fertile races. . . .[82]

And in 1903 President Theodore Roosevelt thundered to the nation the danger of "race suicide":

> Among human beings, as among all other living creatures, if the best specimens do not, and the poorer specimens do, propagate, the type [race] will go down. If Americans of the old stock lead lives of celibate selfishness . . . or if the married are afflicted by that base fear of living which, whether for the sake of themselves or of their children, forbids them to have more than one or two children, disaster awaits the nation.[83]

G. Stanley Hall and other expert observers easily connected the falling WASP birth rate to the epidemic of female invalidism:

> In the United States as a whole from 1860–'90 the birth-rate declined from 25.61 to 19.22. Many women are so exhausted before marriage that after bearing one or two children they become wrecks, and while there is perhaps a growing dread of parturition or of the bother of children, many of the best women feel they have not stamina enough. . . .[84]

He went on to suggest that "if women do not improve," men would have to "have recourse to emigrant wives" or perhaps there would have to be a "new rape of the Sabines."

The genetic challenge posed by the "poorer elements" cast an unflattering light on the female invalid. No matter whether she was "really" suffering, she was clearly not doing her duty. Sympathy begins to give way to the suspicion that she might be deliberately *malingering*. S. Weir Mitchell revealed his private judgment of his patients in his novels, which dwelt on the grasping, selfish invalid, who uses her illness to gain power over others. In *Roland Blake* (1886) the evil invalid "Octapia" tries to squeeze the life out of her gentle cousin Olivia. In *Constance Trescot* (1905) the heroine is a domineering, driven woman, who ruins her husband's life and then relapses into invalidism in an attempt to hold on to her patient sister Susan:

> By degrees Susan also learned that Constance relied on her misfortune and her long illness to insure to her an excess of sympathetic affection and unremitting service. The discoveries thus made troubled the less selfish sister. . . .[85]

The story ends in a stinging rejection for Constance, as Susan leaves her to get married and assume the more womanly role of serving a man. Little did Dr. Mitchell's patients suspect that his ideal woman was not the delicate lady on the bed, but the motherly figure of the nurse in the background! (In fact, Mitchell's rest cure was implicitly based on the idea that his patients were malingerers.) As he explained it, the idea was to provide the patient with a drawn-out experience of invalidism, but without any of the pleasures and perquisites which usually went with that condition.

> To lie abed half the day, and sew a little and read a little, and be interesting and excite sympathy, is all very well, but when they are bidden to stay in bed a month and neither to read, write, nor sew, and to have one nurse,—who is not a relative,—then rest becomes for some women a rather bitter medicine, and they are glad enough to accept the order to rise and go about when the doctor issues a mandate . . .[86]

Many women probably *were* using the sick role as a way to escape their reproductive and domestic duties. For the woman to whom sex really was repugnant, and yet a "duty," or for any woman who wanted to avoid pregnancy, sickness was a way out—and there were few others. The available methods of contraception were unreliable, and not always that available either.[87] Abortion was illegal and risky. So female invalidism may be a direct ancestor of the nocturnal "headache" which so plagued husbands in the mid-twentieth century.

The suspicion of malingering—whether to avoid pregnancy or gain attention—cast a pall over the doctor-patient relationship. If a woman was really sick (as the doctors said she ought to be), then the doctor's efforts, however ineffective, must be construed as appropriate, justifiable, and of course reimbursable. But if she was *not* sick, then the doctor was being made a fool of. His manly, professional attempts at treatment were simply part of a charade directed by and starring the female patient. But how could you tell the real invalids from the frauds? And what did you do when no amount of drugging, cutting, resting, or sheer bullying seemed to make the woman well?

Doctors had wanted women to be sick, but now they found themselves locked in a power struggle with the not-so-feeble patient: Was the illness a construction of the medical imagination, a figment of the patient's imagination, or something "real" which nevertheless eluded the mightiest efforts of medical science? What, after all, was behind "neurasthenia," "hyperesthesia," or the dozens of other labels attached to female invalidism?

But it took a specific syndrome to make the ambiguities in the doctor-patient relationship unbearable, and to finally break the gynecologists' monopoly of the female psyche. This syndrome was hysteria. In many ways, hysteria epitomized the cult of female invalidism. It affected middle- and upper-class women almost exclusively; it had no discernible organic basis; and it was totally resistant to medical treatment. But unlike the more common pattern of invalidism, hysteria was episodic. It came and went in unpredictable, and frequently violent, fits.

According to contemporary descriptions, the victim of hysteria might either faint or throw her limbs about uncontrollably. Her back might arch, with her entire body becoming rigid, or she might beat her chest, tear her hair or attempt to bite herself and others. Aside from fits and fainting, the disease took a variety of forms: hysterical loss of voice, loss of appetite, hysterical coughing or sneezing, and, of course, hysterical screaming, laughing, and crying. The disease spread wildly, not only in the United States, but in England and throughout Europe.

Doctors became obsessed with this "most confusing, mysterious and rebellious of diseases." In some ways, it was the ideal disease for the doctors: it was never fatal, and it required an almost endless amount of medical attention. But it was not an ideal disease from the point of view of the husband and family of the afflicted woman. Gentle invalidism had been one thing; violent fits were quite another. So hysteria put the doctors on the spot. It was essential to their professional self-esteem either to find an organic basis for the disease, and cure it, or to expose it as a clever charade.

There was plenty of evidence for the latter point of view. With mounting suspicion, the medical literature began to observe that hysterics never had fits when alone, and only when there was something soft to fall on. One doctor accused them of pinning their hair in such a way that it would fall luxuriantly when they fainted. The hysterical "type" began to be characterized as a "petty tyrant" with a "taste for power" over her husband, servants, and children, and, if possible, her doctor.

In historian Carroll Smith-Rosenberg's interpretation, the doctor's accusations had some truth to them: the hysterical fit, for many women, must have been the only acceptable outburst—of rage, of despair, or simply of *energy*—possible.[88] Alice James, whose lifelong illness began with a bout of hysteria in adolescence, described her condition as a struggle against uncontrollable physical energy:

Conceive of never being without the sense that if you let yourself go for a moment . . . you must abandon it all, let the dykes break and the flood sweep in, acknowledging yourself abjectly impotent before the immutable laws. When all one's moral and natural stock-in-trade is a temperament forbidding the abandonment of an inch or the relaxation of a muscle, 'tis a never-ending fight. When the fancy took me of a morning at school to *study* my lessons by way of variety instead of shrieking or wiggling through the most impossible sensations of upheaval, violent revolt in my head overtook me, so that I had to "abandon" my brain as it were.[89]

On the whole, however, doctors did continue to insist that hysteria was a real disease—a disease of the uterus, in fact. (Hysteria comes from the Greek word for uterus.) They remained unshaken in their conviction that their own house calls and high physician's fees were absolutely necessary; yet at the same time, in their treatment and in their writing, doctors assumed an increasingly angry and threatening attitude. One doctor wrote, "It will sometimes be advisable to speak in a decided tone, in the presence of the patient, of the necessity of shaving the head, or of giving her a cold shower bath, should she not be soon relieved." He then gave a "scientific" rationalization for this treatment by saying, "The sedative influence of fear may allay, as I have known it to do, the excitement of the nervous centers. . . ."[90]

Carroll Smith-Rosenberg writes that doctors recommended suffocating hysterical women until their fits stopped, beating them across the face and body with wet towels, and embarrassing them in front of family and friends. She quotes Dr. F. C. Skey: "Ridicule to a woman of sensitive mind, is a powerful weapon . . . but there is not an emotion equal to fear and the threat of personal chastisement. . . . They will listen to the voice of authority." The more women became hysterical, the more doctors became punitive toward the disease; and at the same time, they began to see the disease everywhere themselves until they were diagnosing every independent act by a woman, especially a women's rights action, as "hysterical."

With hysteria, the cult of female invalidism was carried to its logical conclusion. Society had assigned affluent women to a life of confinement and inactivity, and medicine had justified this assignment by describing women as innately sick. In the epidemic of hysteria, women were both accepting their inherent "sickness" *and* finding a way to rebel against an intolerable social role. Sickness, having become a way of life, became a way of rebellion, and medical treatment, which had always had strong overtones of coercion, revealed itself as frankly and brutally repressive.

But the deadlock over hysteria was to usher in a new era in the experts' relationship to women. While the conflict between hysterical women and their doctors was escalating in America, Sigmund Freud, in Vienna, was beginning to work on a treatment that would remove the disease altogether from the arena of gynecology.

Freud's cure eliminated the confounding question of whether or not the woman was faking: in either case it was a mental disorder. Psychoanalysis, as Thomas Szasz has pointed out, insists that "malingering *is* an illness—in fact, an illness 'more serious' than hysteria."[91] Freud banished the traumatic "cures" and legitimized a doctor-patient relationship based solely on talking. His therapy urged the patient to confess her resentments and rebelliousness, and then at last to accept her role as a woman. Freud's insight into hysteria at once marked off a new medical specialty: "Psychoanalysis," in the words of feminist historian Carroll Smith-Rosenberg, "is the child of the hysterical woman." In the course of the twentieth century psychologists and psychiatrists would replace doctors as the dominant experts in the lives of women.

For decades into the twentieth century doctors would continue to view menstruation, pregnancy, and menopause as physical diseases and intellectual liabilities. Adolescent girls would still be advised to study less, and mature women would be treated indiscriminately to hysterectomies, the modern substitute for ovariotomies. The female reproductive organs would continue to be viewed as a kind of frontier for chemical and surgical expansionism, untested drugs, and reckless experimentation. But the debate over the Woman Question would never again be phrased in such crudely materialistic terms as those set forth by nineteenth-century medical theory—with brains "battling" uteruses for control of woman's nature. The psychological interpretation of hysteria, and eventually of "neurasthenia" and the other vague syndromes of female invalidism, established once and for all that the brain was in command. The experts of the twentieth century would accept woman's intelligence and energy: the question would no longer be what a woman *could* do, but, rather, what a woman *ought* to do.

FIVE

Microbes and the Manufacture of Housework

At the turn of the new century, the invalid languishing on her chaise longue was at last about to end her morbid existence as a feminine ideal. Female invalidism, the gynecologists' solution to the Woman Question, had always been too exclusive and too demanding. Now a new spirit of activism gripped the women as well as the men of the middle class: American business was expanding into markets all over the world, and at home lay the formidable task of assimilating twenty million immigrant workers on the one hand and civilizing the robber barons on the other. Teddy Roosevelt's rise from an asthmatic boyhood to an obsessively activist manhood stood as an inspiration to the most debilitated and listless veterans of the *fin de siècle*. Everyone wanted to be "on the go," "in the swim," and even the most privileged women were not about to sit out the American Century with a sick headache.

In a burst of pent-up energy middle-class American women were now loosening their garments, riding bicycles and leaving their homes to organize women's clubs, charities, civic reform groups. But they were not, by and large, ready to reject the basic assumptions of sexual romanticism. They were looking for a new version of the romantic ideal—something more democratic than invalidism, something healthier, more activist.

The new ideal carved out in the first decade or so of the century would not be the political activist or social reformer but the housewife. She would be bound to the home just as securely as the invalid had been—not because she was too weak to do anything else, but because she had so much to do there. Bustling, efficient—intellectually as well as emotionally engaged in her tasks—the housewife could stand as a model for all women, not just the wealthier ones. Men could be bank presidents or hod-carriers, professors or coal miners; women, henceforth, would be housewives.

The idea of housekeeping as a full-time profession was elaborated by a new set of experts who were, unlike the doctors, largely women themselves. Making domestic work into a profession meant, of course, making it into a science. Between the late eighteen nineties and the teens of the twentieth century, women organized, discussed, experimented, and drew prodigiously on the advice of male experts in an attempt to lay the basis for a *science* of child raising and a *science* of housework. In the two chapters which follow this one, we will trace the development of "scientific child raising" and its gradual takeover by male experts, doctors, and psychologists. In this chapter we focus on the domestic science, or home economics, experts—their efforts to redefine women's domestic tasks, and to "sell" the new, scientific, housework.

The Domestic Void

Before the industrial revolution, there had never been any question about what women should be doing in the home. Eighteenth- and early-nineteenth-century rural women (and most women then were rural) weren't just making apple pies and embroidered samplers; they were making bread, butter, cloth, clothing, soap, candles, medicines, and other things essential to their families' survival. A New England farmer wrote in 1787 that he had earned $150 from the sale of farm produce in one year, but:

> . . . I never spent more than ten dollars a year which was for salt, nails, and the like. Nothing to eat, drink, or wear was bought, as my farm provided all.[1]

The pre-industrial rural home was a tiny manufacturing center, demanding of its female workers a wide variety of skills and an endless capacity for hard work.

In fact, the pressures of home production left very little time for the tasks which we would recognize today as housework. By all accounts, pre-industrial revolution women were sloppy housekeepers by today's standards. Instead of the daily cleaning or the weekly cleaning, there was the *spring cleaning*. Meals were simple and repetitive; clothes were changed infrequently; and "the household wash was allowed to accumulate, and the washing done once a month, or in some households once in three months."[2] And, since each wash required the carting and heating of many buckets of water, there was a considerable disincentive to achieve higher standards of cleanliness.

Then, beginning in the early nineteenth century, came industrialization and the growth of the Market economy. Bit by bit, wage labor and "business" began to replace agriculture as the American way of life. Young women, adult men, and even children were drawn to the towns to produce for cash, rather than for their families' immediate needs. Yet throughout the nineteenth century, through the upheavals of urbanization, industrialization, war—over 95 per cent of married women remained, like their mothers before them, at home,[3] seemingly untouched by the industrial and social revolution sweeping through American life. But, their lives too were drastically changed: the traditional home crafts were vanishing into the factories. Home textile manufacture, which Alexander Hamilton had hailed as central to the economy of the early republic,[4] practically disappeared between 1825 and 1855.[5] Cloth, and soon candles, soap, and butter, joined buttons and needles as things that most women *bought* rather than made.

By the end of the century, hardly anyone made their own starch or boiled their laundry in a kettle. In the cities, women bought their bread and at least their underwear ready-made, sent their children out to school and probably some clothes out to be laundered, and were debating the merits of canned foods. In middle-class homes the ice box was well established, and easy-to-clean linoleum had made its appearance. "The flow of industry had passed on and had left idle the loom in the attic, the soap kettle in the shed."[6]

With less and less to *make* in the home, it seemed as if there would soon be nothing to *do* in the home. Educators, popular writers and even leading social scientists fretted about the growing void in the home. Sociologist Edward A. Ross observed that "four fifths of the industrial processes carried on in the average American home in 1850 have departed never to return" and demanded an accounting for "the energy released."[7] Economist Thorstein Veblen insisted that even when the affluent housewife did appear to be working in her home, what was left to do was so trivial that it could be counted among the "evidences of wasted effort" which made up the family's round of "conspicuous consumption."[8]

For many working-class women, of course, there was no problem about what to do: they followed their old "women's work" into the factory system—making the textiles, clothing, and soap which had once been made in the home. But in the new urban middle class the domestic void was an urgent problem, tied to the ongoing debate over the Woman Question. If their mothers had been content with a few "accomplishments" such as fancy needlework and sketching, the young women of this class were increasingly demanding—and getting— a full-scale college education. Education only heightened their sense that something was missing in the American home. Some were resentful that male industrialists had pre-empted the productive functions which had once given dignity and purpose to womanhood. When Edward Bok, the influential editor of the *Ladies' Home Journal,* advised women to keep out of politics and stick to their own sphere, a writer in *Woman's Journal* (the national suffrage newspaper) lashed back:

> The baker, the laundry-man, the manufacturer of underwear and ready-made garments, the caterer, the tailor, the man-milliner, and many more would have to go, for if woman is not to encroach on man's especial domain, then he must keep his own side of the fence and not intrude on hers.[9]

Ellen Richards, who was to lead the drive to put housekeeping on a scientific basis, told a male audience:

> . . . I must reiterate [home life] has been robbed by the removal of *creative* work . . . The care of children occupies only five or ten years of the seventy. What are women to do with the rest? . . . You cannot put them where their grandmothers were, while you take to yourselves the spinning, the weaving, the soap-making. The time was when there was always something to *do* in the home. Now there is only something *to be done.*[10] [Her emphasis.]

But others believed that that very "robbery" was woman's greatest opportunity. Feminist Olive Schreiner agreed that the industrial revolution had greatly enriched "man's field of remunerative toil" and had tended to "rob women, not merely in part but almost wholly, of the valuable part of her ancient domain of productive and social labor . . ." But instead of looking nostalgically at the past, she believed, the time had come for women to recognize that the only challenging work for them lay in the male world of industry, science, public affairs. "Give us labor and the training which fits us for labor!" Schreiner demanded, and put her faith in the young woman whom she said was even then knocking on every door that shut off a new field of labor, mental or physical, anxious to fulfill "she knows not what duties, in the years to come!"[11]

And of course there *was* reason to believe that liberation from domestic confinement was just around the corner. All around them in the nineteenth century, feminists had watched as the small, productive workshops—the cobbler, the blacksmith, the potter, the milliner—had been made obsolete by the factory system. Now cities had grown, the physical size of the middle-class home had greatly diminished, and family size had gone down too. Surely, they thought, only a few more steps need be taken to industrialize domestic work completely and free women to join the world of men.

The Romance of the Home

But as it turned out, the home was not just another quaint anachronism which could be tossed aside along with other antique reminders of the past. For every woman like Olive Schreiner or Charlotte Perkins Gilman who was ready to sweep domesticity into the dustbin of history, hundreds more believed that the only answer to the Woman Question lay in preserving the home.

The home was becoming a major issue in and of itself. Clergymen, popular magazines, and politicians continually harped on the sanctity of the home and the dangers besetting it. The 1909 White House Conference on the Care of Dependent Children declared that "home life is the highest and finest product of civilization."[12] The converse idea, that civilization was the product of decent home life, was held to be axiomatic. At the time of the Spanish-American War, Demolins' widely quoted book *Anglo-Saxon Superiority*[13] traced the imperial success of the Anglo-Saxon "race" to an inherent Anglo-Saxon love of home.* Home, with a capital "H," was by this time a word

_____
* We finally came across a "scientific" explanation for this Anglo-Saxon "trait." In his classic work *Social Psychology,* Edward Ross explains what he

which patriotic Americans could hardly breathe without feeling a rush of maudlin sentiment. But at the same time the home seemed to be coming apart. After surveying the last few decades—the rising divorce rates, the apparent indifference of young couples to a settled family life—the social historian Arthur Calhoun warned in 1919 that the future of the home was "problematical."[14]

Paradoxically, throughout the nineteenth century, Americans showed very little reverence for, or even interest in, the home as a physical place. Whole villages had packed up for the westward trek that began in the eighteen twenties. People moved when they ran out of land to support a growing family, or as the story goes, when they felt hemmed in by the sight of a neighbor's hearth smoke. The first of May was "moving day" in eastern cities, when "the streets were a clattering shambles of displaced furniture and families frantically playing the annual game of 'move all,'"—to a few houses or a few blocks away.[15] The parental home, where mother rocked by the fireside, was likely to be remote or even forgotten: grown children, especially sons, were expected to strike out on their own, as far as possible from the maternal apron strings.

During the vast internal migrations of the early and mid-nineteenth century, home had to be realistically redefined as "where mother is" (or, even more minimally, "where you hang your hat"). But industrialization threatened even this scaled-down, stripped-for-action version of home and family. Looking back on the pre-industrial farm home, which grew more alluring with distance, end-of-century social observers could find nothing solid on which to base the modern home. Shared work no longer held the family together; the sources of subsistence lay outside the home in a factory system which valued neither Home, nor Motherhood, nor for that matter childhood—only the labor which could be extracted from individual workers. Even the well-to-do home, with all but the father unemployed, was torn by centrifugal forces: the father poured himself into his career and relaxed in clubs; the mother shopped and visited; the children went out to school. *Life* magazine commented sarcastically:

> The school as a civic center having become overcrowded, it occurred
> to some bright mind to advocate the use of the home as a civic cen-

---

calls the "familism" or family-centeredness of Anglo-Saxons as a result of their being "obliged by climate to centre their lives in the circle about the fireside." It is strange then, that the sociologists did not attribute the greatest racial superiority to the Eskimos and Lapps.

ter. The home is vacant so large a part of the day that it would seem that the highest efficiency would put it to some use other than as a possible place to sleep in after midnight.[16]

But few observers were so cavalier. Historian Calhoun's chapter on "The Precarious Home" quotes dozens of books, articles, special reports anxiously examining the health of the home, "the neglect of the Home," "the subtle danger to the Home," and so forth.[17]

To middle-class observers at the turn of the century, social stability seemed to require that people settle down. The old values of restlessness and adventure—which had been essential to the conquest of the West—were no longer appropriate and possibly dangerous. The frontier had closed. Railroads and ranchers had carved up the West and left little room for pioneering individuals. And the economic frontier was closing rapidly too. Monopolization was setting in, blocking the upward trajectories of would-be Horatio Algers, or confining them to the status of corporate employees. Class lines were being drawn, and in the new industrial order, the reckless values of the frontier could only mean turmoil and instability. People, at least most people, would have to withdraw their aspirations from the wider world and recenter them in the tiny sphere of the home.

In fact, Americans found themselves increasingly drawn to the security of the home. Men who had grown up on farms were now confronting a work world in which a man could no longer control either the work process or the conditions of his employment. In the last decades of the nineteenth century, depressions repeatedly obliterated jobs and wiped out family savings. Even the neighborhood offered little security in the mushrooming cities, where the ethnic composition, and even the street signs, were likely to change every few years. Only the home seemed secure and stable. In his study of a lower-middle-class Chicago neighborhood in the eighteen seventies, historian Richard Sennett documents the retreat to the home—men went out to bars or clubs less often; families did less visiting.[18] Even the trade union movement, which again and again drew thousands of people together in collective struggle, never questioned the middle-class ideal of domesticity and in fact used this ideal to justify demands for higher wages and shorter hours.

Corporate leaders were as vigorous as anyone in advancing the virtues of domesticity. Sociologist Ross encouraged them to see home ownership as a means of social control or, as he put it hygienically, as a "prophylactic against mob mind":

> A wide diffusion of land ownership has long been recognized as fostering a stable and conservative political habit . . . The man owns his home, but in a sense his home owns him, checking his rash impulses, holding him out of the human whirlpool, ever saying inaudibly, 'Heed me, care for me, or you lose me!' "[19]

Right after the great strike of 1892, Carnegie Steel went into the business of subsidizing home ownership for its Homestead workers. In the decades that followed, scores of companies built model villages and offered home loans to their workers. As the welfare director of an (unidentified) large company explained to early-twentieth-century housing reformer Charles Whitaker:

> Get them to invest their savings in their homes and own them. Then they won't leave and they won't strike. It ties them down so they have a stake in our prosperity.[20]

But social control was an investment which only the largest and most farsighted corporations could afford. Most employers could not have cared less how their workers lived, and all, of course, viciously opposed the workers' own attempts to raise their standard of living. Efforts to promote home values among the workers were usually confined to the least expensive, most trivial, measures. For example, the Palmer Manufacturing Company provided basins and towels for its employees so that they could return home looking like "gentlemen," and thus gain a higher respect for home life.[21] Not until the nineteen twenties when business came to see the home as a *market* would the nation's corporate leadership launch a concerted effort to promote domesticity among the workers.

Near the turn of the century, it was the middle class which expressed the greatest commitment to "saving" the home. In the home they saw an ideal which could unite the lowly worker and the corporate mogul: Didn't the workers really want nothing more than a secure and cozy home? Didn't the capitalists know that nothing would be better for "labor peace" than a domesticated work force? Furthermore, the home could be an essential training place in the industrial "virtues." As Rev. Samuel Dike, a leading campaigner against the liberalization of divorce laws explained:

The industrial world should see that its fundamental needs of industry, efficiency, fidelity to tasks, and loyalty to all demands of the situation require qualifications of mind and character that depend very largely on the home behind the workman . . .[22]

Beyond that, the home was an ideal "container" for aspirations which could not be met in an increasingly stratified society: from a middle-class point of view it was a wholesome target for working-class ambitions and from a male point of view it was a safe focus for women's energies.

Many of the reform efforts of this period aimed, directly or indirectly, at the defense of the Home. The best-publicized causes were those which addressed themselves to the external dangers which threatened the home—alcohol, prostitution, poor housing, unregulated female and child labor. The domestic science reformers received far less attention: they had no lurid abuses to expose; they made no claims on the collective conscience of industrialists and politicians. But only they addressed themselves to the danger *within*—the home's eroded core, the Domestic Void. Necessarily their initial priority was the middle-class home, where the void was most palpable and threatening. Better housing, better wages, and legislation to restrict female employment—all of these could not save the home and enforce the romantic solution to the Woman Question if women did not have something useful to *do* within the home. As the *Ladies' Home Journal* editorialized, social stability required that the void be filled:

As a matter of fact, what a certain type of woman needs today more than anything else is some task that "would tie her down." Our whole social fabric would be the better for it. Too many women are dangerously idle.[23]

Domestic Scientists Put the House in Order

Strictly speaking, domestic science was not a "cause," as its advocates liked to think, but a new area of expertise. The idea of systematizing information on housekeeping and making it available to large numbers of women went back several decades. As early as the eighteen forties Catherine Beecher—her English counterpart was the indispensable Mrs. Beeton—had campaigned for an educated approach to household chores, and by the late eighteen hundreds land-grant colleges in the Midwest were offering domestic instruction to future farm wives. By the turn of the century there were several hundred professional women in the United States—chiefly social workers and teachers—who saw themselves as experts on homemaking. As we have already seen, this was the heyday of professionalization: doctors were tightening their ranks and seeking a scientific basis for medicine; the various academic disciplines (sociology, psychology, political science, etc.) were congealing out of the interdisciplinary mush of the mid-nineteenth century; even social work was establishing itself as an exclusive and "scientific" occupation. It was only natural that the homemaking experts would organize to elevate their area of expertise beyond the stage of recipes and household hints and onto the higher ground of scientific professionalism.

Ellen Swallow Richards, a chemist by training, was the woman who led domestic science out of the cookbook stage. The medical profession had required, for its genesis, the combined talents of organizers like Flexner, researchers like Pasteur, and venerable public figures like Osler. For domestic science, there was only Ellen Richards. She did much of the basic research—tested household water purity, foods, and appliances; organized the conferences and journals; and publicized the new field on the international lecture circuit. And unlike the miscellaneous social workers and educators who were drawn to the new domestic science, she had had a genuine scientific education, complete with laboratory training: she represented the necessary link to the transcendent world of science. Contemporary "home ec" texts reserve a place of honor for Ellen Richards, whose photo portrait shows her at the peak of her career—firm-jawed, heavily browed, confident—decked out in the cap and gown which never ceased to represent her highest achievement as a woman.

The story of Ellen Richards' evolution from chemistry to domestic science probably explains as much about her followers—the millions of women who would eventually try to practice "scientific housekeeping"—as it does about herself. She had always struggled to find a wider range for her own abilities than the home, but was hemmed in at every point by the sexual anxieties of male colleagues. As a student, for example, she had to counter her professor (and future husband's) argument that co-education "introduces Feelings, interests [that are] foreign to [the] lecture room."[24] The final outcome of her career—to be honored for founding the science of homemaking—was not so much a triumph as a concession.

As a girl, Ellen Richards had had firsthand experience of the skills which industry had "robbed" from women. The daughter of a stern New England farmer and an invalid mother, Ellen had learned to keep house, cook, sew, garden, and nurse the sick. When she was thirteen, her bread and embroidery won two grand prizes at the county fair. But she had no desire to follow these interests to their usual conclusion in matrimony. From Worcester, where she had gone to study and support herself by tutoring, she wrote a friend that "the young or old gentleman has not yet made his appearance who can entice me away from my free and independent life."[25] Called back from this independence to nurse her mother, Ellen fell into a two-year-long depression. The Woman Question—what does a woman *do* with her life?—weighed down on her, almost crushing her, like her mother, into permanent invalidism.

The answer, for Richards, came with the improbable news that a New York brewer named Matthew Vassar had endowed a college for women. (There were no colleges open to women in New England at the time.) She shook off her depression, scraped together her savings, and set off for Poughkeepsie. From then on, she never paused long enough for depression to catch up with her again. At Vassar she crammed insatiably, even making a practice of carrying a book open in front of her so she could study as she walked between classes. Her hard work and passion for detail (she recorded in her diary the number of steps she climbed each day) endeared her to Vassar professor Maria Mitchell, the astronomer, who encouraged her to crack the male citadel of science.

Ellen (still Swallow at this point) decided to penetrate the inner sanctum: to study chemistry at MIT. Now, it was much more difficult, if possible, for a woman to become an experimental scientist like a chemist, than to be an astronomer or naturalist whose business was to observe nature passively and from a respectful distance. Women might be meticulous observers and note-takers without totally compromising their gender. But the laboratory—chemical or bacteriological—was a scene of *action,* where men backed nature into a corner and beat her secrets out of her.

The faculty of MIT debated for weeks whether to admit Ellen Swallow and finally did so only under the kind of conditions with which a group of surgeons would have invited Typhoid Mary to join them in the operating room. She could only be a "special" student. She had to study separately from male students and work in her own segregated laboratory. She could not earn a graduate degree no matter what she accomplished. And, finally, to make sure she hadn't become "unwomanly" as a result of her studies, the professors would ask her to sort their papers and mend their suspenders: "I try to keep all sorts of such things as needles, thread, pins, scissors, etc., around . . ." She wrote with some satisfaction, "they can't say study spoils me for anything else."[26]

When Ellen Richards graduated from MIT—with a second bachelor's degree—there were still no places for her in the male world of chemistry. MIT graciously lent her a lab where she could train women high school teachers in basic chemistry. But this was not a job, with position and pay, it was just the kind of "good work" that an intelligent faculty wife like Mrs. Richards might be expected to perform. She could assist the male scientists, befriend them, sew for them, even funnel a little of their knowledge off to women teachers, but she could not *be one of them*.

Barred from chemistry, Richards turned her formidable energies toward the creation of a new science in which she *would* have a place on an equal footing with men. In 1873 she announced, in an address to a high society gathering, the birth of the new science of "oekology." One admiring biographer has interpreted this as the premature birth of *ecology,* in the contemporary environmentalist sense, but what she was actually unveiling was the infant version of the "science of right living"; or as she put it then "the science to teach people how to live," which was to blend chemistry, biology, and engineering principles into practical guidelines for daily life. The scientific establishment was not, however, taken in by Richards' stratagem, and dismissed "oekology" as a kind of "hokum" like faith healing and patent medicine. Later Richards tried to launch the "science of right living" again, under the new label of "euthenics"; and was again rebuffed. The scientific community which had rejected her for trying to be a scientist now turned against her for not being scientific enough.

None of these experiences overcame Richards' antipathy to feminism. As a young woman she criticized the early feminist movement for not having ". . . a higher standard of knowledge and responsibility." Neither of her biographers mentions her having any interest in women's rights (or in the abolition of child labor, or any of a dozen of the burning social issues of her lifetime). She did devote considerable energy to expanding higher educational opportunities for women, but her basic stance on the Woman Question was elitist and masculinist: women did not need to struggle collectively; individual women would be "let in" as they proved themselves ready. Thus, despite her own role as the female "first" in MIT, she strongly disapproved when in 1878 MIT decided to start admitting women on the same basis as men. Some of the reasons she listed were obviously contrived: Would the girls be exempted from military drill? If they were, they would be getting a "special privilege" and they would not really be in on the same basis as men. "Finally, and to my mind the most fundamental [reason] of all," she concluded:

> though it grieves me to say it, the present state of public opinion among women themselves does not give reason to believe that, of one hundred young girls of sixteen who might enter if the opportunity was offered, ten would carry the course through. It is demoralizing to have such results in the early stages of scientific education for women.[27]

Decades later, she declined an invitation to serve on the women's board of the World's Columbian Exposition along similar lines:

> Twenty years ago I was glad to work on women's boards for the education of women. The time is now some years past when it seemed to me wise to work that way. Women have now more rights and duties than they are fitted to perform.[28]

But in the end, Richards had to overcome her aversion to working "that way," i.e., with and through women's groups. Domestic Science became the final receptacle for all her ideas of community and household sanitation and "right living" in general. It was a strange place for Ellen Richards to end up, according to Caroline Hunt:

> Considering her passionate desire for equality of educational opportunity for men and women, the preference which she often expressed for working with men and women together and not women alone, and her vigorous protests against special concessions to women, it may seem strange that Mrs. Richards should have interested herself . . . in the home economics movement, which is often thought to interest women chiefly.[29]

In fact, it took a man to convince Richards to try once again to carve out her own distinctive field of human endeavor. No one could have been a better advisor than Melville Dewey, whose life work had consisted of dividing all human knowledge into that system of categories and subcategories known as the Dewey Decimal System. If the period around the turn of the century was characterized by what one historian called "the search for order" on the part of the middle class,[30] then Melville Dewey must have been leading the way with a high-beam searchlight. In addition to inventing the decimal system, he was president of the New York Efficiency Society, whose aim was to spread industrial management techniques into every backwater of human existence. For example, he cut down on waste time in his own life by streamlining his name to Melvil Dewey, and then finally to Melvil Dui. It was Dewey (or Dui for the speedreaders) who finally convinced Richards to give up her efforts to create a new natural science and to be content to launch "right living" as a hybrid between the social and natural sciences; "home economics" was the name he suggested.† He encouraged her to organize the new discipline, and it was near his summer home at Lake Placid in the Adirondacks that the domestic scientists convened every year from 1899 to 1907.

The top domestic science cadre, the few dozen professional men and women who gathered each year at Lake Placid to assess the progress of the new field, were perfectly clear about where they stood on the Woman Question: it was the mission of domestic science to fill the domestic void and thus preserve the home. Ellen Richards often stated her worry that "the family group is in the process of disintegration."[31] Mrs. Alice P. Norton, a University of Chicago professor and a frequent speaker at the Lake Placid Conferences, told her fellow conferees in 1904:

> Many of us are afraid for the future of the home. So many centrifugal forces are working against it, life outside the home is becoming so attractive, that there is danger of the center of social interest losing its normal position in the home. The study of the household arts, if taught in the right spirit, must inevitably tend to make the home a more interesting place . . .[32]‡

† A note on nomenclature: Ellen Richards had been calling her new field "domestic science" since the failure of "oekology" to catch on in 1897. In 1904 the Lake Placid Conference proposed the following official usage: the subject would be called "handwork" in elementary school, "domestic science" in secondary school, "home economics" in normal and professional (i.e., technical) schools, and "euthenics" in colleges and universities. In practice the Lake Placid group tended to use "home economics" and "domestic science" to mean the same thing. Here we use Richards' term "domestic science," although "home economics" became much more common later on.

‡ The hope that education will make housework interesting dies hard. A 1974 home economics text states: "Much has been written in the past few years

When Mrs. Linda Hull Larned, then president of the National Household Economics Association, reported at the 1902 conference on the spread of the domestic science movement among clubwomen, she was able to say:

> Fortunately there are a few thinking, progressive persons in the world besides ourselves and they are just as firm as we are in the belief that homemaking is the most natural and therefore the most desirable vocation for women.[33]

Physicians hastened to support these sentiments with medical arguments. In 1899, the AMA endorsed the need for domestic science education on the grounds that it would lead to reduced "infant mortality, contagious diseases, intemperance (in eating and drinking), divorce, insanity, pauperism, competition of labor between the sexes, men's and women's clubs, etc."[35]

But, as the domestic science professionals knew, it would take much more than a few exhortations on the sanctity of the home to transform homemaking into a career of deep and abiding interest. In the new age of industrial progress, everything had to be justified in the name of an activist, forward-looking, science. As one advocate of domestic science education proclaimed to a women's conference in 1897:

> When the grand meaning and hidden power of her ordained sphere dawn upon her in their full force thru [sic] scientific study, then she [woman] will not sigh because Nature has assigned her special duties which man has deemed safe to be trusted to her instincts, yet in reality need for their performance the highest scientific knowledge.[36]

Crusade Against Germs

The domestic scientists hoped to forge a direct pipeline between the scientific laboratory and the average home. They seized any science, any discipline, any discovery, which could conceivably be used to upgrade a familiar task. Richards believed that biochemistry could

---

concerning the boredom and frustrations of the American homemaker. People who do things poorly are often bored and/or frustrated. The homemaker who is educated for homemaking is able to use her knowledge in a creative way for the attainment of a personally satisfying happy life and for the achievement of the social, economic, aesthetic, and scientific values in successful family life."[34]

eventually transform cooking into a precise laboratory exercise; economics could revolutionize budgeting and shopping; and so forth. As for cleaning, there was now a new, firm scientific foundation to build upon—the bacteriologists' Germ Theory of Disease.

Germ Theory, which became known to the public in the eighteen nineties (though in a somewhat distorted fashion) set off a wave of public anxiety about contagion. Any public place or object was suspect, as these popular magazine titles from the period 1900 to 1904 suggest: "Books Spread Contagion," "Contagion by Telephone," "Infection and Postage Stamps," "Disease from Public Laundries," "Menace of the Barber Shop." Middle-class people were especially fearful of contagion from the "lower" classes. In her household hygiene book, *Women, Plumbers and Doctors, or Household Sanitation,* Mrs. Plunkett warned:

> A man may live on the splendid "avenue," in a mansion plumbed in the latest and costliest style, but if, half a mile away, in range with his open window, there is a "slum," or even a neglected tenement house, the zephyrs will come along and pick up the disease germs and bear them onward, distributing them to whomsoever it meets, whether he be a millionaire or a shillingaire . . .[37]

Not only "zephyrs," but garments, cigars, etc., manufactured in tenement-house factories could carry germs from the poor to the middle-class home, it was feared. Most frightening of all was the possibility that the servants or part-time help could be a kind of fifth column, bringing disease into the family. The case of "Typhoid Mary," the Irish-American cook who left a trail of fifty-two typhoid cases, three of them fatal, in the homes of her employers, stood as a grim warning to the unwary.

In the face of this ubiquitous bacterial menace, who was to be responsible for the public's health? The answer, according to the medical profession, was the housewife. In a speech often quoted by American domestic scientists, the president of the British Medical Association declared that "it is the woman on whom full sanitary light requires to fall." He confided that whenever he made a house call he checked out "the appointments and arrangements and management of the house," since the chances that the disease would spread depended "on the character of the presiding genius of the home, or the woman who rules over that small domain."[38] Along the same lines, the AMA saw the scientifically trained housekeeper as a nurselike ally in the battle against contagion:

> Medical men who know the value of a trained nurse can readily appreciate the value of a training which will not only make American wives prudent, economic and thrifty, but which will establish a sanitary regime in every room in the home as well as in the kitchen and dining room.[39]

For the Domestic Science experts, the Germ Theory of Disease pointed the way to their first victory: the transformation of cleaning from a matter of dilettantish dusting to a sanitary crusade against "dangerous enemies within." Here at last was a challenge suitable to the energy and abilities of educated women. In her book *Household Economics* Helen Campbell described how the old domestic crafts had gradually been taken over by men, but cleaning "can never pass" from women's hands. "To keep the world clean," she exulted, "this is one great task for women."[40]

In the light of Germ Theory, cleaning became a moral responsibility. Mrs. H. M. Plunkett, one of the early popularizers of Germ Theory in relation to household matters, wrote in 1885:

> There is nothing in hygiene she cannot comprehend, and too often does she realize this and begin to study it when, too late, she stands beside the still form of some previous one, slain by one of the preventable diseases that, in the coming sanitary millenium, will be reckoned akin to murder.[41]

This warning was echoed throughout the growth of the domestic science movement: neglect of housecleaning is tantamount to child abuse. Manufacturers of soap and cleansing agents picked up on the theme, with ads which played directly to maternal fears and guilt. Stuart Ewen reports on ads in the twenties:

> . . . Hygeia baby bottles were "safe" and would not "carry germs to your baby". Fly-tox bug killer was presented as the one line of defense for an otherwise "defenseless" child . . . Women were told to follow the dictates of "health authorities" who "tell us that disease germs are everywhere". Lysol divided the house into an assemblage of minutely defined dangers, so mothers were told that they should be aware that "even the doorknobs threaten [children] . . . with disease".[42]

And, at a time when infant mortality (due largely to infectious diseases) ran five times as high as it does today, mothers were likely to listen to anyone who seemed to offer a way to combat disease.

Unfortunately, the scientific content of "scientific cleaning" was extremely thin. The domestic scientists were right about the existence of germs, but neither they nor the actual scientists knew much about the transmission and destruction of germs—which are of course the major issues in domestic disease prevention. For example, the domestic scientists believed that the major household germ carrier was dust and attributed germ-killing qualities to the "damp duster." Helen Campbell ominously described an experiment in which "3000 living organisms" were cultivated from a "pinpoint of dust." "The dry duster had never reached them. The feather duster had no power save for distribution. A damp one alone could render them harmless . . ."[43] Actually, dust is quite innocent, except as a source of allergies. And the damp duster, whatever its other virtues, would be a perfectly comfortable habitat for microbes.

The reader may be interested to know that even today, after decades of further research in bacteriology and epidemiology, professional home economists seem to have very little to offer to the housewife debating what to clean and how to clean it. Here are the results of our own investigation into the scientific basis of house cleaning today. In the summer and fall of 1976 we wrote to six home economics professors at three different universities as well as to the American Home Economics Association, asking:

> 1. What contributions has bacteriology made to our knowledge of good house-cleaning techniques since the early twentieth century? To give one example: is it known today what is the best technique for cleaning surfaces, such as countertops, in order to prevent contagion within the family?
>
> 2. Have any studies been done correlating good house cleaning with lower family morbidity, as from colds, intestinal upsets, etc.? In other words what is known about the actual effectiveness of house cleaning in maintaining family health?

Of the six professors, one did not reply and two referred us to a colleague. Of those who replied, a professor at Purdue admitted she did not know of any studies correlating good house cleaning with family health, and recommended bleach for the countertops. A professor at Cornell replied, confusingly:

Your questions related to housecleaning as researched and taught in home economics are interesting. However, the answers may not be easy to identify. For example, the influence of public health studies and the adaptation of results from these studies to the home may be an important contribution to sanitation in the home, and, in fact, may be more important than research done by home economists.

She went on to cite two studies which indicate "that a relationship exists between good cleaning methods and removal of bacteria," and ignored the question on family health. A third professor (also at Cornell) replied with a diagram showing "home economics" in the center of a large circle, with a ring of smaller overlapping circles containing the words: "Art," "Philosophy and Religion," "Economics," "Political Science," "Sociology," "Psychology," "Biology," "Bacteriology," "Chemistry," "Physics." The American Home Economics Association responded after a three-month delay with a letter from the Information Specialist of their Public Relations department. He had no information on our questions himself and enclosed a list of AHEA publications, which included none on cleaning or subjects related to cleaning.

We concluded from this brief investigation that the home economists' notion of house cleaning is no more scientific today than it was seventy years ago. It is amazing that after so many years this important part of women's work is still dictated by guesswork, tradition, and standards set by the commercial media.

The Manufacture of New Tasks

The domestic scientists of the early twentieth century did not claim to have the last word on scientific cleaning, cooking, or any other task. If they did, housekeeping could be reduced to a mindless routine. On the contrary, Ellen Richards wrote, science transformed housekeeping into an endless adventure, a quest for new knowledge:

It is not a profound knowledge of any one or a dozen sciences which women need, so much as an attitude of mind which leads them to a suspension of judgment on new subjects, and to that interest in the present progress of science which causes them to call in the help of the expert, which impels them to ask, "Can I do better than I am doing?" "Is there any device which I might use?" "Is my house right as to its sanitary arrangements?" "Is my food the best possible?"

"Have I chosen the right colors and the best materials for clothing?"
"Am I making the best use of my time?"[44]

Simply asking such questions—perpetually re-examining one's home-making in the light of a continually unfolding science—was in itself "the best use of time," and the first of the new "white collar" jobs which domestic science added to homemaking.

But domestic science's major white-collar innovation was the task of management. In 1899 Frederick Taylor, one of the first efficiency experts, made history by inducing a Bethlehem Steel Company worker to load 47 tons of pig iron a day instead of his customary 12½, and the middle-class public became as enamored of "efficiency" as it was terrified of germs. The idea, as applied to industry, was to analyze each task down to its component gestures (lift the shovel, take three steps, etc.) and assign these gestures, rather than whole tasks, out to the workers. The premise was that no worker could comprehend the organization of his own work and that time could be saved by putting all thinking, down to the most minute decisions, in the hands of management.[45]

The new "scientific management" meshed immediately with the domestic scientists' goals of eliminating (or redefining) drudgery and elevating housekeeping to a challenging activity. Ellen Richards hated "wasted motions," but it was left to Christine Frederick, writing in 1912, to promote the full managerial revolution in the home. The promise was of course less work (which was especially appealing at a time when the "scientific" approach to cleaning was making more work), and every one of Frederick's articles serialized in the *Ladies' Home Journal*[46] began with a little box containing the pig-iron story, as if the housewife could also expect a fourfold increase in productivity. Much of what she had to say was useful, though hardly startling: ironing boards should be at the proper height to avoid bending; appliances should be chosen with care; schedules should be made for daily and weekly chores; etc. And certainly it seemed to many women that the principles of industrial efficiency could offer the possibility of more free time—without any sacrifice of standards. When Christine Frederick's articles first appeared in the *Ladies' Home Journal,* a record sixteen hundred women wrote in for further information in one month.[47]

Actually, industrial scientific management techniques had almost nothing to offer the housewife. First, the scale of household work was much too small for the savings accrued by time-motion studies to mean much. The seconds saved by peeling potatoes with Frederick's scientific method ("Walk to shelf . . . pick up knife . . ." etc.) might add up to something in a factory processing thousands of potatoes but would be insignificant in the preparation of dinner for four. Second, as later domestic scientists themselves realized, in the household, the manager and the worker are the same person. The whole point of Taylor's management science—to concentrate planning and intellectual skills in management specialists—is necessarily lost in the one-woman kitchen.

For the homemaker, household scientific management turned out to mean *new* work—the new managerial tasks of analyzing one's chores in detail, planning, record-keeping, etc. In fact, much of Frederick's *Journal* series was devoted to the description of this new white-collar work. First, each task had to be studied and timed. (Frederick clocked baby bathing at a remarkably swift fifteen minutes.) Only then could precise weekly and daily schedules be devised. Then there was the massive clerical work of maintaining a family filing system for household accounts, financial records, medical records, "house-hints," birthdays of friends and relatives and (for what use we are not told) a special file for "Jokes, Quotations, etc." —not to mention the recipe files and an inventory file giving the location and condition of each item of clothing possessed by the family.

Nevertheless, Frederick's articles unleashed a near-frenzy for home efficiency. Domestic scientists set up "Housekeeping Experiment Stations" to discover the "principles of domestic engineering." The scientific housekeeper now saw herself not only as a microbe-hunter, but as a manager operating on principles of industrial efficiency. In fact, by the nineteen thirties, domestic scientists considered "management" to be the major thrust of homemaking, practically eclipsing housework itself. Margaret Reid, an Iowa State College domestic scientist categorized all household work into "A. Management," which included "choice-making," "task, time and energy apportionment," "planning," and "supervision"—"B. Performance," which included "housework."[48]

The domestic scientists prepared themselves for the possibility that, despite all the effort scientific management involved, it might lead to greater efficiency and more free time to be filled. Mrs. Alice Norton addressed this problem in a talk at the 1902 Lake Placid Conference entitled "What should we do with the time set free by

modern methods?" After tossing around the possibilities of "self-cul-
tivation," or just plain resting, she went on to say firmly that:

> . . . if a woman undertakes homemaking as her occupation she
> should make that her *business,* and the possibilities of this today are
> almost endless . . . till more instruction is available to fit her for her
> business, she must use part of the time gained in preparing herself.[49]

In other words, she could use the time freed by domestic science to
study domestic science! Christine Frederick also pondered the free
time, but happily concluded that as housewives became more
efficient, their *standards* would rise apace.[50]

And so the Domestic Void began to fill. Old work was invested
with the grandeur of science; new work—challenging, businesslike—
was devised. If homemaking was a full-time career, the Home would
be safe, and the Woman Question would be answered.

Feminism Embraces Domestic Science

The new science rapidly gained public recognition. It was, according to one high school educator, even something of a fad. By
1916–17, 20 per cent of the public high schools offered courses in
domestic science, or home economics as it was more commonly
called by that time. At the college level, home economics made spectacular gains: From a total of 213 home economics students in the
nation in 1905 to 17,778 in 1916, most of them preparing to be
home economics teachers.[51] The Lake Placid Conferences expanded
from a tiny in-group to a major professional organization, the
American Home Economics Association, with 700 charter members
in 1909. Everyone seemed to want to study home economics, or at
least to make sure that the girls did. There had been a joke about the
high school girl who reported to her father, "I have made 100 in al-
gebra, 96 in Latin, 90 in Greek, 88½ in mental philosophy and 95 in
history; are you not satisfied with my record?" To which the father
replied, "Yes, indeed, and if your husband happens to know anything
about housekeeping, sewing and cooking, I am sure your married life
will be very happy."[52] Home economics was the answer: you could
have your Greek and cake too.

It may seem ironic, in retrospect, that one of the most receptive
constituencies for the new science was the women's movement. The
keynote speech at the 1897 meeting of the Woman's Suffrage Associ-

ation had been on the theme of domestic science, and the suffrage press provided a steady outlet for the ideas of the home economics leaders. If this seems strange, we should recall that the women's movement at the turn of the century was hardly a *feminist* movement in the modern sense. The ideology of the movement was sexual romanticism: women deserved the vote because they were homemakers. The wide-ranging, *rationalist* feminism of Susan B. Anthony's generation had been abandoned for a single-minded focus on getting the vote and, secondarily, getting women into college. Domestic science was appealing because it provided a dainty cover-up for both activities. Take the argument that higher education would "de-sex" women. Domestic science had the perfect rejoinder: not only does higher education not destroy women, it makes them better women. Ellen Richards told the Association of Collegiate Alumnae in 1890:

> We [college women] have been treated for some years to discussions from eminent men as to our mental ability, our moral and physical status, our predilection for matrimony, our fitness for voting or for the Presidency; but the kind of home we should make if we did make one, the position we should take on the servant question, the influence we should have on the center and source of political economy, the kitchen, seem to have been ignored.[53]

And it was in the realm of the home that college women were making their most significant contribution, she wrote in 1912:

> It has required many college women (from some 50,000 college women graduates) to build and run houses and families successfully, here one and there another, until the barrel of flour has been leavened. Society is being reorganized, not in sudden, explosive ways, but underneath all the froth and foam, the yeast has been working.[54]

A writer in *Woman's Journal* in 1898 lauded women like Richards for ". . . the very important part college women have played in making everything pertaining to housekeeping a definite science," and concluded:

> Surely studying what men study in men's colleges, has not been able to turn these women out of their "natural sphere"![55]

Domestic science became a way of justifying higher education for women. According to the Lake Placid Conferences the truly scientific housekeeper needed to have studied, at a minimum, chemistry, anatomy, physiology, and hygiene, and to refine her taste for interior decorating, she needed in addition an acquaintance with great works of literature and art. If one couldn't demand to study such things for their own sake—and certainly not for the sake of a "male" career—all that was left was to demand them for the sake of the *home*.

As for the vote, domestic science had nothing to say about suffrage directly, but it did help to guarantee that even voting women would be acceptably housebound. In the *Woman's Journal,* militant articles on suffrage were embedded in columns on homemaking techniques and ads for baking powder and stove cleaners. When women's suffrage passed in Wyoming, a woman wrote to the *Journal* that, contrary to antisuffrage predictions, home life had not fallen apart in that state:

> Were you to visit Wyoming, you would be impressed with the contented, happy expressions of the bread-winners, as they return from the cares of the day to pretty, attractive homes, to a bright fireside and well-ordered dinner, presided over by a home-loving, neatly gowned, womanly wife.[56]

As a matter of fact, there were very few appealing options for educated women outside of the home. For feminists, as for Ellen Richards herself, domestic science seemed to be the way to make the best of a bad deal. If it was impossible to enter a profession and join the public world inhabited by men, a woman could at least ask that the isolated, invisible activity of homemaking be considered equally professional. In an article entitled "Housekeeping as a Profession," an editor of the *Woman's Journal* pointed to the growing prestige of law and medicine and remarked:

> So too, the creation of a body of graduates of Household Science and Art would lift the pursuit into appreciation and honor. Certainly it deserves to be as highly esteemed as medicine, law, or theology. What is so valuable as a good home?[57]

At the same time, from a middle-class point of view, domestic science offered a new approach to the perennial servant problem—another issue which came up frequently in the *Woman's Journal*. Good servants were getting scarcer all the time, as more and more working-class women opted for factory work or nursing over the low pay and indignity of domestic service. Many middle- and upper-class women suspected that the "servant class" was germ-ridden and immoral. Now, thanks to the domestic scientists, housework was becoming too scientific and complex to be performed by uneducated women anyway. Helen Campbell laid out the problem:

> The condition of domestic servitude allows only the development of a certain degree of ability, not sufficient to perform our complex domestic industries. So there we are. When we find a person able to carry on modern household industries, that person will not be our servant. And when we find a person willing to be our servant, that person is unable to carry on modern household industries.[58]

Thus the woman who could not afford, or could not find, a servant was not to be pitied—she had simply realized that this was a job which could no longer be delegated to her social inferiors.

But the feminist embrace of domestic science was not just a matter of sour grapes on the part of unemployed, servantless women. Better to be up and about, briskly scrubbing and organizing, than to pine away as an invalid! And how much better, how much more American, to strive for a single standard for home life: rather than indolence supported by the work of servants in one class, exhausting toil in another, there would now be a single ideal for home life, centered on the classless image of the housewife.

From a feminist point of view, there was something refreshing too about the resolute unsentimentality of the domestic science movement. The architects of domestic science were repelled by the cloying nineteenth-century romanticization of home and womanhood. Lace-bordered images of sweet "little" women placidly awaiting weary breadwinners filled them with revulsion. The home was not a retreat from society, not a haven for personal indulgence; it was just as important as the factory, in fact, it *was* a factory. One domestic science writer upbraided women for "soldiering" (the industrial term for working at less than maximum speed) on the job, for the home, she said, is "part of a great factory for the production of citizens."[59] Henrietta Goodrich told the 1902 Lake Placid gathering:

> Home economics aims to bring the home into harmony with industrial conditions and social ideals that prevail today in the larger world outside the home. This end can never be accomplished till the home in popular conception shall embody something more than the idea of personal relationships to individual homes. Men in general must admit consciously that the home is the social workshop for the

making of men. No home, however isolated, can escape the social obligation that rests on it. . . .[60]

The home existed for the public purpose of "making men," and the scientific home—swept clean of the cobwebs of sentiment, windows opened wide to the light of science—was simply a workplace like any other. No sticky dependencies held the scientific housekeeper to her home, only a clear sense of professional commitment.

But the advocates of domestic science had no wish to follow the logic of rationalized housekeeping through to its conclusions. If the activities of homemaking were indeed the substance of a "profession," then why not literally deprivatize the home and turn its functions over to trained specialists? Ellen Richards and her colleagues agreed that soap-making, spinning, etc., had all been improved by their absorption into outside industry. Why not cooking then, or cleaning, or child care? Why, in fact, have "homes" at all? Of all the American critics of the conventional, unscientific home, only Charlotte Perkins Gilman took this step:

> We are founding chairs of Household Science, we are writing books on Domestic Economics; we are striving mightily to elevate the standard of home industry—and we omit to notice that it is just because it is home industry that all this trouble is necessary.[61]

A social arrangement in which one person cooked or cleaned for three or four others was intrinsically irrational, she argued. No matter how much "science" was myopically applied to it, the very scale of the home precluded the rationalization of domestic work. As for the "making of men," any home—scientific or otherwise—in which women waited upon men was necessarily "a hotbed of self-indulgence," "breeding [in men] a limitless personal selfishness."[62] Gilman pushed the fully rationalist solution: to abolish the home as it was, let people live in apartment communities with centralized, professionally staffed facilities for food preparation, cleaning, child care, laundry. The great majority of women would then be freed for productive work in the world on an equal basis with men.

In practice, many Americans were attracted to lifestyles not unlike that proposed by Gilman. According to Calhoun, large numbers of American families—large enough at least to excite the alarm of the clergy—seemed to prefer "promiscuous hotel [and boarding house] living to the privacy of family life,"[63] apparently because it freed the women from cooking. There were even, in the first decades of the twentieth century, scattered experiments in communal living—among poor immigrant families as well as among the middle class.[64]

But to the advocates of domestic science, Gilman's proposals could hardly have been more distasteful if she had thrown in a request for "free love" (which she emphatically did not). Yet she was only following their own logic. What prevented them from taking the same step was that their romantic commitment to the home—the female-staffed home—went far deeper than their commitment to scientific rationality. According to her biographer and colleague, Caroline Hunt, Ellen Richards

> . . . believed in the family home with a roof of its own and a plot of ground of its own so firmly that she considered its importance beyond argument. The only question was how to preserve it. . . .[65]

"Right Living" in the Slums

When domestic science leaders like Ellen Richards spoke of the endangered home, their first concern was with the middle-class home. It had to be rationalized, sanitized, and, above all, stabilized through the efforts of its resident domestic "scientist," the scientific homemaker. But anyone with a minimum of social awareness could see that the gravest threat to the home, and hence to "civilization," lay in the urban slums.

Professor C. R. Henderson, a former president of the Conference on Charities and Corrections, aroused the 1902 Lake Placid Conference to the slum issue. The danger, he said, came not from foreign ideologies or unionists, but from the very *way the people lived*. "A communistic habitation [by which he meant a tenement house], forces the members of a family to conform insensibly to communistic modes of thought."[66] Worse still, slum living conditions led to evolutionary retrogression:

> It would be unworthy of us to permit a great part of a modern population to descend again to the animal level from which the race has ascended only through aeons of struggle and difficulty.

In the long run the only solution was to disperse the poor and house them in individual private homes, but in the meantime domestic science leaders believed that creeping communism and bestiality could be stemmed by teaching them "the science of right living." In the slums, proclaimed Ellen Richards, "there is ready at hand a field for the Home Economics teacher."[67]

This "field" was, at the time, already being intensively cultivated by a variety of urban reformers, charity organizations, and settlement workers. Philosophies of slum reform ranged from the conservative view (shared by most of the domestic science leaders) of the poor as a threat to be subdued or Americanized as quickly as possible, to the liberal perception of the poor as victims of a corrupt and inhumane society. But from both philosophical perspectives, domestic science was a valuable tool. To conservatives, who blamed poverty on the individual shortcomings of the poor, domestic science instruction was an obvious solution to thriftlessness, intemperance, and general disorderliness. To liberals, it represented a way of helping the poor cope with the debilitating environment of the slums—the substandard housing, filthy streets, and unscrupulous merchants. And to both liberals and conservatives, there was a pragmatic value to teaching the poor to live within their wages. If you could feed a family on ten cents a day, as some domestic scientists proposed, higher wages would be unnecessary.

In fact, domestic science did have a core of useful information for the hard-pressed and frequently bewildered urban slum-dweller. It was clear to reformers like Jane Addams, at any rate, that the poor needed whatever help they could get in making the difficult adjustment to city life. Most of the poor were recent immigrants from rural villages, and many came expecting to recreate their old patterns of life—to raise chickens in the streets, keep livestock in the basements of their tenements, and bake bread on the pavements.[68] But the old ways of life were unworkable in the crowded slums, if not simply unhygienic. Women who were used to raising their own food had to shop; they had to master the technology of the gas or coal stove and the tactics of laundering in tiny kitchens which lacked running water. And there was nothing to prepare them for the dangers of the turn-of-the-century city: uncollected garbage piling up in the streets and courtyards, unreliable water supplies, unsafe milk. For many immigrant women and their daughters, domestic science instruction was a welcome bit of assistance in the struggle for survival.

Wherever there were efforts to uplift, Americanize, or just plain assist the urban poor, domestic science found a ready forum. Public schools and settlement houses offered courses in domestic science. Charity organizations like the New York Association for the Improvement of the Condition of the Poor dispatched trained domestic scientists into poor women's houses. Some domestic scientists set out on their own to establish courses in cooking or household management in the slums.

But along with the useful survival tips which domestic science had to offer came some dubious kinds of messages. First, simply in form, much of the domestic science missionary work was carried out in an arrogant and punitive manner. This was especially true of the voluntary charity organizations, which used domestic science instruction as a substitute, or prerequisite for, more concrete forms of aid. "Friendly visitors" (the charity agency volunteers who were later replaced by trained social workers) were instructed to avoid giving charity at all costs: it corrupted the character of the recipients and destroyed the "friendly" relationship between the classes:

> The visitor should go as a personal *friend*, to enter into the household life, to discover its needs, its weak points and possibilities; to advise, encourage, and suggest; to lend a hand where it is needed, but never to hinder or hamper his [most visitors were women] work by doling out money, food, or raiment.[69]

Not everyone was won over by the friendly approach. Calhoun quotes this sarcastic satire on the role of the charity worker, from a Catholic reformer:

> If the wives of the unsuccessful grow discouraged and become slack before the everlasting problem of how the family can live, cook, eat, sleep, marry, and take in boarders, all in two rooms, let the agents or better still, the wives and aesthetic daughters of the successful go down and investigate and see if the family be worthy; and if they are worthy, let them give—not money (let them never give money to the poor), but let them pour forth good advice, how to economize, how to save, how to make bone soup, how to make something out of nothing, how to save, save, save, till at last worn out by saving, they can go to a better world in a pine coffin.[70]

Friendly visitors typically began a "case" with an appraisal of the family's standard of housekeeping. In her report, "Forty-three Families Treated by Friendly Visiting," Miss Eleanor Hanson described the "filth" and "disorder" of the "untreated" families, and said of successfully treated cases: ". . . order and thrift had been introduced in the house."[71] It was not an easy task—as one sensitive friendly visitor confessed to the 1896 National Conference of Charities and Corrections:

> Before I went to live so near these people, I must confess I sailed
> often into a home and told them to "clean up" in a most righteous
> manner . . . [now] We see the dirt and feel sorry for it, and we hope
> it will be cleaned up and in better condition next time. I have been
> very discouraged about myself, and my inability to tell people to
> clean up. I can't do it.[72]

A more impersonal method was proposed at the 1908 Conference on
Charities and Corrections (later the social workers' professional organization) by Rev. W. J. Kerby: charity organizations could set up
neighborhood housekeeping contests. The whole thing would be inex-
pensive he added, because the prizes "need not be important or
costly."[73]

Even when offered in a context free of degrading associations with
charity, as in the congenial setting of a settlement house, domestic
science instruction represented an effort to discipline and Americanize the urban poor. The useful information—on cooking, shopping,
etc.—which attracted neighborhood women necessarily came pack-
aged with the entire ideology of "right living." And right living meant
living like the American middle class lived, or aspired to live. It
meant thrift, orderliness, and privacy instead of spontaneity and
neighborliness. It meant a life centered on the nuclear family, in a
home cleanly separated from productive labor (chickens and lodgers
would have to go!), ordered with industrial precision—and presided
over by a full-time housekeeper.

Thrift, an obvious virtue, came with a host of assumptions about
what represented worthwhile expenditures: soap, yes, but wine, the
customary dinner beverage of many European immigrants, was outrageous intemperance. Cleanliness, a necessary virtue in the epidemic-
ridden slums, was equated with Americanism itself: the housewife who wished her family to succeed would find a way to send them
out in freshly laundered and ironed white shirts each day. Orderliness
meant adherence to a family schedule: definite times to eat, to sleep—
all necessary to prepare the children for the world of work ahead.
Even cooking lessons had a patriotic, middle-class flavor: emphasis
was on introducing the poor to "American" foods like baked beans
and Indian pudding and weaning them from "foreign" foods like spa-
ghetti. With so much ideological freight, even a little domestic science

instruction could go a long way. As Jane Addams wrote, "an Italian girl who has had lessons in cooking at the public school, will help her mother to connect the entire family with American food and household habits."[74]

Within the domestic science movement, many activists were not satisfied with conveying simply the habits and techniques of "right living" to the poor. The rubric of domestic science was broad enough, they believed, to include many less tangible aspects of middle-class domestic culture. A Miss Talbot mused at the 1905 Lake Placid Conference:

I wonder if it wouldn't be worthwhile to sacrifice half a dozen lessons in cooking for the sake of having the child report what they do in the way of strengthening the life of which they are a part, what is thought right in the family, what they have for diversion, what art galleries they go to, how they spend their money, what their church relations are, what their moral and spiritual life is. . . .[75]

A pioneer in the endeavor to transmit "culture" itself was the Louisa May Alcott Club, a Boston settlement located in an Italian and Russian-Jewish ghetto. Isabel Hyams, Alcott Club charity worker/domestic scientist, reported to the 1905 Lake Placid Conference that her staff's friendly visiting (always "unexpected") had revealed few cases of gross intemperance or extravagance to work on, but:

We did find, however, in most cases untidy homes, filled with unhygienic furnishings, and the food which was good never served in an appetizing manner. So we decided that for us the serving of the food, housekeeping, house furnishing, and decoration, and last but not least, manners were the most important, for, as Thomas Davidson says . . . "It is, to a large extent, the lack of the refinement of manners that unfits the uncultured man for mingling with cultivated people . . . There is no reason in the world why men and women who have to earn their bread by manual labor should not be as refined in manners and bearing as any other class of people. [Final quote marks missing in original.][76]

Seeing that "it is the duty of cultured men and women to try to arouse within these people a desire for right living," the Alcott Club presented itself to the neighborhood as "an idealized home" where "all the activities of a natural home are taught."[77] The neighborhood kids were invited in for afternoon lessons in tidiness, tasteful home decorating, table setting, manners, and the giving of tea parties. Hyams admitted that the lessons were not wholly practical for children from two-room slum flats, but argued that they shaped the children's aspirations for the future:

> While it may be impossible for them at present, owing to poverty-stricken conditions, to make practical use of all they learn, we are teaching for the future and the world, and when the opportunity does present itself they will be able to embrace it intelligently.[78]

Few settlements were as innovative in the teaching of "home values" as the Louisa May Alcott Club but as Jessica Braley of the Boston School of Housekeeping said, "Every settlement has, of course, as a principal aim, to make better homes."[79] As middle-class enclaves in the slums, they were bound to succeed by the force of example: "The settlements are in themselves attractive houses and thus are always an example to the neighborhood." In her autobiography, anarchist leader Emma Goldman described the effects of "successful" settlement work:

> "Teaching the poor to eat with a fork is all very well," I once said to Emma Lee [a nurse who worked in Manhattan's Lower East Side], "but what good does it do if they have not the food? Let them first become the masters of life; then they will know how to eat and how to live." She agreed with my view that, sincere as the settlement house workers were, they were doing more harm than good. They were creating snobbery among the very people they were trying to help. A young girl who had been active in the shirtwaist-makers' strike, for instance, was taken up by them and exhibited as the pet of the settlement. The girl put on airs and constantly talked of the "ignorance of the poor", who lacked understanding for culture and refinement. "The poor are so coarse and vulgar!" she once told Emma. Her wedding was soon to take place at the settlement, and Emma invited me to attend the affair . . . It was very painful to behold, most of all the self-importance of the bride. When I congratulated her on choosing such a fine-looking fellow for her husband, she said: "Yes, he's quite nice, but of course he's not of my sphere. You see, I really am marrying below my station."[80]

The schools too provided an outlet for the more straightforwardly propagandistic aspects of domestic science. A widely used grade-school syllabus prepared by Ellen Richards and Alice Norton and distributed by the Home Education Department of the New York State Library, began as follows:

IDEALS AND STANDARDS OF LIVING
   I. Historic Development of the Family
      a. The darkest ages of history
      b. The beginnings of human society
      c. The psychology of races—expression of the home ideal in races other than the Anglo-Saxon
      d. Early social life of the Anglo-Saxon people
         1. The home life of the Anglo-Saxon vs. the communistic family system[81]

Children began in the first grade with a "comparison of the child's home and mode of living with that of lower animals and primitive peoples." By the third grade, the children had progressed to building model houses and decorating them. Despite the ethnocentrism of the subject matter, one public school domestic scientist reported that "the large proportion of pupils of foreign parentage is not a disadvantage as has been claimed."[82]

In the years that followed, domestic science continued to be an important vehicle for the transmission of middle-class "home values" to ethnic minority groups and the working class generally. The number of high school courses on the "household arts" increased dramatically in the nineteen twenties and thirties. Through "home ec" courses, high schools, YWCA's and other community agencies girls were introduced to "higher ideals," "appreciation and culture" in addition to such esoteric skills as how to prepare "eggs à la goldenrod" for breakfast. Completely furnished "practice cottages" and model homes were used in some cases as laboratory settings. For example, in the twenties the Douglass Community House in Cincinnati set itself up as a homemaking "practice cottage" for "a thousand Negroes":

> The aim is to affect standards of living by making this a model house used by everyone in the community. The girls do all the work in the house . . . The girls love the work, and it is not to be wondered at, when one sees the pleasant home atmosphere and the perfect freedom with which they pursue their various duties.[83]

Most of the recorded descriptions of domestic science courses come, like this one, from professional educators or domestic scientists themselves. There is no real way to judge the impact of domestic science education on the hundreds of thousands of young women who have been exposed to it. But this story, told to us by Elinor Polansky, the daughter of Russian-Jewish immigrants, is suggestive:

> I had domestic science classes in my junior high school in the Bronx in 1949. I remember it very well. They taught us table setting for fancy dinner parties. I can remember the smell of ammonia—they were teaching us to clean rugs. Who had rugs? . . .
>
> What came across was this idea that your home environment was no good and *you* had to make it different. For example, we learned that the only right way to cook was to make everything separately . . . that was the good, wholesome way. Things all mixed together, like stews, that was considered peasant food. I would never have admitted to my teacher that my family ate its food mixed together. There was something repulsive about food *touching*. The string beans weren't supposed to touch the mashed potatoes and so forth . . . Only later did I realize that I hate that kind of cooking. But then I can remember even asking my mother to buy plates with separations in them.
>
> The domestic science class taught us to make the beds a certain way, with "hospital corners" . . . While at home you just took the sheets and shoved them under. At school they took the things we hated to do at home and sort of made them fun. Then I would criticize my mother and she would really get mad at me and say, "this isn't a fancy house." Now that I think back, that's more or less what my mother and I fought about all the time. We were fighting about how life should be in the home.

Domesticity Without the Science

Ellen Richards and her colleagues never doubted the eventual success of their movement. Once she fantasized about "the college woman in 1950":

> She will be so fair to look upon, so gentle and so quiet in her ways, that you will not dream that she is of the same race as the old rebels against the existing order, who, with suspicion in our eyes and tension in our hearts, if not in our fists, confront you now with the question, "What are you going to do about it?"[84]

By the fifties, something had long since been done about "it"— the haphazardly managed, endangered home—though not entirely through the direct efforts of the domestic science experts. In fact, domestic science itself had become almost unnecessary. There was no more need for crusading writers and lecturers to set the standards and dictate the tasks of homemaking. By the mid-twentieth century, the exhortations of the domestic scientists—the principles of "right living"—had been, for a growing proportion of women, built into the material organization of daily life.

Home ownership, long a dream of the domestic scientists, expanded steadily throughout the twentieth century. The domestic science reformers had believed that the single-family, owner-occupied home was the necessary material condition for the full practice of domestic science, if not for the totality of "right living." Business leaders believed that "socialism and communism does [sic] not take root in the ranks of those who have their feet firmly planted in the soil of America through home ownership.[85]* With postwar federal financing, home ownership expanded into the blue-collar working class. By the late nineteen seventies more than 60 per cent of non-farm homes are owner-occupied, compared to 36.5 per cent in 1900.[86] With home ownership, homemaking takes on an importance which goes beyond the maintenance of daily existence; it becomes the maintenance of an *investment*.

Even more important, new taskmasters arose to dictate the regimen of domestic work. Consider the strange effect of "labor-saving" devices which began to be mass-marketed in the nineteen twenties. Historian Heidi Hartmann provides ample documentation to show that the introduction of new appliances has not in any way reduced the time spent on housework.[87] In one recent study, Joann Vanek found that "the time devoted to laundry has actually increased over the past fifty years"—even with the introduction of washers, dryers, and wash-and-wear clothing—"apparently because people have more clothes and wash them more often."[88] Washing machines permit you to do daily, instead of weekly, laundries. Vacuum cleaners and rug shampooers remind you that you do not have to live with dust or countenance a stain on the carpet. Each of them—the dishwasher, the roll warmer, the freezer, the blender—is the material embodiment of a task, a silent imperative to *work*.

So, if they had lived a few more decades, the early domestic sci-

---

* They were probably right. The New York *Times* (October 30, 1974) reports that "Statistically, conservatives tend to be middle-aged, white, Roman Catholic and blue collar; long-term residents of their neighborhoods who travel to work in cars and own their own homes."

ence reformers would have been pleased to see so many of their goals realized: standards of cleanliness have risen to the near-antiseptic; "managerial" chores, such as shopping, have expanded; the problem of the "domestic void" has been all but forgotten. A writer in the May 1930 *Ladies' Home Journal* testified to the expansion of housework which had occurred within her own memory:

> Because we housewives of today have the tools to reach it, we dig every day after the dust that grandmother left to a spring cataclysm. If few of us have nine children for a weekly bath, we have two or three for a daily immersion. If our consciences don't prick us over vacant pie shelves or empty cookie jars, they do over meals in which a vitamin may be omitted or a calorie lacking.[89]

But in one central way the reformers would have had to admit defeat: their promise to feminism—the upgrading of housekeeping to professional status—had been broken along the way. Instead of becoming an elite corps of professionals, homemakers were as surely as ever a vast corps of menial workers. The scientific knowledge of and control over housework passed from the housewives, and even from the domestic science experts, to the corporations which had "robbed" women of their work in the first place.

It was the domestic science leaders themselves who had passed the banner of "right living" on to the manufacturers of appliances, soups, convenience foods, and household aids. Home economists exhibited brand-name equipment at fairs and home shows, and put their professional honor behind the ubiquitous "Good Housekeeping Seal of Approval." Christine Frederick personally provided continuity between the early days of the "cause" and the later days of commercialization, ending up as a market researcher for the appliance industry. In her 1929 book *Selling Mrs. Consumer* (dedicated to Herbert Hoover) she gave the domestic science movement credit for serving as the advance guard of the "appliance revolution" and offered nearly four hundred pages of advice on how advertisers could appeal to the fears, prejudices, and vanities of Mrs. Consumer, the homemaker.[90]

Thirty years later, the home economist was an accepted part of the corporate team—not only helping to develop new product lines, but participating directly in marketing and advertising. "We have always considered the members of our Home Economics Department masters of the soft sell," said Corning (Pyrex) vice-president R. Lee

Waterman, and *Sales Management,* the marketing journal eulogized
the corporate home economist in a 1959 article:

> It takes one to know one—could be said of women, too! Certainly
> only the bravest, or most foolhardy, of the stronger sex claims to
> grasp the workings of the female mind . . . Hence the growing im-
> portance of the home economist in marketing . . .
>
> She has the touch of the sociologist, a creative temperament, a
> background in natural sciences—and the vaunted feminine touch. She
> is the Home Economist in marketing . . . a woman to convince
> women.[91]

By mid-century, the job of the home economist was no longer to
educate, but to "convince." From a corporate point of view, nothing
could be more dangerous than a knowledgeable, "scientific" consumer. The domestic scientists' ideal homemaker—well-versed in
chemistry, sanitation, nutrition and economics—would be as out of
place in a garishly seductive, Muzak-filled supermarket as Mrs. Richards herself would have been at an Avon party.

Housework skills themselves were getting out of style. Consider the
brain-numbing communications to be found on food packaging: One.
Open box. Two. Empty contents into large bowl. . . . Here at last
is genuine "scientific management" in the home: the ultimate task
breakdown, the complete separation of the "worker" (the housewife)
from the "manager" (the manufacturer in a distant office). The
semblance of autonomy remains: you have, after all, selected the
flavor and the brand yourself, and you may, if you wish, add an egg.

The domestic scientists had expected to elevate the homemaker
into partnership with the scientific experts—nutritionists, sanitary engineers, economists. They would have been shocked, at mid-century,
to discover that the homemaker had instead become the *object* of
scientific study. Corporate sociologists probed for her foibles; psychologists worked on techniques to make her dazed and suggestible. As a
result, supermarkets were designed to make the shopping trip as *long*
as possible. Displays were designed to produce enough "sensory
overload" to stimulate "impulse buying." Cereals and candies were
placed, cunningly, at the child's eye level.

Consumer education had become consumer manipulation. Market
researchers had discovered that the most purchase-oriented shopper
is socially isolated, technologically uninformed, and insecure about
her own domestic competence.[92] It was these traits that the new con-

sumer "educators"—the manufacturers and admen—sought to culti-
vate. The TV housewife is anxious about the brightness of her wash,
the flavor of her coffee, or the luster of her floors. Enter the male
"expert"—a professional-looking man or perhaps a magician-helper
like "Janitor in a Drum" or "Mr. Clean"—whose product, "studies
show," will set things right. The actress-housewife beams with gratitude, and testifies to the impact that Hamburger Helper or Brillo
soap pads have on her life, if not on her total self-image. As far as
the manufacturer goes, the homemaker is still (thankfully) a domestic but *not* (hopefully) a scientist.

SIX

The Century of the Child

There was always something missing from the world of the domestic scientists. There was a curious silence in the dustless rooms, an absence in the gleaming kitchen and pantry. For all the things the domestic scientists concerned themselves with—the correct ways of cleaning, sorting, scheduling—were only the stage setting, and not the central drama. Now we turn to the human actor for whom the stage was set. And in the twentieth century that is no longer the patriarchal husband, but the Child. Right at the turn of the century, America "discovered" the child as the leading figure in the family, if not in history itself.

"If I were asked what is to be accounted the great discovery of this century," the school superintendent of the State of Georgia told the National Education Association in late 1899:

I would pass by all the splendid achievements that men have wrought in wood and stone and iron and brass. I would not go to the volume that catalogs the printing-press, the loom, the steam-engine, the steamship, the ocean cable, the telegraph, the wireless telegraphy, the telephone, the phonograph, I would not call for the Roentgen ray that promises to revolutionize the study of the human brain as well as the human body.

Above and beyond all these the index finger of the world's progress, in the march of time, would point unerringly to the little child as the one great discovery of the century now speeding to its close.[1]

"On the whole it cannot be doubted that America has entered upon 'the century of the child,'" wrote social historian Calhoun. ". . . As befits a civilization with a broadening future, the child is becoming the center of life."[2]

The discovery of the child by adult male public figures, scientists and experts of various kinds, was a step filled with humanistic promise. Perhaps women had always known what the male authorities were now asserting: that the child is not just a stunted adult, but a creature with its own needs, capabilities, charms. Now, with public recognition of the special needs of children, the door was potentially opened to public *responsibility* for meeting those needs: vastly expanded programs for child welfare and health, free public day care, community resources for dealing with problems which arise in child raising, and so forth. But, except for the expansion of the public school system in the early twentieth century, very little of this promise was realized. The children who had been "discovered" with so much fanfare would remain the individual responsibility of their mothers. What historian Calhoun failed to explain was that the child was becoming the "center of life" only for women. Any larger social interest in the child would be expressed by the emerging group of child-raising *experts*—and they of course had no material help to offer, but only a stream of advice, warnings, instructions to be consumed by each woman in her isolation.

The rise of the child-raising experts, which we will trace in this chapter, depended on the elaboration of a *scientific* approach to child raising. This, too, was a promising endeavor. A scientific approach, even if it stayed within the framework which made mothers solely responsible for their children's care, could potentially be based on the real needs of children, as well as the needs and feelings of mothers. But the child-raising science which developed was a masculinist science, framed at an increasing distance from women and children themselves. It was a science which drew more and more on the judgments and studies of the experts, less and less on the experience of mothers—until, as we shall see, it comes to see the mothers not only as the major agents of child development but also as the major *obstacles* to it.

Discovery of the Child

What had happened near the turn of the century to bring the child out of the background and into the spotlight of public attention? The discovery of the child as a unique and novel form of life, like the discovery of women as an "anomaly" or question, could not have been made in the Old Order. Even a hundred years earlier, the individual child was hardly a figure to command the attention of adult men. Women had, on the average, seven live births in the course of their lives; a third or a half would not survive to the age of five. Each individual child had to be seen as a possibly temporary visitor. Frontier parents often left their infants nameless for many months, lest they "waste" a favorite name; and mothers spoke not only of how many children they had raised, but of how many they had buried. This note in a local Wisconsin paper, October 1885, was typical for an era when it was the young, not the mature, who lived in the shadow of death:

> The malignant diphtheria epidemic in Louis Valley, La Crosse County, proved fatal to all the children in Martin Molloy's family, 5 in number. Three died in a day. The house and furniture was burned.[3]

By 1900 child mortality was already declining—not because of anything the medical profession had accomplished, but because of general improvements in sanitation and nutrition.[4] Meanwhile the birthrate had dropped to an average of about three and a half; women expected each baby to live and were already taking measures to prevent more than the desired number of pregnancies.[5] From a strictly biological standpoint then, children were beginning to come into their own.

Economic changes too pushed the child into sudden prominence at the turn of the century. Those fabled, pre-industrial children who were "seen, but not heard," were, most of the time, hard at work— weeding, sewing, fetching water and kindling, feeding the animals, watching the baby. Today, a four-year-old who can tie his or her own shoes is impressive. In colonial times, four-year-old girls knitted stockings and mittens and could produce intricate embroidery; at age six they spun wool.[6] A good, industrious little girl was called "Mrs." instead of "Miss" in appreciation of her contribution to the family economy: she was not, strictly speaking, a child.

But when production left the household, sweeping away the dozens of chores which had filled the child's day, childhood began to stand out as a distinct and fascinating phase of life. It was as if the late Victorian imagination, still unsettled by Darwin's apes, suddenly looked down and discovered, right at knee-level, the evolutionary missing link. Here was the pristine innocence which adult men romanticized, and of course, here, in miniature, was the future which today's adult men could not hope to enter in person. In the child lay the key to the *control* of human evolution. Its habits, its pastimes, its companions were no longer trivial matters, but issues of gravest importance to the entire species.

This sudden fascination with the child came at a time in American history when child abuse—in the most literal and physical sense—was becoming an institutional feature of the expanding industrial economy. Near the turn of the century, an estimated 2,250,000 American children under fifteen[7] were full-time laborers—in coal mines, glass factories, textile mills, canning factories, in the cigar industry, and in the homes of the wealthy—in short, wherever cheap and docile labor could be used. There can be no comparison between the conditions of work for a farm child (who was also in most cases a beloved family member) and the conditions of work for industrial child laborers. Four-year-olds worked sixteen-hour days sorting beads or rolling cigars in New York City tenements; five-year-old girls worked the night shift in southern cotton mills.

> So long as enough girls can be kept working, and only a few of them faint, the mills are kept going; but when faintings are so many and so frequent that it does not pay to keep going, the mills are closed.[8]

These children grew up hunched and rickety, sometimes blinded by fine work or the intense heat of furnaces, lungs ruined by coal dust or cotton dust—when they grew up at all. Not for them the "century of the child," or childhood in any form:

> The golf links lie so near the mill
> That almost every day
> The laboring children can look out
> And see the men at play.[9]

Child labor had its ideological defenders: educational philosophers who extolled the lessons of factory discipline, the Catholic hierarchy which argued that it was a father's patriarchal right to dispose of his children's labor, and of course the mill owners themselves. But for the reform-oriented, middle-class citizen the spectacle of machines tearing at baby flesh, of factories sucking in files of hunched-over children each morning, inspired not only public indignation, but a kind of personal horror. Here was the ultimate "rationalization" contained in the logic of the Market: all members of the family reduced alike to wage slavery, all human relations, including the most ancient and intimate, dissolved in the cash nexus. Who could refute the logic of it? There was no rationale (within the terms of the Market) for supporting idle, dependent children. There were no ties of economic self-interest to preserve the family. Child labor represented a long step toward that ultimate "anti-utopia" which always seemed to be germinating in capitalist development: a world engorged by the Market, a world without love.

So, on the one hand, the turn-of-the-century focus on the child was an assertion of what were felt to be traditional human values against the horrors of industrial capitalism. The child represented, as it had for decades, a romanticized past—rural, home-centered, governed by natural rhythms rather than by the industrial time-clock. Psychologist G. Stanley Hall saw children as a race related to the "savages" of Africa—gentle, spontaneous, and badly in need of protection by grown (white) men.

But it was not only the romantic, pastoral image of childhood which inspired the "century of the child." The Little Child in whose name so many reform campaigns were waged—for compulsory education, public health programs, etc.—was not only a symbol of the past but of the industrial future. Addressing a women's meeting in 1898, Dr. W. N. Hailman refuted the "primitive" image of the child as either a "little animal" or "an embryo savage" and presented children as the evolutionary vanguard of the race:

> Childhood is not a makeshift to keep mankind from dying out; but it is the very abrogation of death, the continued life of humanity in its onward march to its divine destiny . . . It is childhood's teachableness that has enabled man to overcome heredity with history . . . The very meaning and mission of childhood is the continuous progress of humanity. It, and it alone, renders life worth living.[10]

The exaltation of the child for its "teachableness" and pliancy reflected a growing sense that children might be actually better suited to the industrial world than adults. Turn-of-the-century America was suffering from a massive case of "future shock." Technology seemed to remold the world anew each day: What good was experience? How could "maturity" mean anything other than obsolescence? With the introduction of scientific management and assembly-line procedures, industry was coming to need the pliant youth more than the seasoned craftsman. The rise of the child (and decline of the patriarchal father) was probably most wrenching in immigrant working-class families: the parents often remained, in their attitudes and language, uprooted peasants; helplessly dependent on the son or daughter who had gone to an American school, knew English, and understood the ways of the big city.

The idea that the child was the key to the future, banal as it sounds, had a definite political message. To say that the child alone held the key to social change was to say that the present generation of adults did not. That, contrary to the hopes of socialists and militant unionists, the social structure could not be transformed within a single generation. Child-centrist ideology pictured society inching toward reform generation by generation. The professional or businessman of Yankee stock and the Polish laborer might appear, temporarily, to be members of different species, but, with an "American" upbringing, there would be less of a gap between their sons, even less between their grandsons, and so forth. Social distinctions would dissolve, over time, through mass public education, while improved methods of child raising would produce a "higher" type of human personality. By concentrating on the child—rather than on, say, political agitation, union organizing, or other hasty alternatives—the just society could be achieved painlessly, albeit a little slowly.

Thus the turn-of-the-century exaltation of the child was both romantic and rationalist, conservative and progressive. The child was "primitive" but this meant it was also malleable, hence really more "modern" than anyone else. The child was the reason to seek reforms, and also a reason to defer them. The child was the "founder of the family," the foundation of the home; it was also the only member of the family truly prepared (by virtue of its very inexperience) for the technological turmoil of the outside world. Only the figure of the child held the key to a future which could contain both behemoth factories and nurturing hearthsides, the cold logic of Wall Street and the sentimental warmth of Christmas.

The "Child Question" and the Woman Question

If it was not always crystal clear how a concentration on the child would solve such social problems as labor unrest or urban corruption, it was obvious at once that the child held the answer to the Woman Question. The child was no longer "a mere incident in the preservation of the species" but the potential link to a higher plateau of evolutionary development. Since no one else was going to take responsibility for the child, it fell to the individual mother to forge that link. The Swedish writer Ellen Key's 1909 bestseller, *The Century of the Child,* spelled out the new evolutionary responsibilities of womanhood:

> Women in parliament and in journalism, their representation in the local and general government, in peace congresses and workingmen's meetings, science and literature, all this will produce small results until women realize that the transformation of society begins with the unborn child . . . This transformation requires an entirely new conception of the vocation of mother, a tremendous effort of will, continuous inspiration.[11]

According to Key, only by dint of a total focus on children, for several generations, could women hope to bring forth "the completed man—the Superman." Key's proposals were radical—she argued that even monogamy should be abandoned if it got in the way of women's selection of evolutionarily suitable mates—but other than that her thinking was completely in tune with the establishment's romantic line. Nothing could be more important than motherhood, President Roosevelt told a gathering of women:

> The good mother, the wise mother—you cannot really be a good mother if you are not a wise mother—is more important to the community than even the ablest man; her career is more worthy of honor and is more useful to the community than the career of any man, no matter how successful, can be . . .
>
> But . . . the woman who, whether from cowardice, from selfishness, from having a false and vacuous ideal shirks her duty as wife and mother, earns the right to our contempt, just as does the man who, from any motive, fears to do his duty in battle when the country calls him.[12]

Many women agreed, either because they were proud to find themselves in such an important career, or because, as the President warned, the only alternative was contempt. An American female speaker told an international conference on motherhood in 1908:

> With clear eyes we must see the goal of our effort and with unfaltering steps journey towards it. The goal is nothing less than the redemption of the world through the better education of those who are

172 FOR HER OWN GOOD

able to shape it and make it. The keeper of the gates of to-morrow is the little child upon a mother's arms. The way of that kingdom which is to come on earth, as in heaven, is placed in the hands of a child, and that child's hands a woman holds.[13]

In the reflected glory of the child, motherhood could no longer be seen as a biological condition or a part-time occupation; it was becoming a "noble calling."

So stridently does a "century of the child" cry out for a cult of motherhood that it would be easy enough, in retrospect, to dismiss the whole fixation on children as just another advertisement for female domesticity. In part it was: a woman's home can have no sturdier gatekeeper than a tiny child. Yet something else was going on too: the discovery of the child was, in one sense, a discovery of the *power* of women. In the official ideology of the time, woman was already sequestered in the realm of private life, which was, after all, "her sphere." Here, because of the triviality of domestic concerns, she was even allowed to "reign," just as the man supposedly did outside. But now it is as if the masculinist imagination takes a glance over its shoulder and discovers it has left something important behind in "woman's sphere"—the child. This child—the new child of the twentieth century—is not valued, like the child of patriarchy, simply as an heir. This child is conceived as a kind of evolutionary protoplasm, a means of *control* over society's not-so-distant future. This child cannot be left to women.

It follows that if children must be left with their mothers, they must not be left *alone* with them. A new figure will enter the family tableau—a man equipped to manage both children and mothers *and* to direct the interaction between them—the scientific expert in child raising.

The rapid rise of the child-raising experts reflected the growing prestige of experts in other areas of women's lives. The male takeover of healing had weakened the communal bonds among women—the networks of skill and information sharing—and had created a model for professional authority in all areas of domestic activity. But the terrain that the psychomedical experts began to chart with the "discovery" of the child was, if anything, more ancient, more essentially female, than healing had been. Healing itself is an outgrowth of mothering, a response to the exigencies of childbirth, sick babies, winter colds, etc. When the experts enter the area of child raising, they step into what had been, for better or for worse, the irreducible core of women's existence, the last refuge of her skills and dignity.

The Mothers' Movement

The experts did not, however, come uninvited. The "modern" educated young woman near the turn of the century refused to see child raising as something instinctive, like appetite, or automatic, like uterine contractions. Everything else was coming into conformity with the industrial age and becoming "scientific"—why not the ancient activity of child raising? In 1888 a group of upper-middle-class New York City mothers constituted themselves the Society for the Study of Child Nature and set out to explore every facet of child "nature"—from music appreciation to the concept of private property. These women, according to historian Bernard Wishy "were eager to defer as much as possible to the best ideas, but they now wanted their information directly from experts trained in child study rather than from popular writers."[14] Within the next decade, the idea of women gathering to study and discuss child raising caught on throughout the country. Child study and mothers' clubs sprang up by the score, child study lecturers toured the land, pamphlets and articles proliferated—as if American womanhood was busily cramming for the upcoming "century of the child."

The "mothers' movement"—for they did consider themselves a movement—was a response to some of the same forces which brought forth the domestic science movement. If, in the pre-industrial farm home "housekeeping" had never been an issue, neither had child raising. The mother-child relationship had been shaped by the round of daily tasks; it was always in part an apprenticeship relationship. "Child raising" meant teaching children the skills and discipline required to keep the home industries running. It was not something that one *did,* so much as it was something that happened, or had to happen, if the family's work was to be done.

But within the Domestic Void of the modern home, there is no longer any "natural" way to raise children. There are fewer and fewer skills to acquire in the home, and those that there are bear little relation to the skills that the child (especially the male child) might eventually need in the outside world. Learning to help Mother pick up around the house will not help Johnny pass the college boards ten years later or teach Susy to type. With the separation of home and work, private and public realms, the standards for "success" in child raising came to be set outside the home, beyond the mother's control. Paradoxically, the "better" the mother—the more singlemindedly home-oriented she is—the less experience she will have had in the outside world where her efforts will eventually be judged. In the sexually segregated society built by industrial capitalism on the ruins of the Old Order, there is, in the end, no way for *women* to raise *men*.

The mothers' movement, like the domestic science movement, was an attempt to make a dignified response to this difficult and contradictory situation. In the setting of the Domestic Void, housekeeping priorities were unclear, child raising was baffling. Women were naturally drawn together to discuss domestic issues, share information, and study whatever scientific advice was available. In their recognition that child raising was not a matter of instinct, or mere supervision, they had made real progress over the women (two generations earlier) who had no time to think of children as anything but miniature assistants. But if the women who gathered in the turn-of-the-century mothers' clubs were prepared to confront the problems posed by their new situation as mothers, they were *not* prepared to challenge that situation itself. The domestic science leaders who had gazed, with horror, into the Domestic Void, did not propose to abandon the home. And the mothers' movement was not about to suggest that there might be more congenial, collective settings for child raising.

In fact, when the mothers' movement took institutional form as the National Congress of Mothers in 1897, its concern over the preservation of the home seemed almost to outweigh its concern for children. For example, in the Congress' 1908 Declaration of Principles the word "home" appears four times in the first four principles: "child" or "children" only twice. The opening principles begin, "Whereas, the home is the basis of society . . ." continuing:

> Whereas, the God-given function of parenthood is the highest, most far reaching duty of humanity, and the performance and sacredness of marriage is the foundation of society . . .
> Whereas, All students of social conditions seeking the causes of crime and disease trace them to inefficient homes . . .
> Whereas, Homes are inefficient because there is nothing in education to fit young people [i.e., women] for wise home makers . . .[15]

The national mothers' conferences did give women a chance to hear from the few child-raising experts of the day—G. Stanley Hall and the Rockefellers' pediatrician Emmett Holt (see Chapter 3)—but to judge from the conference proceedings, the real issue at hand was the Woman Question. As Mrs. Birney asked at the first conference, ". . . How, I ask, can we divorce the woman question from the child question?"[16] Neither the movement's leaders—upper-class women like Mrs. Adlai Stevenson and millionaire Phoebe Hearst—nor the rank and file which consisted of middle-American clubwomen—were in any sense feminists. If anything, the National Congress of Mothers represented a contemporary backlash against feminism, like the "right-to-life" movement in the nineteen seventies. "We need not care who makes the laws," one speaker asserted, "if we, as mothers, will make *them* what they should be."[17] Mrs. Birney, the Congress president for several years, expressed her faith that the inherent Anglo-Saxon love of home (see Chapter 5) would "eventually turn back into the home the tide of femininity which is now streaming outward in search of a career."[18]

But contemporary feminists, as we have already seen, were as thoroughly committed to the cult of domesticity as were their more conservative sisters in the mothers' movement. "Woman is the mother of the race," gushed Boston suffragist Julia Ward Howe, "the guardian of its helpless infancy, its earliest teacher, its most zealous champion. Woman is also the homemaker, upon her devolve the details which bless and beautify family life."[19] A more scientific approach to child raising promised to elevate the status of woman's traditional occupation, and the higher the status of woman (in any role) the stronger the argument for female suffrage. What's more, feminists could use the "mother heart" as an excuse for almost every area of female activism—social welfare and reform, even the suffrage struggle. "The age of Feminism," declared feminist Beatrice Hale, "is also the age of the child. The qualms of the timorous should be allayed by this fact, which proves that women, in gaining in humanity do not lose in womanliness."[20] And feminists had good reason to try to disguise their activities as an expanded form of mothering: the tenor of the times was such that even the National Congress of Mothers was criticized for drawing women out of their homes.

In a speech which both feminists and antifeminists (or perhaps we should say suffragists and antisuffragists) could probably have agreed with, a Mrs. Harriet Hickox Heller expressed her confidence at the second annual National Congress of Mothers that higher education would not destroy the maternal instinct:

. . . all the "isms" and "ologies" known, all the languages living and dead; all the caps and gowns; even all the eyeglasses, are not sufficient to eradicate from any feminine heart the desire to nurture the young of her kind.[21]

Yet, she admitted, higher education could somewhat *attenuate* that instinct. Child care was not sufficiently challenging to the woman who had had a taste of "isms" and "ologies." If it was to absorb the whole woman, it would have to be redefined, amplified and enriched. Just as the domestic scientists had declared their intention of filling the Domestic Void, Mrs. Heller exhorted: *"Let us discover the lens that will focus all a woman's power upon her motherhood."* [Emphasis hers.]

The immediate solution—exactly as in the case of housework—was to reinterpret motherhood as a *profession.* "It seems to me," National Congress of Mothers' president Birney told the second annual convention

that we should all perceive what intelligent parenthood means for the race, and that to attain it is as well worth our effort and attention as the study of Greek, Latin, higher mathematics, medicine, law or *any* other profession.[22]

A writer in *Cosmopolitan* magazine urged that motherhood be formally instituted as a profession, open only to those who could demonstrate "fitness." "Doctors and lawyers and teachers and clergymen fit themselves to have charge of human lives. Why should not mothers?"[23] And even Charlotte Perkins Gilman was arguing, though from a position of rationalist feminism, that mothering must become "brain work and soul work" rather than "brute instinct."[24]

The idea that motherhood was a profession, potentially requiring advanced degrees and licenses, may have been unsettling to the average, uncredentialed mother. But there was also something reassuring about it. To insist on the need for "professionals" rather than old-fashioned amateurs was at least to admit that child raising had indeed become a tricky business. The mother who felt isolated, confused, and irritated reminded herself that her occupation was known to be a difficult and challenging career. She was confined to her home but within those confines she could be as purposeful and rational as any enterprising man of the world. And indeed, given the contradictions built into child raising in this privatized and strangely peripheral setting, she would have to be.

The Experts Move In

But the birth of the "professional mother" was shadowed, from the start, by the simultaneous birth of another kind of professional—one who would make it *his* specialty to tell the mothers what to do. The new child-raising experts would be drawn of course from medicine, but also from the brand-new discipline of psychology. In less rigorous days, medicine had blithely pursued the workings of the uterus or ovaries into the nether reaches of the psyche; it discoursed with equal comfort on fractures and fantasies, tissues and tantrums. But medicine lacked the tools to dissect the intangibles of personality and feeling. When psychology entered the scene in the eighteen eighties and nineties, medicine was forced, for official purposes, to retreat back down below the neck. Psychology claimed the psyche; medicine was left with the hard-core soma (the material body). In practice this division of labor left both disciplines free to talk about those areas which happen to involve both body and mind, such as child raising, family life, and most other aspects of human social and biological existence.

Unlike medicine, psychology had no commercial past. It was born a science (becoming implicated in commercialism only later on). According to historian Eli Zaretsky, the need for a full-scale science of psychology reflects the split between public and private spheres of existence.[25] The interior life of the individual could no longer be assumed to be a simple reflection of what went on in the observable world "outside." Real people were not like the fully rational, calculating men assumed by economists to inhabit the Market. Real people have quirks, they make errors of judgment, they do not always do things out of clear-cut self-interest—they do things, as we say, for "psychological" reasons. The rupture between the world of the Market and the world of private life thus revealed human nature itself to be something anomalous and unaccountable—something to be studied, analyzed, and if possible, controlled.

Potentially, this was the most daring step yet taken by science. Evolutionary theory, if viewed without comforting overlays of religious moralism, had revealed a natural history of pitiless and probably purposeless struggle. Now psychology proposed to take as its object of study nothing less than the soul itself. Subjected to the ruthless inquisition of modern experimental science, would not "man's" higher nature turn out to be mere biology—mere matter—like the body itself? This, in fact, was the project of psychology: to take feelings, sensations, ideas, etc., and reduce them to a matter of nerve impulses; to take the traditional material of *philosophy* and seize it for *biology*. William James, the first American psychologist, realized this with considerable personal anguish (resolved by his philosophical construction of a special preserve where religious feelings, mysticism, and other transcendent experiences could dwell without fear of scientific pursuit). President Gilman of Johns Hopkins realized it when he made G. Stanley Hall, the university's first professor of psychology, promise to keep his researches strictly away from the subject of religion—lest the trustees take offense.

As it turned out, there was not much to worry about. The great achievement of early psychology (and this applies, to an extent, right up to the present) was not to transform philosophy into biology, but the reverse: to transmute biology into a kind of generalized philosophy. The necessary stage setting for this bit of twentieth-century alchemy was the modern experimental laboratory. Recall what laboratories had done for medicine. By acquiring laboratories (among other reforms of course) medicine became "scientific" and gained absolute authority to speak on anything related to the human physical condition. At roughly the same time, psychologists acquired laboratories and gained the authority to speak on anything related to the human condition—period. The laboratory bench metamorphosed itself into the speakers' podium, from which the psychologist could hold forth on sexuality, criminology, ethnic differences in intelligence, industrial productivity, child raising, labor unrest—to give just a few of the areas to which early twentieth-century American psychologists lent their expertise.

There is some dispute over who established the first psychological laboratory and thus launched American psychology. William James set up a lab at Harvard as early as 1875, but it is not clear that he ever used it. By his own admission, he "hated" experimental work. Credit for the first working American laboratory should probably go to G. Stanley Hall, the former theology student, English tutor, and lecturer on education who had studied with the great German experimental psychologist Wundt in Leipzig. Returning to the United States to take a position at Hopkins, Hall proceeded to organize, first his laboratory, and then the entire profession of psychology. His prime concern was to make psychology as rigorous and quantitative a discipline as, say, physics. Under Hall's influence "a wave of laboratory-founding swept over America" and the laboratory became, as someone cunningly put it, the *"hall*mark" of American psychology.[26] Even William James, who was as eager as anyone to see psychology established as a sound scientific discipline, felt Hall took the laboratory fetish a little too far, describing Hall as

> a wonderful creature. Never an articulate conception comes out of him, but instead of it a sort of palpitating influence making all men believe that the way to save their souls psychologically lies through the infinite assimilation of jaw-breaking German laboratory articles.[27]

Hall himself did no experimental work of any note. By the late eighteen eighties he had already abandoned the tedious empiricism of the lab (measuring reflex times, spatial perception, etc.) to found the new field of child study. His experimental efforts in this field were, by ordinary scientific standards, little short of grotesque. In one study, he attempted to take an "inventory" of the six-year-old mind by, of course, asking the six-year-olds about everything. In an even more ambitious study, he mailed out 102 questionnaires to parents, asking about their children's moods, fears, dolls, imagination, speech, religious sentiments, affection, games, sense of self and—as if that weren't enough for one questionnaire, inquiring about the parents' own feelings about old age, disease and death, ownership vs. loss, pity, menstruation, education for women, and religious conversion.[28] (No results were published.) E. L. Thorndike, one of the younger generation of psychologists raised in the experimental tradition which Hall himself had created, recalled with a shudder

> The possibility that the pseudo-scientific pretensions of the child-study movement might be mistaken for educational psychology was too horrible to contemplate.[29]

Yet to the educated public near the turn of the century, Hall was a man of science par excellence, his name indelibly linked with the image of the psychology laboratory. As a popular lecturer, he awed his audiences with glimpses into mysterious Germanic investigations, and simultaneously reassured them with his verbose reverence for childhood, motherhood, adolescence, nature, etc. The mothers' movement adored him. In fact, in the long relationship between the American mother and the child-raising expert, it was Hall who did the initial courting. His presence at the National Congress of Mothers meetings, seemingly trailing faint emanations of laboratory chemicals, promised a glorious union of science and motherhood. Whether he described his own research, or gave practical advice (such as that children need exercise), or simply exhorted the mothers to be more "scientific," women in the mothers' movement found him uplifting. As one mother wrote, reflecting the influence of Hall and his colleagues in the child study field:

> Scientific motherhood means more than a casual thought can grasp. It means a grander, nobler race, an altruistic humanity which shall fit the earth for the Saviour's advent. It means the reformation of the drunkard, the redemption of the criminal, the repentence of the murderer, the abolition of asylums for the blind, dumb and insane . . . the elimination of selfishness, the death of oppression, the birth of brotherly love, the uplifting of mankind through true spiritual Christianity . . .[30]

But in a way it was the very absence of scientific content which gave "scientific motherhood" dignity. If child raising was to be a science, then the "laws" of that science had not yet been discovered. Experimental psychology had nothing to offer, neither did medicine. This meant that the mothers themselves could be scientists, or at least assistants to the real scientists, in the effort to discover the scientific laws which could govern human development. In Hall's view, the truly scientific mother did not simply raise her child, she studied it, making notes which could serve as field data for the male academic experts. Hall urged mothers to keep a "life book" for each child, recording "all incidents, traits of character, etc., with frequent photographs, parental anxieties, plans, hopes, etc."[31] Mrs. Emily Talbot, of the American Social Science Association, established a "Register of Infant Development" to collect parental observations and make them available to academicians.[32] To the "professional" scientific mother, ". . . the child was no longer merely a beloved offspring or the nation's future in microcosm but a home-laboratory experiment as well."[33]

The mother's career as a scientist—taking notes on her child's behavior, comparing observations with those of other mothers, etc.—was bound to be short-lived, however. Psychologists like Hall and his colleagues welcomed the partnership of mothers, at least as data gatherers. But the younger generation of experts in the early nineteen hundreds was not interested in the amateurish contributions of mothers. As far as they were concerned, only scientists could gather the data and formulate the rules: all that was left for mothers was to follow the instructions. Consider this stern observation from Dr. Holt, whose 1896 book *The Care and Feeding of Infants* made him the Dr. Spock of his period:

> If a man wishes to raise the best grain or vegetables, or the finest cattle or horses, all admit that he must study the conditions under which alone such things are possible. If he is in doubt regarding these matters he may apply to the Agriculture Department at Washington, and be furnished with the reports of the best scientific work on these subjects by experts who make these matters their study under government supervision. But instinct and maternal love are too often assumed to be a sufficient guide for a mother.[34]

What could be simpler? The uncertain mother, like the farmer aiming to produce "the best grain or vegetables," had only to send for the latest scientific information and apply it faithfully.

Early-twentieth-century child-raising experts like Holt drew their prestige from science, but the content of their advice—what they actually had to tell mothers—came much less from the laboratory than the *factory*. Hall had romanticized youth; he wanted its spontaneity and openness protected from the ugly realities of the adult world. But the vulnerability of the child aroused very different impulses in most child-raising experts of the time. If the child was pliant, then the child could be molded. And if the child could be molded, why not begin shaping it at once to fit the "real" world of modern industry?

The goal was industrial man—disciplined, efficient, precise— whether it was his lot to be an industrial laborer, a corporate leader, or another expert himself. The key to producing such a man was *regularity*. It was never too early to introduce the child to the rhythms of industrial life, as Dr. Winfield Hall explained at the Chicago Child Welfare Exhibit in 1911:

> This period of early childhood is the period during which the child is acquiring habits which may last him through life . . . and many a mother will begin almost with the first day of the life of her infant to guard its habits and to introduce the element of regularity into its life . . .[35]

The federal government's twenty-five-cent pamphlet *Infant Care,* which was the best-selling publication of the Government Printing Office during the late teens, counseled similarly:

> In order to establish good habits in the baby, the mother must first be aware what they are, and then how to induce them. Perhaps the first and most essential habit is that of regularity. This begins at birth, and applies to all the physical functions of the baby—eating, sleeping and bowel movements.[36]

In the interests of industrial regularity, spontaneity would have to be strangled in the cradle. "The rule that parents should not play with the baby may seem hard," advised the government pamphlet cited above, "but it is no doubt a safe one." Inciting a baby to laugh in "apparent delight" was to impose a dangerous strain on its nervous system. Picking up a baby between scheduled feedings was to invite future mental disease or at least moral laxity. Dr. Winfield Hall painted a lurid picture for the indulgent mother:

> Eating a thing because it tastes good, or drinking a thing because it tastes good, is doing a thing that gratifies the sensual! Mothers, if you begin that way with the child on these simple senses of taste and smell, and the flavor of food and drink, what are you going to do fifteen years later when the primordial urge gets into that young person's blood and he looks out at the world and turns to the right and to the left for other forms of sense gratification?[37]

The industrial approach to child raising met with instant approval from domestic science leaders. In one of her rare mentions of children Ellen Richards wrote:

> Most powers are the result of habits. Let the furrows be plowed deeply enough while the brain cells are plastic, then human energies will result in efficiency and the line of least resistance will be the right line . . . To the woman, the home worker, we say, "You must have the will power, for the sake of your child, to bring to his service all that has been discovered for the promotion of human efficiency, so that he may have the habit, the *technique*."[38]

Besides, scientific housekeeping was incompatible with anything but the most obedient, well-programed child. Christine Frederick described how her children, ages two and four, accommodated themselves to her schedule:

> Some of my friends laugh at what they call my "schedule babies" because their hours of sleeping and feeding and play are quite regu-

lar. Most normally healthy babies can be trained easily to regular habits.[39]

The development of the industrial model of child raising automatically undermined the professional aspirations of the mothers' movement and contributed to the movement's decline in the teens. Mrs. Helen Gardener, speaking at the 1897 National Congress of Mothers convention had asked:

What profession in the world, then, needs so wide an outlook, so perfect a poise, so fine an individual development, such breadth and scope, such depths of comprehension, such fullness of philosophy as the lightly considered profession of motherhood?[40]

But how much depth of comprehension or "fullness of philosophy" did one need to follow the instructions which usually included the exact times for waking, feeding, bathing, etc.? Gone too, in the industrial scheme, were the ennobling side effects of contact with children which the mothers' movement had celebrated ("Would you know yourself? Would you understand the human race? *Go, read your child.*")[41] The child was not an exemplary human being to be studied, but the object of the mothers' work—raw material to be molded and channeled. And the work itself was not that of a professional— but that of a semiskilled employee with punched-card instructions to follow.

The industrial approach to child raising finally achieved a scientific footing in the late teens, with the development of "behaviorism." John B. Watson, one of the first of generations of psychologists to begin his academic career with the study of rats in mazes, formulated the new theory at Johns Hopkins in the early nineteen hundreds. Behaviorism, as he developed it, was not so much a theory devised to explain certain facts as it was a flat assertion about the nature of human nature. Briefly, Watson's behaviorism abolished mind, soul, subjectivity, consciousness, and all other shadowy philosophic notions. Only the observable exists and only behavior is observable. Subjective experience is simply the "behavior" of various muscles and chemicals. For example, he suggested that feelings would turn out to be the "tumescence and detumescence of genital tissues"; thought would turn out to consist of "tiny laryngeal movements," producing an inaudible monologue.[42] (It did not seem to bother him that these hypothetical "tiny movements" were not observable themselves, any more than thought itself was.)

Other expert proponents of the industrial model of child raising had insisted that the child could be trained to behave like a machine, or at least to fit into a world requiring machinelike regularity and discipline. Watson added the "scientific" assertion that the human person was in fact a machine—a thing: the problem in child raising was simply to program the little machines to fit into the larger industrial world. They could, he noted, be programed to fit any given culture; as a behaviorist, he was concerned only with the practical problem of fitting them into the culture they were actually born into. This particular culture demanded stoicism, independence, and iron discipline—presumably the qualities to which Watson attributed his own success. The ideal child, he wrote, is

> a child who never cries unless actually stuck by a pin, illustratively speaking . . . who soon builds up a wealth of habits that tides him over dark and rainy days—who puts on such habits of politeness and neatness and cleanliness that adults are willing to be around him at least part of the day . . . who eats what is set before him—who sleeps and rests when put to bed for sleep and rest—who puts away two year old habits when the third year has to be faced . . . who finally enters manhood so bulwarked with stable work and emotional habits that no adversity can quite overwhelm him.[43]

The production of these model children would require a very different kind of mother from the one who had been celebrated by the National Congress of Mothers. The mothers' movement had conceded that instinct could not provide a practical guide to child raising, but still clung to it as the underlying emotional force behind all the activities of motherhood. Their ideal mother, for all her efforts to be "scientific," was a woman driven by uncontrollable maternal instincts and given to melting fits of tenderness at the invocation of the Little Child. All this was anathema to the behaviorist:

> There is a sensible way of treating children. Treat them as though they were young adults. Dress them, bathe them with care and circumspection. Let your behavior always be objective and kindly firm. Never hug and kiss them, never let them sit on your lap. If you must, kiss them once on the forehead when they say good night. Shake hands with them in the morning . . .[44]

Nothing disturbed Watson more than the possibility of irrational, emotional elements in the mother-child relationship. In fact the spectacle of spontaneous affection was enough to push Watson to the brink of an emotional outburst himself:

> If you expect a dog to grow up and be useful as a watch dog, a bird dog, a fox hound, useful for anything except a lap dog, you wouldn't dare treat it the way you treat your child. When I hear a mother say "Bless its little heart" when it falls down, or stubs its toe, or suffers some other ill, I usually have to walk a block or two to let off steam.[45]

By the nineteen twenties, when Watson's synthesis of behaviorist child-raising theory, *The Psychological Care of Infant and Child* appeared, the mothers' movement was dead, the National Congress of Mothers itself had been absorbed into the newly organized National Congress of Parents and Teachers. The century had begun with middle-class mothers organizing to search out the "science" of child raising. Now that science had been found, or so it seemed, and there was very little room in it for mothers. "It is a serious question in my mind," Watson wrote,

> whether there should be individual homes for children—or even whether children should know their own parents. There are undoubtedly more scientific ways of bringing up children which probably mean finer and happier children.[46]

For despite the neuter wording of this statement Watson grasped that vexing problem: How could *women* raise *men?* The middle-class mother had not been tempered by the discipline of the outside work world. How could the child-raising expert, remote in his university office, trust her to control her perverse impulses to cuddle, fondle, and otherwise corrupt the young? Without supervision how could she produce anything but a generation of "lap dogs"? Watson bemoaned the unaccountable "mores" that stood in the way of fully scientific, motherless, child raising:

> The home we have with us—inevitably and inexorably with us. Even though it is proven unsuccessful, we shall always have it. The behaviorist has to accept the home and make the best of it.[47]

While Watson was manfully accepting the limitations of the middle-class home, an even more serious menace lurked in the neighborhoods of the poor. The mothers' movement and its attendant experts had paid scant attention to the "lower" classes, partly on account of the middle-class prejudice that the poor should not be

bearing children in the first place. Certainly, if the mothers' movement's dream of professionalization had been realized, the average
working-class woman would never have qualified for a license to raise
children. Watson himself disqualified the poor with the simple rule
that no one should have a child until she could afford to give the
child a room of its own. But poor and working-class people defiantly
went ahead and had children, and at a greater rate than the better-off
WASPs. This posed a serious problem to the would-be reformer: if
the middle-class woman could not always be counted on to follow instructions, she could at least be counted on to read the experts'
books. What about the woman who did not read English, or did not
read at all? What about the working mother who had no time to attend mothers' meetings or lectures by experts? Furthermore, it was
widely known, or suspected, that the poor were *more* impulsive and
affectionate with their children than the "better" classes. A settlement-house worker had reported disapprovingly in 1900 that in the
homes of the poor "there is no meal hour and no bedtime, the children retiring late with the parents and eating where and when they
please . . ."[48]

Lillian Wald, the famous nurse and settlement-house worker, observed

> We are not always mindful of the fact that children in normal [i.e.,
> middle class] homes get education apart from formal lessons and in-
> struction. Sitting down to a table at definite hours, to eat food prop-
> erly served, is training, and so is the orderly organization of the
> home . . .
>
>   Contrast this regulated domestic life with the experience of chil-
> dren—a large number in New York—who may never have been
> seated around a table in an orderly manner, at a given time, for a
> family meal . . .[49]

As a product of the "disorganized tenement home," Wald cited sev-
enteen-year-old Emil. Emil was an able high school junior who
managed to support himself by teaching his fellow immigrants at
night. But he betrayed his lowly origins one weekend by arriving em-
barrassingly late for a party at the country home of one of the settlement workers. The problem: he had not realized that trains only
leave at definite scheduled times—an obvious consequence (to Wald)
of irregular childhood habits.

Inevitably the challenge of the working class child attracted the interest of wealthy and powerful forces. If the baby Emils ate when they wanted to, what were the chances that they would ever get to work on time as grown men? Or follow the instructions of the foreman? The industrial line on child raising, buttressed by behaviorist psychological theory, seemed to offer an irresistible key to future productivity. Methods existed, or were about to be discovered, in modern psychological laboratories, for instilling workers with obedience, punctuality, and good citizenship while they were still in the cradle, and long before they had ever heard of trade unions or socialism. Vistas of infallible social control, with the techniques developed in psychological laboratories finding instant application in factories and slums, stretched before the Rockefellers and like-minded men.

In the early twenties the Laura Spelman Rockefeller Memorial Foundation turned its attention to the problem of child raising. Set up by John D. Rockefeller as a memorial to his wife, the foundation's over-all goal was to promote "scientific" solutions to social problems. As the foundation's final, summary report put it in 1933:

> It was felt that through the social sciences might come more intelligent measures of social control that would reduce such irrationalities as are represented by poverty, class conflict, and war between nations.[50]

Beardsley Ruml, director of the L. S. R. Memorial, had always had a special interest in psychology as a potential tool for social control[51] and child raising was an obvious point of intervention. If the "irrationalities" of poverty, class conflict, etc. were to be abolished, then why not begin with the irrationalities of child raising? According to the L. S. R. Memorial final report, "the management of the child in the home and the school" suffered from a basic ignorance of child-raising techniques and a lack of psychological insight. The only way to rationalize and standardize child raising, given that it is carried out in the privacy of individual homes, was to train a battery of experts, skilled in scientific methods, to reach out to all the ignorant and isolated mothers.

Between 1923 and 1929 the Laura Spelman Rockefeller Foundation spent over $7 million to achieve its vision of standardized, expert-controlled child raising. Money went to set up "institutes" and "research stations" at universities across the country; to bring together experts from many disciplines (fifteen hundred of them met for a full week in 1925 at a Rockefeller-sponsored conference); to train home economists and teachers to be "parent educators" on the side. A late-twenties' survey found seventy-five *"major"* organizations involved in parent education, thanks largely to stimulation by the Rockefeller money. These included government agencies (the federal government had begun sponsoring mass education in housekeeping and child raising in 1914), public colleges and schools, voluntary social welfare agencies, religious organizations, nursery schools, health agencies and national organizations such as the Child Study Association of America (descended from that little group of New York mothers who first met in 1888).[52]

Orville Brim, the historian of the parent education "movement," gives the Rockefeller foundation credit for rapid "professionalization" of the child-raising business in the twenties. But the new professionals were not, as the early mothers' movement might have hoped, mothers themselves. Where there had been a mothers' movement, there were now the twin disciplines of child study and parent education. Where there had been gatherings of mothers—ordinary lay women—there were now formal conferences of academic experts. No one thought of mothers as potential research assistants any more, much less as professionals themselves. But the parent educators, the demi-experts who distilled the works of psychologists and physicians into popular pamphlets and courses, were already organizing themselves into an independent profession complete with credentialing, professional publications, and research on new techniques of reaching the grassroots mother.

The financial crash of 1929 brought the Rockefeller-sponsored parent education movement to a sudden halt. Without foundation funding, parent education could not become an independent profession, supplying educators to fan out across the country, penetrating the most recalcitrant homes. The Rockefeller vision of standardized child raising, in tune with corporate needs, guaranteeing a future free of social "irrationality"—was temporarily abandoned. But the efforts to make child raising more "scientific"—beginning with the mothers' movement and leading up to the professional (and foundation) dominated parent education movement—had by no means been wasted. There existed, by the twenties, a nationwide apparatus for diffusing expert advice on child raising to the working class, as well as to the educated and wealthy, to the small towns as well as cosmopolitan cities. And, thanks in part to the early organizing by the mothers' movement, there existed a mass demand for whatever the experts had to say. The Lynds, in their classic study of "Middletown," a small midwestern city in the twenties, noted:

> The attitude that child-rearing is something not to be taken for granted but to be studied appears in parents of both groups [working class and "business class"]. One cannot talk with Middletown mothers without being continually impressed by the eagerness of many to lay hold of every available resource for help in training their children: . . .[53]

In their search for guidance, Middletown mothers turned to doctors, home economists, government pamphlets, church-sponsored lessons on child raising, popular women's magazines (which increasingly featured expert child-raising advice), and books such as Emmett Holt's still trusted *Care and Feeding of Infants*. Looking back on the growth of maternal reliance on experts, Dorothy Canfield Fisher recalled in the nineteen fifties how her own older relatives mocked "mothers who bring their babies up *by a book!*" But times were changing fast, and by the second and third decades of the twentieth century, Dr. Holt's "name was revered by the young mothers as much as it was mocked at by their grandmothers,"[54] who no doubt could not comprehend how difficult and anxious an endeavor child raising had become.

These then, were the achievements of the "century of the child" in its first three decades: mothers had not become professionals; child raising had not become "scientific." But it had come to be seen as a more challenging, all-engulfing activity than ever before. "I accommodate my entire life to my little girl," one business-class mother told the Lynds.[55] "Life was simpler for my mother," observed another Middletown mother. "In those days one did not realize that there was so much to be known about the care of children."[56] The Little Child had provided what seemed to be an effective and final answer to the Woman Question, but the child had not, in the process, been *given over* to women. For the other great achievement of the early "century of the child" was the creation of the child-raising expert, and his installation in the home as a new source of patriarchal authority.

SEVEN

Motherhood as Pathology

The goal of scientific motherhood, according to the experts, had been to "bring the home into harmony with industrial conditions." Mothers were supposed to seek their ideals as well as their methods in the laboratories and commercial centers of the "outside" world. If the home could attain industrial standards of discipline, efficiency, and thrift, then its little child-products would be able to roll effortlessly along the conveyor belt leading from the family into the big world of business. A mother's success would be measured, ultimately, along a yardstick calibrated in a distant factory.

But in the course of the twentieth century, a major cultural inversion takes place: private life becomes an end in itself, and effort in the outside world becomes merely instrumental to greater *private* fulfillment. From the nineteen twenties on, the "progressive" mother would no more think of looking to the factory or office for her standards of child raising than she would look to the old-fashioned ideas of her grandmothers. Child raising comes unhinged from any external goals—an end in itself which will invite women to enter deeper and deeper into a shadow world of feelings and suspected feelings, guilt, self-analysis, and every nuance of ambivalence.

In this increasingly self-enclosed world of the nursery, the expert looms larger and more authoritative than ever before—yet over time even he ceases to represent an "objective" external standard, scientific or industrial. It is as if he himself were drawn into the intense, interiorized life of the family, to become the pivotal figure in the new mid-twentieth century drama of the Mother, the Child, and

the Expert. In this chapter we are concerned with the character of
the expert as it unfolds (through his published advice) from the late
twenties to the sixties: beginning with a spirit of good-natured opti-
mism and—as his task becomes more and more frustrating—giving
way to undisguised horror at women and punitive outrage toward
children.

The new spirit which would dominate the multiplicity of twentieth-
century child-raising techniques was *permissiveness*. In the broadest
sense, permissiveness was about much more than child raising—it was
like a national mood, a wind of change which swept through everything. The American economy was becoming more and more dependent on individual consumption—of cars, housing, and an ever-expand-
ing panoply of domestic goods—and the ethos of permissiveness
flourished in the climate of consumption. The experts who had been
concerned with discipline and self-control now discovered that self-
indulgence was healthy for the individual personality just as it was
good for the entire economy.

Corporate leaders and psychological experts alike agreed on the
need for drastic reshaping of the American character. The old Puritan habits, work-hard and make-do, were obsolete and had to be replaced by new "antihabits" of consumption and leisure. The period
of deprivation imposed by the Depression and World War II was
only an anticipatory pause as people got used to the idea that deprivation was as unnecessary as it was unpleasant. Commercial prosperity
now *required* that people attempt to gratify themselves through individual consumption, and anyone who saw it differently was factually
wrong, possibly un-American, and worst of all—"old-fashioned."
Throughout the century, the steadily climbing index of consumer
spending would be matched by a decline in the old inhibitions—in
sex, in dress, in attitudes and etiquette.

The new emphasis on personal enjoyment was inevitably fatal to
feminism and the other reform efforts which had occupied middle-
class women in the first decades of the twentieth century. In Mary
McCarthy's novel *The Group,* Mrs. Renfrew, a member of one of the
earliest crops of Vassar graduates, reflects on the "gulf between the
generations" to her daughter, Dottie (class of '33), who is about to
make a marriage of convenience to a rich man:

". . . Women in my day, women of all sorts, were willing to make
sacrifices for love, or for some ideal, like the vote or Lucy Sto-

nerism. They got themselves put out of hotels for registering as Miss
and Mr. when they were legally married. Look at your teachers,
look what they gave up. Or at women doctors and social workers."
"That was your day, Mother," Dottie said patiently. "Sacrifices
aren't necessary anymore. Nobody has to choose between getting
married and being a teacher. If they ever did. It was the homeliest
members of your class who became teachers—admit it. . . . Sacrifice is a dated idea. A superstition, really, Mother, like burning
widows in India. What society is aiming at now is the full development of the individual."[1]

But the female individuality which would be developed in the "age
of enjoyment" would be as relentlessly domestic as anything Ellen
Richards had ever imagined. The home, which rationalist feminists
had once been able to criticize as a backwater, out of the mainstream
of change, was now clearly at the center of things—economically and
socially. By 1929, more than 80 per cent of the family's needs were
satisfied by purchases by women. There was no need to rush off to
the world of male endeavor if that world only existed to supply the
home with the goods, the cash and the information it needed. From
now on the energies of mothers would pour into the job of nurturing
the kind of American youth who, from the cradle on, would fit the
mold of the consumer society.

The Expert Allies with the Child

Permissiveness in child raising represented a 180-degree turn away
from early-twentieth-century theories. The change came so fast that it
could make a mother's head spin. Many women found themselves
replacing their methods in the middle of their child-raising careers.
One mother described her sudden recognition—one evening at dinner-
time—of how her ideas had changed: "I was serving a new vegetable
to the boys. Suddenly I realized that I expected Peter, the oldest, to
clean his plate. Daniel, the middle one, didn't have to eat it but he
had to taste it. And little Billy, as far as I was concerned, could do
whatever he wanted."[2] Even Dr. Spock and his wife changed horses
in midstream: their first child was raised according to the rigid schedules of behaviorism.

The behaviorists had seen the child as a piece of raw material to
be hammered into shape. Its natural impulses—to eat when and what
it liked, to play, etc.—had to be suppressed as firmly as bed-wetting

and thumb-sucking. On the contrary, the permissivist proclaimed that the child's spontaneous impulses were good and sensible and that the child, instead of being a *tabula rasa*, actually *knew,* in some sense, what was right for itself.

Lawrence Frank, an executive of the Laura Spelman Rockefeller Fund and a leading policy maker in the foundation world, warned parents that children were better advised to adapt to their peers, rather than their elders, if they were to succeed:

> It should never be forgotten that youth must follow its own group, for it is within this group that mating, social life, and economic status must be achieved. When this is blocked or prevented by parental control, devastating conflicts are often set up . . .[3]

Floyd Dell, a leading writer of the twenties and thirties seconded Frank's advice: ". . . it is fatuous," he wrote in *Love in the Machine Age,* "for parents to suppose they can set the style for their adolescent children."[4]

The one area in which it would seem that parents might have played an authoritative role, even from the experts' point of view, was in preparing youth for family life. But even here the experts were distrustful. A subcommittee report prepared for the 1932 White House Conference on Child Health and Protection found, paradoxically:

> There is indisputable evidence that the home today, laboring under disadvantages imposed upon it by modern conditions, cannot alone cope with the problem of teaching its children how to adjust themselves to family living.[5]

Starting in the second decade of the twentieth century, the weight of expert opinion had it that all the details of home life—from toothbrushing to parent-child relationships and dating—could only be successfully taught outside of the home—by experts in the schools. Children and experts turned to each other in agreement: How could parents who were themselves products of the *old* child raising ever hope to know how to raise the children of the *new* child raising? Here is an excerpt from the record of a teen-age discussion group in *Middletown* on the topic, "What's Wrong With the Home":

> BOY: "Parents don't know anything about their children and what they're doing."
> GIRL: "They don't want to know."
> GIRL: "We won't let them know."

BOY: "Ours is a speedy world and they're old."

BOY: "Parents ought to stand together. Usually one is easy and one is hard. They don't stand together."

BOY: "Parents ought to have a third party to whom they could go for advice."

(*Chorus of "Yes"*)[6]

It was not only teen-agers to whom the new permissiveness in child raising applied. Teen-agers were the first to reap the benefits, but the change in attitude soon trickled down to the smallest infant. Martha Wolfenstein studied the government's *Infant Care* bulletin (a fair guide to the state of expert theory) and found that in the editions released between 1914 and 1942 the baby has undergone an "extreme transformation" from a fierce little animal to a mellow and temperate creature:

> The earlier infant was described as one afflicted with dangerous and harmful impulses, such as the practices of masturbation and thumb-sucking. . . . The mother must be ceaselessly vigilant; she must wage a relentless battle against the child's sinful nature. She is told that masturbation "must be eradicated . . . treatment consists in mechanical restraints." . . . The mother's zeal against thumb-sucking is assumed to be so great that she is reminded to allow the child to have his hands free some of the time so that he may develop legitimate manual skills. . . ."[7]

But by the later date:

> . . . the baby has been transformed into almost complete harmlessness . . . the intense and concentrated impulses of the past have disappeared. . . . Instead we find impulses of a much more diffuse and moderate character. The baby is interested in exploring his world. If he happens to put his thumb in his mouth, or to touch his genitals, these are merely incidents, and unimportant ones at that, in his overall exploratory progress . . . Everything amuses him, nothing is excessively exciting.[8]

Gone were the wicked urges which the behaviorist had sought to tame. In this late-model baby, what the baby wants is what it needs. Crying is no longer due to "contrariness" but to a specific need—for food, drink, or attention. Play, which was once an activity strictly confined to certain times of the day, has become the "healthful development of motor activities." Thus the babies, like the teen-agers, no longer need their mothers to limit them, to teach them discipline or to set a model that they could aspire to—instead, they need their mothers only to follow them around and meet their needs for stimulation, play, and nurturance. From now on, the child itself would set the pace of child care. Diligent mothers found more and more of their time given over to keeping up with their children on the one hand the experts on the other. As a Middletown mother said:

> I have given up church work and club work since the children came. I always like to be here when they come home from school so that I can keep in touch with their games and their friends. Any extra time goes into reading books on nutrition and character building.[9]

The Doctors Demand Permissiveness

In Mary McCarthy's novel *The Group* two mothers (Vassar, class of '33) are following their toddlers through Central Park. "Have you heard about Gesell's studies at Yale?" one asks. "Finally we're going to have a scientific picture of the child."[10] If the permissive mother's job was to indulge her child's wishes, it was the task of science to translate seemingly incomprehensible childish behavior into a pattern of cues for the mother to follow. Dr. Arnold Gesell, researcher, pediatrician, and authority to the later authority, Benjamin Spock, took the decisive step of placing the child itself in the laboratory. With support from the Rockefeller and Carnegie Foundations, Gesell set up a guidance nursery at the Yale School of Medicine, where teams of professionals studied children's every move as they played in rooms flanked by one-way mirrors.

The result was a theory of stages of development—source of the commonplace, "He's just going through a stage." In each stage a child followed perfectly predictable patterns of behavior. Thus Gesell could lay out a two-year-old's "behavior day" with all the detail of a screenplay:

BEHAVIOR DAY
The two year old child wakes somewhat slowly at, say 7 o'clock in the morning. He is happy to wake but not interested in getting out of his crib at once. He wakes wet but tolerates this conditon and plays contentedly for about half an hour. He has a ready greeting for his mother, who toilets him and puts him in a bathrobe for an interim. He likes to go into the bathroom during this interim to watch his father shave. He is also content when he is returned to his room where he munches a cracker and plays behind the closed gate. At breakfast

he accepts considerable help from his mother but contributes in small dabs of self-help. (He will take over more completely at the noon meal.)[11]

With this self-determined baby, the function of the mother is never to "mold," and hardly even to "influence":

First of all, recognize your child's individuality for what it is and give up the notion that you either produce (except through inheritance) or that you can basically change it. Recognize it, understand it, accept it. . . .[12]

The ideal mother of scientific permissiveness applies her understanding of the vicissitudes of child development, encouraging certain behaviors and discouraging others, with inexhaustible patience and always through indirection—showing her "willingness to use endless techniques to get around rigidities and rituals and stubbornness."[13] Sensitive mothers follow the child's lead, never bucking a "phase." The moody seven-year-old, for example, has good days and bad days. "An aware teacher will shift her intellectual fare on these different days. And a wise mother will keep her child at home if his bad day starts the minute he gets out of bed, as it so often does."[14]

Gesell and his colleagues suggested techniques of "household engineering" through which the well-organized mother could simply eliminate family conflict. As Gesell Institute authorities Ilg and Ames explained:

A factory manager doesn't simply tell his workers that they *ought* to produce more. Instead he tries to arrange things so that higher production is possible. Similarly, a little creative thinking about some of the most ordinary household routines can often result in improved behavior on the part of the child.[15]

"The possibilities, of course, are endless," they wrote:

For instance, suppose that two brothers or sisters cannot be together for any length of time without fighting. You may, if you wish, try to deal with this problem by warning, scolding, punishing. Simpler and more effective is to separate them physically. If you don't have the space to do this, you can often work wonders by rearranging their schedules. Hours of naps can be shifted. Sometimes it even pays to have children eat separately.[16]

The idea of "household engineering" recalls the crusades of Ellen Richards and the domestic scientists to turn the housewife into a professional domestic "engineer," economizing on time, money, and work. Transformed by the permissive ideology, household engineering has come to mean that the mother can, through hard work, planning, and diligence, save not time—not money—but stress. Her child's stress, that is. The imperative which faces her now is: no effort should be spared which might smooth the way of the free and natural child. For example, they suggest the following set of "General Rules to Help Children Enjoy Food":

1. Serve food attractively
2. Give small helpings
3. Serve food without comment
4. Do not stress amount of food to be eaten. . . .
5. Try to maintain a calm, unworried attitude. . . .[17]

In the early-twentieth-century "scientific" phase, the mother had been the representative of the expert in the home, imposing his regimens on the child. But now it is the child who acts as a junior field representative of the expert, instructing the mother in the routines of daily life.

Gesell recommended that the spontaneity of the infant be recorded, twenty-four hours a day, on specially designed charts with appropriate symbols for the taking of orange juice, for sleep, for elimination, crying, dreaming, etc. The adoption of the "self-demand" policy of feeding, he wrote, "creates a favorable atmosphere for the kind of observation which will enable the mother to really learn the basic characteristics of her infant":

> Instead of looking at the clock on the wall, she shifts her interest to the total behavior day of the baby as it records itself on the daily chart . . . It simply comes to this: She has made the baby (with all his inborn wisdom) a working partner. He helps her to work out an optimal and a flexible schedule suited to his changing needs.[18]

The scientific mother who once speculated on the nature of childhood, and who saved her observations for G. Stanley Hall, has been reduced to a painstaking—but essentially passive—marker of charts.

Libidinal Motherhood

The child of permissiveness had no use for parental authority or even guidance. Gesell's toddlers developed to the ticking of an internal clock, which parents could not hope to reset. Frank's teen-agers followed their impulses—and their pals—into a future which adults could neither understand nor control. But, according to the experts who developed the theory of permissiveness further in the thirties and forties, there was one thing that the child did need from its parents (read "mother"), and that was love—unquestioning, spontaneous, warm, all-enfolding *love*.

In fact, love was the necessary condition, the essential premise, of permissiveness. As Dr. Spock, the world-wide popularizer of permissiveness, put it, "children raised in loving families *want* to learn, *want* to conform, *want* to grow up. If the relationships are good they don't have to be forced to eat, forced to learn to use the toilet."[19]

Only an atmosphere of loving approval could allow a child to develop into a well-adjusted member of the new consumer society. Therefore, mothers must provide, not only a deftly managed stress-free environment, but loving encouragement to each childish impulse. To the child-raising experts of the thirties and forties, to love is a mother's *job*.

The love demanded by the permissive experts was not the measured love of the scientific mother, the austere love of the morally righteous mother, or the long-suffering love of the martyred mother—or any other variety of love to be found in nineteenth-century maternal iconography. It was a force of nature, an instinct. Even Gesell, so quantitative and rationalistic when it came to child development, seemed to lose his scientific grip at the thought of mother love. Describing appropriate motherly attributes, he lists "a pleasing voice . . . nimbleness and manual facility . . . leisureness of tempo combined with quickness of reaction . . . a fundamental knowledge of the theory and principles of child development" and other traits which presumably a dedicated woman might attempt to develop. But after all the analysis is said and done he allows that mothering is a "natural aptitude" and goes on astonishingly to state:

> It is also well known that among the colored race there are many women who are supremely endowed with almost unique emotional equipment which makes their services ideal for infants and young children.[20]

The black woman—impressed in Gesell's imagination as a warm and simple soul, a nanny—symbolized for him the primitive essence of mother-love.

It would take another kind of expert—the psychoanalyst—to claim mother-love as an area of scientific expertise. The psychoanalysts discovered the maternal instinct in much the same spirit as if they had isolated a new chemical element to be found only in women. Obviously, love is the only ingredient of child raising which cannot be mechanized, merchandised, or farmed out to outside institutions. It is the intangible core of the mother-child relationship, the glue which alone could hold the mother to the child and the woman to the home. Psychoanalysis now took up the project which nineteenth-century gynecology had attempted earlier: To anchor female domesticity in the bedrock of female *biology:* "Mothering behavior," declared psychoanalyst Therese Benedek, "is regulated by a pituitary hormone."[21]

The psychoanalysts agreed with Gesell that it was a mother's job, not to attempt any outright molding of the child, but to provide a perfectly nourishing environment. However, the psychoanalytically oriented experts observed with kindly disapproval, marking charts all day long would help her to accomplish this not one bit. Child raising, from their point of view, would be better described as being like an extension of pregnancy. If a woman was healthy, her maternal aura would contain all the proper, precious nutrients as naturally and miraculously as her body had nourished the child in her womb.

The psychoanalysts had constructed the ideal mother to go with the permissively raised child—one who would find passionate fulfillment in the details of child care. Through her new found biological instincts, this new "libidinal mother" was an even better match than the "household engineer" for the liberated child of permissive theory. Not only would she naturally fulfill her child's needs, but she would find her *own* fulfillment only in meeting the needs of the child. The libidinal mother would rejoice in pregnancy and breast-feeding. She would seek no richer companionship than that of her own child, no more serious concern than the daily details of child care. She instinctively needed her child as much as her child needed her. She would avoid outside commitments so as not to "miss" a fascinating stage of development, or "deprive" herself of a rewarding phase of motherhood. No longer would motherhood be reckoned as a "duty," or child raising as a disciplined profession. Instead, mother and child could enjoy each other, fulfilling one another's needs perfectly, instinctively, as if Nature in her infinite wisdom had created them, two happily matched consumers consuming each other.

The theory of libidinal motherhood left the field of rational interpretation as the sole province of the professionals. The child-guidance books now told women simply to trust their instincts—though of course, they insisted on defining for women exactly what those instincts ought to be. No need for scientific study, comparing notes with other mothers or "keeping up" with the latest developments, the books exulted. The good mother is the instinctive mother. Just—relax!

Education—or even thought—was once again viewed as a threat to motherliness—not because it caused "atrophy of the uterus" but because it would alienate a woman from her instincts. Norinne, in *The Group*, was educated enough to understand this:

> "Our Vassar education made it tough for me to accept my womanly role . . . [admitted Norinne] . . . The trouble is my brains . . . I was formed as an intellectual by Lockwood [a Vassar professor] and those other gals." Priss was surprised . . . Brains, she thought to herself, were supposed to help you organize your life more efficiently. . . . "You really feel our education was a mistake?" Priss asked anxiously. Sloan [her husband, a pediatrician] had often expressed the same view, but that was because it had given her ideas he disagreed with. "Oh, completely," said Norinne. "I've been crippled for life."[22]

So the gulf between the scientific expert and the instinctual mommy opened, and the gap between mother and child closed as *their* natures came to appear markedly similar.

Psychoanalysts like Therese Benedek did not flinch from the realization that this romantic bond, the mother-infant love affair, could only be based on maternal *regression*—or reversion to a childlike state. Regrettably, she thought, in our culture many women may develop an "active, extroverted ego-ideal" before marriage. Since this conflicts with the "natural, intuitive" ease with which she should care for her baby, she theorized that a woman would have to "undo" her masculine ego-ideal:

> In order to become a mother, women experience a biologic regression with each phase of their reproductive physiology. Men, in contrast, have to overcome their regressive tendencies to assert their virility in the heterosexual act and they have to integrate active extroverted psychic potentials to fulfill the role of father as protector and provider.[23]

In psychoanalytic parlance, motherliness had become "a normal characteristic of woman's psychosexual maturity." Yet, this "psycho-sexual maturity" began with regression: women could only "grow up" by becoming more infantile!* The explanation for this paradox, according to the psychoanalysts, was that only through regression could a woman overcome her girlhood penis envy. The regression allowed her to unconsciously accept the baby as the symbolic "gift" of a penis, compensating her for her own long-resented "castration." Conciliated at last, the woman is able to accept her femininity and submit without envy to her husband's love:

> Feelings of incompletion and deprivation in being a girl have been compensated . . . Her love for the husband who has made such a completion possible deepens. She does not wish the child just for herself but as a meaningful outcome of her relationship to her husband, pleasing him with a gift that is part of him that he has placed in her to nurture but also something of herself that her husband will cherish. To some extent, the baby is herself, loved by a benevolent father.[24]

Marcel Heiman, an obstetrician much influenced by Benedek, applied the theory of maternal regression to his patients, suggesting that ". . . . more than any other physician, the obstetrician needs to understand intimately feminine psychology." In a paper entitled "A Psychoanalytic View of Pregnancy," he wrote:

> . . . regression in the course of pregnancy is universal and normal, and pregnancy has aptly been called a "normal illness". . . . just as the regression of the pregnant woman brings to the surface childhood fears, so we find the pregnant woman as suggestible as a child. This is reminiscent of some of the fears children commonly have; all the mother has to do at times is to take the child in her arms and say "Now, there, there . . ." and thus establish in the child a feeling of security that eradicates the fears. . . . This is the reason for the success authoritarian obstetricians have with their patients. . . .[25]

(Along the same lines, Dr. Spock described women's greater willingness to take advice and listen to professionals as one of the most basic differences between the sexes.)[26]

The breakdown of maternal integrity was complete: the mother

---

* The psychological idea that female maturity is accomplished through regression is an uncanny echo of the nineteenth-century biological theory that for females evolutionary advance meant sinking into an ever more primitive animalistic condition.

has herself been turned into a child. Regressed to a psychological replay of her own infancy by the experience of motherhood, she is expected to turn an obedient and worshipful ear to the father figures who will coach her in her new role. Accordingly, the voice of the professional becomes insidiously paternalistic. After commenting modestly that "I cannot tell you exactly what to do, but I can write about what it all means," Dr. Winnicott, once president of the British Psychoanalytic Association, and author of *Mother and Child: A Primer of First Relationships,* addressed this condescending reassurance to the young mother:

> You do not have to be clever, and you do not even have to think if you do not want to. You may have been hopeless at arithmetic at school; or perhaps all your friends got scholarships but you couldn't stand the sight of a history book and so failed and left school early; or perhaps you would have done well if you hadn't had measles just before the exam. Or you may be really clever. But all this does not matter, and it hasn't anything to do with whether or not you are a good mother. If a child can play with a doll, you can be an ordinary devoted mother. . . .[27]

Naturally it was only the wholly domestic, nonworking mother who could hope to release the libidinal unself-consciousness, the blissful ignorance, that was now the *sine qua non* of good mothering. Working mothers of the late forties and fifties were urged to quit and give into the instincts they had been fighting. For example, one woman wrote to *Child Study* (a parent-oriented periodical whose advisory board included Lawrence Frank, Benjamin Spock, and leading psychiatrists René Spitz and David Levy):

> I am a professional woman with a son five years old, afraid that in my busy life I'm not giving him all he needs . . . though I keep planning to quit, so far I haven't. . . . Realizing as I do that I'm evidently not the domestic type, I'm not at all sure it would be wise for me to give up my work and try to be just a mother.

After chiding her for that final phrase "just a mother"—the *Child Study* staff responded encouragingly:

> Perhaps you honestly do feel that you lack whatever it takes to give the term "domestic" [this] fuller meaning. If so, you may want to get some help from professional sources in finding out what has caused you to lose confidence in your capacities. It may be that you're more the "domestic type" than you think and that under the

right circumstances your powers as wife and mother could be liberated in the service of your child, your husband and—last but by no
means least—for your own enduring satisfaction.[28]

It was assumed, of course, that all women had husbands and that
their husbands could support the family singlehandedly. The mass
media poured out the same advice to women of all classes: women
who worked, no matter what the reasons, were depriving their children and denying their deepest instincts.

Bad Mothers

Psychoanalytic theory did not linger too long in front of the romantic tableau of the mother-child relationship. Even at the height of
libidinal motherhood theory, the suspicion arose that American
women were not really natural mothers—and this suspicion only grew
stronger in the late forties and fifties. Psychiatrists, after all, are
medical men, trained to search for the pathology—the dark lesions,
the hidden microbial spores—which lie under the healthiest exterior.
As they peered into the rosy picture of the mother-child relationship
with the X-ray vision of psychoanalytic insight, a core of hideous
pathology revealed itself and came to dominate mid-twentieth-
century child-raising theory.

The symptoms abounded in the waiting rooms of school psychologists, psychiatric social workers, and (for wealthier parents) psychoanalysts themselves. There were cranky children, destructive children, withdrawn children, frightened and disturbed children, babies
who cried inconsolably, babies who masturbated obsessively, and so
on—despite a scientific theory which locked mother and child together in mutual bliss, and despite the honeymoon isolation which the
mother and child were now supposed to enjoy in so many middle-
class and working-class homes. It did not enter the experts' minds to
question the theory or to be alarmed at the terrible solitude in which
most women were now attempting to raise their children.† The
theory was solid; the home was sacred; it was the woman who had
failed.

† Evaluating anthropological reports on child raising in many other cultures,
sociologist Jessie Bernard reports that the isolation and exclusivity with which
American mothers raise their children is both historically new and culturally
unique.[29]

As psychoanalytic attention shifted from the normal to the deviant, from the "healthy" to the pathological, the theory of instinctual motherhood quickly lost whatever comfort it might have held for women. The instinct theory asserted, at best, that women did know something about child raising independently of the experts. They did not have to master techniques and methods formulated in the psychologists' lab or clinic. But with the new emphasis on pathology, "instinct" proved to be a harsher taskmaster for women than discipline and study had ever been. If anything should go awry in the mother-child relationship or in the child's development the finger of blame would no longer point at the mother's faulty technique, but at her defective instincts. What really mattered now was not what the mother read or thought, what she wanted to do or tried to do, but what her unconscious motivations were. And instincts couldn't be faked.

As she played out her subconscious urges through the act of mothering, a woman wrote on the baby's psyche, as it were, with invisible ink. In time the ink would become legible to the expert, who would read it—and judge.

The emphasis on pathology reinforced the child-raising experts' heroic image of themselves as public health crusaders—working for a healthy future just as sanitation experts worked for a healthy present. In the period of scientific motherhood, the challenge to child-raising experts as public health officials had been to inform the maternal intellect. Now the challenge was to probe the maternal subconscious, searching for the neuroses which could infect a generation of children with the germs of mental illness. René Spitz led a generation of psychoanalysts in the effort to trace each childhood disorder to a specific disorder in the mother, just as the bacteriologists sought to trace each disease to a specific type of microbe.

Using the language of the pathology lab, Spitz identified the "psychotoxic diseases of infancy." These were the diseases in which "the mother's personality acts as the disease-provoking agent, as a psychological toxin." He devoted a major portion of his book, *The First Year of Life,* to connecting each of the following maternal attitudes with a corresponding infantile disturbance: "Primary Anxious Overpermissiveness" (which he said produces the three-month colic); "Hostility in the Guise of Manifest Anxiety" (infantile eczema); "Oscillation between Pampering and Hostility" (rocking in infants); "Cyclical Mood Swings of the Mother" (fecal play and coprophagia); "Maternal Hostility Consciously Compensated" (the hyperthymic child).[30]‡ Mothers could seek no escape from the instinctual imperative. A deficient mother would be exposed by the very symptoms of her child's pathology. So pretending to have a good time washing the baby wasn't enough—you had to *really* enjoy it. Psychoanalytic theory identified two broad categories of bad mothers—the rejecting mother and the overprotecting mother—mirror images and equally malevolent. The indictment of the "rejecting mother" became so widespread in clinical practice and popular literature that even psychoanalyst Anna Freud eventually regretted its overuse:

> . . . the idea of being rejected by the mother suddenly began to overrun the fields of clinical work and casework. On the clinical side, more and more of the gravest disturbances (such as autism, atypical and psychotic development, mental backwardness, retardation of speech, etc.) were attributed to the presence of rejection. On the caseworker's side, more and more mothers were pronounced to be cold, not outgoing, unresponsive, unloving, hating, in short, rejecting their children. This caused much heart-searching and also much self-accusation, especially among the mothers of abnormal children.[32]

Few mothers could read about the maternal rejection syndrome without a pang of conscience. Every woman has, at some time, turned away from a two-year-old's tenth teasing demand to know "why"; left a toddler alone for an interminable fifteen minutes to cry it out; let her mind wander during a conversation with a four-year-old—or otherwise "rejected" her child. Full-time mothers, struggling to keep a home spotless and tidy, know what it is to resent, and fleetingly hate, an infant or a pre-schooler as if it were a full-grown adversary. If motherhood was "fulfillment" then these flashes of hostility must be traitorous, and implicitly destructive of all that was normal, good and decent. Science could not account for these feelings except as perversions—serpents in the Eden of the mother-child relationship. The result was agonizing self-doubt: the mother who is

‡ In 1973, in the *New England Journal of Medicine* Lennane and Lennane examined the scientific literature that traced infantile behavior disturbances, especially colic, to maternal psychogenesis. They found that what scientific evidence exists tends to disprove the psychogenic theory, while it tends to confirm the existence of certain organic causes. Nevertheless, as they show, the prejudice about maternal causation persists among doctors, as for example in a standard pediatric textbook which lists colic under "Psychological Disorders."[31]

blamed for her "hostility," her "aggressiveness," and also (if she was seeing a child-raising or mental health expert) for "disguising" it, is a mother whose own internal life has been rendered inhuman and unintelligible. As her own wants and needs are interpreted as destructive toxins, she drifts toward actual psychosis. Adrienne Rich, who raised her own children in the fifties and early sixties, writes of "the invisible violence of the institution of motherhood":

> . . . the guilt, the powerless responsibility for human lives, the judgments and condemnations, the fear of her own power, the guilt, the guilt, the guilt. So much of this heart of darkness is an undramatic, undramatized suffering: the woman who serves her family their food but cannot sit down with them, the woman who cannot get out of bed in the morning, the woman polishing the same place on the table over and over, reading labels in the supermarket as if they were in a foreign language, looking into a drawer where there is a butcher knife.[33]

Twenty or thirty years later, women gathered in consciousness-raising groups or workshops would discover that suppressed maternal violence was as widespread among full-time mothers as migraine headaches or "excess" pounds. It can be cured, before any overt violence occurs, if day care is available, supportive women's groups, responsible fathers, etc. (Recent studies show that mothers who do have help—for example from a grandmother—are "more stable and emotionally consistent" in their responses to their children.) But mid-twentieth-century science had no comfort to offer the average ambivalent mother. In the nineteen fifties, influenced by John Bowlby's study *Maternal Care and Mental Health,* the experts posted their final, most devastating accusation against the rejecting mother: The mother who harbored hostile and rejecting feelings for her child was not only planting the seeds of neurosis, she was actually and materially destroying her child. To think of violence, even subconsciously, was to commit it. The intent of John Bowlby's 1950 study was unquestionably humanistic. At the end of the Second World War he was commissioned to study the needs of war orphans, children who had been hospitalized for long periods, and children who had been boarded in rural areas to protect them from air raids. Bowlby's review of the literature on these children makes somber reading: they rated low on Gesell-type development tests and standard I.Q. tests; they were emotionally withdrawn and often autistic, and—perhaps most horrifying—they were likely to be physically stunted and sickly. Describing the homeless infant, Bowlby wrote:

The emotional tone is one of apprehension and sadness, there is withdrawal from the environment amounting to rejection of it. . . . Activities are retarded and the child often sits or lies inert in a dazed stupor. Insomnia is common and lack of appetite universal. Weight is lost and the child becomes prone to intercurrent infections.[34]

Bowlby concluded with a series of practical recommendations—ranging from cconomic aid to mothers in distress to phasing out institutional care in favor of care in loving, homelike situations.

So far so good. But Bowlby nimbly leaped beyond his data base to the child *in* the home. His conclusions imply that the dire consequences of maternal deprivation can occur wherever there was less than singlehanded, full-time provision of maternal attention. For example, in an analysis of why families fail, he lists "fulltime employment of mother," without qualification, on a par with such items as, "Death of a parent," "Imprisonment of a parent," "Social calamity—war, famine," etc.[35]

Even within the home which had not been visited by the calamity of maternal employment, there could be insidious "partial deprivation" due, of course, to maternal rcjection. Bowlby did not define "partial deprivation," but the standard he set for "good mothering" left an enormous amount of room for it:

> Just as the baby needs to feel that he belongs to his mother, the mother needs to feel that she belongs to her child and it is only when she has thc satisfaction of this feeling that it is easy for her to devote herself to him. The provision of constant attention day and night, scven days a week and 365 in the year, is possible only for a woman who derives profound satisfaction from seeing her child grow from babyhood, through the many phases of childhood, to bccome an independent man or woman, and knows that it is her care which has made this possible.[36]

Bowlby believed that child-guidance counselors should search out these cases of partial deprivation and "give as much time to the therapy of the parents as to that of the children." He called for a public health campaign to detect cases of deprivation on a mass scale, likening such an effort to the turn-of-the-century public health campaigns which had focused on microbial disease-bearers:

> Deprived children, whether in their own homes or out of them, are a source of social infection as real and serious as are carriers of diphtheria and typhoid. . . .[37]

Bowlby's followers continued the search for "deprivation" in the average American home. Writing in *Deprivation of Maternal Care: A Reassessment of Its Effects,* a volume of professional commentary on Bowlby's original monograph, child psychiatrists Dane Prugh and Robert Harlow observed solemnly

> . . . it is to be emphasized that instances of "masked" or covert deprivation may have as devastating effects upon emotional development as the more gross maternal deprivations highlighted by Bowlby.[38]

Psychologists demonstrated the noxious effects of maternal deprivation of baby monkeys, baby rats, and baby ducks, including weight loss, enlarged adrenal glands, heightened susceptibility to infectious diseases and chemical poisons, and stunted growth. In the logic of the experts, it followed that the mother who failed to meet their exaggerated standards of mother-love might as well be watering her baby's milk.

Popular books on child raising began to feature ominous references to orphaned animals and institutionalized children:

> The best of food and shelter, the finest medical care will not suffice him [the child]—without love. In a foundling hospital babies have been known to wither away and die, not that the doctors and nurses did not try their scientific utmost to save them, but because there were not enough loving arms to cuddle and comfort them.[39]

If the mid-twentieth-century studies of maternal deprivation did not lead to any striking improvements in public care for neglected children, they did impress on the average mother's mind the tragic picture of the maternally deprived child—sunken eyes above wan cheeks, limbs thin and flaccid, prey to every passing infection—all presumably, for lack of "constant attention day and night, seven days a week and 365 in the year."

The second specter to haunt the sweet maternal ideal was the feared and hated "overprotective" mother—the mirror-opposite of her "rejecting" sister. The ubiquitous "overprotective" mother *had* immersed herself in child care—too much. In fact, she seemed to have taken advantage of her domestic isolation, and her husband's absence, to increase her own power and influence over the children.

In 1943 Dr. David Levy singled out this problem mother for attention, and gave the syndrome a name with the publication of *Maternal*

Overprotection. According to his diagnosis certain women had "made maternity into a disease" which had "symptoms . . . as clearly as organic symptoms."*[40] Levy had culled through thousands of case records at the family guidance center he directed, and specially selected out twenty cases of what he considered "pure" overprotection (in nineteen out of twenty of the cases, the overprotected children he singled out were boys).

These overprotecting mothers proved to have little in common; their methods ran from extreme authoritarianism to extreme permissiveness. Not at all deterred by this finding, Levy divided the mothers into two broad categories; the "submissive" mother and the "domineering" mother. Predictably enough, the children of the domineering mothers were submissive, while those of the submissive mothers were dominating. The "symptoms" of the overprotected, then, ran from tyrannical aggression all the way to docility and "too good" behavior. Levy lumped all these symptoms together as "infantilization" by mothers who refused to let their children grow up.

The "libidinal mothers" who had been working hard in the thirties and forties at not rejecting their children might have been relieved to find out that there *was* such a thing as overprotection. But it soon developed that a woman could be *both* rejecting and overprotecting at the same time—in fact if she was one, she probably was the other. Levy's central conclusion about the overprotecting mothers was that they were all "aggressive"—in psychoanalytic terms, no light judgment, and practically an equation with "hostile" and "destructive." Now aggression was also considered by him to be the main ingredient in the *rejecting* mother. Levy hypothesized that overprotection and rejection represented two alternate ways a woman might express her "unconscious hostilities." The factor which determined which way a woman went (toward overprotection or rejection) was probably the "strength of the maternal tendency" or the amount of maternal-type hormones the woman possessed.

Levy's theories hung from his "data" by the slenderest of threads.

---

* Levy echoes nineteenth-century evolutionary theory [see Chapter IV] in his belief that reproductivity links women more closely than men to animals. He looked forward to the day when science would prove the hormonal basis of all maternal behavior, but doubted that similar findings would be made about the other human drives, which are shared by the two sexes. He speculated, "It may be true that the maternal drive, a drive so basic to survival, has a higher degree of resemblance in man [i.e. woman] and animals than the sex drive."[41]

Not only did his overprotective mothers fail to exhibit common personality traits—his overprotected children failed to develop a common neurosis. Follow-up studies showed there was little to differentiate the grown-up overprotected children from any other random sample of young adults. Quite a few of them, in fact, appeared to be happy and well-adjusted.†

But all this mattered little. "Overprotection" had entered the vocabulary of the reading public and the front-line child-raising experts. The vision of the grasping, power-hungry mother frightened women into new torments of self-doubt, which were no doubt exacerbated by the fact that the malicious, overprotecting mother so closely resembled the ideal mother of just a short while before. Betty Friedan quotes Dr. Edward Strecker, consultant to the Surgeon General of the Army and Navy, describing the type of mother whom he "found guilty" for emasculating the nation's potential soldiers:

> . . . From dawn until late at night she finds her happiness in doing for her children. The house belongs to them. It must be "just so"; the meals on the minute, hot and tempting . . . Everything is in its proper place. Mom knows where it is. Uncomplainingly, gladly, she puts things where they belong after the children have strewn them about, here, there, everywhere . . . Anything the children need or want, mom will cheerfully get for them. It is the perfect home . . . Failing to find a comparable peaceful haven in the outside world, it is quite likely that one or more of the brood will remain or return to the happy home, forever enwombed.[43]

"Overprotectiveness" became an accusation hurled not only at individual women but at whole cultures such as the Italians and the Jews. Progressive-minded women, who tried to keep up with the latest scientific information, examined themselves anxiously for signs of this

† Actually, Levy's research methodology is so sloppy by conventional scientific standards that it's impossible to tell what the long-term results of "overprotection" might be. His twenty overprotected children are not compared to a control group of any kind (though admittedly it would be hard to select a control group for a sample as heterogeneous as the overprotected twenty). Furthermore, the psychiatric evaluations of these twenty as adults are extremely biased. The research team tended to give "normal" ratings to subjects who had attained white-collar jobs, and to rate as only "partially adjusted" subjects who did blue-collar work. "Normal" type ratings went with judgments such as "reliable, stable, industrious" and "partially adjusted" ratings went with judgments such as "stupid." One subject was described in the case summary as a "good-natured, lazy, genial fat man."[42]

new danger. In her memoirs Margaret Mead describes her own docile reaction to Levy and his theories:

> . . . I had been a "baby carriage peeker," as Dr. David Levy described the child with an absorbing interest in babies, and he identified this as one of the traits that predisposed one to become an over-protective mother. When I told him, in a telephone conversation, that I was expecting a baby, he asked, in that marvelous therapeutic voice which he could project even over the telephone, "Are you going to be an over-protective mother?" I answered, "I'm going to try not to be. . . ."

Mead recalled,

> "I knew that I would have to work hard not to overprotect my child."[44]

Steering a course between the cliffs of maternal rejection and the shoals of overprotection was indeed hard work. The beautiful libidinal bond between mother and baby had turned out, under closer professional scrutiny, to be an intense libidinal conflict—in which the child's psychological integrity, if not its very life, was at stake. Dr. Joseph Rheingold of Harvard Medical School carried the experts' suspicions of maternal pathology to their logical extreme: every mother was subconsciously trying to *kill* her child. Maternal destructiveness was built into the female psyche, he wrote, and it arose from a fundamental horror of being female, which was the "basic conflict of the woman's personality." Having a baby confirms to a woman that indeed she *is* a woman and, ". . . To save herself she must disown motherhood by destroying the child and rejecting it. Only this extremity of fear, this infantile terror, gives rise to the self-preservative need to undo motherhood. It is kill or be killed. Most mothers do not murder or totally reject their children, but death pervades the relationship between mother and child."[45]

"Momism" and the Crisis in American Masculinity

The experts' disillusionment with libidinal mothering reflected a widespread anxiety that something was going wrong with America— or Americans. World War II brought the problem into sharp focus. Psychological screening methods were used for the first time by American draft boards, and over 2,000,000 men were rejected or discharged for psychiatric reasons because, according to one medical authority, they lacked "the ability to face life, live with others, think for themselves and stand on their own two feet."[46] Who was to blame? Obviously, their mothers. The spirit of the American male was being broken in babyhood.

Betty Friedan, who lived through it, recalls the deep mood of misogyny that settled over the country in the nineteen forties, fifties, and early sixties:

> It was suddenly discovered that the mother could be blamed for almost everything. In every case history of the troubled child; alcoholic, suicidal, schizophrenic, psychopathic, neurotic adult; impotent, homosexual male; frigid, promiscuous female: ulcerous, asthmatic, and otherwise disturbed American, could be found a mother. A frustrated, repressed, disturbed, martyred, never satisfied, unhappy woman. A demanding, nagging, shrewish wife. A rejecting, overprotecting, dominating mother.[47]

At first sight, the American mother might seem to be an unlikely target for public expressions of misogyny. The strongest disapproval had always been reserved for the "loose" woman, the "bad" woman, or the ambitious woman who dared to break with the romantic expectations about her place and role. Psychiatrist Marynia Farnham and sociologist Ferdinand Lundberg, authors of the 1947 best-seller *Modern Woman: The Lost Sex,* a pop-Freudian diatribe against women, acknowledged that the American mother was "not a feminist or a courtesan type,"—she *had* been attempting to do her job as a woman. But she was still "afflicted very often with penis envy"—that unwomanly drive to power which, in the confines of the home, could only fester until it destroyed the people around her.[48]

In the popular imagination, the American mother had become actually *more* powerful than any career woman could hope to be, and probably more powerful than her own husband. She had accepted the romantic solution, but now it appeared that within the privacy of the home she had secretly been accreting more and more power unto herself: first, power over the children, and now—it seemed from a masculinist standpoint—power over the *economy*.

The housewife may have been economically invisible in the accumulation-oriented economy of the nineteenth century, but in the consumption-oriented economy of the twentieth century she had become a force to be reckoned with. "Never underestimate the power of a woman," became the *Ladies' Home Journal*'s motto in the nineteen forties, and the power they were referring to was clearly *pur-*

chasing power. Marketing men raved about "Woman USA: The World's Greatest Consuming Phenomenon." Admen aimed their psychological artillery at her. It seemed as if, by some strange quirk of history—despite the collapse of feminism in the nineteen twenties and despite the unchallenged hegemony of sexual romanticism—women had taken over the country. Women had been granted the home as "their sphere," and now they had stealthily extended their dominion to the Market. A popular child-raising book from the fifties observed anxiously that the American woman "rules her husband, she rules her children, and to an ever-increasing degree she is beginning to own, if not rule, American business."[49]

The real power of housewives in the consumption economy consisted of the power to choose between Ivory and Lux, between Bendix and Westinghouse, between Cheerios and Sugar Pops. And of course the admen, the retailers, and the marketing men all conspired to stupefy her to such an extent that even these trivial decisions were hardly hers. Nevertheless the popular wisdom advanced by novelists, cartoonists, politicians, and experts, insisted that America had not only achieved sexual equality, but had somehow overshot the mark and become a *matriarchy*.

Philip Wylie, novelist and social commentator, sounded the alarm with his 1942 best-seller *Generation of Vipers*. The romantic insistence on seeing Mother as a figure in a Norman Rockwell painting, perpetually bearing hot pies to the table, had blinded men to her true nature—which was cunning, ruthless, and power-hungry. And while American men had foolishly held the doors open for them, the mothers of the land had rushed in and staged a cultural coup d'état. America had its own dictator, as vicious as any produced by European fascism, and her name was Mom:

> . . . megaloid momworship has got completely out of hand. Our land, subjectively mapped, would have more silver cords and apron strings criss-crossing it than railroads and telephone wires. Mom is everywhere and everything and damned near everybody, and from her depends all the rest of the U.S. Disguised as good old mom, dear old mom, sweet old mom, your loving mom, and so on, she is the bride at every funeral and the corpse at every wedding.[50]

The accusative "Mom," coined by Wylie, quickly bounced upward into the language of professional acceptability. Psychoanalyst Erik Erikson for example, accepted "Momism" as if it were a scientific diagnostic term coined by clinical researchers, and offered this devastating analysis:

> . . . "Mom" is a woman in whose life cycle remnants of infantility join advanced senility to crowd out the middle range of mature womanhood, which thus becomes self-absorbed and stagnant.[51]

The towering figure of "Mom" reflected no change in the social and occupational position of women, which, if anything, had reached a nadir for the twentieth century. Behind the hatred and fear of the mother was a growing sense that *men* had somehow lost power—that they were no longer "real men."

The end of World War II brought millions of men to sudden consciousness of their situation: they had been away for months or years in the most masculine endeavor of all, where nothing counted more than male solidarity, stamina and "balls." Then one day sometime after the war had ended, the American male woke up to find himself driving a blue Ford (like the hundreds of others on the highway) between a job he found no meaning in and a tract house he could identify only by looking at the street number. Thus the flip side of the megalomaniac Mom was the degraded Dad—the mid-century middle-class man who sensed that he was powerless, a conformist, adrift in a world that had no use for his manhood.

The mid-twentieth-century masculinity crisis hit the middle class—which the experts themselves belonged to—hardest. A generation ago the growing urban middle class had seen a heroic role for themselves as the tamers and "rationalizers" of capitalist society. They had carved out the professions and made themselves indispensable to industry as managers, lawyers, and researchers. Now their sons faced a world which, if anything, seemed to be overly mechanized, rationalized, and organized. Research had been bureaucratized during the war; medicine was increasingly organized around the large, bureaucratic hospital; universities were becoming more like corporations; and corporations themselves were becoming more like medium-sized nations, with vast and intricate systems of internal government. William H. Whyte wrote that the bureaucratization of the work world was calling forth a new type of man—the "organization man":

> Blood brother to the business trainee off to join Du Pont is the seminary student who will end up in the church hierarchy, the doctor headed for the corporate clinic, the physics Ph.D. in a government laboratory, the intellectual on the foundation-sponsored team proj-

ect, the engineering graduate in the huge drafting room at Lockheed, the young apprentice in a Wall Street law factory.[52]

The classic description of the change in American manhood was David Riesman's 1950 book, *The Lonely Crowd*. Earlier Americans, he argued, had been "inner-directed"—self-motivated achievers spurred by the Protestant work ethic. But ". . . the 'scarcity psychology' of many inner directed people, which was socially adaptive during the period of heavy capital accumulation . . . needs to give way to an 'abundance psychology' capable of 'wasteful' luxury consumption of leisure and of the surplus product."[53] The new "other-directed" men of post-accumulation capitalism were relaxed consumers and adaptable bureaucratic workers. No inner drive to achieve propelled them, no obsessions lurked in their subconscious minds—they wanted only to "get along" at work and cash in their earnings for a private life of suburban leisure.

The decline in ambitious individualism documented by Whyte and Riesman did not go unlamented. To a not inconsiderable extent the emergence of the bureaucratic order seemed to be an attack on maleness itself. Liberal and conservative alike, social commentators studied the American man with distaste. They found him "absurd," and "alienated." He was the man in the gray flannel suit, the cog in the machine and worst of all, they were *him,* or rapidly becoming so. Yet the corporation was so comfortable, so safe, so secure, that according to novelist Alan Harrington you gradually swallow your self-disgust and

> . . . become accustomed to the Utopian drift. Soon another inhibition may make you even more amenable. If you have been in easy circumstances for a number of years, you feel that you are out of shape. Even in younger men the hard muscle of ambition tends to go slack, and you hesitate to take a chance in the jungle again. . . . Apparently when you remove fear from a man's life you also remove his stinger.‡[54]

‡ Women, of course, had never had the hard muscle that goes slack. Women were to be envied or dismissed, because they so easily escaped the bureaucratic transformation of the work world. For example, in *Growing Up Absurd* Paul Goodman addressed himself to "young men and boys" ". . . because the problems I want to discuss . . . belong primarily, in our society, to the boys: how to be useful and make something of oneself. A girl does not *have* to, she is not expected to, 'make something' of herself. Her career does not have to be self-justifying, for she will have children. . . ."[55] Riesman also ignored women. He noted that the change from the inner-directed to the other-directed personal-

For men who had nothing to fear at work but the loss of their "stinger," home offered the only chance of masculine redemption. The "collectivized" work world no longer provided a sure sense of maleness; perhaps private life—suitably augmented with power tools, do-it-yourself hobbies and home-repair projects—could make things right. Wasn't a man's home his castle—the only place he could count on to give him a feeling of individuality, autonomy and control? But, unfortunately for all concerned, someone had gotten there ahead of him—the American woman.

The American housewife, as so many GIs noted with disappointment on their return, was no geisha girl or French coquette. She was a busy mother, housekeeper, and household finance manager. In the small space of the home, her much-vaunted economic power had some real meaning. It was the husband's job to earn, but it was *her* job to spend. And in a consumer society centered on private life, her job often seemed more important. From the vantage point of the home, all that mattered about the man's job was the size of the check it produced, and this the housewife stood prepared to measure against all the family's needs, wants, and expectations. Did he bring home seventy-eight dollars a week? Then there might be a baby-sitter for Saturday night but no vacation trip. Did he bring home two hundred dollars? Then there would be summer camp for the kids but no new furniture until next year. So long as she did the buying and budgeting, it was largely her decision. After all, sexual-romanticist ideology had insisted for decades that private life was "woman's sphere." Now men were furious to find women dominating the home, and there was nowhere to tell them to go.

Mass culture became obsessed with the diminution of the American male. In cartoons, the average male was shorter than his wife, who habitually entered the frame in curlers, wielding a rolling pin over her cowering husband. TV squeezed the American male's diminished sense of manhood for whatever laughs—or thrills—were left. The domesticated Dad, who was most hilarious when he tried to be manly and enterprising, was the butt of all the situation comedies. Danny Thomas, Ozzie Nelson, Robert Young, and (though not a father) Jackie Gleason in "The Honeymooners," were funny only as pint-sized caricatures of the patriarchs, frontiersmen, and adventurers

---

ity was more marked in men than in women, but without troubling over the reasons for the difference, he concluded that "characterological change in the West seems to occur first with men."

who once defined American manhood. Meanwhile, cowboy shows
provided men with an escape into a world where men were men, and
women were—absent. In literature, Norman Mailer glorified
America's suppressed masculinity as a subversive principle which
might overthrow "the system" as well as the dominating woman.
(Two of the most memorable novels of female domination and male
revolt were written in the sixties: *Portnoy's Complaint* [1969] and
One Flew Over the Cuckoo's Nest [1962].)

Psychomedical science was quick to ratify the idea that women
were dominating the American male. With their usual anatomical
precision, the experts announced that American women were, in fact,
castrating men. "The 'Battle of the Sexes' is a reality," wrote Farnham and Lundberg, "and one of its results has been rather extensive
psychological castration of the male."[56] Naturally the combat which
most concerned the child-raising experts was the unequally matched
one between the mother—now known to the world of science as well
as to the misogynist-on-the-street as "Mom"—and her little boy. Science had already concluded that the mother-child relationship was
full of mortal dangers for the child. In the light of mid-century misogyny, it became clear that what was at stake, in the case of the sons,
was not only life and sanity, but something possibly more precious—
their manhood.

The Obligatory Oedipus Complex

By the mid-twentieth century the experts were grimly acknowledging that despite their constant vigilance the American mother was
failing at her job. There was only one person to turn to now, and that
was the long-neglected father. Parent advice articles in the media
began to feature titles like "What Every Father Should Know," "Let
Daddy Take Over!" and "Men Make Wonderful Mothers." But as
the experts made abundantly clear, Dad was not being called home
just to "help out." He was needed to *protect the children,* and especially the sons. Levy, the discoverer of "overprotection," believed
that overprotected patients had to "fight" for release from the
mother. "When the father entered the picture," he observed in one
study, "the patient had an ally in this battle."[57] By returning to active
duty in the home, a man could defend his children and at the same
time regain his own endangered masculinity.

In the post-war period the experts mapped out two key functions for Dad in the home. One had to do with sex: Only sex could drain off the poisonous energies Mom might otherwise direct at her children, and of course, only Dad could provide the sex. The other had to do with gender: left to herself, Mom would produce emasculated males and equally Mom-ish females. According to expert theory, only Dad could undo the damage and guide the boys toward manliness and the girls toward true womanliness. It was a brilliant stroke—calling in Dad to perform these tasks. Not only would the children be saved, or so the experts hoped, but something would at last be found for poor old Dad to do—a job which was not make-work, like puttering with tools, and was not women's work, like drying the dishes, but was quintessentially male. "Being a real father is not 'sissy' business," a psychiatrist wrote in *Parents' Magazine* in 1947, "It is not an avocation, a hobby to be pursued in spare moments. It is an occupation. And for the father and his children, it is the most important occupation in the world and for the world."[58]

Levy had been one of the first to hypothesize that sex might be necessary not only for the conception of children, but for the successful raising of them. Levy argued that a woman could protect herself and her children from overprotectiveness by immersing herself in heterosexual femininity:

> A wife devoted to her husband cannot be exclusively a mother. In a more fundamental sense, the release of libido through satisfactory sexual relationship shunts off energy that must otherwise flow in other directions—in the case of our group, in the direction of maternity. The child must bear the brunt of the unsatisfied love life of the mother. One might theoretically infer that a woman sexually well adjusted could not become overprotective to an extreme degree.[59]

From Levy's hypothesis in 1943 the idea matured into this self-confident assertion in a 1959 child-care book:

> The truly feminine mother, fulfilled in her marriage to a truly masculine father, does not overprotect, dominate, or over-fondle her children. She lets them judiciously alone. She knows exactly what they need of food, shelter or clothing, because she waits until they tell her. . . .[60]

It followed that it was the husband's duty *as a father* to keep his wife sexually satisfied:

> A man who is a good lover to his wife is his children's best friend. . . . Child care is play to a woman who is happy. And only

a man can make a woman happy. In deepest truth, a father's first duty to his children is to make their mother feel fulfilled as a woman.[61]

Good sex had been discovered as the antidote to bad mothering. It cured Momism and overprotectiveness, rejection of the female role, and disparagement of the father. Furthermore, the experts suggested subtly, it could act as a preventative against future male homosexuality. "That mother-bound boy, so uncreative in work and love, is a casualty of his mother's mis-mating."[62]

From the thirties to the fifties the sexologists spawned a brood of marriage manuals, directed primarily at husbands, which alerted them to the need for wifely satisfaction and instructed (or misinstructed) them in the techniques to bring it about. While the husband was reading the marriage manual, the wife was reading the child-care book, and they both got the same message. Marital sex was not only permissible, it was obligatory. Sex, in fact, had a therapeutic function for the whole family. "Your Sexual Happiness Is Your Child's Emotional Security" blared a chapter title in the parent's guide quoted above, declaring "The happy lovers are the potentially effective parents . . . Unless you love each other, you cannot really love your children!"[63]

On the one hand, the linking of sex and parenthood was a tremendous breakthrough for women. Recall the late-nineteenth-century denial (and fear) of female sexuality. Now the experts were not only acknowledging female sexuality, but welcoming it as they insisted that it was the husband's duty to satisfy it. But there was also a hint of a threat to women in the new insistence on marital joy. At no time was a woman to "let herself go" in terms of grooming or dress—lest she cease to be "feminine." Apparently this stricture applied even to the primal act of childbirth. In Mary McCarthy's novel The Group, Priss Crockett has just given birth to her son Stephen:

> She was wearing a pale blue bed jacket, and her thin ashy hair was set in waves; the student nurse had done it for her that morning. On her lips, which were dry, was a new shade of lipstick, by Tussy; her doctor had ordered her to put on lipstick and powder right in the middle of labor; he and Sloan [her husband, Dr. Sloan Crockett, a pediatrician] both thought it was important for a maternity patient to keep herself up to the mark. . . . She would have been more comfortable in the short cotton hospital nightshirt that tied in back,

but the floor nurses every morning made her struggle into a satin-and-lace "nightie" from her trousseau. Doctors orders, they said.[64]

The woman who didn't make the effort to be sexy and feminine at all times might not only damage her children; she might lose her husband. "Husbands are often neglected," wrote child-raising expert Goodman. "Some of them feel pretty bad about this, though they don't say much. Some go wandering, and that's never good. Smart wives see to it that it doesn't happen."[65] In fact, the kind of sex being recommended at this time was actually almost wholly husband-centered: vaginal penetration with little attention to the clitoris. (Freudian theory branded clitoral sexuality as "immature"—more on this in the next chapter.) The "smart wife" would just have to pretend that she liked it. "It is good advice to recommend to the women the advantage of *innocent simulation* of sex responsiveness," a 1952 gynecology text advised doctors, "and as a matter of fact many women in their desire to please their husbands learned the advantage of such innocent deception."[66] [Emphasis added.]

What was really supposed to save the children was not the sex itself, but the wife's efforts to remain sexually attractive to her husband. Thus the marriage of sex and parenthood laid the basis for a new "energy economy" for the American family: the wife would work hard to be attractive and thus hold the husband in the home. The husband in turn would strive to make the wife feel more womanly so that she could face her children with a serene, laissez-faire attitude. As a result, the female energy which might have destroyed the children would be safely shunted off into marital coquetry, and everyone, presumably, would be happy. In the nineteen fifties this arrangement was celebrated as "togetherness."

Having sex with Mom was just the first step in Dad's new task of preventing her from messing up the kids. His second important function was to use a firm hand to guide the kids toward their proper sexual identifications—masculinity for the boys and femininity for the girls. His function as a sex partner contributed to this of course, by draining off some of the maternal energies which might have gone into overprotecting—hence emasculating—the sons. But if the family was once again to produce "real men" and "real women," a little more fine tuning was called for. In the nineteen forties and fifties sociologists, psychologists, and child-raising experts became obsessed by the problem of "socializing" children into their appropriate "gender" or "sex role."

Previous generations had not even bothered to distinguish "sex" from "gender," so complacent were they that people's behavior would end up matching their genital organs. "Boys will be boys," went the comfortable old adage, as if masculinity were a genetic potential which would simply unfold in time. (If there was any problem, it was with the girls, whose brains, as we recall, could undo the influence of the uterus and ovaries.) But from the midst of the mid-century masculinity crisis things did not seem so simple. Any lingering hopes of biological predestination were destroyed by anthropologists' reports of cultures where women did "masculine" things, like engaging in trade, and men did "feminine" things like watching the children. While old-fashioned psychoanalysts clung to "maternal instinct" and other innate sex-linked drives, social psychologists, sociologists, and behaviorist psychologists took the less biological position that sex identification was not natural—it had to be learned. You were born with a sex, but not with a gender. In the new terminology coined at the interface of psychology and sociology, gender-appropriate behavior was not something built into your genes or etched on your neural circuitry by hormonal tides—it was a "role," like a part in a high school play.

But scientists agreed that sex-roles were not something that could be learned as easily as the Latin declensions or the names of the presidents. Sex roles obviously sank deeper, becoming part of the self in a permanent way. Certainly, mere knowledge *about* sex roles was not enough, as one expert noted with concern:

> There are many individuals who have knowledge of sex-role norms but prefer to behave in an opposite sex manner. For example, a boy can be aware that he is a male and possess knowledge about sex-typed toys yet prefer to play with girls' toys.[67]

So the experts agreed that sex roles would have to be inculcated. Child-raising advice books began to pay more and more attention to instructing the parents in how to produce the appropriate sex-roles in their children. The first step, obviously, was for the parents to get a tight grip on their own sex-roles, so they could provide "role models" for their children. "Live Your Gender!" exhorts a chapter title in the 1959 child-raising book cited before. "What kind of parents are best for children?" the author demands of his readers. "Manly men and

womanly women. They provide a harmonious home and a sound heredity."[68] Lundberg and Farnham asserted that girls would have little problem so long as the mother was in the home, performing womanly functions:

> . . . it is her mother's grasp on femininity on which the girl chiefly
> depends . . . If the girl has the good fortune to have a mother who
> finds complete satisfaction, without conflict or anxiety, in living out
> her role as wife and mother, it is unlikely that she will experience se-
> rious difficulties.[69]

With boys it was a slightly more difficult problem, since the traditional male sex role involved not being present in the home at all, at
least not enough to be a successful role model. Experts agreed that
fathers would have to be present occasionally to play their part in
sex-role production. More important than the amount of time he
spent at home, though, was the father's strict adherence to the masculine role while he was present: "Imitation of the father enhances
the boy's masculine development only if the father displays masculine
behavior in the presence of his son."[70] [!] He should spend *time*
with his children to be sure, but yet not get so involved in domestic
affairs as to undermine the value of his presence by confusing the
children as to his sex role:

> A crucial factor in the father-present boy's masculine development is
> the degree to which his father exhibits masculine behavior . . . ado-
> lescent boys low in masculinity of interests often came from homes
> in which the father played a traditionally feminine role. The fathers
> of these boys took over such activities as cooking and household
> chores . . .[71]

In practice, the problem of what sort of masculine behavior the father should "display" or "exhibit" (like the plumage of a male
bird) was solved by sports. The world of sports became a sort of all-
male subdrama within the larger family sex-role performance—the
only setting where fathers could pass on the ancient male values of
competitiveness, male solidarity, and physical prowess. Besides,
unlike work, or religious duties, or the tasks of citizenship (all integral aspects of an earlier male experience) sports appealed to the
permissively raised, pleasure-oriented boys. The new masculine ideal
of fatherhood was not the patriarch, but the "pal." "The emergence
of the father as an imp of fun," Jules Henry observed about life in
the fifties, "is a revolution in our time."[72]

Parents had to do more than provide sex-role models, though. They had to actively guide the children toward the proper roles, and in this endeavor the father turned out to be far superior to the mother, despite the relatively small amount of time he put in with the kids. According to Talcott Parsons, "dean" of American sociology and author of most of the seminal sex-role theory, fathers (and men generally) play "instrumental" roles in society, meaning they serve technical, executive and judicial functions. Mothers were "expressive"—emotional, supportive, and nurturing. Being "instrumental," or rationally in control of themselves, fathers were able to act *differently* with their sons and daughters in ways which would condition masculinity and femininity respectively. As one psychologist explained Parsons' theory:

> . . . the mother has a primarily expressive relationship with both boys and girls; in contrast, the father rewards his male and female children differently, encouraging instrumental behavior in his son and expressive behavior in his daughter. The father is supposed to be the principal transmitter of culturally based conceptions of masculinity and femininity.[73]

Thus a competently instrumental father could make up for the harmful effects of even an unfeminine mother.

The sociologist's terminology—"transmitter," "instrumental"—made the imposition of gender sound more like a problem in engineering than an issue in human psychic development. But there was a deeper, emotional level, the sociologically oriented experts conceded, though this too could be understood and manipulated. Talcott Parsons explained that people assume their roles in order to satisfy their deeper "relational needs." For example, a little girl has a relational need to be loved: she learns that if she takes on the feminine sex role she will be loved and that she will not be loved if she takes on the role of a man. The purpose of the family as a small social system, in Parsonian language, was to tailor the girl's social options to her relational needs in such a way that the appropriate role-outcomes occur. In simpler terms, parents could turn on a little heterosexual charm to coax along the kids' sex role development. Spock wrote: "I'm thinking of the little things he [the father] can do, like complimenting her on her dress, or hair-do, or the cookies she's made."[74]

These little cross-sex, cross-age flirtations which were so essential for sex-role socialization could never go on in a well-run nursery school or first grade. Only the family could provide the appropriate Oedipal nest for the hatching of infant gender identities. Parsons and the host of child-raising experts who followed him not only acknowledged the Oedipus and Elektra complexes, they virtually insisted that families should provide them for their children. Boys would not become men unless they fell in love with their mothers and then gradually shifted their allegiance to the father; girls would not become women unless they competed with their mothers for a heterosexual attachment to the father, and so on.

In this melding of psychoanalytic theory with sociological role theory, a funny thing happened to the Oedipus Complex. Freud had conceived it as a psychic crisis so profoundly disturbing that its memory could only be unearthed by psychoanalysis, and then only after breaking through layers of resistance and denial. In Freud's theory, the little boy automatically forms an initial erotic attachment to his mother. But he is rudely awakened from this incestuous fantasy by the powerful figure of the father, who (in the boy's subconscious mind) threatens castration if the boy should attempt to act on his desires. As a result of this traumatic insight, the boy abandons his subversive goal of sleeping with the mother and patterns his behavior on the father, who is, after all, the most powerful figure around. Girls went through a somewhat parallel, but less intense "Elektra Complex," in which they learned that they could not *become* the father, and would have to settle for his love. But now that the Oedipus Complex and its female counterpart, the Elektra Complex, were seen as ordinary stages in "sex-role socialization," the drama lost its tragic quality, not to mention its shock value. Parsons and his followers managed to transform Freud's stormy epic into an orderly series of functional necessities.

Parents would have to gently direct the child through the steps of the Complex. Children who were a bit slow to want to kill the parent of the same sex and marry the parent of the opposite sex would need a little coaching. Baby books rushed to print with the plot and characters of the drama, complete with suggested lines and entrance and exit cues. Here are typical instructions from Dr. Spock:

> We believe that a boy's attraction to his mother in the three-to-six-year old period is vital in establishing an idealistic romantic pattern for his future life as an adult . . . [But in] the ordinary family he is prevented from feeling that he can have her all to himself by three interrelated factors: his awe of his father, his realization that his

mother's romantic love belongs to her husband, her tactful refusal to let the boy become too intensely affectionate toward her in a physical sense.[75]

The reformulation of the Oedipus Complex as a hygienic family routine went hand in hand with the new realities of American manhood. Dad the "organization man" and domestic "imp of fun" was hardly a model of male mastery: (if he had been the experts wouldn't have found it necessary to legislate the Oedipus Complex in the first place). He was still given a starring role in the drama. But he would have been miscast in the part of the vengeful patriarch. In the new social psychological child-raising theory, Dad was simply a skilled domestic sex-role engineer doing his job. This job was to coax the daughter into feminine sex-role identification and rescue the son from the erotic thralldom of the mother—not with the threat of castration (as it went in the original script), but perhaps with two tickets to a Yankees game.

By the mid-fifties child-raising theory had become so dependent on the father that the experts could only contemplate the "father-absent" situation with alarm and confusion. In the paternally deprived home, the full dramatic burden of the family sex-role performance would fall upon the woman. But this did not mean that she should take on a masculine, instrumental role in child-raising—far from it: the absence of a father required her to ham up her feminine sex-role performance even more: ". . . even in a father's absence, an appropriately identified mother will respond to the boy 'as if' he were a male [sic] and will expect him to treat her as a male would treat a female."[76] Dr. Spock even suggested that the very helplessness felt by the single mother confronted with the task of raising sons could be turned to good account, since to admit inadequacy was to be more fully a woman:

. . . I myself think it's a good sign when a mother confesses that boys are more mysterious to her than girls, in some respects; it means that she's very much a woman herself and has a respect for the male sex as somewhat different. . . . When a mother can admit she's only a woman it should foster the chivalrousness of her son, whether he's four or sixteen.[77]

But it was not enough for the single mother to be ultrafeminine to compensate for her unnatural situation. She also had the dramatic responsibility of creating a *mythical* father to preside over the family.

No matter what the real father had been like, this ghostly father figure had to be a strong and positive image of manhood for his sons. Spock felt so strongly about this that he even advocated lying to the children, which was rare for him. For the woman who had a hard time making up a good story about the departed daddy, or perhaps the father who had never lingered long enough for the birth of the baby (this was well before the legalization of abortion), Spock suggested the following complete speech:

> Your daddy and I loved each other very much and we got married. We wanted to have a little boy to take care of and to love. Then you were born and I loved you very much and your daddy loved you very much. But after a while your daddy and I didn't get along so well. We began to have arguments and fights just the way you and Tommy have arguments and fights. . . . Finally your daddy got so upset that he thought it would be better if he went away. He thought he would feel better and I would feel better if there were no more arguments around here. But he felt bad to leave you because he loved you very much. He loved to hold you and play with you. I'm sure he still thinks about you a lot and wishes he could live with you. But I think he is afraid if he came back to see us the arguing and fighting would start all over again.[78]

Spock admitted that: "A mother who has been indignant about the father's lack of affection for the child may think that some of these statements about how he loved the child are a bit thick." But when she considered that the little boy's manhood was at stake, a good mother would be willing to stick to the script.

Communism and the Crisis of Overpermissiveness

The mid-century family drama, as directed by the child-raising expert, was a performance put on solely for the benefit of the child. It was for the child's sake that the mother strove to regress into a formless "expressiveness"—or pulled back so that her love would not turn into a seductive quicksand capable of swallowing the sons. It was for the child's sake, too, that the father made himself available as a backyard example of masculinity—always careful to present it, in the spirit of permissiveness, as a new source of fun. And it was for the child's sake that the parents worked at their respective jobs, relaxed on weekends, and even made love after the kids were in bed. But the reign of the child was to be short-lived. Even beginning in the early fifties the experts were beginning to view the American child with a cold and critical eye. By the end of the sixties the alliance of the expert and the child would end in a climax every bit as violent as the original Oedipal drama: the experts would turn, in a patriarchal fury, against the very children they had nurtured and protected.

To understand what happened we have to draw back from the closed world of the suburban "wreck-room" with its festering entanglements between expert, mother, and child. While Americans had spent the post World War II years in a great national celebration of private life, the political geography of the world was being reorganized on a vast scale. Poland, Czechoslovakia, Hungary, Rumania, and China all "fell" to communism in a few short years after 1945. To American children growing up in the fifties, this development was experienced as a spreading red stain on the *Weekly Reader* maps of the world. What went on there behind the "Iron Curtain" seemed too horrible to contemplate (there were stories of "purges," "liquidations," "forced labor camps," etc.) but with the exception of a few inexplicable home-grown "spies" and "traitors," it was all safely removed from us in the heartland of the Free World.

But as the fifties progressed the threat of communism began to loom larger and larger in the middle-class American psyche. On the one hand, communism as portrayed in the U.S. press represented everything that Americans were against: religion had been abolished; two-dimensional "socialist realism" dominated art; all life centered around production. Worst of all, the sanctity of the family had been violated. Muscular women swept the streets while their children were raised by the state.

In short, *communism* looked like nothing so much as the rationalist nightmare which had always been latent in industrial *capitalism*—a world without love, without poetry, without illusion. In describing the "communist mentality" in his 1958 scare book *Masters of Deceit,* J. Edgar Hoover used the very language which could have described the mentality of a hardheaded capitalist—"systematic, purposive and conscious. . . ." Hoover's book describes rationalist communism not so much as a threat to the state or the capitalist economy, but to "the happiness of the community, the safety of every individual, and the continuance of every home and fireside."[79]

The horror of communism as the rationalist anti-utopia found expression in the developing genre of science-fiction movies. During the McCarthy era, men from Outer Space repeatedly invaded the American screen, and they were remarkably similar to the popular conception of men from beyond the Iron Curtain—cold, purposeful, emotionless humanoids. In movies like *Invaders from Mars* [1953], *The Creeping Unknown* [1955], *Invasion of the Body Snatchers* [1956], and *The Invisible Invaders* [1959], aliens bent on world conquest infiltrated cozy neighborhoods and homey rural towns. (The subtheme was the budding romantic love between the female lead and the brave young scientist. With the aliens licked, the two would be free to set up housekeeping and settle into all-American family life.)

But at the same time, the experts had to acknowledge, communism provided an external standard which could be used to measure American children, parents, and, ultimately, America's most sacred values. While middle-class Americans had been relaxing in the new consumption-centered economy, the Soviets had been "catching up" with American industry, and there was no telling what the Chinese were doing. Waking up to the imperatives of the Cold War, Americans began to see child raising as another "race" like the Arms Race and the Space Race.

Figuratively speaking, the American child first encountered communism face-to-face in Korea. Experts later agreed that the Korean confrontation provided a critical test for the whole American way of life—and we failed dismally. Close to seven thousand American soldiers were captured by the North Korean and Chinese armies. By all accounts, they responded with a high level of demoralization. No one obeyed the American officers; the strong stole from the weak and sick; many simply curled up and died from what psychiatrists later termed "give-up-itis."[80] Most alarming of all to American analysts, a whopping one-seventh of the prisoners seem to have succumbed to "brainwashing"; i.e., they came to agree with their captors' seemingly bizarre claim (this was before Vietnam) that the war was a result of U.S. imperialism and aggressiveness. With this, the first suspicions were raised that something might be amiss in the nursery. American youth was too soft to bear the rigors of war and too confused to tell the difference between communism and "freedom."

To make matters worse, American youth was fast becoming a pressing social problem at home. Throughout the fifties there were repeated explosions of violence from male youth gangs. Most delinquency was concentrated among the urban poor, a group usually ignored by child-raising experts, but it appeared to be a "symptom" which could easily infect even "wholesome normal environments."

Pulitzer Prize-winning journalist Harrison Salisbury suggested a link between juvenile delinquency at home and communism abroad:

> The teenage problem and the Russian problem—there was, I suspected, a somewhat closer connection between the great issues of our times than many imagined. They might, even, be regarded as two faces of one coin. . . .[81]

Concern over Korean War POWs and domestic JDs sent the child-raising experts scurrying back to the drawing boards. Even Dr. Spock asked himself: Are American youth underdisciplined, overcoddled? Spock began to rethink permissiveness and decided that American mothers had been carried away by his original advice—they were guilty of "overpermissiveness":

> Overpermissiveness seems to be *much* commoner in America than in any other country . . . I have talked with dozens of professional people from other countries, visiting the United States for the first time, who have had trouble concealing their surprise and irritation at the behavior of certain children they have seen here.[82]

In contrast, American child-raising professionals were coming back from their first visits to Soviet schools and nurseries with glowing reports about the kids; Dr. Spock quotes the report of Dr. Milton Senn, a professor of pediatrics and child psychiatry at Yale, who "though a scientist not given to easy enthusiasm" was moved to report:

> They are good-humored, easygoing, carefree and friendly . . . They play together in notable harmony, even when there is a remarkable disparity in their ages. They never seem to whine; they cry only when they hurt themselves, and then only briefly. They are warm, spontaneous, polite and generous . . .[83]

The Communists' obvious lead in the child-raising race inspired Dr. Spock and a group of other well-known educators and psychologists to organize a special Cold War parent education project— Parenthood in a Free Nation, which, according to its literature, was funded "by a grant from a foundation that recognized the strategic importance of parents in the preservation of a free world."[84] In its hundreds of study groups, Parenthood in a Free Nation educators emphasized "the importance of setting limits appropriate to the child's stage of development and to the realities of the environmental situation." "Limits" became the new catchword of expert child-raising argot: A child could not do *just anything;* it would have to give up a little power, a little freedom, for the sake of the larger interests of the Free World. Just as there would be "containment" abroad, there would be "limits" at home.

But even "limits" were not enough, the experts realized. Just as Cold War propagandists understood the need for not only missiles and tanks but for "a crusading faith to counter communism"[85] child-raising experts recognized the need for some positive "values" to guide child raising. After all, the Communists had firm values, as J. Edgar Hoover stressed emotionally in *Masters of Deceit:*

> Let us not blind ourselves to the fact that communists do have a "faith." True, it is falsely placed, but still it inspires them to sacrifice, devotion and a perverted idealism.
>
> The late Mother Bloor, the [Communist] Party's woman "hero," often praised Walt Whitman's "The Mystic Trumpeter" as the poem she loved best. It seemed, she said, to prophesy the coming of a "new world":
>
> > War, sorrow, suffering gone—the rank
> > earth purged—nothing but joy left!
> > The ocean fill'd with joy—the atmosphere
> > all joy!
> > Joy! Joy! in freedom, worship, love!
> > joy in the ecstasy of life!
> > Enough merely to be! enough to breathe!
> > Joy! Joy! all over joy!

Hoover was apparently as taken with this poem as Mother Bloor was. He comments with pique:

> She is trying to identify communism with the dream of a world of joy. She is exploiting Walt Whitman. Yet her feeling shows the lure of communist "faith." If communists can be so inspired from error, falsehood, and hate, just think what we could do with truth, justice, and love! I thrill to think of the even greater wonders America could fashion from its rich, glorious, and deep tradition. All we need is faith, *real faith.*[86]

Spock and other child-raising experts had to agree that the Russians were inspired by their values and that this no doubt gave them their advantage in child raising:

> . . . the great majority of the Russian people have a very strong sense of common purpose. They are convinced that they are creating a nobler political and economic system than has ever existed be-

fore. . . . They are proud to be playing their individual roles in such a mighty effort.[87]

But what values did we have? There had been nothing in the self-absorbed, libidinal approach to child raising to suggest that children had to grow up at all, much less face a world inhabited by hordes of Communist "fanatics."

In fact there was a widespread suspicion that Americans had no values at all. Intellectuals were suffering through a mass case of "alienation." Housewives were showing the first signs of the boredom which would later be considered their characteristic occupational disease. Teen-agers were beginning to assume their now-familiar mien of sullen anomie. The heroes of the time, such heroes as there were, were distinguished by their very lack of values: James Dean of *Rebel Without a Cause* and Marlon Brando of *The Wild One*—aimless, inarticulate loners.

Throughout the fifties, child-raising experts joined forces with educators and government officials to unearth some truly American values for mothers to inculcate and children to absorb. The results, though, were disappointing. In 1951 the National Education Association and the American Association of School Administrators concluded a study with the finding that "the basic moral and spiritual value in American life" was "the supreme importance of the individual personality."[88] Similarly, a 1960 Presidential Commission on Goals for Americans announced that "the paramount goal of the United States . . . is to guard the rights of the individual, and to enlarge his opportunity."[89]

Now, "individualism" can be a reason for fighting courageously, but it can also be the rationale for defecting to the enemy, betraying a friend, or terrorizing old people on the streets. Besides, individualism is hardly a unifying value. Dr. Spock observed sadly that the American emphasis on individual success "does not bind us together, but puts us in competition with one another." It wasn't that American ideals were "unworthy," he wrote, "it is only that they do not serve to unite and inspire us." In the age of POW turncoats and juvenile delinquents, the child-raising experts uneasily faced the fact that America did not have any transcendent, unifying "values": nor could it, because the imposition of any other overarching value would undercut the first value, "individualism," and thus would be a step toward totalitarianism.

On October 4, 1957, something happened to take the experts' minds off the American dilemma about "values" and to give them a concrete challenge to think about. The Soviets launched Sputnik, the world's first orbital satellite, and it hit like a spitball in the eyes of American child-raising experts, educators, and Cold War propagandists. American psychologists who had visited the Soviet Union had been willing to concede that Communist children were co-operative and good-tempered to a degree that was almost eerie compared to the Dennis-the-Menace personality deemed acceptable in American kids. But the very niceness of the Soviet children was presumed by the experts to be achieved by some process of indoctrination. They must be basically robots—utterly lacking in "individuality." Or so it seemed until Sputnik raised the possibility that at least some of them were *more* creatively daring and imaginative than their American counterparts.

Sputnik created an "almost instantaneous national mood of panic and alarm."[90] Conservative public opinion—and at this time, any opinions which were not conservative were not public—turned against American kids with vicious impatience. A public service advertisement printed in *Newsweek* and *Reader's Digest* a few months after Sputnik's launching warned (with a grammatical recklessness that only seems to reinforce the point):

> Johnny had *better* learn to read. It no longer matters whether he wants to or would like to or may learn to read—and read well—or we may wind up in a world where no English is written any more . . . We Americans don't want to move the world. But we don't want anyone else to, either. So Johnny had *better* learn to read. Because you can bet Ivan is spending a lot of time on his books.[91]

A best-seller of 1955, *Why Johnny Can't Read* was soon followed ominously by *Why Ivan Can Read*. "Ivan," who a few years ago had been only an insignificant speck on the red part of the map, seemed to have moved right into the classroom, where he sat apple-cheeked and alert, as conversant with logs and vectors as "Johnny" was with batting averages and *TV Guide*. With Ivan around, American children ceased to be regarded as a national hobby and became a national military resource—a status memorialized in the National *Defense* Education Act of 1958.

Faced with the Soviet military threat, experts discovered that the toddler—who had been indulged in every way in the last decades of libidinal luxury—was in fact, a malingerer. Leading educator Dr. George Shuster snapped:

> That learning to read at 3 can be for some children as exciting as stringing beads or jumping was news to a certain school of pedagogy until experiment began to prove it was truth. We have, in short, been wasting a lot of the nation's time.[92]

Experts discovered overnight that not only toddlers but babies of ten months could learn to read. The Sputnik scare, combined with rising competition for entry to colleges, set off a kind of hysteria among upwardly mobile parents. The permissiveness that still hung over the physical side of child raising stood in sharp contrast to the new intellectual pushiness of the fifties and early sixties: the psychologically ideal three-year-old of 1960 might soil its diapers, drink from a bottle and cling to a tiny rag-fetish, but it could recite the alphabet and was showing the first signs of aptitude for the new math.

The new standards for juvenile achievement gave the image of "Mom" a much-needed boost in status. Experts now stressed that the infant I.Q. needed constant stimulation to nurture its growth—without stimulation even infants could slip into boredom, apathy, and, ultimately, retardation. Obviously the American mother would have to be resurrected from the primeval muck of instinct laid down by past generations of psychoanalysts. In a merciful lapse of memory, the experts forgot the iron laws governing sex-role socialization, and decreed that Mother could now play an instrumental role in child raising: it was her job to keep the child's sensory apparatus employed full-time. Gone were the days when all a mother had to do was provide a womblike environment, a sort of constant-temperature bath gently rocking the baby in ambient love. Mothers who responded to the Cold War alert were supposed to keep the environment challenging, noisy, colorful, and ever-changing. Mobiles should be strung above the baby's crib; even patterned sheets could help tickle an infant nerve cell into life. For the toddler, the home should be stocked with toys such as that advertised as

> . . . one of the hundreds of Creative Playthings that psychologists say can help add 20 points to your child's I.Q. rating before the first day of school. What a true Christmas blessing to give your child.[93]

For the older child, there should be a smorgasbord of extracurricular lessons and activities, gentle pressure at homework time, and a chemistry set for Christmas.

Experts suddenly found themselves prizing some of the very characteristics they had denounced in the domineering mom: properly channeled into I.Q. production, even the "penis envy" of the frustrated middle-class housewife could turn out to be an asset in the Space Race. Meanwhile the black mother, who had seemed to be a "natural" to Gesell in the days of libidinal mothering, fell out of favor: now it appeared to the experts that the black mother did not provide her children with enough of the right kind of "stimulation." According to the logic behind Project Headstart (a federally sponsored day care program), poor black children required a year or more of remedial stimulation to make up for the "cultural deprivation" they suffered at home.

But by this time we have moved well into the sixties, the decade in which the expert and the child will have their final falling out. The great concern of the fifties and early sixties had been whether American kids would have what it takes to face the Enemy. Korea revealed that American youth was soft; Sputnik showed it was stupid. At the beginning of Kennedy's New Frontier, the director of the newly formed Peace Corps program confessed that many public figures, here and abroad, had expressed doubts that American youth had the physical stamina or moral dedication to carry out their Peace Corps missions.[94] President Kennedy revealed that five out of seven men called for army service had to be rejected as physically or mentally defective.[95] Clearly American youth was unfit to face the Enemy. Then the movements of the sixties came along and revealed that youth *was* the enemy.

Anyone who—like most of our child-raising experts—followed "the movement" on TV or from a safe distance in an academic office, would not have seen the years of community organizing, the endless discussions, the door-to-door campaigns, the thousands of "alternative" projects which built up a mass radical movement in this country. Instead they would have seen what looked like a headlong rush to violent insurrection: the black movement seemed to leap from Civil Rights (which was respectable enough in the North), to mass rioting, to the disciplined and openly pro-Communist activities of the Black Panthers. The antiwar movement, which began with staid teach-ins, came to a media climax in the late sixties with bombings, bank burnings, and building takeovers. Then there was the GI movement, which made the Korean War turncoats look almost patriotic by comparison. U.S. soldiers refused to fight, fragged their officers, and proudly raised the enemy flag at demonstrations. It seemed like a "black revolution," a "student revolution," and a "sexual revolution" all at once. "We are the people our parents warned us against," proclaimed the demonstrators. In the nervous middle-aged and middle-class imagination, the black nationalist, the antiwar activist, the hippie, the homosexual, and the subteen groupie, all merged into a composite figure threatening political and moral chaos.

If there was one thing that all the miscellaneous strands of the movement did have in common it was *youth*. For anyone who couldn't or didn't want to understand the issues that motivated the movement there was the convenient explanation of the "generation gap." And it seemed to make sense. Middle-aged black leader Bayard Rustin had no more in common with Panther leader Huey Newton than, say, veteran white liberal Michael Harrington had with SDS leader Mark Rudd. What's more, youth was beginning to identify itself *as a class,* with its own interests, its own culture, and a unique ability to change the world.

The age dimension allowed the experts to psychologize away what was actually a serious political uprising. Calling the problem a "generation gap" made it sound as though the whole thing was a family dispute, an unexpected Oedipal flare-up. Freudians found that when young people demonstrated they were really committing "symbolic patricide" (father murder), and that they couldn't be expected to control themselves because their "driving energy came from unconscious sources."[96] But the specific historical explanation—why the movement happened *when* it did—as any street-corner psychologist could tell you, was that American child raising had been too permissive for the last two decades. (Actually, "the movement" drew about as many people from authoritarian backgrounds as from permissive backgrounds.) Campaigning in 1968, Spiro Agnew repeatedly lashed out against the "permissiveness" which he found in the homes, in the schools, and in the Democratic administration. The activists, he charged, were "spoiled brats who never had a good spanking."[97] In Spokane, when a young man interrupted Agnew with shouts of "Warmonger!" Agnew intoned paternally (as police beat the heckler to the ground), "It is really tragic that somewhere somebody in that young man's life has failed him."[98]

The finger of blame inevitably turned to the stately, white-haired figure of Dr. Benjamin Spock, the original giver of pediatric "permission" to the world's children. The New York *Times* summarized the criticism of Spock: He ". . . turned out a generation of infants who developed into demanding little tyrants. And now the world is reaping a whirlwind, they say. The small monsters have grown up to be unkempt, irresponsible, destructive, anarchical, drug-oriented, hedonistic non-members of society."[99] Critics called the youthful rebels the "Spock-marked generation," as if they had been inflicted in infancy with a disfiguring disease. And when Columbia students seized the campus's main buildings to protest the university's complicity in the war and its racist relation to the Harlem community, university vice-president Dr. David Truman blamed the whole thing on the elderly physician.[100]

Dr. Spock's own behavior in the sixties only confirmed the conservatives' worst suspicions about the link between permissiveness and subversion. He had always been a humanist (though not, as we know, a feminist), and we have seen the anguish he experienced in the fifties over America's lack of "values." In the early sixties he had campaigned for disarmament. The Vietnam War—with its scorched villages, napalmed children, and pregnant women impaled on bayonets—was too much for Dr. Spock. With an agility deemed unusual in anyone over thirty, much less sixty, he leaped the generation gap and joined the rebels. When the New York *Times* asked him if it was true that his influence had helped create the "youth rebellion," he responded with humility: "I would be proud if the idealism and militancy of youth today were caused by my book. I would be delighted. But I think the influence in that way is very small."[101] Young activists welcomed Dr. Spock to their ranks. He had been their champion in infancy; he was one of their heroes now. His name, a comforting household word for more than twenty years, now appeared on demonstrators' posters as SP☮CK

Very few prominent child-raising experts followed Dr. Spock into active resistance to the war. There was an initial reaction of confusion and panic: the experts began to bicker in public over what had gone wrong. One exonerated parents, pointing to China's rebellious Red Guards who, being Communists, could not have been raised permissively.[102] Another suggested that parental authoritarianism could be as much a problem as permissiveness.[103] Yet another got the experts off the hook by proposing that mothers had not been reading child-raising advice books carefully all these years; they had just picked out what they wanted to hear.[104] The experts were breaking rank. It became almost a literary convention to preface child-raising advice books with a disclaimer of all previous "expert" theories.

By the end of the sixties the experts' mood hardened into outright hostility to kids. Bruno Bettelheim, an elder statesman of the child psychiatry establishment, sounded the new note of punitiveness. His long work with disturbed children, his studies of collective child raising in Israel, his many academic and lay publications, gave him a stature in the academic community far greater than that of popularizers like Spock. He had always been a political liberal, but he had no sympathy for the new activists. Some student protestors, he told a congressional subcommittee on education, "had not matured emotionally beyond the temper tantrum level."[105] Because they had never experienced authoritarian guidance in their own homes, they now looked to Ho Chi Minh and Mao Tse-Tung as "strong fathers." In their fanaticism, he told Congress, they bore a sinister resemblance to the Hitler Youth. (He did concede, however, that the fact that Nazi youth were racist while American youth were fighting racism, might be "an important difference.") To bring youth back into line, parents would have to take on the responsibility of implanting "inner controls" at an early age. By this he did not mean just an ordinary sense of right and wrong. The violent "crack-up" of modern youth had discredited liberal approaches to child raising. In April 1969, one year before the shootings of students at Kent State and Jackson State, Bettelheim argued that little children would have to be taught to *fear*.[106]

The antichild mood of the late sixties quickly found its way into the child-raising advice literature. Where there had once been some tentative talk about "limits," there was now a frank demand for law and order. Titles like *Power to the Parents!* [1972], *Raising a Responsible Child* [1971], and *Dare to Discipline* [1972] began to crowd the fading copies of Spock and Ribble on suburban library shelves. Commonly they began with a little synopsis of the failure of permissiveness, with reference, in varying degrees of explicitness, to the resultant dope addicts, homosexuals, and revolutionaries. Then the reader is reassured that there is a technique, set forth in this book, by which children can be managed without resort to brute force. For example, the inside cover of *You Can Raise Decent Children* tells us:

> Some leaders still flatter "the Kids" of the Spock-marked generation, but most parents are worried sick. Is it possible to raise children who won't turn into hippies, drug freaks, radicals or dropouts? Two eminent doctors say yes, and show us how. They spell it out, in words any parent can understand, the importance of discipline; how to discipline firmly and with love; why permissiveness spawns violence; the foundations of masculinity and femininity; and how parents can reinforce them in these days of Women's Liberation and open homosexuality. . . .[107]

It is almost as if we had come full circle back to the days of "scientific motherhood," when experts joined mothers to manufacture upright citizens out of unruly infants. But things never quite repeat themselves. Five decades of historical twists and turns—in the political atmosphere, the economy, and in the content of science—had warped the old mother-child-expert triangle beyond all recognition. For one thing the experts had lost status. They had quarreled too often, and they had changed their minds too often in the memory of living women. First there was industrial-style behaviorism, then permissiveness, and finally the reaction against it in the fifties and sixties. "Science," applied to child raising, began to look like a chameleon which could match any national mood or corporate need.

The other thing that had changed was the status of the child. Remember that this began as the Century of the Child: The Child was the hope of the future, the mechanism of evolutionary progress, the symbol of America, the goal and the purpose of all women's lives. But the "failure" of kids in the Korean War, followed by their "betrayal" in the Vietnamese War, raised the disturbing possibility that perhaps, after so many decades of official child-centrism—children could not really be trusted with the future. Certainly, after the long parade of youthful turncoats, radicals, homosexuals, juvenile delinquents, etc., through the establishment media, it was getting harder to argue that a woman could have no more exalted destiny than the raising of children.

The cultural image of children changed swiftly after the sixties, as the endearing kid stars of the forties and fifties—Margaret O'Brien, Ricky Nelson, Beaver Cleaver, the Mouseketeers—gave way to child-figures who were either possessed by the devil, employed by the devil, or fathered by the devil. *Rosemary's Baby* [1970] depicts a female dilemma which would have been unthinkable twenty years earlier—to have wanted a baby, like any normal young wife, and find yourself carrying a fetal Satan. A recent film carries the horror of children one step further: "There's only one thing wrong with the Davis baby," say the ads of this precociously homicidal infant, *"it's alive!"* And this is a criticism which, one begins to suspect, will be leveled any day now at millions of real-life children. The Century of the Child was over by 1970, thirty years ahead of time.

The Fall of the Experts

EIGHT

From Masochistic Motherhood to the Sexual Marketplace

While the experts were worrying that children had been overfed with permissiveness, no one noticed that one member of the family—Mom —had never even had a taste of it. Permissiveness was for the kids, and secondarily for Dad. The kids were free from adult rules and schedules, and (at least in the mass media's ideal family) Dad was free to relax—have a few beers, pitch a few balls and perhaps contemplate the need for a new lawn mower. But the lotus scent of permissiveness which wafted through the nursery and the den was never meant to penetrate to the kitchen. *Someone* had to pick up the toys when the kids didn't feel like it and do the dishes while Dad watched TV. Not for her the cultural imperative to relax, enjoy, indulge. Even as a consumer she worked in other people's interests, translating the family's demands into the appropriate snack foods, home furnishings, soft drinks. By some curious asymmetry in the permissive ideology, everyone else in the family lived for themselves, and she lived for *them*.

The experts clung for as long as they could to the romantic ideal of femininity. But gradually the tension between the culture of self-gratification, on the one hand, and the experts' ideal of maternal self-sacrifice, on the other, became unbearable. To bridge the contradiction, psychomedical theory would become ever more tortured and bizarre—until once again femininity could only be explained as a kind of disease—"masochism." By the sixties the experts' theories would become hopelessly out of touch with women's own aspirations. Women would be ready for a completely new self-image, and even the advertisers and market researchers who had profited so much from the old image would help to promote the new one. The "new woman" of the sixties and seventies contradicted more than a century of scientific romanticism. This new woman, when she came, would be such a radical break from the old romantic ideal that she would require her own experts, her own "lifestyle": even the idea of "life-styles" with its promise of freedom and gratification, was born with her.

Mid-century Masochism

Mid-century psychoanalytic theory repeatedly insisted on the need for female self-denial. The path to healthy adult femininity, according to the experts, was paved with sacrifice. In her authoritative two-volume study of women, psychoanalyst Helene Deutsch described all the things that a woman had to *give up* in order to be feminine. First she had to give up all adolescent ambitions and submit to the necessity of motherhood—the feminine "reality principle." True motherliness, according to Deutsch, "is achieved only when all masculine wishes have been given up or sublimated into other goals. If 'the old factor of lack of a penis has not yet forfeited its power,' complete motherliness remains still to be achieved."[1]

A woman could renounce her "masculine" ambitions by transferring them to the child (if the child was a son). Deutsch quotes with approval these words of Freud's: "the mother can transfer to the son the ambition that she was compelled to repress in herself. She expects him to gratify everything that has remained in her of her own masculinity complex."[2] But no sooner has the mother reconciled herself to her diminished ego expectations by projecting them onto her child than she must give up any hope that the child will actually fulfill her ambitions: "A mother must not strive to achieve any other goals through her child than those of its existence," Deutsch warns. At last she makes the final renunciation: she gracefully gives up the child itself. "Woman's two great tasks are to shape her unity with the child in a harmonious manner and later to dissolve it harmoniously."

Deutsch described all this as "the tragic destiny of motherhood" and proposed this solace: "Probably the path traced by nature is the most successful: having many children is the best protection against the tragic loss."*[3]

It was hard to reconcile the self-denying "essence" of woman's nature with the cultural atmosphere created by a consumption-centered economy. Here was a society which claimed to value individualism above all and which exhorted everyone to devote themselves to the search for personal gratification. Yet one half the population seemed to be committed, by their very anatomy, to a life of renunciation and self-denial. The obvious objective sorts of explanations—that most women were economically dependent on their husbands, that abortions and day care were virtually unavailable—had no place in the psychoanalytic world-view. The only logical way to reconcile woman's commitment to suffering with the over-all cultural commitment to pleasure was to assert that, for women, suffering *was* pleasurable. The psychoanalytic construction of the female personality found mounting cultural acceptance from the thirties on, and by the forties and fifties—the height of the permissive era—the Freudian faith in female masochism stood almost undisputed.

For women, even sex was to be an exercise in happy self-denial. Female sexual pleasure had become respectable enough, by this time, for therapists to prescribe it in cases of overprotection or other forms of maternal maladjustment. But a woman's journey to mature female sexuality, like the way to "true motherliness," was a mournful pilgrimage. First—as she outgrew her girlhood—a woman had to renounce the pleasures of the clitoris and attempt to transfer all sexual feeling to the vagina. In Freudian theory the clitoris was a tiny—and laughably inadequate—version of the penis. To cling to the clitoris was only to invite humiliation by comparison to the large and masterful male organ.† When a woman accomplished the task of aban-

* However, Deutsch herself had only one child. In a 1973 interview she recalled how he was raised mostly by a nurse named Paula. "Busy with her work, his mother recalls, 'I had to slip a $5 note under her door to see my son.' Dr. Deutsch doesn't approve of this sort of substitute mothering and suffered guilt over it, but she says the experience doesn't seem to have harmed her son."[4]

† For example, psychoanalyst Marie Bonaparte described the clitoris as "a phallus, atrophied in comparison with the male penis. . . ." This "rudimentary" organ is "never destined to achieve, even in its owner's imagination, the degree of activity to which the penis can lay claim, for in this respect the male organ is far better endowed by nature." Yet in the same paragraph Bonaparte reveals

doning the clitoris, she symbolically set aside all masculine strivings (penis envy) and accepted a life of passivity. The "rich reward" for all this was supposed to be the pleasure of heterosexual vaginal sex, which the penis-envying, clitoris-identified woman could never achieve. (Lundberg and Farnham said of the penis-envying bed partner, "The woman's unconscious wish to herself to possess the organ upon which she must depend militates greatly against her ability to accept its vast power to satisfy her when proffered to her in love."[5]) But in psychoanalytic theory vaginal sexuality actually provided a fresh experience of powerlessness and debasement; Helene Deutsch described it as an experience of "being masochistically subjugated by the penis." Psychoanalyst Marie Bonaparte took the theory a step further, commenting that woman's masochism, "combining with her passivity in coitus, impels her to welcome and to value some measure of brutality on the man's part." Bonaparte seems to chuckle reassuringly as she adds, "actually, normal vaginal coitus does not hurt a woman; quite the contrary."[7]

Needless to say, masochistic sex was intimately linked to masochistic maternity.

> The wish for maternity . . . is a factor so favorable to vaginalization [the transfer of sexual feelings to the vagina] that . . . highly domestic women are often best adapted to their erotic function . . . Psychical inacceptance of the maternal function and defective maternal instinct [are] . . . frequently related to the normal failure in women to establish the erotic function.[8]

Carrying the theory of female masochism to an extreme, Helene Deutsch argued that the relationship between orgasm and labor was so great that the two experiences were really "one process," and one might speak of orgasm as a "missed labor."[9]

The idea that women were masochistic seemed to solve everything. Woman's lot, from a masculinist point of view, consisted of menial labor and sexual humiliation. But as a masochist, these were precisely the things that she liked and needed. (The explanation of "masochism" is so convenient and totalistic that we can only wonder why the psychomedical experts didn't think to extend it to other groups, like the poor and racial minorities.) But at the same time, the idea of female masochism signaled the mounting bankruptcy of sexual roman-

---

that "the functional maladjustment of women of the clitoridal type" is that the clitoris is "too highly charged with active impulses."[6]

ticist theory. Once, women had been lured into domesticity with promises of intellectual challenge, activity, and power over the household and children. No one had argued, in the early-twentieth-century mothers' movement or domestic science movement, that women had to *resign* themselves to motherhood, that they had to give up anything. Energy, intelligence, and ambition were precisely the character traits the scientific mother needed to run her household and raise her children. To say now, at mid-century, that it was not energy, but passivity, that held a woman to her home, not ambition, but resignation, not enjoyment, but pain—was to say that from a masculinist point of view the female role was unthinkable, and that those who fit into it were in some sense insane. The theory of female masochism stood as an admission from the psychomedical experts that the feminine ideal they had helped construct was not only difficult to achieve, but probably impossible.

If the task of becoming a woman was so arduous, it followed that "real women"—mature, vaginal women—were the exceptions. The psychomedical experts, themselves in the grip of the mid-century crisis of masculinity, became convinced that America was suffering from an epidemic of unwomanliness. With the zeal of medieval witch hunters searching out the marks of demonic possession, doctors and therapists organized to flush out the millions of women who must be "rejecting their femininity" in one way or another.

Psychotherapists found "rejection of femininity" in every frustrated or unhappy patient. Under any circumstances woman must "travel a twisted road in order to reach her 'true nature' " wrote Dr. Hendrik Ruitenbeek in the introduction to his anthology, *Psychoanalysis and Female Sexuality*, but under modern social conditions the "female movement to passivity has been made more difficult." There were too many women, he explained, who "want to do or to get something for themselves rather than merely to reflect the achievement of their husbands." These "clitoridal women," even when they avoid professional training, marry early, and have large families, show their resistance to their lot in their inability to have vaginal orgasms:

> In a world where male activity sets the standards of worth—and analysts point out that both physiologically and psychologically, male sexual performance is an achievement—female experience in sex as in other aspects of life takes on the character of a peculiarly ambiguous struggle against male domination.[10]

It was clear then, that all the women who complained of sexual frigidity were really "in a state of rebellion against the passivity which nature and society impose upon them." But even the apparently feminine woman might be cleverly "overcompensating" for her inner masculine strivings. Analyst Joan Riviere alerted her fellow therapists to "the female who dons womanliness as a mask to conceal her anxiety and to ward off the retribution she fears from the men whose prerogative she wishes to usurp."[11] Ruitenbeek concluded that the possibility that modern women could ever achieve "normal" vaginal sexuality was so remote that most women should reconcile themselves to being satisfied with simpler pleasures, such as "awareness that she is desireable, ability to excite a man sexually, child-bearing, and the aim-deflected sexual pleasures of affection and tenderness."[12]

Gynecology as Psychotherapy

In the nineteen fifties, gynecologists joined the psychiatrists in the search for "rejection of femininity" and, sure enough, began to find it in every patient. The gynecologists' claim to the female psyche as a terrain for intervention and investigation had been challenged early in the century by Freud himself. Then, in the twenties, the discovery of hormones had given the doctors a new license to extend their practice into female psychology. To the gynecologists, hormones provided the long-suspected material link between the brain and the uterus: female reproductive functions are in part regulated by the pituitary gland, which is in turn subject to the activity of the hypothalamus in the brain (the apparent locus of many basic emotions and drives). The link between the hypothalamus and the uterus paved the way for a new interdisciplinary approach to women. Obviously the psychiatrist, whose professional turf included the hypothalamus, had a great deal to say about the lower regions claimed by the gynecologists. Conversely, the gynecologist, through his access to the uterus, was in a position to detect malfunctions in the psychiatrist's traditional realm.

The doctors accepted their new areas of responsibility with enthusiasm, almost abandoning the female reproductive organs in their haste to pass judgments on the female psyche. An article in the professional journal *Obstetrics and Gynecology* stated:

As evidence has accumulated linking pelvic function and psychological factors, the obstetrician-gynecologist has tended to undertake a broader role in the management of the total patient . . . He has also found it appropriate to relate the presenting pelvic symptoms to underlying emotional stress rather than to organic disease.[13]

Thus millions of women who would never have sought help from a psychotherapist and perhaps were unaware of any emotional stress, were, without knowing it, being analyzed by their gynecologists. The pelvic examination itself could be a valuable aid in diagnosis of the patient's mental problems. In the doctor's imagination, the pelvic exam simulated heterosexual intercourse. Thus the examination could be used to evaluate a woman's sexual adjustment. All the doctor had to do was to redirect his attention from the patient's cervix, uterus, etc. to her *reactions* to the exam:

> The overly seductive patient may have underlying hysterical symptoms, and vaginismus and extreme anxiety during the pelvic examination may be linked with frigidity—and occasionally with failure to consummate a marriage.[14]

Psychoanalysts like Therese Benedek (whom we quoted in the last chapter on the subject of maternal regression) encouraged gynecologists to join the hunt for "rejection of femininity":

> . . . women incorporating the value-system of a modern society may develop personalities with rigid ego-defenses against their biological needs. The conflicts which arise from this can be observed clinically not only in the office of the psychiatrist, but also in the office of the gynecologist and even of the endocrinologist.[15]

Echoing Benedek, gynecologists Sturgis and Menzer-Benaron wrote in the introduction to their 1962 monograph, *The Gynecological Patient: A Psycho-Endocrine Study:*

> We feel this discipline [gynecology] should embrace those disturbances in function or structure of any part of the female organism that influence or are affected by the performance of the reproductive system. We are impressed in particular with the dictum that much of the physical and mental ill health of the individual woman can be properly understood only in the light of her conscious or unconscious acceptance of her feminine role.[16]

Once this "dictum" (note: not "fact," "hypothesis," or "theory," but *"dictum"*) was accepted, there seemed to be few, if any, gynecological complaints which were not actually symptoms of the rejection of femininity. Among the conditions which gynecologists in the fifties and sixties began to view as psychogenic, or caused in one way or another by "incomplete feminization," were: dysmenorrhea, excessive pain in labor, menstrual irregularity, pelvic pain, infertility, a tendency to miscarry or to deliver prematurely, excessive nausea in pregnancy, toxemia of pregnancy, and complications of labor.[17] Women everywhere seemed to be "battling their femininity," and the gynecologist must have felt at times overwhelmed by the stream of casualties that poured into his office. In the beginning of a section on gender, a 1959 child-raising advice book offers this sketch of the gynecologists' task:

> At the end of a hard working day, a woman gynecologist sat in her office smoking a cigarette and reflecting on the many patients she has seen during office hours. Some had mysterious functional disorders for which she could find no physical cause. Others had come just for a pre- or post-childbirth check-up and had asserted with smiling emphasis that they felt fine.
>
> As the doctor reviewed the two types of patients in her mind, an idea dawned on her with the shock of a great realization. The women with the "mysterious" functional disorders had one thing in common: they regretted being women. They thought men had the best of it. It was their discontent with their gender that had caused these functional disorders. The other women, the happy, healthy ones, were glad to be women, diaper-dirty babies and tobacco-smelling husbands and all. Unfortunately, hardly half of modern womankind can be said to belong to this truly feminine category.‡[18]

Pregnancy offered the doctors a chance for long-term surveillance of women during a critical period of their feminine development. During pregnancy, psychoanalysts gravely observed, a woman is confronted with undeniable "proof" that she is a woman. Her reaction might understandably be revulsion and horror. A chapter by Dr. Stuart Asch in a 1965 textbook of obstetrics tells us that pregnancy

---

‡ It is striking that the author chose a female gynecologist for this fictional anecdote. Not more than 5 per cent of gynecologists were women at this time, and one could hardly imagine a less "truly feminine" woman than a woman physician. In fact, the author has this doctor smoking a cigarette, while we are told that her feminine patients have made a masochistic adjustment to their husbands' smoking. Apparently there was room for a few masculinized, scientific women, so long as they made their careers out of exposing the unfemininity of other women—as did Marynia Farnham, Helene Deutsch, and Therese Benedek in real life.

. . . will shake the most mentally healthy person. Thus one finds
that *some* manifestation of anxiety is *always* present during pregnancy. In the most serious reactions this can take the form of any
possible psychiatric picture, including phobias, depressions, and psy-
choses.

It was only logical for pregnant women to resent their condition, this
author continues, since pregnancy "gives us [sic] pain" and "makes
us ugly."[19]

Thus *all* pregnant women must be regarded as temporarily neurotic and in need of the gynecologist's covert psychotherapy. Particularly "dangerous," according to a chapter by Marcel Heiman in
the same text, were

. . . those patients who consider themselves more "socially aware."
They are not necessarily more mature but are trying, by their active
interest in everything "avant garde," socially as well as medically, to
persuade themselves and others that they are . . . This is the patient
who is interested in such methods as "natural childbirth," hypnosis,
or using childbirth as an "experience."[20]

In fact, the "socially aware," assertive patient who was interested in
participating in her own childbirth experience was probably more infantile and neurotic than the average patient. Heiman warned that
"the childlike suggestibility of the pregnant woman has been wittingly
and unwittingly used and/or exploited by some of the proponents of
'natural childbirth' methods,"[21] implying that the pro-natural childbirth patient was really a dupe. Dr. Asch offers this "note of caution"
with reference to "the occasional woman who is fanatic in her zeal
for 'natural childbirth' ":

The intensity of her demands and her uncompromising attitude on
the subject are danger signals, frequently indicating severe psychopathology . . . A patient of this sort is *not* a candidate for natural
childbirth and requires close and constant psychiatric support.[22]

For all women, prenatal care was to be regarded as an opportunity
for psychiatric care, in which the patient could gradually be brought
to accept her femininity. A 1969 case study reported in the professional nursing journal *Nursing Forum* showed what success could be
achieved by blending subtle counseling with the physical side of prenatal care. "Judy," a twenty-year-old prenatal patient and object of
intensive counseling by the nurse-author of this article, was one of

those unfortunate failures of family sex-role socialization. Her father could hardly be faulted. He had been so conscientious about his instrumental role as sex-role imparter, that, when Judy won an athletic prize in sixth grade, he was "horrified" and presented her with a pair of ruffled panties with a note urging her to work harder at being a girl. Despite all this, Judy's nurse-therapist noted, "she appeared unable to assume the culturally accepted passive, yet creative, role of housewife and homemaker."[23] She wore "blue jeans with her husband's sweaters," and dominated her husband, who, the nurse observed, "spoke in a high-pitched voice." (Another failure of sex-role socialization?) But, with prolonged help from the nurse-therapist, who evidently considers herself a role-model of successful femininity, Judy comes to accept her own maternal destiny and develops a more appropriate, submissive attitude toward her husband.

Once gynecologists had accepted responsibility for the mental health of their patients, it was only a short step to taking responsibility for the social well-being of the entire nation. Since gynecological problems were really psychological problems and psychological problems inevitably manifested themselves as social problems, the gynecologist was not really treating vaginitis or menstrual discomfort or whatever—he was really treating the "family life of our country." In the conclusion to their monograph on *The Gynecological Patient*, Sturgis and Menzer-Benaron cited as an "index of the gynecological health of our country's women" the "tally of sexual unhappiness, broken homes, illegitimacy, septic abortions and sterility," later adding sexual deviancy and delinquency. After making a quick and alarming estimate of the numbers of divorces, abortions, illegitimate births, etc., plus the "10 million married couples in our country battling with the frustrations of infertility" the authors blame the whole mess on the "state of ill health in the reproductive functioning of the women of our nation."[24]

Once, they argue, the general practitioner had been "the friend, guardian and teacher" of his clientele.

> With the priest or pastor, he stood as a bulwark against illegitimacy, abortions and divorce . . . Today, in the medical profession, obstetricians and gynecologists are perhaps best able to fill this position. . . .

Gynecologists should establish themselves as their patients' counselors as early as possible, for example at the premarital visit, when "a girl . . . will undergo a pelvic examination without resentment."[25] Then, in the difficult task of achieving mature femininity, a woman would need the constant supervision of her doctor, helping her to accept her marriage and her lot as a mother. Without this guidance, the entire social fabric of the nation might come unraveled. Sturgis and Menzer-Benaron lamented that "it is unlikely that there ever will be sufficient numbers of trained workers" to guide each woman and hence each family to a successful adjustment.

The Revolt of the Masochistic Mom

The medical perception that American women were massively rejecting their femininity helped to soothe masculine insecurity, and, of course, suggested endless possibilities for professional self-advancement. But it also contained a hard kernel of truth. Women simply would not flog themselves to live up to the masochistic ideal: they *were* rejecting their "femininity." By the early sixties women would be reaching for a new feminine ideal—one which was so scornfully different from all previous psychomedical inventions—invalids, scientific housekeepers, libidinal mothers, etc. that the old scientific authorities would never quite recover from the shock.

Even the ideology of female masochism had not been able to muffle the signs of real discontent among American housewives. In September 1960, *Redbook* ran an article called "Why Young Mothers Feel Trapped" (which, given its cautious tone, might have been titled "Why Young Mothers Sometimes Feel Conflicted"). Readers had been invited to send written responses to the article, drawn from their own experience. The editors expected to receive a few hundred manuscripts at most. But within one month 1,000 manuscripts had arrived; within four years, there were 50,000. Most were "coping" stories—how I coped with depression, lack of money, or twins, etc.—cheerful, but with a faint undertone of disillusionment.[26]

A new genre of female literature developed out of the mounting domestic discontent. In the nineteenth century, women had relieved their despair with novels and diaries; in the mid-twentieth century, they wrote "humor." There was Peg Bracken's *I Hate to Cook Book* and Jean Kerr's best-seller *Please Don't Eat the Daisies*. (Erma Bombeck's *The Grass Is Always Greener Over the Septic Tank* is a latter-day example.) It was a self-deprecating kind of humor, as befitted the essentially masochistic role of the housewife, with the author continually cast as straight man to devilish kids, nonchalant repairmen, and thoughtless neighbors. At the same time, the genre of domestic humor provided a furtive outlet for hostility to kids, husbands, and experts. Kerr recalled being "younger and full of Dr. Spock," and starts her book with the assertion that her children will

> never have to pay a psychiatrist twenty-five dollars an hour to find out why we rejected them. We'll tell them why we rejected them. Because they're impossible, that's why.[27]

But this breezy cynicism never developed into a real critique of the housewife's situation. At the end of every exhausting chronicle of domestic slapstick there was always some piece of childish gallantry—a sticky kiss or a love offering sculpted out of Mom's best cold cream—that made it all worthwhile. Besides, the domestic-humor books implied, the woman who was warm and witty enough to squeeze a few laughs out of her daily trials really didn't need much more compensation. "Our life may not be endlessly rewarding," concluded one housewife-author, "but it can be very funny."[28]

Not everyone could laugh her way through day after day of infant colic, malfunctioning refrigerators, whooping cough, and grape juice spills. Doctors and magazines began to identify a new female malady —"housewife's syndrome." It might take the form of neurotic behavior: One woman would wake up one morning and decide to stay in bed, permanently. Another woman would suffer from uncontrollable weeping. Or the syndrome might show up in the form of physical symptoms—exhaustion, insomnia, palpitations, headaches, trembling hands, drastic weight gain or loss, fainting. Gabrielle Burton, author, mother of five, and former housewife, writes of having flashes of inexplicable rage and periods of exhaustion:

> I attributed these imbalances to various things. They were probably post-partum, pre-partum, or intra-partum depressions. The pill took responsibility for a while. I didn't like to think about it too much because I was afraid that there was something wrong with me—some basic lack that kept me from being truly fulfilled . . .
> I slept inordinate amounts. It made me very guilty, but it also made the day go away and that was more important . . . I asked a doctor once for some pep pills to keep me awake long enough so that I could change my pattern of afternoon naps . . . He laughed (kindly) and said (paternally), "Now don't you worry about it. You're normal." I *knew* I was normal. My whole block was snoring. I just wanted to be vertical.[29]

Many women took their symptoms to a doctor, who prescribed uppers like Dexedrine or downers like Miltown along with instructions to cheer up and "buy a new hat" or to go home and "relax." (Sixty-seven per cent of the psychoactive drugs prescribed in this country, i.e., tranquilizers and "mood elevators," are prescribed to women. One third of American women over thirty are given a prescription for a psychoactive drug each year.[30]) Other women coped in their own way, with alcohol—a mid-afternoon drink before the kids got home, martinis before dinner and a few snorts with the barbiturates before bed. Sociologist Jessie Bernard concluded in the early sixties that "the housewife syndrome might well be viewed as public health problem number one."[31]

In 1960, according to Betty Friedan, "the problem that has no name burst like a boil through the image of the happy American housewife."[32] There was a CBS-TV special on "The Trapped Housewife." Magazine analysts speculated on whether the problem was overeducation, overwork, or maybe just incompetent appliance repairmen. Even the *Ladies' Home Journal,* propagandist of domestic felicity for three generations of women, had to acknowledge that there was trouble brewing. In between the regular features like "Pat Boone's Advice to Teenagers," "Making Marriage Work," and Dr. Spock's column, some disturbing headlines began to appear: "Who *Me? An Alcoholic?*" and "How to Recognize Suicidal Depression." Meanwhile, in the literary world, one best-seller after another was nurtured on the suburb's "atmosphere of brooding sexual anxiety and frustration," which by 1960 had already generated the middle-class diversion of "wife-swapping" and party games featuring intercouple petting. Anyone who might have thought that the Woman Question was safely buried in a suburban dream house would have to acknowledge that there was, in author John Keats' words, "a crack in the picture window."[33]

It wasn't only that the life of the full-time housewife was becoming psychologically untenable. It was also turning out to be *financially* untenable. There was a fatal catch in the mid-century domestic ideal. The picture of the "good life" included a house (Cape, ranch, or pseudo-colonial), three or four kids, and of course the full-time homemaker who held everything else together. The problem was the first two items (house and kids) turned out to be so expensive that the third (full-time mother) often had to go.

Life had been cheaper when most people lived in close-knit, urban

neighborhoods. There a woman could wash her clothes in the corner
laundromat (and meet with friends while she did it), leave the kids
with a grandmother for an evening, borrow a vacuum cleaner from a
neighbor. Most likely her first set of furniture was handed down from
within the family. But once she moved to a housing development, she
had to own her own washer and (unless the house was to be strung
with dripping laundry on rainy days) a dryer too. The furniture
would be bought new—probably a cheap set at first, which could be
replaced as the family got ahead. One car would be a necessity, and
soon, two. There was less borrowing and sharing than there had been
in the old neighborhoods: you had to have your own vacuum cleaner,
`pay for a baby-sitter, buy *new* clothes for the kids every spring and
fall.

There were mounting psychological pressures to consume too. Between 1950 and 1960, television invaded nearly every American
home, with its standardized image of how Americans *should* live, and
how you, too, *could* be living right now. High school home ec courses
offered state-sanctioned advertising for GE, Singer, General Foods,
etc. Every woman's magazine from *Seventeen* to *Bride* to *Woman's
Day* pushed a female lifestyle of relentless consumption. In 1961 a
Gallup poll conducted for the *Ladies' Home Journal* showed that
young women already had a clear sense of what they wanted out
of life by the time they were sixteen to twenty-one, and could define
it with a surreal catalogue of future purchases:

> . . . I want a split-level brick with four bedrooms with French Pro-
> vincial cherrywood furniture.

> . . . I'd like a built-in oven and range, counters only 34 inches high
> with Formica on them.

> . . . I would like a lot of finished wood for warmth and beauty.

> . . . My living room would be long with a high ceiling of exposed
> beams. I would have a large fireplace on one wall, with a lot of cop-
> per and brass around and on the face of the fireplace, I would have
> Moroccan carpets, with some areas in cinnamon tones. My kitchen
> would be very like old Virginian ones—fireplace and oven.[34]

Fantasies like these—plus the inescapable new expenses of suburban
life—guaranteed a lifelong sense of privation. The *Ladies' Home
Journal's* popular "How America Lives" department was a series of
case studies in the financial struggles of couples caught between
seven- or eight-thousand-dollar incomes and twenty-thousand-dollar a

year dreams (multiply by two to get the equivalent figures today). There were all the small economies: macaroni dinners until the car payments were finished, hand-made Christmas gifts, a moratorium on "going out." And finally the agonizing decision—was it worth two or three thousand dollars a year for the wife to go out and get a job?

Increasingly, the answer was yes, and so, unnoticed by the woman's magazines, child-raising experts, and psychoanalysts, women started sneaking out to work right after the postwar job shakedown in the late forties. In 1950 only about a third of American women held paying jobs; in the mid-sixties 40 per cent were jobholders; today the figure is about 50 per cent and still rising. Some women had been working right along, of course, despite every effort to dissuade them, from the experts' theories of maternal rejection to the help-wanted ads that began "opportunity for ambitious young man . . ." Half the nation's black women, for example, held jobs in 1950 and this figure has not changed substantially since. Poor women, widows, divorcees, and a few die-hard professional women had always expected to work. But the women who began to pour into the labor force in the sixties had by and large grown up expecting to enter permanent retirement somewhere between the honeymoon and the first baby shower. They went out to work now because they needed the money and, in many cases, because they were "going nuts."

Ads in the sixties continued to feature the full-time homemaker who had time to ponder her husband's cholesterol intake, rethink the bedroom color scheme, and worry about kitchen odors. But the marketing men were falling in love with a different sort of woman: she was at least high school educated and usually more, mobile, possessed of a driver's license, and, best of all, she made money. No one expected her (yet) to bring home the bacon, but she was certainly bringing home the Baco-bits. Discretionary income brought in by working wives was fueling unprecedented family spending, the business magazines exulted in articles like "The Ladies . . . Bless their Little Incomes."[35]

By the sixties, with close to 30 million women employed and a quarter of them not even married, the discrepancy between the romantic ideal and economic reality was getting out of hand. The contradiction was acute for the working "housewives," torn between a romantic ideal which demanded masochistic servitude, and the reality of a double life which barely left time for an occasional laundry, much less memorable home cooking. The growing number of self-supporting single women could find even less to identify with in the ideal of feminine self-sacrifice. The times called for a new feminine image—one which would reflect the working woman's new sense of independence and self-worth. It all happened so quickly that the psychomedical authorities were caught unprepared—with no time to revise their theories or rewrite their advice.

The Rise of the Single Girl

In 1955, or even 1960, no one looking for a likely new culture heroine would have thought of the single woman. For one thing, she was hard to find, appearing in the women's media only as a short-lived premarital phase, or, in her later years (twenty-five plus) as a vexing problem for hostesses. She was the odd woman in a couple-oriented culture, an object of pity to her married sisters, something of a freak to the medical profession. She might be brilliant, famous, visibly pleased with herself, successful in every way—but the judgment hung over her that she had "failed as a woman." The woman who remained single long enough for the condition to appear to be chronic was written off as a sexual cripple, a biological anomaly.

The "single girl" who burst out into the media in the early sixties corresponded to a new social reality: the single woman, divorced or never-married, who lived alone and supported herself. In the early sixties, a trend-setting minority of single women had begun to crowd into the "singles ghettos" of New York, San Francisco, Washington, D.C., and Seattle. They were secretaries, stewardesses, social workers, "gal fridays," and "assistants" of various kinds in publishing houses, banks, department stores, etc. They wanted to get married sometime, but not to be "just a housewife." They went to bars (the first "singles bar" opened in 1964 on New York's Upper East Side) to meet men. They saved for ski weekends. They skipped meals so they could afford (and fit) the latest clothes. They had "relationships."

For many real-life "single girls," the new sexual freedom that went with life in the big city was not exactly a libidinal romp. In the sixties most clerical jobs *required* women to look sexy—as if women's entry into the marketplace had to be masked with an ever-more determined facade of "femininity." And it took a certain desperation for women to thrust themselves into the after-hours social scene: the successful singles bars soon became known cynically as "meat markets." But from a distance it all looked glamorous enough: the big-city single girl wore the latest fashions from the pages of *Cosmo* or *Glamour*. She took the pill and lived in an apartment with a double bed. She spent her money on herself and men spent attention on her. She was the old feminist ideal of the independent woman with a new twist —she was sexy.

It was Helen Gurley Brown, more than anyone else, who was responsible for the transformation of the "spinster" of the forties and fifties into "the newest glamour girl of our times." Her book *Sex and the Single Girl* announced the new woman in 1962; her magazine, *Cosmopolitan,* has promoted the single-girl image since Brown's takeover as editor in 1965. An ex-single girl herself, who worked her way up from clerical jobs to the top of the publishing industry, Brown knew from personal experience what it took to create—and hold onto—a sexy image. "When I got married," she confides in *Sex and the Single Girl,* "I moved in with six-pound dumb-bells, slant board, an electronic device for erasing wrinkles . . . and enough high-powered vitamins to generate life in a statue." "I'm sure of this," she exhorted her readers. "You're not too fat, too thin, too tall, too small, too dumb, or too myopic to have married women gazing at you wistfully."[36]

Brown's message was more than a pep talk for insecure singles. She grasped the appalling fact that "magazines never deal with, that single women are too brainwashed to figure out, that married women know but won't admit. . . ." namely, that men *didn't like* the suburban housewives of the romantic ideal. Expert ideology had so thoroughly knitted sex to reproduction that there was supposed to be one continuous blur of female regression linking sexual intercourse, childbirth, and Jimmy's first Little League game. Brown understood how tenuous the links really were: who wanted to embrace a woman who had baby drool on her shoulder and chocolate fingerprints all over her blouse? Sex could be peeled away from the home and family scene as easily as clingy sweaters could be peeled off the willing starlets in James Bond movies. When the single girl walked away with female sexuality, then the housewife would indeed have nothing to do but gaze wistfully after her.

Brown, perhaps even more than feminist Betty Friedan, whose *Feminine Mystique* followed *Sex and the Single Girl* in 1963, sensed the profound misogyny which was spreading under the suburban "dream houses" like seepage from a leaky septic tank. Men resented

their domestication, and hated the company of sexless "Moms."
Brown advised her single girls to avoid the Formica practicality of
the suburbs and transform their apartments into lairs of erotic fascination. But the new single girl was not using her sexiness simply to
drag a man down into a world of female "trivia." Her world, like his,
was the world of the Market:

> . . . a single woman, even if she is a file clerk, moves in the world
> of men. She knows their language, the language of retailing, adver-
> tising, motion pictures, exporting, shipbuilding. Her world is a far
> more colorful world than the one of P.T.A., Dr. Spock and the
> jammed clothes dryer.[37]

The single girl had the pizazz which came from facing the real world
on the same terms as a man (though for only a fraction of the pay):

> She is engaging because she lives by her wits. She supports herself
> . . . She is not a parasite, a dependent, a scrounger, a sponger or a
> bum. She is a giver, not a taker, a winner and not a loser.[38]

The housewife, by implication, *was* a parasite, a dependent, a
"bum." While the single girl braved the rigors of the business world,
the housewife lived a life of sheltered ease. To Brown, the wife deserved no quarter; the worst that could happen to her was that she
too would get a taste of the single life. "I'm afraid I have a rather
cavalier attitude about wives," Brown wrote. Husbands were fair
game for the single girl, who after all, had no desire to take the wife's
place behind a vacuum cleaner in Levittown. The new single girl was
not just a sexy object; she needed male attention and she went after it
—wives, children, mortgages, and the *Ladies' Home Journal* notwithstanding.

The triumph of the single girl was complete by the late sixties and
early seventies. *Cosmopolitan,* which reached a circulation of about
two and a half million, was followed by *Viva* and *Playgirl,* while the
hard-core propagandists of domesticity—*Woman's Day* and *Family
Circle*—held on only at the supermarket checkout stands (where they
remain leading sellers). Debbie Reynolds, Doris Day, and Lucille
Ball vanished into the canyons of Beverly Hills to make way for
tough new heroines like Faye Dunaway and Angie Dickinson, and at
last the single working girl burst into family viewing time in the engaging persona of Mary Tyler Moore.

Meanwhile, in the popular media, the full-time housewife had sunk to approximately the level of prestige once occupied by single women. She was more and more likely to be portrayed as the object of pity— an infantile neurotic who got through the day with the aid of "mother's little helper" (tranquilizers) and three-hour doses of soap operas. *Diary of a Mad Housewife* showed her pacing in the confinement of her family; in *A Woman Under the Influence,* she breaks out —to a mental hospital. TV's favorite housewife in the mid-seventies was Mary Hartman—who has a neurotic relationship with her daughter, an affair with a policeman, a dramatic mental breakdown—all the while remaining distracted by the details of housekeeping, like the "waxy yellow build-up" on the kitchen floor. Eventually the housewife's reputation got so bad that even the *Ladies' Home Journal* dropped her, preferring to be known henceforth as "LHJ," and tellings its advertisers:

LHJ stands for Ladies' Home Journal.

And Ladies' Home Journal stands for the woman who never stands still . . .

One moment, she's off to the mountains for some skiing. The next moment, she's off to the islands for some tennis. And in between, she's a growing family [sic], an exciting career and creative way of life that's hers and hers alone.[39]

The Spread of the Singles Culture

American capitalism crossed the culture gap from *LHJ* to *Cosmo,* from the shopping mall to the discothèque, with barely a tremor of discomfort. To be sure, presidential proclamations on the importance of the family to the American way of life have become a bipartisan tradition, and there are continuing right-wing attempts to revive a romantic ideal of femininity. But the marketing men were, on the whole, delighted with the new singles lifestyle. First of all, in just a physical sense, the singles lifestyle meant more demand for the basic necessities like appliances and furniture. In a suburban home, four or more people might use one TV set; in a singles apartment, one person used one set. If everyone could be induced to live alone (including children, for the sake of the argument), the demand for TV sets would increase fourfold or more, with no increase in population. The director of market research for a major U.S.-based multinational corporation (who asked that neither he nor the corporation be identified) explained this principle to us in a 1974 interview. Asked what he thought of the trend toward women delaying marriage and living alone, he said:

> There's nothing in this that business would be opposed to. People living alone need the same things as people living in families. The difference is there's no sharing. So really this trend is good because it means you sell more products. The only trend in living arrangements that I think business does not look favorably on is this thing of communes, because here you have a number of people using the same products.*

In addition to expanding the market for familiar products like TVs, blenders, and vacuum cleaners, the singles lifestyle represented a new *kind* of market, centered on travel, liquor, hi fi and sports equipment, clothing, and cosmetics. The theme was instant gratification. American families spent their best years *saving*—for the kids' college education or for a larger house someday, or they channeled it into home improvements and durable goods. But there was nothing to stop the single from enjoying her (or his) money now. For example, an ad for *Psychology Today* magazine, directed at potential advertisers, shows what is supposed to be a typical reader: A young woman, sitting on her living room floor, wearing a scuba mask and flippers, holding ski poles, with a tennis racket tucked under one arm. The caption says, in bold lettering, **"I love me."** "I'm not conceited," the ad goes on:

> I'm just a good friend to myself.

> And I like to do what ever makes me feel good.

> Me, myself and I used to sit around, putting things off until tomorrow.

> Tomorrow we'll buy new ski equipment, and look at the new compact cars. And pick up that new camera.

> The only trouble is that tomorrow always turned into the next tomorrow.

> And I never had a good time "today" . . .

> [But now] **I live my dreams today, not tomorrow.**[40]

---

* He went on to explain that the way "business" dealt with the commune threat was by keeping them out of the media. Thus there are no situation comedies about life in a commune, no ads, etc. The glamour of singleness, however, is continually extolled.

It had to happen. Ever since the first warm winds of "permissiveness" swept America in the twenties, something like this had been in the air. In the thirties, forties, and fifties women were told to "express themselves," to follow their "instincts," by all means to have fun. Then the experts and the admen told them that "fun" meant a house and babies, that it in fact meant hard work and sacrifice. Sooner or later someone had to discover that there was desperately little pleasure to be gotten out of new aluminum siding, or a fifteen-hundred-dollar living room set which is kept under plastic until company comes. The media which reflected—and promoted—the new singles lifestyle spoke in a subversive whisper to a generation of young women: "Why wait? Why sacrifice? You don't need any excuses to indulge yourself. It's OK to have fun right now—for yourself." No one denied that a woman should fulfill herself even though "fulfillment" might mean masochistic suffering. But if fulfillment meant casual sex and new cameras, instead of freckled kids and a lawn free of crab grass—what was wrong with that?

A clear-headed capitalist could only rejoice at the new self-indulgent mood of young women. Sexual romanticism had sustained a market for single family homes, for large cars, heavy appliances, and fruit-flavored breakfast cereals. But it was now becoming clear that one sybaritic single could outconsume a family of four. Spending no longer had to be justified in terms of the house, the kids, the future. For example, an advertisement for ad space in *Mademoiselle* magazine shows a relaxed and elegant young woman above the headline, "I could be happy with less, but I prefer being happy with more," with the text:

> Mademoiselle readers don't live beyond their means. But they see no reason to live below them.
>
> They are young women who have acquired a taste for the better things in life, and have earned the means to acquire them.
>
> Mademoiselle has the highest index of readers of all young women's magazines who own audio components . . .
>
> And, as you might expect, the highest index of successfully employed young women.[41]

To keep up with the times, an intelligent corporation had only to rewrite its ad copy, scale down its products to singles' size (e.g., the single-serving can of Campbell's soup, the one-hamburger frying pan, the compact car instead of the station wagon, etc.) and if possible, acquire a subsidiary in the booming "leisure industry."

Spread of the Singles Culture

There was no way to contain the new lifestyle to the singles ghettos of a few cosmopolitan cities. With its intrinsic "sex appeal" and, by the late sixties, plentiful corporate promotion, the singles lifestyle spread with amazing speed—to the married. Young newlyweds especially began to throw out the old *Saturday Evening Post* images of white picket fences and backyard swing sets for dreams fashioned out of the pages of *Cosmo* or *Playboy.* The majority of *Cosmo*'s readers were not really "Cosmo Girls," who select their lovers to match their moods and astrological forecasts, but married women. And the men who read *Playboy, Penthouse,* and the slew of imitators who followed, were, on the whole, not playboys but hard-working husbands. By 1969, the new lifestyle had become so popular that the market for private homes, which had been expanding since the Second World War, suddenly went soft.† Half the new housing starts that year were for apartments—not only for singles, but for the increasing number of marrieds who now had other ways to spend their money than on lawnmowers and wood paneling for the den. A 1967 "motivational research study" cited in *Fortune,* noted the trend away from houses and towards "fun" spending:

> . . . a new car or a Caribbean cruise can connote youth and vibrancy to a man. In 1966, $20 billion was spent by the U.S. public on nonbusiness and family travel; only $4 billion more went to housing. As a consumer item, the house is underconsumed.[42]

In fact, there was getting to be less and less objective difference between the condition of marriage and singleness. Sometime in the late sixties, "living together" before or instead of marriage ceased to be a bohemian eccentricity and became a more or less thinkable alternative for millions of ordinary secretaries, schoolteachers, and college students. (The *Ladies' Home Journal,* which in the early sixties had faced the etiquette problems posed by the single woman dinner guest, confronted in the seventies the difficult problem of making sleeping arrangements for a grown son or daughter's "roommate.")

† This turned out to be a temporary decline. Today many childless couples and even singles are investing in suburban homes.

At the same time, the divorce rate began to reach record heights—from 9.2 per 1,000 married women in 1960 to 16.9 in 1970,[43] eventually reaching the point where some 40 per cent of marriages end in divorce. Marriage and singleness were no longer opposite conditions for women, requiring completely different ways of life, but "phases" marked off (in the language of the enormous literature which deals with psychological coping) by periods of "transition."

Manufacturers of household goods made a quick adjustment to the new marital instability. For years they'd banked on the indissoluble all-American family, with its steady savings and gradual accretion of durable goods. But the new "marriage cycle"—marriage, divorce, second marriage, and so on—offered a dizzying multiplication of sales opportunities. "It used to be that we thought in terms of one big point where we 'sold' a couple," the market research man we interviewed told us. "That was when they got married and started buying for their house. Later on, bit by bit, they would upgrade the items they had bought originally. But now we think more in terms of two big points. One when they first get married, and a second one ten or fifteen years later when they get divorced and have to duplicate many of the things they've held in common—from furniture and appliances to record albums and houseplants." Along these lines, the New York *Times* reported in 1977 that the housing industry was pinning its hopes for recovery on the country's one million annual divorces: "Eventually, 80 percent of divorced people remarry, but in the meantime they need a place to stay."[44]

The most dramatic indicator of the success of the "singles" lifestyle was the great "baby bust" of the sixties and seventies. Back in the post-World War II years of nationwide nest-building, the birth rate had risen like the curve of a pregnant belly. The *Ladies' Home Journal*'s 1961 poll of young women age sixteen to twenty-one found that "most" wanted four children, and "many" wanted five. But even by then the trend was starting to reverse itself. The birth rate began to fall after 1957, plummeting with the nineteen sixties' "youth rebellion" and reaching a nadir of "zero population growth" in the mid-seventies. The results are well known: hospitals began to close their obstetrical wards; obstetricians compensated for the loss of income by performing more hysterectomies and (when a pregnant woman did come along) Caesarian sections. Suburban schools were shut down. Manufacturers of infant formulas—like Nestlé's—transplanted their promotional campaigns to the baby-rich countries of the Third World.‡

The moral excuse for childlessness was the "population explosion" discovered by demographers and futurists in the mid-sixties, but the real reason, for most young couples, was that children just didn't fit into the lifestyle they had become accustomed to as singles. For every idealist, like the Mills College valedictorian of 1969, who declared, "Our days as a race on this planet are numbered . . . I AM TERRIBLY SADDENED BY THE FACT THAT THE MOST HUMANE THING FOR ME TO DO IS TO HAVE NO CHILDREN AT ALL,"[45] there were now dozens of women who saw no reason to defend their childlessness in anything but personal terms. Gael Greene, of *New York* magazine, laid out the self-indulgent arguments against parenthood as early as 1963:

> We [her husband and herself] treasure the freedom to pick up and disappear for a weekend or a month or even a year, to sleep odd hours, to breakfast at three A.M. or three P.M., to hang out the DO NOT DISTURB sign, to slam a door and be alone, or alone together, to indulge in foolish extravagances, to get out of bed at seven A.M. and go horseback riding in the park before work . . . to have champagne with dinner for no special reason at all, to tease and love anywhere, any hour, without a nagging guilt that a child is being neglected.[46]

Of course, most women were not weighing the possibility of a child against morning horseback rides and champagne dinners, but weighing a second or third child against a family vacation trip, a chance to go back to college or just a stack of unpaid bills. The pill made the decision easier, as did the lack of day care for children and the declining number of grandmothers willing to make a second career of baby-sitting. The point is, whether you lived on the luxurious fringe of Central Park or simply on the fringe of solvency, children were becoming just an option—and not the most appealing option at that. "Children didn't make much sense," explained one young couple in the New York *Times Magazine:* "The population explosion, the high fees of orthodontists. And who wants to sit home and fill the vapor-

‡ With tragic results—the substitution of formula-feeding for breast-feeding, often promoted by saleswomen dressed as medical personnel, has led to increased infant mortality due to intestinal infections and malnutrition, since poor women often overdilute the formula to make it go further, and because they lack refrigeration. See "Exporting Infant Malnutrition" by Leah Margulies, *HealthRight*, Spring 1977.

izer and sort the bibs? And why produce a child just to deliver it to some church basement every morning?" This particular couple nevertheless made the unusual decision to have a child, though observing ruefully: ". . . we get the impression that babies figure in the new scheme of things roughly the way ocelots and coatimundis did a few years ago—as rare domestic pets."[47]

By the seventies, statements of outright hostility to babies which would have had a ring of treason in the years of the Cold War and warm cribs were beginning to sound like common sense. "Babies are a liability," explained a political science professor in *New York* magazine, "A drag. And the notion that people will ever stop viewing them that way is ridiculous."[48] In 1973, "NON," the National Organization for Non-parenthood, appeared on the scene with two thousand members, including actress Shirley MacLaine and philanthropist Stewart Mott, to combat what they described as the "pervasive pronatalism" of American society. "People do not deserve honor and respect simply for having a baby," according to a psychiatrist who spoke at the 1975 NON convention. "Children are not that perfect—or likable, either."[49]

Attitudes changed rapidly: the plump, jowly Gerber's baby began to look, from a personal standpoint, like a highly uncertain investment; from an ultimate social standpoint, he or she was manifestly little more than *pollution*. The mother of three or four who, in the fifties, had looked "fulfilled," was beginning to look like a felon.

After the baby had been thrown out, the next thing to go was the bath water of sexual masochism. Women began to speak up for their subjective sexual experience as a *fact,* not a neurosis. In the new atmosphere of sexual liberation, the theoretical ties which had bound vaginal orgasms to maternal instinct and marital fidelity began to fray like worn apron strings. The long-suppressed clitoris could be held back no longer. Masters and Johnson, who became the world's leading experts in the new field of sex therapy performed the ritualistic act,* escorting the clitoris into the laboratory and observing it in ac-

* Actually scientific and sociological evidence of the primary role of the clitoris in female sexuality had never been lacking. Havelock Ellis, at the beginning of the century, and Alfred Kinsey, in the middle of the century, had both on the basis of their research disagreed with the Freudian distinction between a vaginal and a clitoral orgasm and had declared that the clitoris was the chief organ of female sexual pleasure. Kinsey, for example, pointed out that female masturbatory and lesbian practices showed the relative unimportance of penile penetration to female orgasm. Furthermore, physiological evidence available

tion. They emerged convinced of its exhaustive powers (which now made the penis seem feeble by comparison) and gave their scientific imprimatur to a new era of female sexuality—in which pleasure could potentially be divorced from its last ties to marriage, babies, and even men themselves.

With the spread of the "singles lifestyle" in the sixties and seventies, the media rushed to celebrate the "liberation" of the American woman. The kitchen and the nursery no longer beckoned as the unique arena for female creativity. Babies were no longer the self-evident climax of adult life. Work was crowding out of the peripheries of women's lives and into what had once been the peak years of reproductivity. And sex, once supposed to be the glue of perpetual matrimony, had become detached from any commitments—it was something a woman did for *herself*. Hip men and "sensitive" advertisers congratulated the sexy, self-supporting woman: "You've come a long way, Baby."

But for women it was an ambiguous kind of liberation. After the old dependency came the new insecurity of shifting relationships, a competitive work world, unstable marriages—an insecurity from which no woman could count herself "safe" and settled. There was a sense of being adrift, but now there was no one to turn to. The old romantic ideology, buttressed by 150 years of psychomedical theory, was transparently useless, and the old experts were increasingly discredited. The post-romantic era called for a new ethos, a new ideology, new rules for "right living."

Popular Psychology and the Single Girl

The corpse of romantic psychomedicine was barely cold before an entirely new school of experts made their dashing entrance on the scene. The proponents of the new popular psychology, or "pop psychology," broke with Freud, with medical science, and ultimately

---

from at least the late nineteen forties on contradicted psychoanalysis, since female sexual nerve-ends for the perception of orgasm were absent in the vagina and abundant in the clitoris. But despite the clinical, physiological, anatomical and sociological evidence, not to mention the possibilities of personal observation, mid-century doctors and psychiatrists had struggled manfully against the persistent appearance of the clitoris in female sexual activity. Until women themselves began to take apart the edifice of sexual masochism, the wealth of evidence was simply ignored.

with science itself. They made few claims to "data," laboratory studies, or clinical experience. The new psychology would become, openly and without intellectual pretension, the mass ideology of the consumer society, the lore of the adman and the Market researcher, condensed into easy-to-read guidelines for daily living.

The new "marketplace psychology" was of course aimed at men and women—anyone who could pay fifteen to thirty dollars for a group-therapy session or $2.95 for a paperback. But its most revolutionary message was for women. The pop psychologists took the step which the neo-Freudians had drawn back from: they accepted permissiveness as a program of universal liberation—not only for infants, teen-agers and work-weary dads—but for women too. The new psychology was distinctly, and vociferously, *antimasochistic*. Suddenly the epidemic of "rejection of femininity" went the way of hysteria and other obsolete diseases. The new experts were concerned with a new and equally widespread syndrome: "femininity" itself. Women had been "brainwashed" (by their mothers, said the experts) to be passive and submissive. Taking a tip from Helen Gurley Brown, the experts now revealed that men weren't interested in the old "stereotypes," as they were now called. "Men don't want relationships with frail baby-dolls," announces the title page of an assertiveness training manual, "they want the excitement of a fully grown woman."[50] And trusted popular writers like Dr. Joyce Brothers brought the message back from the frontiers of urban experimentation to the backwoods of middle American marriage: the time had come even for wives to "put themselves first."[51]

The new pop psychology was invigorating, even lifesaving, news to the millions of women it reached through therapy groups, talk-show experts, self-help books and magazine articles. So they hadn't been crazy all along to blow up at that inverted bowl of Rice Krispies on the floor and the dirty socks on the coffee table. So it was all right for a woman to want something for herself, whether it was better sex or a higher salary or a little bit of recognition. Pop psychology amplified the youthful voice of the new feminism: It's OK to be angry; it's OK to be a woman; it's OK to be *you*. Summing up her own transformation by the new psychology, one woman wrote:

> *I'm entitled.* That's what I learned . . . . I'm entitled to a life of my own. I don't have to do everything *they* want. I'm not bad for wanting to do what they don't approve of—my mother, my husband, my sons.[52]

But ultimately the new psychology turned out to be as misogynistic as anything that might creep out from under the fallen log of sexual romanticism. Romanticist ideology, finding no place for the values of love and nurturance in the Market, had fastened them onto woman. More precisely, nailed them into her flesh. Women would love in a world that did not honor love, so, as it was put in the final neo-Freudian debacle, women would have to love *pain*. But the new ideology was willing to accept the values of the marketplace as *universal* principles; in the world of the marketplace psychologists there was *no* place for the old "human" values of love and caring—not even on the backs of women. In a flash all the feminine traits which had been glorified as natural and instinctual were exposed as the trappings of a "socialized sex role," which—almost overnight—had become obsolete.

The marketplace psychology that would set guidelines for the new woman of the sixties and seventies was first born in the expansive, almost rebellious atmosphere of the Human Potential Movement. The HPM grew out of the broad spectrum of psychological methods and styles which flourished together in the iconoclastic atmosphere of the nineteen sixties. The thrust of the movement grew from the work of "Third Force" ("humanist") psychologists—neither Freudians nor behaviorists—optimistically dedicated to the "self-actualization" of a psyche presumed to be possessed of an almost infinite capacity for expansion. By the mid-sixties, psychotherapists from every kind of professional background were becoming excited by the mass appeal of the movement, its dramatic techniques (such as group work, physical touch, and direct expression of feelings) and its utopian vision of mass psychological transformation.

Because it was concerned with the "expansion of human potential," the new psychology was for everyone. "If there is one statement true of every living person it must be this: he hasn't achieved his full potential."[53] HPM methods were not about "making sick people well"—they were about "making well people better." In fact, the new techniques worked best on people who were "healthy" and "open" (encounter group leaders learned that psychotics and neurotics had to be screened *out* or the new "expansion" techniques would only worsen them by bringing up "unmanageable material").

The point of achieving one's full potential, according to HPM ideologues, was not to be able to get more work done, or make a greater contribution to society, or any other old-fashioned "inner-directed" goal—but simply to have more fun. In *Joy,* an early mani-

festo of the HPM, Dr. Schutz tells us that the worst aspect of unful-
filled potential is that it "robs us of pleasure and joy in living." With
the techniques he recommends (developed in experiments in the Air
Force and various corporations) as well as at Esalen, the institutional
mecca of the HPM, he promises a return to the bliss of childhood:
"Perhaps we can recapture some joy, regain some of the body-pleas-
ures, share again the joy with other people that was once possible."[54]
Schutz looked at his own newborn son as a creature who was in
danger of losing his infant joyousness as he grew up, unless *Joy* techniques were widely practiced: "We'd better hurry," he warned, "The
culture is already getting to him—Ethan looks as if he is beginning
to feel frightened and guilty."†[55]

A major theme of the HPM and the various schools of pop psychology which followed it was that you didn't *have* to grow up, at
least not in any old-fashioned, repressive, Freudian sense. Why be
forced to give up the pleasures of a permissive childhood at any age?
Characteristically, pop psychology sought psychic liberation through
sensual indulgence, peer-group closeness, sexual experience, and
other characteristic discoveries of adolescence transported to the
world of adults. It gave a place of honor to "the child within us" as a
permanent inhabitant, as if the Gesellian infant "with all his inborn
wisdom" remained within each of us in a state of perfect preservation, lovable and hedonistic. While the birth rate fell throughout the
sixties and seventies, more and more adult Americans were looking
within themselves to find the "child" that they would nurture.

But the fact that you didn't have to grow up didn't mean you
didn't have to *change*. HPM theory implied that it is not only a pleasure to expand oneself but almost an obligation: Who could be sure
that their personality didn't need improvement? Any rejection, any
dead-end relationship, any failure to advance at work could point to
the need for psychological help.

In the context of the singles culture, with its rapid-turnover "relationships," compulsive sexiness, and nervous pressure to have "fun,"
this message took on special urgency. People were easily convinced

---

† Writing in the sixties, Shutz had political ambitions that HPM techniques
could be useful in containing youthful radicalism. He hoped that what he had
to teach would ease the "current 'credibility gap' . . . that is eroding a political
administration," and that it would answer "youth's demand that we 'tell it like
it is.'" He even went so far as to suggest that the new techniques might match
the joys of the drug culture.

that their personalities did need work, and hundreds of thousands of
seekers from every kind of background converged at the sites of the
new psychological practices. HPM workshops of every stripe
flourished in locations as disparate as suburban community centers,
college and high school campuses, corporation boardrooms, in every
conceivable type of professional and semiprofessional training program, in political organizations, and even in churches. Speaking of
encounter groups alone, psychiatrist Joel Kovel writes:

> . . . such groups constitute a major social phenomenon, albeit one
> that seems, like acid rock, to have peaked in the late Sixties. It had
> to. At the rate it was growing then, the movement would have en-
> gulfed all other forms of social organization by now had it not
> slowed. I recall being told during a visit to Palo Alto, California, in
> 1969 that that modest-sized town sported something like 360 ongo-
> ing groups.[56]

When encounter groups peaked, other therapies had already begun to
fill the gap, including Psychodrama, Gestalt, Transactional Analysis,
Primal Therapy, more unorthodox new ones (such as "est") and
even "traditional" methods—like Jungian, Reichian, or Sullivanian approaches—plus a hundred "eclectic" variations on all of them. In addition there were "theme" groups—groups for the married, or the
divorced, groups for smokers, or overeaters, or insomniacs. "Joy is
burgeoning" exulted Schutz prophetically in 1967, exclaiming that if
things kept going right, all of our institutions and even "the establishment" would soon be hooked on joy.[57]

With this mass demand for psychological counsel, psychotherapy
became a growth industry in itself, and soon a degree in psychology
became one of the best bets for a college graduate looking for guaranteed status and money. But "pop psych" was too much of a bo-
nanza to be contained by any mere academic discipline. Only a psychoanalyst can psychoanalyze you, but lots of people can be
"marriage counselors" or "group leaders," and just about anyone
with a typewriter can write a book advising millions of people on how
to live. A horde of new psychological experts, loosely educated with a
few inhalations of HPM doctrine, rushed in to meet the demand for
guidelines in the confusing new singles culture. Frontrunners in the
psychological gold rush were the veterans of the manipulation industries (marketing and advertising) who, recognizing that this was their
natural turf, began the mass production of self-help books in the

nineteen seventies. Jean Owen, whose background is in television audience and opinion research is the interviewer-editor of the best-selling *How to Be Your Own Best Friend*. *I Ain't Much, Baby—but I'm All I've Got*, a popular book followed up with *I Ain't Well—but I Sure Am Better* were written by Jess Lair, who had a successful career as a marketing and management consultant before getting a Ph.D. in psychology.

Success Through Transactional Analysis, by Jut Meininger, applies TA directly to business. *How to Say No Without Feeling Guilty* was co-authored by Dr. Herbert Fensterheim and Jean Baer (his wife) the former public relations director of *Seventeen* magazine. After the success of *How to Say No,* Jean Baer broke into the psych market on her own with *How to Be an Assertive (Not Aggressive) Woman*.

Soon even the strongholds of academic psychomedicine, finding themselves left holding the old bag of romantic-masochistic formulas, had to stoop to learn from the paperback book racks. Jean Baer co-led an assertiveness training pilot study program at the Payne Whitney clinic of the New York Hospital. Eric Berne, who was denied admittance to the American Psychoanalytic Association in light of his Transactional Analysis theories, would, had he lived, have had the satisfaction of seeing TA taught in medical schools and Ph.D. programs. Freud was relegated to the back shelves while the more progressive M.D. and Ph.D. programs rushed to catch up with Gestalt, TA, "behavior mod" and their more overtly commercial variations.

With the seventies' boom in self-help book sales, modern market-place psychology, composed of one part HPM philosophy (drawn eclectically from the burgeoning new pop psych tendencies) and two parts sheer hardheaded marketing cunning, really took off as a mass cultural phenomenon on its own. Marketplace psychology took the cheerful expansiveness of the HPM and transformed it into a philosophy of ruthless self-centeredness. In the post-romantic world, where the old ties no longer bind, all that matters is *you:* you can be what you *want* to be; you *choose* your life, your environment, even your appearance and your emotions. Nothing "happens to" you. There are no "can'ts," only "won'ts." You don't have to be the victim even of your own emotional reactions: you choose to feel what you *want* to feel. "You are free when you accept the responsibility for your choices," write Newman and Berkowitz in *How to Be Your Own Best Friend,* adding that the only obstacles they know of are that "people cling to their chains." Similarly, Transactional Analysis is "realistic,"

according to popularizer Thomas Harris, M.D., ". . . in that it confronts the patient with the fact that he is responsible for what happens in the future no matter what has happened in the past."[58] In pop
psychology logic it followed that the only thing that held women back
was a "negative mental set": ". . . women don't think of themselves
as equal to men so they don't act equal; consequently men, employers, relatives, society do not treat them as equal."[59]

The corollary of the proposition that you are totally responsible for
your feelings is that you are *not* responsible for anything else: "You
don't have to live up to anyone's expectations." Selfishness is not
a "dirty word"—it is merely an "expression of the law of self-preservation."[60] A behavior-modification book warns you that when you embark on their program people will accuse you of being selfish, egotistical, or egocentric. Don't worry. The person who does this "is himself
self-centered and is merely saying, indirectly: You are not centering
enough on ME."[61] Book after book assumes that the only way to
avoid being "stepped on" is to "put yourself first." They promise to
help you look out for Number One, or to help the person you love the
most—yourself!: "Selfishness (self-ness) is simply the recognition and
acceptance of the reality that each person is the most important person in the world to himself."[62] The flip side of "Don't be a victim"
is "Don't rescue" any other victims. The "Gestalt Prayer" which found
its way onto thousands of posters, greeting cards, and coffee mugs,
puts it best:

> I do my thing, and you do your thing.
> I am not in this world to live up to
>   your expectations
> And you are not in this world to live
>   up to mine.
> You are you and I am I, and if by chance
>   we find each other, it's beautiful
> If not, it can't be helped.[63]

If you are not responsible to anyone but yourself, it follows that
relationships with other people are merely there to be exploited when
(emotionally) profitable, and terminated when they cease to be
profitable. The primary assumption is that each person in a relationship has a set of emotional, sexual, or other "needs" which he or
she wants met. If they are no longer being satisfied by a friend or sexual partner, then that bond may be broken just as reasonably as a

buyer would take his business away from a seller if he found a better price. The *needs* have an inherent legitimacy—the *people* are replaceable.

Thus, a bad relationship is one where you "put in" more than you "get out." Relationships—especially marriages—are in reality financial/emotional "contracts" in which rights and responsibilities should be clearly agreed on, and preferably spelled out in writing, down to the last intimate expectation. With this the veil of sentimentality is finally torn away from what Charlotte Perkins Gilman had called the "sexuo-economic relation." Marriage, it is revealed, is a deal like any other which begins when two people "sell" themselves to each other. Robert Ringer (former real estate salesman and author of *Winning Through Intimidation* and *Looking Out for Number One*) sets forth these four steps for successful personal "selling":

1) Obtain a product to sell (e.g., a woman's "product" could very well be *herself*—as a wife),
2) Locate a market for the product (in the above example this would consist of available men who would meet her standards),
3) Implement a marketing method (put into effect a procedure for selling herself), and
4) Be able to close the sale (get the stiff to sign on the dotted line and hand over the ring).[64]

Once you're in a relationship, according to another advice book, its success will be based on such conditions as "the desire and ability of both partners to reinforce the expectations of each in a trade negotiation sufficiently balanced to maintain consonance." For example, an assertiveness training manual recommends that couples follow certain rules for "behavior exchange contracts" in which couples alter their behavior for each other. Some of the rules include:

a. Each partner gets something he/she wants from the other. For instance, you contract to "wear a nice robe in the morning instead of that torn one." He agrees to "come home for dinner on time instead of drinking with the boys." You start with simple behaviors and progress to more complex ("She should initiate more sex . . ." "He should kiss me more.") . . .

d. Whenever possible, keep track of the target behavior with graphs, charts, points, or tokens.
e. Avoid disagreements about the contract by writing it out. Keep

it in a spot where you both can see it easily. Many couples put it on
the refrigerator or bedroom door. When you effect one Behavior Exchange Contract to your mutual satisfaction, go on to another.[65]

Should such negotiations break down, according to a different
book, there can be a "successful divorce,"—by no means to be
thought of as a failure—but one which "has been pre-considered in
terms of personal upward mobility, with stress laid not nearly so
much on what is being left, and may therefore be lost, as on what
lies ahead that may be incorporated into a new and better image."[66]
After the successful divorce, this behavior-modification book tells us,
"Little Affairs" may be useful for many reasons, including "the opportunity to replace lovers who have contributed sexual dissonance
with others more able to contribute consonance." The person with a
"Positive Self Image" need not worry about promiscuity. *All* these
affairs will be "meaningful" because they will all contribute to the
"self's reservoir of experiences."

If relationships are business transactions, the Self is now an
owner, an investor, and a consumer. One can almost hear the
scratching of pencil on paper as the "strokes" are counted and the
tabulations of love-given/love-received are totaled up. In the language of psycho-business, we are smart to capitalize on our assets
and cut our losses, maximize the return on our (emotional) investments, and in general put all our relationships—whether with lovers,
co-workers, or family members—on the psychic equivalent of a cash
'n' carry basis.

From the business metaphor for relationships, it's a quick leap to
the "game" metaphor—already so stylish in the real business world.
Marketplace psychology divides the world into two categories of people—"winners" and "losers." *The Winner's Notebook, Born to Win,
Winners and Losers,* and *Winning Through Intimidation* are only a
few titles from the self-help book rack. (In the nineteenth-century
economy, everyone knew that most people would be "losers." But in
the modern consumption-centered economy, where "winning"
doesn't necessarily mean gaining wealth and power, but having fun—
suddenly everyone can be a "winner": it just takes the right frame of
mind.) "What is called for is concentration on the forthcoming material and the desire to minimize losing streaks while maximizing winning ones," says *Winners and Losers.* "In poker, it's done every day
in the week: Cut your losses; throw in the bad or "maybe" hands and

bet big on the good ones."[67] And don't get too upset about anything—it's only a game!

As an abstract system, marketplace psychology postulates an emotional "economy" in which standardized "players" interact, like real businessmen, according to definite rules of possession and exchange. Standardizing the players is the hard part, since they are, of course, human. The first step is to dismiss, as much as possible, the unique personal past. Almost all the marketplace psychologists pride themselves on their avoidance of time-consuming and confusing history: One Gestalt book dismisses the past with the words, ". . . reality exists only in the present. A person's memory of the past (despite his sincere denials of this fact) is a collection of obsolete distortions and misperceptions." With their personal autobiographies eradicated, people do appear more similar, and can be analyzed in terms of their needs and their behavior in the here-and-now: "What we do and how we function *is* our self."[68] The conception of the self is simplified, and whenever possible, mechanized. "The brain functions as a high-fidelity tape recorder" says Harris. "The Adult [ego-state] is a data-processing computer." When they're not tape-recorders or computers, people most often appear as robots whose "programming" keeps them from taking in "positive input" or from stopping other robots, who are looking for "negative payoffs," from pushing their "anger buttons." "Freedom," is, of course, "standing at your own controls."

The rules of possession are clear: First of all, concentrate on "owning yourself" and "owning your feelings," because everyone else will be busy doing the same. No more will love be sung to the tune of romantic bondage—"we belong to each other," "I gave my heart to him," "I'm going to make her mine" and so forth. No, in the new game you never give yourself away completely:

> . . . an adult, when he loves, does not risk his whole identity. That he already has, and will have however the other responds. If he loses his lover, he will still have himself. But if you look to someone else to establish your identity for you in some way, losing that person can make you really feel destroyed.[69]

To this self-possessed adult in a universe of standardized "selves," not even death makes too much of an impact. One of the psychiatrist-authors of *How to Be Your Own Best Friend* recalls:

> I once was seeing a man who was grieving deeply. The person he had been closest to had died, and he felt utterly desolate. I sat with

him and could feel the depths of his sorrow. Finally, I said to him,
"You look as if you had lost your best friend." He said, "Well, I
have." And I said, "Don't you know who your best friend is?" He
looked at me, surprised. He thought a moment, and tears came into
his eyes. Then he said, "I guess it's true—you are your own best
friend."[70]

In the world of standardized, interchangeable "players," all relationships are governed by the marketplace principle of equivalent exchange. If the two of you can establish an equitable stroke exchange:
beautiful. If not, it can't be helped: move on to another player. The
old hierarchies of protection and dependency no longer exist, there
are only free contracts, freely terminated. The marketplace, which
had long ago expanded to include the relations of production, has
now expanded to include *all* relationships.

The new psychology recognized at once that women were entering
the expanded emotional-economic marketplace with a special handi-
cap: they had been prepared since childhood for a life of unqualified
giving, in a framework of stable, protective relationships. This handi-
cap called for a special sort of mass therapy—something which could
provide women with the "survival skills" they would now need in a
world dominated by the singles culture. Assertiveness Training, as the
new therapy was labeled, called for nothing short of a complete psychological make-over. According to the introduction to one manual,
women were recognizing that "there was a kind of disability in our
femininity"[71] and that if they were not going to go under in the fierce
personal and occupational race, they would have to change—fast.

With very little hesitation, the assertiveness-training books fastened on male behavior as the model. They observed that most men
don't have assertiveness problems; their socialization has given them
the proper degree of self-centeredness. But "Society has never
impressed on women as it has on men the absolute necessity of putting yourself first."[72] The assertiveness training books enviously
praise the emotional upbringing of boys in stark contrast to the experiences of girls:

> Had you been born a boy, you'd probably have been welcomed
> warmly, with expectations of either following in Father's footsteps
> (if they're big ones) or of surpassing him. As a girl, however, your
> greeting may be more subdued—particularly if you already have an
> older sister. "Oh, well, maybe we'll try again," Dad might say. "She
> *is* a pretty little thing." . . . If you have in fact put yourself first,

you've learned to feel guilty afterward, in contrast to boys, who can assert themselves, say what they want—and even fight to get it![73]

The fortunate men have no trouble with the marketplace or with marketplace psychology—but women have to unlearn their socialization and imitate the male style. One book on how women can make it in managerial jobs counsels: "Above all, don't show emotion and *never* cry in front of a male co-worker. Men have spent their lives learning to repress tears; women have a lot of catching up to do."[74]

Assertiveness training, like popular psychology generally, is meant to be applied to all situations—work, sexual relationships, friendships. One assertiveness-training book opens with the following illustration of how to be "assertive" with a woman friend: In the story, "you" are at home alone, the housework done. You have some free time—two hours "just for yourself." Then the phone rings. It's a friend asking if you would please, as a very special favor, watch her two-year-old daughter Alison for the morning while she goes out to a meeting. You have a "familiar sinking feeling in your stomach." You *really* wanted those two hours for yourself:

> If you were non-assertive you could simply deny your own wishes, and agree to care for Alison: "Well, I was going to do something else, but it really doesn't matter. O.K., bring her over."
>
> Or you could say, *assertively*, "I know it's a drag to take Alison with you, but I've set aside two hours for myself this morning, so I won't be able to take her today."[75]

The book promises to help you learn to do what you want to do. Neatly evaded is the annoying question of what is *right* to do. There is no room here for you to balance Alison's mother's need to go to the meeting against your need to have two hours alone; nor of Alison's mother's relative hardships against your own. The only possible reason to take care of Alison is because you *want* to do it (which in fact the authors assume you don't). The acknowledgment, "I know it's a drag to take Alison with you" is nothing but a psychological "technique" intended to make the friend *feel* that you sympathize, even as you refuse to help. One is left to wonder what will become of Alison's mother when she arrives at her meeting, child-in-tow, only to be told—assertively—that they really don't want children at the meetings any more.

But in the dog-eat-dog sexual marketplace no woman can afford an old-fashioned sense of responsibility to other women. One assertiveness training book lists a series of single women's rights, including the right to—"date a married man":

> Do you want this right? It's a decision only you can make. Today, in these days of urban renewal, Back Street has practically ceased to exist. The Other Woman is alive, well, and living everywhere from one-room efficiency to posh pad. . . . today's OW may suffer some guilts, but she . . . does not consider herself immoral; she sees herself as a moral, self-respecting woman who is in the Other Woman situation.[76]

Like a boomerang, this denial of the existence of any moral values comes back to strike at all women. The marketplace model purports to be egalitarian or even feminist. But in fact it assumes a false equality, and denies that women have any special needs or experience any special discrimination as women. Even the ideal object of marketplace psychology, the single girl with no family responsibilities, has "handicaps" which can't be overcome by any amount of psychotherapy or paperback self-help. Assertiveness training doesn't remove the hazards of contraception, the risks of pregnancy, the price of an abortion.

But it is over the issue of children that marketplace psychology completely breaks down as a practical philosophy for women. The relationships in the pop psychology books are never relationships with children, and when a child appears, like little Alison, it is assumed that *nobody* wants her. After all, how can you run a relationship with a child on the principle of equivalent exchange? Do you ignore the infant who doesn't give you enough "strokes"? Refuse to make breakfast for the two-year-old who peed on its sheets last night? Desert a child who doesn't meet your needs (kindly reciting the Gestalt Prayer as you go)? When confronted with the problem of children—always introduced as a "problem," an obstacle to women's mobility—the marketplace psychologists suddenly become rigid, judgmental and even scolding:

> I'm not against day care or careers for women. But having children is—or ought to be—a choice. If women want to have babies, they should. If they don't want to raise children, they shouldn't have them . . . They can lobby for day-care centers if they like, but they shouldn't feel like victims.[77]

And in *Winners and Losers,* the authors ask themselves: "Aren't divorced men better off, because they're usually without children, in-

volved in work, and also freer to find social and sexual partners?"
and answer:

> If men are better off in any area of divorce, it's because they choose
> to be better off; if women are worse off, it's because they've chosen
> to be worse off . . . As for freedom from children, the best way to
> be free from children is not to conceive them. . . .[78]

Psychological ideology had swung 180 degrees from the neo-
Freudian theories of libidinal motherhood and female masochism.
From being the only source of fulfillment in a woman's life children
had become an obstacle to her freedom. From being a symbolic act
of submission, sex had become a pleasurable commodity which
women as well as men had a right to demand. The old rationalist
promise that the forces of the Market would break the ancient ties of
the family seemed to be coming true, and the ideology of sexual
romanticism at last began to crumble. But if the rules imposed by
sexual romanticism had denied women any future other than service
to the family, the new psychology seemed to deny human bonds altogether for women or for men. Pop psychology, which had begun
with the effusive evocation of universal joy, ended up with the grim
"realism" of the lifeboat strategy: not everyone can get on board, so
survival depends on learning how to fight it out on the way to "getting yours." Despite their radical break with sexual romanticism,
the experts of marketplace psychology ended up promoting an ideal
of women's nature which was no less distorted and limiting than the
ideal which had once been advanced by nineteenth-century gynecology.

Afterword:
The End of the Romance

Like the period we began with, when Charlotte Perkins Gilman, Jane Addams, and so many others of their generation faced the Woman Question, this is a turning point in the lives of women. Sexual romanticism as a systematic ideology, buttressed by science and propagated by an army of professionals—has collapsed. The rules which governed women's lives for generations have been broken. But what lies ahead is unclear.

There is an improvised quality to women's lives, as each woman tries to piece together a pattern that will be, she hopes, stable without being confining, varied without being chaotic. One woman succeeds as a single working woman, only to be panic-stricken, in her mid-thirties, not to have had children. Another woman devotes herself to her children, as her mother had done before her, only to collapse into a profound depression, in her forties, over what now looks to her like a "wasted" life. A housewife leaves a comfortable home and growing family to join a lesbian commune . . . a single working woman goes on welfare to raise a child out of wedlock . . . There are too many choices . . . or there are not enough. The possibilities are exhilarating . . . and they are terrifying.

We are living in the aftermath of an economic and social transformation—not as cataclysmic as the one which opened up the Woman Question in the first place—but thoroughgoing enough to have shaken the firmest assumptions about woman's nature and woman's place. It is the end of the period of sexual romanticism, the end of the ideology which had "solved" the Woman Question and sealed it shut for over a century and a half.

The romantic solution persisted for as long as it did because it had *moral* force. It asserted, in however trivialized and sentimental a fashion, the supreme value of love as against self-interest, human persons as against dead things. It affirmed the human needs which could not be met in the marketplace—needs for love and intimacy, for nurturance and caring. It upheld the weak, the infant, the elderly, in an economic world which rewarded only the victorious and the strong.

But the romantic "solution" was to take all the responsibility for love and caring and place it squarely on the backs of women: individual women, each one in isolation, holding out against the anarchy of the marketplace. And in this lay the fatal moral compromise of sexual romanticism: it chose not to remake the world, but to demand that women *make-up for it*. From the beginning (even when the pedestal seemed most secure), this was a task which could only lead to humiliation. Women worked to maintain the home as a sanctuary for human values. But there was no honor in this work. Women's domestic efforts had been so marginalized as to be scarcely visible (and offered less financial reward than that of the most menial labor). Women tried to be "feminine," and found themselves forced to be the negation of everything purposive and dynamic. In demanding that women "humanize" society, sexual romanticism ended by dehumanizing women.

The romantic reality had already been seriously undermined by the mid-sixties. But it took a conscious, organized effort to overthrow sexual romanticism from its position as the dominant ideology: and this was the work of the feminist movement of the late sixties and seventies. The movement was in one sense a coming-to-consciousness of the changes which were already reshaping women's lives—the decline of the sexual double standard, the mass entry of women into the work force, the new opportunities, and dangers, of independence. But feminism quickly transcended and even contradicted the "singles culture" articulated by corporate ideologues. It represented a new *moral* force, one capable of exposing (as *Cosmo* and its followers could never do) the moral corruption of sexual romanticism.

The founders of the early feminist movement were activists schooled in the civil rights and antiwar movements. Like the men of their generation, they had seen beyond the bucolic peacefulness of the suburbs to the war zone at the perimeter—the ghetto rebellions in the cities, the guerrilla struggles in the Third World. They had come to understand that the force which held the status quo together was not consensus, but force itself. Inevitably they drew the analogy between women and blacks, between women and all other "oppressed people." Where sociologists saw "roles" and "institutions," psychiatrists saw "feminine adjustment" and the medical authorities saw "biological destiny," feminists saw *oppression*. Sexual romanticism, for all its chivalry and sentiment, existed only to conceal the most ancient injustice: the forcible rule of men over women.

Armed with moral insight into the coercive side of sexual romanticism, feminists proceeded to challenge its "scientific" basis. The terms of the debate were those that the experts had long ago chosen themselves—the rules and logic of science. Again and again feminist critics matched male "science" against a superior rationality. In pamphlets, books, underground newspapers, and scholarly articles, women cut to the theoretical core of sexual romanticism. In consciousness-raising groups, in women's study groups, and in college classrooms women held the scientific theories up to their own experience, and the old "facts" went up in smoke as myths. The immutable maternal instinct . . . the sanctity of vaginal orgasms . . . the child's need for exclusive mothering . . . the theory of female masochism—all the shibboleths of mid-century psychomedical theory—shriveled in the light of the feminist critique.

At the same time, the beneficent "care" which masked the ideology dispensed by the gynecologists came in for a blistering appraisal. Exposés of the hazards of the pill, intrauterine devices, and hormone treatments for menopausal women raised serious questions about the doctors' integrity, if not their basic competence. Doctors were found to be cutting into the female body with something of the same abandon which had characterized nineteenth-century gynecology. (Half of the hysterectomies performed each year in the United States are estimated to be medically unnecessary.) Perhaps most shocking was the feminist dissection of professional obstetrical care: the routine use of anesthesia, and common resort to forceps, chemical induction of labor, and Caesarian sections turned out to be hazardous for mother and child, though convenient and probably gratifying to the physician. "Scientific" childbirth, for the sake of which the midwives had been outlawed, was revealed by the feminist critics as a drama of misogyny and greed.*

* Important feminist exposés of medical practices include: Ellen Frankfort's *Vaginal Politics* (New York: Quadrangle Press, 1972), the Boston Women's Health Collective's *Our Bodies, Ourselves* (New York: Simon and Schuster, 1976), Barbara Seaman's *Free and Female* (Greenwich, Fawcett Crest, 1972),

The feminist assault on the experts was soon echoing in kitchens and clinic waiting rooms. By the seventies, the label of "Freudian" was enough to seriously damage a would-be therapist's practice or discredit a best-selling child-raising expert. Women began to question their doctor's opinion on their cervix, not to mention his ideas about sexuality, marriage, or femininity.

The great romance between women and the experts was over, and it ended because the experts had betrayed the trust that women had put in them. Claiming the purity of science, they had persisted in the commercialism inherent in a commoditized system of healing. Claiming the objectivity of science, they had advanced the doctrines of sexual romanticism. They turned out not to be scientists—for all their talk of data, laboratory findings, clinical trials—but apologists for the status quo. Confronted with something resembling the essence of real scientific thought—the critical and rationalist spirit of the new feminism—they could only bluster defensively or mumble in embarrassment.

The collapse of the authorities who had upheld sexual romanticism was sudden and catastrophic. Within less than a decade, the entire edifice of romanticist theory—with its foundation of biological metaphors, its pillars of Freudian dogma, its embellishments of gynecological wisdom—tumbled down like an ornate Victorian mansion in the face of a hurricane. It had no grounds—moral or scientific—from which to resist the feminist assault.

As the old authorities fell into disgrace, and as the weight of sexual romanticist ideology began to lift, it became possible for women to ask once again the old questions: What is our nature as women?

Adrienne Rich's *Of Woman Born* (New York, W. W. Norton and Co., 1976), Doris Haire's *The Cultural Warping of Childbirth* (Seattle: International Childbirth Education Association), Naomi Weisstein's essay "Psychology Constructs the Female" in V. Gornick and B. K. Moran, eds., *Women in Sexist Society* (New York, Signet/New American Library, 1971). Two new anthologies including important feminist writings on medicine are: Claudia Dreifus' *Seizing Our Bodies: The Politics of Women's Health Care* (New York: Vintage, 1978) and John Ehrenreich's *The Cultural Crisis of Modern Medicine* (New York: Monthly Review Press, 1978).

Bibliographies of recent writings on women and medicine can be found in Jane B. Sprague, "Women and Health Bookshelf," *American Journal of Public Health* 65, 741–46 (July 1975) and in *Women and Health Care: A Bibliography with Selected Annotation,* Program on Women, Northwestern University, Evanston, Illinois, 1975.

What are our needs? How shall we live? And, too, the deeper questions which had once been "solved" by sexual romanticism: Is there a place for love and caring within a masculinist society? What is woman's responsibility for it? Or anyone's? The Woman Question, prematurely "solved" a hundred and fifty years ago and sealed shut with all the weight of science, has been reopened.

On the one hand, there has been an enormous release, a joyful overflowing, as the female energy once channeled toward domesticity pours out in all directions. Suburban housewives organize women's centers, newspapers, conferences, hot lines. The Girl Scouts discuss sexuality, and little girls join Little League. Women workers stop being subservient and housewifely: clerical workers join unions, nurses strike, here and there a secretary refuses to serve coffee any more. Mothers organize and fight for high-quality, low-cost day care for their children. Women who had been afraid to speak out become leaders. Women who had been "ugly" become radiant. A women's culture flourishes: women's studies courses, women's poetry and music, new approaches to language, art, relationships. And, prophetically, there is a return of the female healer—embodied in today's lay midwives, self-help teachers, founders of women's clinics, abortion counselors—women dedicated to returning the skills of women to the community of women.

An Ambiguous Liberation

But on the other hand there is crisis and confusion, even a sense of loss. The expectation that women will have to support themselves (and probably others) has changed some of the more oppressive features of female education, but it has not changed the nature of the jobs available. The imperative to work—to supplement a husband's income or support the children of an absent father—does not send most women into careers as TV newscasters or tennis stars. Women of all races join black men and youths in a weary army of subsistence wage-earners to make two to three dollars an hour for typing, cleaning, fetching, soldering, stitching. From a permanent position on the assembly line or in the typing pool it does not look so terribly degraded to bake cookies for spoiled children or to fake orgasms for an uninspiring husband. At home you can be "yourself," a person with intrinsic significance to others. In the Market you are abstractly interchangeable with any other quantum of human energy which can be had for the same price.

But meanwhile, the old ideal of blissful and secure domesticity is getting harder to find than a $25,000 ranch house. The suburban diaspora of the fifties atomized middle- and working-class America into nuclear families; the "singles culture" of the sixties seemed to split even these atoms into individual particles flying off on their own trajectories. We have already noted the rising divorce rates, the increase in the chronically single: today only a tiny proportion of American households (seven out of a hundred) are the typical nuclear families of twenty years ago, with a working father, children, and an unemployed wife. Instead of marriage as an eternal union, guaranteeing a woman long-term financial security, we have the speeded up "marriage cycle" whose inexorable rotations spin off the most domesticated woman as well as the young and independent. Even woman's biological vulnerability, her bond to the children, no longer seems to guarantee male protectiveness. Most divorced fathers vanish within a year to avoid paying child support to an ex-wife. And for the young woman old-fashioned enough to think that an unplanned pregnancy might provoke a proposal: she'll be lucky if her boy friend is chivalrous enough to split the costs of an abortion.

Even sex, supposedly one of the big payoffs of women's "liberation" in the sixties and seventies, probably leads to anxiety more often than release. Mercifully detached from reproduction, sex is rapidly parting company from human commitment and even simple affection. Mid-century culture veiled sex in romance and then sublimated it off into the purchase of "sexy" cars, cigarettes, even furniture. But when the adult "permissiveness" of the sixties licensed sex for direct (rather than vicarious or sublimated) consumption, the veil was ripped away. Sex became another commodity with its own "marketplaces"—bars, resorts, offices, and suburban backyards. The middle-aged housewife knows, to her terror, that she somehow inhabits the same sexual free market as the expensive young women on *Viva* covers or the braless female detectives on TV.

So the world opening up to women today is not exactly the halcyon vista of "careers," options, relationships portrayed by our more positive-thinking feminist leaders. For every sexually successful single there must be a hundred unsuccessful, unslim, "unattractive" housewives. For every careerwoman, there are dozens of low-paid woman job-holders. For every divorce that frees a woman, there are others

that throw women into poverty or loneliness. The alternative to the
suffocation of domesticity turns out to be the old rationalist nightmare: a world dominated by the Market, socially atomized, bereft of
"human" values. At best sexual romanticism had aimed to set women
apart in an oasis of love and nurturance. Most of the time the "oasis"
turned out to be a mirage covering a patch of quicksand. But now
even this much seems unattainable, or too thoroughly discredited to
bother with: there is only the desert.

Out of the real confusion in women's lives—the ambivalence, impatience, disillusionment—a terrifying version of the romanticist/ra-
tionalist dialectic is emerging, one in which neither pole has the
moral force of a "solution," and both agree ultimately only in their
cynicism. On the one side is the neo-romanticist ideology represented
by the anti-abortion movement, the anti-equal rights movement, and
mass self-improvement courses like Total Woman and Fascinating
Womanhood. The constituency for neo-romanticism is the vast number of women who see themselves as potential "losers" in the sexual
free marketplace: housewives who have no alternative means of support to their husbands' income and, they fear, no alternative to their
present husbands.

For these women every advance in women's legal status seems to
represent a further erosion of male responsibility. "Equal rights"
seem to threaten the only security a woman has left when her husband's sexual interest wanes—alimony and child support. Abortion is
threatening simply because it does make pregnancy a "woman's
choice," rather than something that men inflict and must be held responsible for (and at the same time, of course, abortion makes it
easier for other women to "play around.") And in a society which licenses casual couplings and uncouplings but has nothing to offer a
discarded wife but welfare, these fears are real enough.

But today's neo-romanticism is at best a degenerate descendant of
the sexual romanticism of the nineteenth century. It makes no claims
to intellectual rigor. When a higher justification is needed, it skips
backward over the corpse of romanticist science and appeals to the
ghosts of patriarchal religion: *God* has decreed unequal rights, invol-
untary pregnancies, monogamy, male domination, and if worse comes
to worst, alimony. But, except when he contemplates homosexuality
or the mixing of the races, the God of neo-romanticist ideology is a
strangely mellowed, permissive version of the old God of Abraham or
Calvin. He is a God who has made His peace with the consumer soci-

ety, we are led to believe by Mirabel Morgan (who advises in *Total Woman* on how to exchange sex for "gifts")—a God who smiles benignly on the wife who serves dinner topless to earn a new living room rug and approves when she performs fellatio to win a weekend in Miami.

But there is a deeper level of corruption to today's neo romanticism. Nineteenth-century romanticist ideology upheld the home as a negation of the Market, one small haven for Christian values within the moral wasteland created by capitalism. But the contemporary middle- to upper-middle-class home defended by neo-romanticism can hardly be said to stand in moral antagonism to the Market; it has been too thoroughly colonized, for too long. Its ideals do not come from the Bible or from some autonomous principle of womanly virtue, but from Madison Avenue, CBS, General Electric, Procter & Gamble. To hold up the home designed by Frigidaire, Bendix, RCA, and General Foods as a social ideal is not to challenge, in however indirect a way, the inhumanity of the marketplace, but to defend the material wealth of a particular class and race of people. For all its emphasis on the "right to life," neo-romanticist ideology does not even have a charitable nod for poor black children, for welfare mothers, and for that majority of the world's people who do not have indoor plumbing, much less Whirlpool baths and lawn sprinkler systems. All these must be simply kept at bay, along with the "women's libbers" who would unleash sexual anarchy if anyone were so foolish as to give them equal rights and free access to abortions.

The alternative to neo-romanticism which most forcefully and publicly competes for women's allegiance today is not, alas, rationalist feminism, but the marketplace psychology purveyed in the "self-help" literature, popular magazines, psychotherapy programs, and occasionally, feminist literature itself. As an ideology for women, marketplace psychology bears a superficial resemblance to the old rationalist feminism. It emphasizes autonomy and opportunity; it implicitly acknowledges the need for formal equality between the sexes. It offers techniques, some similar to feminist consciousness-raising, to build women's confidence and self-reliance. But there the resemblance ends. For rationalist feminism had always had a program of *social* change, and not just individual improvement. Women would not be liberated one by one, but through political efforts to socialize the caring functions they had performed in the home. In Charlotte Perkins Gilman's vision (and she remains one of the most radi-

cal rationalist feminist thinkers of this century), women would not
simply desert the home, they would organize for the collective dining
halls, day care centers, laundries, etc., which alone would make all
women free of domestic labor.

But marketplace psychology, at least in its most cynical forms,
would see in such collective organizing efforts only the snivelings of
people afflicted with a "victim mentality." There is no justification
for mutual help or social change in an ideology which holds each person wholly responsible for her own condition, from the welfare mother
to the million-dollar-a-year TV star. They each "chose" to be what
they are, and they *could* choose to be something else. The "neo-rationalist" program for women, then, is to break out into the marketplace, but without making any social provision for the children who
are left behind or for all the women who are not educated enough,
wealthy enough, or pretty enough, to make it on their own too. If
neo-romanticism wants to concentrate the principle of nurturance
and caring within the fortress of the home; today's neo-rationalist
thinking seems happy to abandon them altogether. Let the "losers"
look out for themselves!

These then are the ideological poles which dominate sexual politics
in the late twentieth century—the "romanticism" of the sun-belt suburbs or the "rationalism" of the paperback self-help shelf. Claus-
trophobia or agoraphobia. Suffocation or free-fall. Neither projects a
vision of moral redemption or social transformation. Neither upholds
any higher value than material self-interest in a world of scarcity. The
neo-romanticists huddle in their fortress and the neo-rationalists
strike out in the lifeboat: both are strategies of defense and desperation. As rallying points for idealists they are embarrassing, as living
options for women they are bankrupt.

These are, in extreme and distorted form, the age-old options
which masculinist culture presents to women. Only today the experts
refuse to arbitrate. The monolithic grip of the old romanticist experts
has been broken, and the horde of pop psychologists, sex therapists,
counselors, liberal gynecologists, etc., who take their place offer no
answer—or all answers. Their only clear and consistent interest in the
Woman Question is that it remain, insofar as possible, privatized—
compressed into the psyche of each individual woman, for this is the
only terrain on which they can operate. They will not presume, as
psychomedical science did before them, to pass judgment on what is
right or wrong. The most sophisticated raise their agnosticism to the

status of a therapeutic principle: "I can't tell you anything; only you can help yourself," an admission which unfortunately does not obviate the need for payment.

And where is feminism in all this—the force which reopened the Woman Question in the first place? Is it prepared to project a new ideal, a moral outlook, a way for women—and men—to live? After all, it was feminism which comprehended the violence implicit in sexual romanticism. It saw through the psychomedical defense of domesticity, the systematic segregation of women workers, the corporate sell directed at women, the imposition of phallic sexuality. But now it hangs back, as if it had exhausted its moral energy in the assault on sexual romanticism. Feminism hesitates, unable to intervene in the dominant polarization between neo-romanticist and neo-rationalist ideologies.

In its uncertainty, feminism at this moment hedges with a philosophy of individual choice: let there be rights; let there be choices; let there be no right or wrong way for all women. Neo-rationalism is thus condoned (after all it champions the right to individual choices). And neo-romanticism is condemned only for its absolutism, for its hostility to free choice. As neo-romanticist ideology gains ground, fueled by the subjective crisis in women's lives, feminism seems to become ever more determined about its undeterminedness, more nervously defensive of "choice" for its own sake, less and less prone to pass judgment on the alternatives, or to ask how these came to be the choices in the first place.

The reason we hang back is because there are no answers left but the most radical ones. We cannot assimilate into a masculinist society without doing violence to our own nature, which is, of course, *human* nature. But neither can we retreat into domestic isolation, clinging to an archaic feminine ideal. Nor can we deny that the dilemma is a social issue, and abandon each other to our own "free choices" when the choices are not of our making and we are not "free."

The Woman Question in the end is not the question of *women*. It is not we who are the problem and it is not our needs which are the mystery. From our subjective perspective (denied by centuries of masculinist "science" and analysis), the Woman Question becomes the question of how shall we all—women and children and men—organize our lives together. This is a question which has no answer in the marketplace or among the throng of experts who sell their wisdom there. And this is the *only* question.

There are clues to the answer in the distant past, in a gynocentric era that linked woman's nurturance to a tradition of skill, caring to craft. There are the outlines of a solution in the contours of the industrial era, with its promise of a collective strength and knowledge surpassing all past human efforts to provide for human needs. And there are impulses toward the truth in each one of us. In our very confusion, in our legacy of repressed energy and half-forgotten wisdom, lies the understanding that it is not *we* who must change but the social order which marginalized women in the first place and with us all "human values."

The romantic/rationalist alternative is no longer acceptable: we refuse to remain on the margins of society, and we refuse to enter that society on its terms. If we reject these alternatives, then the challenge is to frame a moral outlook which proceeds from women's needs and experiences but which cannot be trivialized, sentimentalized, or domesticated. A synthesis which transcends both the rationalist and romanticist poles must necessarily challenge the masculinist social order itself. It must insist that the human values that women were assigned to preserve expand out of the confines of private life and become the organizing principles of society. This is the vision that is implicit in feminism—a society that is organized around human needs: a society in which child raising is not dismissed as each woman's individual problem, but in which the nurturance and well-being of all children is a transcendent public priority . . . a society in which healing is not a commodity distributed according to the dictates of profit but is integral to the network of community life . . . in which wisdom about daily life is not hoarded by "experts" or doled out as a commodity but is drawn from the experience of all people and freely shared among them.

This is the most radical vision but there are no human alternatives. The Market, with its financial abstractions, deformed science, and obsession with dead things—must be pushed back to the margins. And the "womanly" values of community and caring must rise to the center as the only *human* principles.

Notes

NOTES TO CHAPTER ONE

1. Charlotte Perkins Gilman, *The Living of Charlotte Perkins Gilman* (New York: Harper Colophon Books, 1975), p. 91.

2. Karl Marx and Friedrich Engels, "The Communist Manifesto," in *A Handbook on Marxism* (New York: International Publishers, 1935), p. 26.

3. Fernand Braudel, *Capitalism and Material Life 1400–1800* (New York: Harper Colophon Books, 1975), p. ix.

4. Quoted in William F. Ogburn and M. F. Nimkoff, *Technology and the Changing Family* (Boston and New York: Houghton Mifflin Co., 1955), p. 167.

5. Edmund S. Morgan, *The Puritan Family* (New York: Harper Torchbooks, 1966), pp. 44–45.

6. Mary P. Ryan, *Womanhood in America: From Colonial Times to the Present* (New York: New Viewpoints, 1975), p. 31.

7. See, for example: Arthur W. Calhoun, *Social History of the American Family, Volume III: Since the Civil War* (Cleveland: The Arthur H. Clark Co., 1919); Floyd Dell, *Love in the Machine Age* (New York: Octagon Books, 1973); Ogburn and Nimkoff, op. cit.

8. Alexandra Kollontai, "The New Woman," in *The Autobiography of a Sexually Emancipated Communist Woman* (New York: Schocken Books, 1975), p. 55.

9. Sigmund Freud, "Femininity," in James Strachey (ed.), *The Complete Introductory Lectures on Psychoanalysis* (New York: W. W. Norton, 1966), p. 577.

10. Quoted in E. J. Hobsbawm, *The Age of Revolution 1789–1848* (New York: Mentor, 1962), p. 327.

11. Quoted in Eva Figes, *Patriarchal Attitudes* (New York: Stein and Day, 1970), p. 114.

12. Olive Schreiner, *Woman and Labor* (New York: Frederick A. Stokes, 1911), p. 65.

13. R. H. Tawney, *Religion and the Rise of Capitalism* (Gloucester, Massachusetts: Peter Smith, 1962), p. 228.

14. Quoted in Kate Millett, *Sexual Politics* (New York: Avon, 1969), pp. 139–40.

15. G. Stanley Hall, "The Relations between Higher and Lower Races," reprint of the Massachusetts Historical Society, January 1903 (unpaginated).

16. Quoted in Figes, op. cit., p. 107.

17. Olive Schreiner, *The Story of an African Farm* (New York: Fawcett Premier, 1968), p. 167.

NOTES TO CHAPTER TWO

1. See Jules Michelet, *Satanism and Witchcraft* (Secaucus, New Jersey: Citadel Press, 1939); Margaret Alice Murray, *The Witch-Cult in Western Europe* (New York: Oxford University Press, 1921); Christina Hole, *A Mirror of Witchcraft* (London: Chatto and Windus, 1957); Alan C. Kors and Edward Peters, *Witchcraft in Europe: 1100–1700* (Philadelphia: University of Pennsylvania Press, 1972); Pennethorne Hughes, *Witchcraft* (London: Penguin Books, 1952).

2. Quoted in Thomas S. Szasz, *The Manufacture of Madness* (New York: Dell Publishing Co., 1970), p. 89.

3. Heinrich Kramer and Jacob Sprenger, *Malleus Maleficarum: The Hammer of Witches,* Pennethorne Hughes (ed.), Montague Summers (trans.) (London: The Folio Society, 1968), p. 218.

4. Ibid., p. 30.

5. Ibid., p. 150.

6. Ibid., p. 128.

7. Susan B. Blum, "Women, Witches and Herbals," *The Morris Arboretum Bulletin, 25,* September, 1974, p. 43.

8. Quoted in Szasz, op. cit., p. 85.

9. Muriel Joy Hughes, *Women Healers in Medieval Life and Literature* (New York: King's Crown Press, 1943), p. 90.

10. Joseph Kett, *The Formation of the American Medical Profession: The Role of Institutions, 1780–1860* (New Haven: Yale University Press, 1968), p. 108.

11. Jethro Kloss, *Back to Eden* (Santa Barbara, California: Woodbridge Publishing Co., 1972, first published 1934), p. 226.

12. Sarah Orne Jewett, "The Courting of Sister Wisby," in Gail Parker (ed.), *The Oven Birds: American Women on Womanhood 1820–1920* (Garden City, New York: Doubleday/Anchor, 1972), p. 221.

13. Samuel Haber, "The Professions and Higher Education in America: A Historical View," in Margaret S. Gordon (ed.), *Higher Education and the Labor Market* (New York: McGraw-Hill, 1974), p. 241.

14. Whitfield J. Bell, Jr., "A Portrait of the Colonial Physician," in *The Colonial Physician and Other Essays* (New York: Science History Publications, 1975), p. 22.

15. See Carl A. Binger, *Revolutionary Doctor, Benjamin Rush* (New York: W. W. Norton, 1966).

16. Haber, loc. cit.

17. William G. Rothstein, *American Physicians in the Nineteenth Century* (Baltimore: The Johns Hopkins University Press, 1972), p. 27.

18. Quoted in Binger, op. cit., p. 88.

19. Dolores Burns (ed.), *The Greatest Health Discovery: Natural Hygiene, and Its Evolution Past, Present and Future* (Chicago: Natural Hygiene Press, 1972), p. 30.

20. Richard Harrison Shryock, *Medicine and Society in America: 1660–1860* (Ithaca, New York: Great Seal Books, 1960), p. 17.

21. Rothstein, op. cit., p. 43.

22. Binger, op. cit., p. 217.

23. Quoted in Rothstein, op. cit., p. 47.

24. Ibid., p. 51.

25. Shryock, op. cit., p. 70.

26. Rothstein, op. cit., pp. 333–39.

27. Shryock, op. cit., p. 131.

28. Quoted in Philip S. Foner, *History of the Labor Movement in the United States, Vol. I: From Colonial Times to the Founding of the American Federation of Labor* (New York: International Publishers, 1962), p. 132.

29. Mary P. Ryan, *Womanhood in America: From Colonial Times to the Present* (New York: New Viewpoints, 1975), p. 128.

30. Elizabeth Cady Stanton, "Motherhood," in Alice S. Rossi (ed.), *The Feminist Papers: From Adams to De Beauvoir* (New York and London: Columbia University Press, 1973), p. 399.

31. Ibid., p. 401.

32. Richard Harrison Shryock, *Medicine in America: Historical Essays* (Baltimore: The Johns Hopkins University Press, 1966), p. 117.

33. Arthur M. Schlesinger, Jr., *The Age of Jackson* (Boston: Little, Brown, 1953), p. 181.

34. Quoted in Schlesinger, op. cit., p. 183.

35. Schlesinger, loc. cit.

36. Marcia Altman, David Kubrin, John Kwasnik, and Tina Logan, "The People's Healers: Health Care and Class Struggle in the United States in the 19th Century," 1974, mimeo, p. 18.

37. Quoted in Rothstein, op. cit., p. 129.

38. Ibid., p. 131.

39. Altman et al., op. cit., p. 23.

40. Rothstein, op. cit., p. 141.

41. Kett, op. cit., p. 119.

42. Altman et al., op. cit., p. 27.

43. Quoted in Kett, op. cit., p. 110.

44. Burns, op. cit., p. 137.

45. Rothstein, op. cit., p. 333.

46. Quoted in Altman et al., op. cit., p. 39.

47. Ibid., p. 40.

48. Quoted in Burns, op. cit., p. 122.

49. Richard H. Shryock, quoted in Burns, op. cit., p. 126.

50. Burns, op. cit., p. 124.

51. Rothstein, op. cit., p. 156.

52. Ibid., p. 108.

53. Ibid., p. 108.

54. Gerald E. Markowitz and David Karl Rosner, "Doctors in Crisis: A Study of the Use of Medical Education Reform to Establish Modern Professional Elitism in Medicine," *American Quarterly* 25, March 1973, p. 88.

55. Quoted in Thomas Woody, *A History of Women's Education in the United States,* Vol. II (New York: Octagon Books, 1974), p. 348.

56. Altman et al., op. cit., p. 25.

57. Quoted in Woody, op. cit., p. 343.

58. Catherine Beecher, "On Female Health in America," in Nancy Cott (ed.), *Root of Bitterness: Documents of the Social History of American Women* (New York: E. P. Dutton, 1972), p. 269.

59. Quoted in Woody, op. cit., pp. 344–45.

60. Quoted in Woody, op. cit., p. 349.

61. Ibid., p. 322.

62. Ibid., p. 360.

63. *Journal of the American Medical Association* 37, 1901, p. 1403.

64. Woody, op. cit., p. 349.

65. Constance Rover, *The Punch Book of Women's Rights* (South Brunswick, New Jersey: A. S. Barnes, 1967), p. 81.

66. Quoted in G. J. Barker-Benfield, *The Horrors of the Half-Known Life: Male Attitudes Toward Women and Sexuality in Nineteenth Century America* (New York: Harper & Row, 1976), p. 87.

67. Quoted in Shryock, *Medicine in America: Historical Essays*, p. 185.

68. Quoted in Woody, op. cit., p. 346.

69. Ibid., p. 361.

70. Quoted in Shryock, *Medicine in America: Historical Essays*, p. 184.

71. Quoted in Burns, op. cit., p. 118.

72. Ibid., p. 116.

73. Markowitz and Rosner, op. cit., p. 95.

74. Quoted in Haber, op. cit., p. 264.

NOTES TO CHAPTER THREE

1. Sir William Osler, *Aequanimitas: With Other Addresses to Medical Students, Nurses and Practitioners of Medicine* (Philadelphia: P. Blakiston's Sons, 1932), p. 219.

2. See Robert H. Wiebe, *The Search for Order* (New York: Hill and Wang, 1967) and Barbara and John Ehrenreich, "The Professional/Managerial Class," *Radical America,* March–April and May–June, 1977.

3. Quoted in Samuel Haber, *Efficiency and Uplift: Scientific Management in the Progressive Era 1890–1920* (Chicago: University of Chicago Press, 1964), p. 99.

4. Quoted in Richard Hofstadter, *Anti-Intellectualism in American Life* (New York: Alfred A. Knopf, 1963), p. 200.

5. Quoted in Edwin T. Layton, *The Revolt of the Engineers: Social Responsi-*

bility and the American Engineering Profession (Cleveland: Case Western Reserve University Press, 1971), p. 67.

6. Edward A. Ross, *The Social Trend* (New York: Century, 1922), p. 171.

7. Quoted in Paul F. Boller, Jr., *American Thought in Transition: The Impact of Evolutionary Naturalism 1865–1900* (Chicago: Rand-McNally, 1969), p. 120.

8. Sinclair Lewis, *Arrowsmith* (New York: Signet, 1961), pp. 84–85.

9. Ibid., p. 13.

10. Ibid., p. 25.

11. Boller, op. cit., p. 23.

12. Charlotte Perkins Gilman, *Women and Economics*, Carl N. Degler (ed.) (New York: Harper & Row, 1966), pp. 330–31.

13. Elizabeth Chesser, *Perfect Health for Women and Children* (London: Methuen, 1912), p. 49.

14. Quoted in Geraldine J. Clifford, "E. L. Thorndike: The Psychologist as Professional Man of Science," in *Historical Conceptions of Psychology,* Mary Henle, Julian Jaynes, and John J. Sullivan (eds.) (New York: Springer Publishing, 1973), p. 234.

15. Quoted in Anna Robeson Burr, *Weir Mitchell: His Life and Letters* (New York: Duffield and Co., 1929), pp. 82–83.

16. Lewis, op. cit., p. 265.

17. Ibid., pp. 268–69.

18. William G. Rothstein, *American Physicians in the Nineteenth Century* (Baltimore: The Johns Hopkins University Press, 1972), p. 262.

19. George Bernard Shaw, *The Doctor's Dilemma* (Baltimore: Penguin, 1954), pp. 107–8.

20. John H. Knowles, M.D., "The Responsibility of the Individual," in John H. Knowles, M.D. (ed.), *Doing Better and Feeling Worse: Health in the United States* (New York: W. W. Norton and Co., 1977), p. 63.

21. Samuel Haber, "The Professions and Higher Education in America: A Historical View," in *Higher Education and the Labor Market*, Margaret S. Gordon (ed.) (New York: McGraw-Hill, 1974), p. 264.

22. Allan Nevins, *John D. Rockefeller* (New York: Scribner, 1959), pp. 279–80.

23. Joseph F. Wall, *Andrew Carnegie* (New York: Oxford University Press, 1970), p. 833.

24. Ibid., p. 67.

25. E. Richard Brown, *Rockefeller Medicine Men: Medicine and Capitalism in the Progressive Era* (Berkeley: University of California Press, in press), p. 99.

26. Brown, loc. cit.

27. Lewis, op. cit., pp. 271–72.

28. Abraham Flexner, *Medical Education in the U.S. and Canada* (New York: Carnegie Foundation, 1910) (available from University Microfilms, Ltd., Ann Arbor, Michigan).

29. Rosemary Stevens, *American Medicine and the Public Interest* (New Haven: Yale University Press, 1971), p. 56.

30. Brown, op. cit., p. 138.

31. Gerald Markowitz and David K. Rosner, "Doctors in Crisis: A Study of the Use of Medical Education Reform to Establish Modern Professional Elitism in Medicine," *American Quarterly* 25 (1973), p. 83.

32. Rothstein, op. cit., p. 265.

33. Ibid., p. 266.

34. Haber, "The Professions and Higher Education in America," p. 265.

35. J. E. Stubbs, "What Shall Be Our Attitude Toward Professional Mistakes?" *Journal of the American Medical Association* 32 (1899), p. 1176.

36. Haber, "The Professions and Higher Education in America," p. 266.

37. Quoted in Harvey Williams Cushing, *The Life of Sir William Osler,* Vol. I (New York: Oxford University Press, 1940), p. 222.

38. Ibid., p. 223.

39. Quoted in Robert B. Bean, M.D., *Sir William Osler: Aphorisms,* William B. Bean, M.D. (ed.) (New York: Henry Schuman, 1950), p. 114.

40. Cushing, op. cit., p. 354.

41. Osler, *Aequanimitas,* p. 286.

42. Ibid., p. 260.

43. Frances E. Kobrin, "The American Midwife Controversy: A Crisis of Professionalization," *Bulletin of the History of Medicine,* July–August 1966, p. 350.

44. Molly C. Dougherty, "Southern Lay Midwives as Ritual Specialists," paper presented at the American Anthropological Association Annual Meeting, Mexico City, 1974.

45. Austin Flint, M.D., "The Use and Abuse of Medical Charities in Medical Education," *Proceedings of the National Conference on Charities and Corrections,* 1898, p. 331.

46. Quoted in Ann H. Sablosky, "The Power of the Forceps: A Study of the Development of Midwifery in the United States," Master's Thesis, Graduate School of Social Work and Social Research, Bryn Mawr College, May 1975, p. 15.

47. Quoted in Ursula Gilbert, "Midwifery as a Deviant Occupation in America," unpublished paper, 1975.

48. G. J. Barker-Benfield, *The Horrors of the Half-Known Life* (New York: Harper & Row, 1976), p. 63.

49. Sablosky, op. cit., p. 16.

50. Barker-Benfield, op. cit., p. 69.

51. Sablosky, op. cit., p. 17.

52. Barker-Benfield, op. cit., p. 69.

53. See Doris Haire, "The Cultural Warping of Childbirth," *International Childbirth Education Association News,* Spring 1972; Suzanne Arms, *Immaculate Deception* (San Francisco: San Francisco Book Co., 1976).

54. Kobrin, op. cit.

NOTES TO CHAPTER FOUR

1. Anna Robeson Burr, *Weir Mitchell: His Life and Letters* (New York: Duffield and Co., 1929), p. 289.

2. Charlotte Perkins Gilman, *The Living of Charlotte Perkins Gilman: An Autobiography* (New York: Harper Colophon Books, 1975), p. 96.

3. Gilman, loc. cit.

4. Charlotte Perkins Gilman, *The Yellow Wallpaper* (Old Westbury, New York: The Feminist Press, 1973).

5. Gilman, *Autobiography,* p. 121.

6. Catherine Beecher, "Statistics of Female Health," in Gail Parker (ed.), *The Oven Birds: American Women on Womanhood 1820–1920* (Garden City, New York: Doubleday/Anchor, 1972), p. 165.

7. Ilza Veith, *Hysteria: The History of a Disease* (Chicago and London: The University of Chicago Press, 1965), p. 216.

8. Quoted in F. O. Matthiessen, *The James Family* (New York: Alfred A. Knopf, 1961), p. 272.

9. Quoted in Irving H. Bartlett, *Wendell Phillips: Brahmin Radical* (Boston: Beacon Press, 1961), p. 78.

10. Quoted in Leon Edel (ed.), *The Diary of Alice James* (New York: Dodd, Mead, 1964), p. 14.

11. We thank medical historian Rick Brown for sharing this story with us.

12. Thorstein Veblen, *Theory of the Leisure Class* (New York: Modern Library, 1934).

13. Burr, op. cit., p. 176.

14. Olive Schreiner, *Woman and Labor* (New York: Frederick A. Stokes, 1911), p. 98.

15. John C. Gunn, M.D., *Gunn's New Family Physician* (New York: Saalfield Publishing, 1924), p. 120.

16. New York Public Library Picture Collection, no source given.

17. Dr. Mary Putnam Jacobi, "On Female Invalidism," in Nancy F. Cott (ed.), *Root of Bitterness: Documents of the Social History of American Women* (New York: E. P. Dutton, 1972), p. 307.

18. John S. Haller, Jr., and Robin M. Haller, *The Physician and Sexuality in Victorian America* (Urbana, Illinois: University of Illinois Press, 1974), pp. 143–44.

19. Ibid., p. 168.

20. Ibid., p. 31.

21. Ibid., p. 28.

22. Gilman, *The Yellow Wallpaper,* pp. 9–10.

23. Quoted in G. Stanley Hall, *Adolescence, Vol. II* (New York: D. Appleton, 1905), p. 588.

24. Gunn, op. cit., p. 421.

25. W. C. Taylor, M.D., *A Physician's Counsels to Woman in Health and Disease* (Springfield: W. J. Holland and Co., 1871), pp. 284–85.

26. Winfield Scott Hall, Ph.D., M.D., *Sexual Knowledge* (Philadelphia: John C. Winston, 1916), pp. 202–3.

27. U. S. Bureau of the Census, *Historical Statistics of the United States, Colonial Times to 1957,* Washington, D.C., 1960, p. 25.

28. Rachel Gillett Fruchter, "Women's Weakness: Consumption and Women in the 19th Century," Columbia University School of Public Health, unpublished paper, 1973.

29. Haller and Haller, op. cit., p. 59.

30. Emma Goldman, *Living My Life,* Vol. I (New York: Dover Publications, Inc., 1970, first published 1931), pp. 185–86.

31. Carroll D. Wright, *The Working Girls of Boston* (Boston: Wright and Potter Printing, State Printers, 1889), p. 71.

32. Ibid., pp. 117–18.

33. Lucien C. Warner, M.D., *A Popular Treatise on the Functions and Diseases of Woman* (New York: Manhattan Publishing, 1874), p. 109.

34. Quoted in Dr. Alice Moqué, "The Mistakes of Mothers," *Proceedings of the National Congress of Mothers Second Annual Convention,* Washington, D.C., May 1898, p. 43.

35. Goldman, op. cit., p. 187.

36. Quoted in G. J. Barker-Benfield, *The Horrors of the Half-Known Life: Male Attitudes Toward Women and Sexuality in Nineteenth-Century America* (New York: Harper & Row, 1976), p. 128.

37. Quoted in Elaine and English Showalter, "Victorian Women and Menstruation," in Martha Vicinus (ed.), *Suffer and Be Still: Women in the Victorian Age* (Bloomington: Indiana University Press, 1972), p. 43.

38. "Mary Livermore's Recommendatory Letter," in Cott, op. cit., p. 292.

39. Mary Putnam Jacobi, M.D., in Cott, op. cit., p. 307.

40. Quoted in Haller and Haller, op. cit., p. 73.

41. Ibid., p. 47.

42. Quoted in Haller and Haller, op. cit., p. 51.

43. Hall, op. cit., p. 578.

44. Quoted in Haller and Haller, op. cit., p. 56.

45. Hall, op. cit., p. 56.

46. Ibid., p. 562.

47. Loc. cit.

48. Frederick Hollick, M.D., *The Diseases of Women, Their Cause and Cure Familiarly Explained* (New York: T. W. Strong, 1849).

49. Quoted in Ann Douglas Wood, "The 'Fashionable Diseases': Women's Complaints and their Treatment in Nineteenth-Century America," *Journal of Interdisciplinary History* 4, Summer 1973, p. 29.

50. Quoted in Rita Arditti, "Women as Objects: Science and Sexual Politics," *Science for the People,* September 1974, p. 8.

51. W. W. Bliss, *Woman and Her Thirty-Years' Pilgrimage* (Boston: B. B. Russell, 1870), p. 96.

52. Quoted in Haller and Haller, op. cit., p. 101.

53. Quoted in Veith, op. cit., p. 205.

54. M. E. Dirix, M.D., *Woman's Complete Guide to Health* (New York: W. A. Townsend and Adams, 1869), pp. 23–24.

55. Quoted in Fruchter, op. cit.

56. Wood, op. cit., p. 30.

57. Barker-Benfield, op. cit., pp. 121–24.

58. Ben Barker-Benfield, "The Spermatic Economy: A Nineteenth Century View of Sexuality," *Feminist Studies* 1, Summer 1972, pp. 45–74.

59. Barker-Benfield, *Horrors of the Half-Known Life,* p. 122.

60. Ibid., p. 30.

61. Ibid., pp. 96–102.

62. Haller and Haller, op. cit., p. 103.

63. Thomas Woody, *A History of Women's Education in the United States,* Vol. II (New York: Octagon Books, 1974).

64. Haller and Haller, op. cit., p. 61.

65. Edward H. Clarke, M.D., *Sex in Education, or a Fair Chance for the Girls* (Boston: James R. Osgood, 1873. Reprint edition by Arno Press Inc., 1972).

66. Quoted in Haller and Haller, op. cit., p. 39.

67. Vern L. Bullough and Bonnie Bullough, *The Subordinate Sex: A History of Attitudes Toward Women* (Urbana: University of Illinois Press, 1973), p. 323.

68. Wood, op. cit., p. 207.

69. Hall, op. cit., p. 632.

70. Ibid., p. 633.

71. Quoted in Haller and Haller, op. cit., p. 81.

72. Burr, op. cit., p. 374.

73. Woody, op. cit., p. 154.

74. Quoted in Haller and Haller, op. cit., pp. 29–30.

75. Rosalind Rosenberg, "In Search of Woman's Nature: 1850–1920," *Feminist Studies* 3, Fall 1975, p. 141.

76. Quoted in Woody, op. cit., p. 153.

77. Burr, op. cit., p. 183.

78. Jane Addams, *Twenty Years at Hull-House* (New York: Macmillan, 1960), p. 65.

79. Burr, op. cit., p. 290.

80. Quoted in Wood, op. cit., p. 38.

81. Burr, op. cit., p. 184.

82. Quoted in Theodore Roosevelt, "Birth Reform, From the Positive, Not the Negative Side," in *Complete Works of Theodore Roosevelt,* Vol. XIX (New York: Scribner, 1926), p. 163.

83. Roosevelt, op. cit., p. 161.

84. Hall, op. cit., p. 579.

85. S. Weir Mitchell, *Constance Trescot* (New York: The Century Co., 1905), p. 382.

86. Quoted in Veith, op. cit., p. 217.

87. See Linda Gordon, *Woman's Body, Woman's Right: A Social History of Birth Control in America* (New York: Grossman, 1977).

88. Carroll Smith-Rosenberg, "The Hysterial Woman: Sex Roles in Nineteenth Century America," *Social Research,* 39, Winter 1972, pp. 652–78.

89. Quoted in Matthiessen, op. cit., p. 276.

90. Dirix, op. cit., p. 60.

91. Thomas S. Szasz, *The Myth of Mental Illness* (New York: Dell, 1961), p. 48.

NOTES TO CHAPTER FIVE

1. Quoted in Margaret Reid, *Economics of Household Production* (New York: John Wiley and Sons, 1934), p. 43.

2. William F. Ogburn and M. F. Nimkoff, *Technology and the Changing Family* (Boston and New York: Houghton Mifflin, 1955), p. 152.

3. U. S. Bureau of the Census, *Historical Statistics of the United States, Colonial Times to 1957*, Washington, D.C., 1960.

4. Elizabeth F. Baker, *Technology and Women's Work* (New York: Columbia University Press, 1964), p. 4.

5. Reid, op. cit., p. 52.

6. Caroline L. Hunt, *The Life of Ellen H. Richards* (Washington, D.C.: The American Home Economics Association, 1958), p. 141.

7. Edward A. Ross, *The Social Trend* (New York: Century Co., 1922), p. 80.

8. Thorstein Veblen, *Theory of the Leisure Class* (New York: Modern Library, 1934), pp. 81–82.

9. Fannie Perry Gay, *Woman's Journal*, November 12, 1889, p. 365.

10. Quoted in Hunt, op. cit., p. 159.

11. Olive Schreiner, *Woman and Labor* (New York: Frederick A. Stokes, 1911), pp. 45–46.

12. Quoted in Robert H. Bremner, *Children and Youth in America, A Documentary History, Volume II, 1866–1932* (Cambridge, Massachusetts: Harvard University Press, 1971), p. 365.

13. Edmond Demolins, *Anglo-Saxon Superiority: To What Is It Due?* (New York: R. F. Fenne, 1898).

14. Arthur W. Calhoun, *The Social History of the American Family from Colonial Times to the Present, Volume III: Since the Civil War* (Cleveland: Arthur H. Clark, 1919), p. 197.

15. Russell Lynes, *The Domesticated Americans* (New York: Harper & Row, 1957), p. 11.

16. Quoted in Calhoun, op. cit., p. 197.

17. Calhoun, op. cit., pp. 179–98.

18. Richard Sennett, *Families Against the City: Middle Class Homes of Industrial Chicago 1872–1890* (Cambridge, Massachusetts: Harvard University Press, 1970).

19. Edward A. Ross, *Social Psychology* (New York: Macmillan, 1917), p. 89.

20. Charles H. Whitaker, *The Joke About Housing* (College Park, Maryland: McGrath Publishing, 1969, first published 1920), p. 9.

21. David J. Pivar, *The New Abolitionism: The Quest for Social Purity* (Ann Arbor, Michigan: University Microfilms, 1965), p. 283.

22. Quoted in Calhoun, op. cit., pp. 197–98.

23. Editorial, *Ladies' Home Journal*, October 1911, p. 6.

24. Robert Clarke, *Ellen Swallow: The Woman Who Founded Ecology* (Chicago: Follett, 1973), p. 51.

25. Ibid., p. 12.

26. Ibid., pp. 32–33.

27. Hunt, op. cit., p. 78.

28. Clarke, op. cit., p. 157.

29. Hunt, op. cit., p. 157.

30. Robert H. Wiebe, *The Search for Order* (New York: Hill and Wang, 1967).

31. Proceedings of the Sixth Annual Conference on Home Economics, Lake Placid, New York, 1904, p. 64.

32. Ibid., p. 16.

33. Proceedings of the Fourth Annual Conference on Home Economics, Lake Placid, New York, 1902, p. 85.

34. Eileen E. Quigley, *Introduction to Home Economics* (New York: Macmillan, 1974), pp. 58–59.

35. Editorial on "Public School Instruction in Cooking," *Journal of the American Medical Association,* 32, 1899, p. 1183.

36. Sallie S. Cotten, "A National Training School for Women," in *The Work and Words of the National Congress of Mothers* (New York: D. Appleton, 1897), p. 280.

37. Mrs. H. M. Plunkett, *Women, Plumbers and Doctors, or Household Sanitation* (New York: D. Appleton, 1897), p. 203.

38. Ibid., p. 11.

39. Editorial, *Journal of the American Medical Association,* 32, 1899, p. 1183.

40. Helen Campbell, *Household Economics* (New York: G. P. Putnam, 1907), p. 206.

41. Plunkett, op. cit., p. 10.

42. Stuart Ewen, *Captains of Consciousness: Advertising and the Social Roots of Consumer Culture* (New York: McGraw-Hill, 1976), pp. 169 70.

43. Campbell, op. cit., p. 196.

44. Quoted in Hunt, op. cit., p. 161.

45. Harry Braverman, *Labor and Monopoly Capital: The Degradation of Work in the Twentieth Century* (New York: Monthly Review Press, 1974), pp. 85–123.

46. Christine Frederick, "The New Housekeeping," serialized in the *Ladies' Home Journal,* September–December 1912.

47. Samuel Haber, *Efficiency and Uplift: Scientific Management in the Progressive Era, 1890–1920* (Chicago: University of Chicago Press, 1964), p. 2.

48. Reid, op. cit., pp. 75–76.

49. Proceedings of the Fourth Annual Conference on Home Economics, Lake Placid, New York, 1902, p. 59.

50. Carol Lopate, "Ironies of the Home Economics Movement," *Edcentric: A Journal of Educational Change,* no. 31/32, November 1974, p. 40.

51. Thomas Woody, *A History of Women's Education in the United States,* Vol. II (New York: Octagon Books, 1974), pp. 60–61.

52. Quoted in Woody, op. cit., p. 52.

53. Hunt, op. cit., p. 113.

54. Ellen Richards, *Euthenics: The Science of Controllable Environment* (Boston: Whitcomb and Barrows, 1912), p. 154.

55. Letter from "E.W.S.," *Woman's Journal,* September 10, 1898, p. 293.

56. Letter from Mrs. Vivia A. B. Henderson, *Woman's Journal,* November 19, 1898, p. 375.

57. H. B. B. Blackwell, "Housework as a Profession," *Woman's Journal,* August 27, 1898, p. 276.

58. Campbell, op. cit., p. 219.

59. Haber, op. cit., p. 62.

60. Proceedings of the Fourth Annual Conference on Home Economics, Lake Placid, New York, 1902, p. 36.

61. Charlotte Perkins Gilman, *The Home: Its Work and Influence* (Urbana: University of Illinois Press, 1972, first published 1903), p. 93.

62. Ibid., pp. 179–81.

63. Calhoun, op. cit., p. 180.

64. Ibid., p. 185.

65. Hunt, op. cit., p. 161.

66. Quoted in Richards, op. cit., p. 160.

67. Quoted in Hunt, op. cit., p. 163.

68. Jane Addams, *Twenty Years at Hull-House* (New York: Macmillan, 1960, first published 1910), p. 294.

69. Mrs. L. P. Rowland, "The Friendly Visitor," in Proceedings of the National Conference on Charities and Corrections 1897, p. 256.

70. Calhoun, op. cit., p. 77.

71. Miss Eleanor Hanson, "Forty-three Families Treated by Friendly Visiting," Proceedings of the National Conference on Charities and Corrections 1907, p. 315.

72. Mary E. McDowell, "Friendly Visiting," Proceedings of the National Conference on Charities and Corrections 1896, p. 253.

73. Reverend W. J. Kerby, "Self-help in the Home," Proceedings of the National Conference on Charities and Corrections 1908, p. 81.

74. Addams, op. cit., p. 253.

75. Quoted in Proceedings of the Seventh Annual Conference on Home Economics, Lake Placid, New York, 1905, p. 67.

76. Isabel F. Hyams, "Teaching of Home Economics in Social Settlements," Proceedings of the Seventh Annual Conference on Home Economics, Lake Placid, New York, 1905, pp. 56–57.

77. Isabel F. Hyams, "The Louisa May Alcott Club," Proceedings of the Second Annual Conference on Home Economics, Lake Placid, New York, 1900, p. 18.

78. Ibid., p. 19.

79. Jessica Braley, "Ideals and Standards as Reflected in Work for Social Service," Proceedings of the Fourth Annual Conference on Home Economics, Lake Placid, New York, 1902, p. 49.

80. Emma Goldman, *Living My Life,* Vol. I (New York: Dover Publications, 1970, first published 1931), p. 160.

81. Quoted in Proceedings of the Third Annual Conference on Home Economics, Lake Placid, New York, 1901, p. 93.

82. Ibid., p. 69.

83. Subcommittee on Preparental Education, White House Conference on

Child Health and Protection, *Education for Home and Family Life, Part I: In Elementary and Secondary Schools* (New York: Century, 1932), pp. 78–79.

84. Hunt, op. cit., p. 109.

85. Allie S. Freed (Chairman of the Committee for Economic Recovery), "Home Building by Private Enterprise," address to the Cambridge League of Women Voters, February 26, 1936.

86. United States Bureau of the Census, Statistical Abstract of the United States, 1973, Washington, D.C., 1973.

87. Heidi Irmgard Hartmann, "Capitalism and Women's Work in the Home 1900–1930," unpublished doctoral dissertation, Yale University, 1974 (available from University Microfilms, Ann Arbor), pp. 212–75.

88. Joann Vanek, "Time Spent in Housework," *Scientific American*, November 1974, p. 116.

89. Quoted in Reid, op. cit., pp. 89–90.

90. Christine Frederick, *Selling Mrs. Consumer* (New York: The Business Bourse, 1929), p. 169.

91. "Wonders Women Work in Marketing," *Sales Management*, October 2, 1959, p. 33.

92. See Lee Rainwater, Richard P. Coleman, and Gerald Handel, *Workingman's Wife* (New York: McFadden-Bartell, 1959).

NOTES TO CHAPTER SIX

1. Richard Hofstadter, *Anti-Intellectualism in American Life* (New York: Alfred A. Knopf, 1963), p. 364.

2. Arthur W. Calhoun, *Social History of the American Family, Volume III: Since the Civil War* (Cleveland: The Arthur H. Clark Co., 1919), p. 131.

3. Quoted in Michael Lesy, *Wisconsin Death Trip* (New York: Pantheon, 1973) (unpaginated).

4. See René Dubos, *The Mirage of Health* (New York: Harper, 1959); René Dubos, *Man Adapting* (New Haven: Yale University Press, 1965); Thomas McKeown, *Medicine in Modern Society* (London: Allen and Unwin, 1965); A. L. Cochrane, *Effectiveness and Efficiency: Random Reflections on Health Services* (London: Oxford University Press, 1972).

5. See Linda Gordon, *Woman's Body, Woman's Right: A Social History of Birth Control in America* (New York: Grossman, 1977).

6. William F. Ogburn and M. F. Nimkoff, *Technology and the Changing Family* (Boston and New York: Houghton Mifflin, 1955), p. 195.

7. John Spargo, *The Bitter Cry of the Children* (New York and London: Johnson Reprint Corp., 1969, first published 1906), p. 145.

8. Quoted in Spargo, op. cit., p. 179.

9. Sarah N. Cleghorn, quoted in "Child Labor," *Encyclopedia Americana*, Vol. 6 (New York: Americana Corp., 1974), p. 460.

10. Dr. W. N. Hailman, "Mission of Childhood," Proceedings of the National Congress of Mothers Second Annual Convention, May 1898, p. 171.

11. Ellen Key, *The Century of the Child* (New York: G. P. Putnam, 1909), pp. 100–1.

12. Theodore Roosevelt, Address to the First International Congress in Amer-

ica on the Welfare of the Child, under the auspices of the National Congress of Mothers, Washington, D.C., March 1908.

13. Lucy Wheelock, "The Right Education of Young Women," speech given at the First International Congress in America on the Welfare of the Child, Washington, D.C., March 1908.

14. Bernard Wishy, *The Child and the Republic: The Dawn of Modern American Child Nurture* (Philadelphia: University of Pennsylvania Press, 1968), p. 117.

15. Declaration of Principles, First International Congress in America on the Welfare of the Child, Washington, D.C., March 1908.

16. Mrs. Theodore W. Birney, "Address of Welcome," *The Work and Words of the National Congress of Mothers* (New York: D. Appleton, 1897), p. 7.

17. Dr. Alice Moqué, "The Mistakes of Mothers," Proceedings of the National Congress of Mothers Second Annual Convention, Washington, D.C., May 1898, p. 44.

18. Mrs. Theodore W. Birney, "Presidential Address," Proceedings of the Third Annual Convention of the National Congress of Mothers, Washington, D.C., February 1899, p. 198.

19. Julia Ward Howe, quoted in William L. O'Neill, *Everyone Was Brave: A History of Feminism in America* (New York: Quadrangle/The New York Times Book Co., 1974), p. 36.

20. Beatrice Forbes-Robertson Hale, *What Women Want: An Interpretation of the Feminist Movement* (New York: Frederick A. Stokes Co., 1914), p. 276.

21. Mrs. Harriet Hickox Heller, "Childhood, an Interpretation," Proceedings of the National Congress of Mothers Second Annual Convention, Washington, D.C., May 1898, p. 81.

22. Mrs. Theodore W. Birney, "Address of Welcome," Proceedings of the National Congress of Mothers Second Annual Convention, p. 17.

23. John Brisben Walker, "Motherhood as a Profession," *Cosmopolitan,* May 1898, p. 89.

24. Wishy, op. cit., p. 120.

25. Eli Zaretsky, *Capitalism, the Family and Personal Life* (New York: Harper Colophon Books, 1976), p. 31.

26. A. A. Roback, *History of American Psychology* (New York: Library Publishers, 1952), p. 129.

27. Quoted in Dorothy Ross, *G. Stanley Hall: The Psychologist as Prophet* (Chicago: University of Chicago Press, 1972), p. 177.

28. Edwin G. Boring, *A History of Experimental Psychology* (New York: Appleton-Century-Crofts, 1950), p. 569.

29. Geraldine J. Clifford, "E. L. Thorndike: The Psychologist as a Professional Man of Science," in Mary Henle, Julian Jaynes, and John J. Sullivan (eds.), *Historical Conceptions of Psychology* (New York: Springer Publishing Co., 1973), p. 242.

30. Mrs. Sallie S. Cotten, "A National Training School for Women," in *The Work and Words of the National Congress of Mothers* (New York: D. Appleton, 1897), p. 280.

31. G. Stanley Hall, "Some Practical Results of Child Study," in *The Work and Words of the National Congress of Mothers,* p. 165.

32. Arnold Gesell, M.D., "A Half Century of Science and the American Child," in *Child Study,* November 1938, p. 36.

33. Wishy, op. cit., p. 119.

34. Dr. L. Emmett Holt, "Physical Care of Children," in Proceedings of the Third Annual Convention of the National Congress of Mothers, Washington, D.C., February 1899, p. 233.

35. Winfield S. Hall, Ph.D., M.D., "The Nutrition of Children Under Seven Years," in *The Child in the City,* papers presented at the conference held during the Chicago Child Welfare Exhibit, 1911, published by the Chicago School of Civics and Philanthropy, 1912, pp. 81–82.

36. Mrs. Max West, "Infant Care," in Robert H. Bremner (ed.), *Children and Youth in America, A Documentary History, Volume II, 1866–1932* (Cambridge, Massachusetts: Harvard University Press, 1971), p. 37.

37. Winfield S. Hall, op. cit., p. 85.

38. Ellen Richards, *Euthenics: The Science of Controllable Environment* (Boston: Whitcomb and Barrows, 1912), pp. 82–83.

39. Christine Fredericks, "The New Housekeeping: How It Helps the Woman Who Does Her Own Work," *Ladies' Home Journal,* October 1912, p. 20.

40. Mrs. Helen H. Gardener, "The Moral Responsibility of Women in Heredity," in *The Work and Words of the National Congress of Mothers,* p. 143.

41. Heller, loc. cit.

42. Boring, op. cit., pp. 643–44.

43. John B. Watson, *Psychological Care of Infant and Child* (New York: W. W. Norton and Co., 1928), pp. 9–10.

44. Ibid., pp. 81–82.

45. Ibid., p. 82.

46. Ibid., pp. 5–6.

47. Ibid., p. 6.

48. Isabel F. Hyams, "The Louisa May Alcott Club," Proceedings of the Second Annual Lake Placid Conference on Home Economics, 1900, p. 18.

49. Lillian D. Wald, *The House on Henry Street* (New York: Dover Publications, 1971), p. 111.

50. The Laura Spelman Memorial Final Report, New York, 1933, pp. 10–11.

51. See Ruml's remarks in the transcript of the Conference of Psychologists called by the Laura Spelman Rockefeller Memorial, Hanover, New Hampshire, August 26–September 3, 1925 (mimeo).

52. Orville Brim, *Education for Child Raising* (New York: Russell Sage, 1959), p. 328.

53. Robert S. Lynd and Helen Merrill Lynd, *Middletown: A Study in Contemporary American Culture* (New York: Harcourt, Brace, 1929), p. 149.

54. Dorothy Canfield Fisher, "Introduction," in Sidonie Matsner Gruenberg (ed.), *Our Children Today: A Guide to their Needs from Infancy Through Adolescence* (New York: Viking, 1955), pp. xiii–xiv.

55. Quoted in Lynd and Lynd, op. cit., p. 146.

56. Ibid., p. 151.

NOTES TO CHAPTER SEVEN

1. Mary McCarthy, *The Group* (New York: Harcourt, Brace and World, 1954), p. 178.

2. Our thanks to Mary Bolton for telling us this story.

3. Lawrence K. Frank, "Life-Values for the Machine-Age," in Dorothy Canfield Fisher and Sidonie Matsner Gruenberg (eds.), *Our Children: A Handbook for Parents* (New York: Viking, 1932), p. 303.

4. Floyd Dell, *Love in the Machine Age* (New York: Octagon Books, 1973, first published, 1930), p. 107.

5. White House Conference on Child Health and Protection, *Report of the Subcommittee on Preparental Education* (New York: Century, 1932), p. 3.

6. Robert Lynd and Helen Merrill Lynd, *Middletown: A Study in Modern American Culture* (New York: Harcourt, Brace, 1929), p. 152.

7. Martha Wolfenstein, "Fun Morality: An Analysis of Recent American Child-training Literature," in Margaret Mead and Martha Wolfenstein (eds.), *Childhood in Contemporary Cultures* (Chicago: The University of Chicago Press, 1955), p. 169.

8. Ibid., p. 170.

9. Lynd and Lynd, op. cit., p. 147.

10. McCarthy, op. cit., p. 342.

11. Arnold Gesell and Frances L. Ilg, *Infant and Child in the Culture of Today* (New York and London: Harper, 1943), p. 162.

12. Frances L. Ilg and Louise Bates Ames, *Child Behavior* (New York: Harper & Row, 1951), p. 64.

13. Ibid., p. 27.

14. Ibid., p. 37.

15. Ibid., p. 346.

16. Ibid., pp. 343–44.

17. Ibid., p. 82.

18. Gesell and Ilg, op. cit., p. 56.

19. Benjamin Spock, M.D., *Problems of Parents* (Greenwich, Connecticut: Crest/Fawcett Publications, 1962, first published 1955), p. 237.

20. Gesell and Ilg, op. cit., p. 273.

21. E. James Anthony and Therese Benedek, M.D., *Parenthood: Its Psychology and Psychopathology* (Boston: Little, Brown, 1970), p. 179.

22. McCarthy, op. cit., p. 345.

23. Anthony and Benedek, op. cit., p. 173.

24. Dr. Theodore Lidz, quoted in Angela Barron McBride, *The Growth and Development of Mothers* (New York: Harper & Row, 1973), p. 5.

25. Marcel Heiman, M.D., "A Psychoanalytic View of Pregnancy," in Joseph J. Rovinsky, M.D., and Alan F. Guttmacher, M.D. (eds.), *Medical, Surgical and Gynecological Complications of Pregnancy* (second edition) (Baltimore: The Williams and Wilkins Co., 1965), pp. 480–81.

26. Spock, op. cit., p. 110.

27. D. W. Winnicott, M.D., *Mother and Child: A Primer of First Relationships* (New York: Basic Books, 1957), p. vii.

28. "Parents' Questions," *Child Study*, Spring 1952, pp. 37–38.

29. Jessie Bernard, *The Future of Motherhood* (New York: Penguin Books, 1974), p. 9.

30. René Spitz, *The First Year of Life: A Psychoanalytic Study of Normal and Deviant Development of Object Relations* (New York: International Universities Press, 1965), p. 206.

31. K. Jean Lennane, M.B., M.R.A.C.P. and R. John Lennane, M.B., "Alleged Psychogenic Disorders in Women—A Possible Manifestation of Sexual Prejudice," *The New England Journal of Medicine* 288, 1973, p. 288.

32. Anna Freud, "The Concept of the Rejecting Mother," in Anthony and Benedek, op. cit., p. 377.

33. Adrienne Rich, *Of Woman Born: Motherhood as Experience and Institution* (New York: W. W. Norton, 1976), p. 277.

34. John Bowlby, *Maternal Care and Mental Health* (New York: Schocken Books, 1966, first published 1951), p. 22.

35. Ibid., p. 73.

36. Ibid., p. 67.

37. Ibid., p. 157.

38. Mary D. Ainsworth et al., *Deprivation of Maternal Care: A Reassessment of Its Effects* (New York: Schocken Books, 1966), p. 206.

39. Dr. David Goodman, *A Parents' Guide to the Emotional Needs of Children* (New York: Hawthorne Books, 1959), p. 25.

40. David M. Levy, M.D., *Maternal Overprotection* (New York: W. W. Norton, 1966, first published 1943), p. 213.

41. Ibid., p. 150.

42. Ibid., pp. 242–351.

43. Quoted in Betty Friedan, *The Feminine Mystique* (New York: W. W. Norton, 1963), p. 191.

44. Margaret Mead, *Blackberry Winter: My Earlier Years* (New York: Pocket Books, 1975), p. 275.

45. Joseph Rheingold, M.D., Ph.D., *The Fear of Being a Woman: A Theory of Maternal Destructiveness* (New York, London: Grune and Stratton, 1964), p. 143.

46. Dr. Edward Strecker, quoted in Friedan, op. cit., p. 191.

47. Friedan, op. cit., p. 189.

48. Ferdinand Lundberg and Marynia Farnham, "Some Aspects of Women's Psyche," in Elaine Showalter (ed.), *Women's Liberation and Literature* (New York: Harcourt Brace Jovanovich, 1971), pp. 233–48.

49. Goodman, op. cit., pp. 51–52.

50. Philip Wylie, *Generation of Vipers* (New York: Holt, Rinehart and Winston, 1955), p. 198.

51. Erik Erikson, *Childhood and Society* (New York: W. W. Norton and Co., 1950), p. 291.

52. William Whyte, *The Organization Man* (New York: Simon and Schuster, 1956), pp. 3–4.

53. David Riesman, *The Lonely Crowd* (New Haven: Yale University Press, 1961, first published 1950), p. 18.

54. Alan Harrington, "Life in the Crystal Palace," in Eric Josephson and

Mary Josephson (eds.), *Man Alone: Alienation and Modern Society* (New York: Dell Publishing Co., 1962), pp. 136–37.

55. Paul Goodman, *Growing Up Absurd* (New York: Vintage Books, 1956), p. 13.

56. Lundberg and Farnham, op. cit., p. 244.

57. Levy, op. cit., p. 214.

58. Quoted in Peter Gabriel Filene, *Him/Her Self: Sex Roles in Modern America* (New York: Mentor/New American Library, 1974), p. 179.

59. Levy, op. cit., p. 121.

60. Dr. David Goodman, op. cit., p. 55.

61. Ibid., p. 33.

62. Ibid., p. 34.

63. Ibid., p. 64.

64. McCarthy, op. cit., p. 224.

65. Goodman, op. cit., p. 35.

66. Quoted in Diana Scully and Pauline Bart, "A Funny Thing Happened on the Way to the Orifice: Women in Gynecology Textbooks," *American Journal of Sociology* 78, January, 1973, p. 1045.

67. Henry B. Biller, *Father, Child and Sex Role* (Lexington, Massachusetts: D. C. Heath, 1971), p. 45.

68. Goodman, op. cit., p. 56.

69. Lundberg and Farnham, op. cit., p. 238.

70. Biller, op. cit., p. 24.

71. Biller, loc. cit.

72. Jules Henry, *Culture Against Man* (New York: Vintage Books, 1963), p. 140.

73. Biller, op. cit., p. 107.

74. Benjamin Spock, M.D., *Baby and Child Care* (New York: Cardinal/Pocket Books, 1957), p. 315.

75. Spock, *Problems of Parents,* p. 192.

76. T. Colley, quoted in Biller, op. cit., p. 97.

77. Spock, *Problems of Parents,* p. 194.

78. Ibid., pp. 187–89.

79. J. Edgar Hoover, *Masters of Deceit: The Story of Communism in America and How to Fight It* (New York: Cardinal/Pocket Books, 1958), p. vi.

80. Eugene Kinkead, *Every War But One* (New York: W. W. Norton and Co., 1959), p. 18.

81. Harrison Salisbury, *The Shook-Up Generation* (Greenwich, Connecticut: Fawcett Publications, 1958), p. 8.

82. Spock, *Problems of Parents,* p. 235.

83. Spock, op. cit., p. 244.

84. Ethel Kawin, *Parenthood in a Free Nation.* Vol. I: *Basic Concepts for Parents* (New York: Macmillan, 1967, first published 1954), p. v.

85. Barbara Ward, "A Crusading Faith to Counter Communism," New York *Times Magazine,* July 16, 1950.

86. Hoover, op. cit., pp. 313–14.

87. Spock, *Problems of Parents,* pp. 245–46.

88. Kawin, op. cit., p. 104.

89. Ibid., p. 105.

90. Willis Rudy, *Schools in an Age of Mass Culture* (Englewood, New Jersey: Prentice-Hall, 1965), p. 175.

91. Quoted in Rudy, loc. cit.

92. Quoted in Eda Le Shan, *The Conspiracy Against Childhood* (New York: Atheneum, 1967), p. 104.

93. Ibid., p. 105.

94. Albert D. Biderman, *March to Calumny* (New York: Macmillan, 1963), pp. 2–3.

95. Rudy, op. cit., p. 131.

96. Lewis Feuer, quoted in the New York *Times,* February 14, 1969, p. 24.

97. The New York *Times,* September 29, 1968, p. 74.

98. The New York *Times,* October 13, 1968, p. 79.

99. The New York *Times,* November 8, 1968, p. 54.

100. The New York *Times,* May 28, 1968, p. 46.

101. The New York *Times,* November 8, 1968, p. 54.

102. Fred Brown, quoted in the New York *Times,* May 12, 1968, p. 52.

103. U. S. Education Commissioner Harold Howe, 2nd, in the New York *Times,* May 24, 1968, p. 51.

104. Samuel Kausner, quoted in the New York *Times,* July 29, 1969, p. 40.

105. The New York *Times,* March 21, 1969, p. 3.

106. Bruno Bettelheim, "Children Must Learn to Fear," the New York *Times Magazine,* April 13, 1969, p. 125.

107. Berthold Schwarz, M.D., and Bartholomew Ruggieri, *You CAN Raise Decent Children* (New Rochelle, New York: Arlington House, 1971).

NOTES TO CHAPTER EIGHT

1. Helene Deutsch, *The Psychology of Women.* Vol. II, *Motherhood* (New York: Bantam Books, 1973), p. 321.

2. Deutsch, loc. cit.

3. Ibid., pp. 308–48.

4. Helen Dudar, "Female—and Freudian," the New York *Post,* July 14, 1973.

5. Ferdinand Lundberg and Marynia Farnham, "Some Aspects of Woman's Psyche," in Elaine Showalter (ed.), *Women's Liberation and Literature* (New York: Harcourt Brace Jovanovich, 1971), p. 245.

6. Marie Bonaparte, "Passivity, Masochism and Femininity," in Jean Strouse (ed.), *Women and Analysis* (New York: Laurel Editions, 1975), p. 286.

7. Ibid., p. 284.

8. Marie Bonaparte, *Female Sexuality* (New York: International Universities Press, 1973), p. 48.

9. Helene Deutsch, "The Psychology of Women in Relation to the Functions of Reproduction," in Jean Strouse (ed.), *Women and Analysis* (New York: Laurel Editions, 1975), p. 180.

10. Hendrik M. Ruitenbeek, M.D., *Psychoanalysis and Female Sexuality* (New Haven: College and University Press, 1966), p. 11.

11. Ibid., p. 17.

12. Ibid., p. 14.

13. Howard J. Osofsky, M.D., "Women's Reactions to Pelvic Examinations," *Obstetrics and Gynecology,* 30 (1967), p. 146.

14. Osofsky, loc. cit.

15. Therese Benedek, M.D., "Infertility as a Psychosomatic Disease," *Fertility and Sterility,* 3 (1952), p. 527.

16. Somers H. Sturgis and Doris Menzer-Benaron, *The Gynecological Patient: A Psycho-Endocrine Study* (New York: Grune and Stratton, 1962), p. xiv.

17. See Osofsky, op. cit., and Sturgis and Menzer-Benaron, op. cit.

18. Dr. David Goodman, *A Parents' Guide to the Emotional Needs of Children* (New York: Hawthorne Books, 1959), p. 51.

19. Stuart S. Asch, M.D., "Psychiatric Complications: Mental and Emotional Problems," in Joseph J. Rovinsky and Alan F. Guttmacher (eds.), *Medical, Surgical and Gynecological Complications of Pregnancy,* 2nd edition (Baltimore: Williams and Wilkins Co., 1965), pp. 461–62.

20. Marcel Heiman, M.D., "Psychiatric Complications: A Psychoanalytic View of Pregnancy," in Rovinsky and Guttmacher, op. cit., p. 476.

21. Heiman, op. cit., p. 481.

22. Asch, op. cit., pp. 463–64.

23. Louise H. Warwick, R.N., M.S., "Femininity, Sexuality and Mothering," *Nursing Forum* 8 (1969), p. 216.

24. Sturgis and Menzer-Benaron, op. cit., p. 237.

25. Ibid., p. 238.

26. Robert Stein (ed.), *Why Young Mothers Feel Trapped* (New York: Trident Press, 1965).

27. Jean Kerr, *Please Don't Eat the Daisies* (Garden City, New York: Doubleday, 1957), p. 21.

28. Carol Bartholomew, *Most of Us Are Mainly Mothers* (New York: Macmillan, 1966), p. 203.

29. Gabrielle Burton, *I'm Running Away from Home, But I'm Not Allowed to Cross the Street* (New York: Avon Books, 1972), pp. 22–25.

30. Daniel Zwerdling, "Pills, Profits, People's Problems," *Progressive,* October 1973, p. 46. Also Linda Fidell, "Put Her Down on Drugs," available from KNOW, Inc., Box 86031, Pittsburgh, Pa., 15221.

31. Quoted in Shirley Radl, *Mother's Day Is Over* (New York: Charterhouse, 1973), p. 86.

32. Betty Friedan, *The Feminine Mystique* (New York, W. W. Norton, 1963), p. 22.

33. John Keats, *The Crack in the Picture Window* (Boston: Houghton Mifflin, 1956).

34. "Shaping the '60's . . . Foreshadowing the '70's," *Ladies' Home Journal,* January 1962, p. 30.

35. "The Ladies . . . Bless Their Little Incomes," *Sales Management,* July 16, 1965, p. 46.

36. Helen Gurley Brown, *Sex and the Single Girl* (New York: Giant Cardinal Edition, Pocket Books, 1963), pp. 7–8.

37. Brown, op. cit., p. 4.

38. Brown, op. cit., p. 3.
39. The New York *Times*, January 19, 1977.
40. The New York *Times*, October 24, 1975.
41. The New York *Times Magazine*, June 5, 1977, p. 85.
42. Quoted in Walter McQuade, "Why People Don't Buy Houses," *Fortune*, December, 1967, p. 153.
43. U. S. Bureau of the Census, Statistical Abstract of the United States 1975 (96th edition), Washington, D.C., 1975, p. 67.
44. "One Divorce—Two Houses," the New York *Times*, January 16, 1977.
45. Quoted in Ellen Peck and Judith Senderowitz, *Pronatalism: The Myth of Mom and Apple Pie* (New York: Crowell, 1974), p. 270.
46. Quoted in Peck and Senderowitz, op. cit., p. 266.
47. Nancy and Chip McGrath, "Why Have a Baby?" the New York *Times Magazine*, May 25, 1975, p. 10.
48. Quoted in Linda Wolfe, "The Coming Baby Boom," *New York* magazine, January 1, 1977, p. 38.
49. Dr. Robert Gould, quoted in Judy Klemesrud, "The State of Being Childless, They Say, Is No Cause for Guilt," the New York *Times*, February 3, 1975, p. 28.
50. Jean Baer, *How to Be an Assertive (Not Aggressive) Woman*, (New York: New American Library, 1976).
51. Dr. Joyce Brothers, *The Brothers' System for Liberated Love and Marriage* (New York: Avon Books, 1972), p. 190.
52. Emily Coleman, *How to Make Friends with the Opposite Sex* (Los Angeles: Nash, 1972), p. xii.
53. William C. Schutz, *Joy: Expanding Human Awareness* (New York: Grove Press, 1967), p. 15.
54. Ibid., p. 10.
55. Ibid., p. 12.
56. Joel Kovel, M.D., *A Complete Guide to Therapy: From Psychoanalysis to Behavior Modification* (New York: Pantheon Books, 1976), p. 166.
57. Schutz, op. cit., p. 223.
58. Thomas A. Harris, M.D., *I'm O.K.—You're O.K.* (New York: Avon Books, 1967), p. 14.
59. Jean Baer, op. cit., p. 12.
60. Dr. Jerry Greenwald, *Be the Person You Were Meant to Be* (New York: Dell, 1973), p. 19.
61. Howard M. Newberger, Ph.D. and Marjorie Lee, *Winners and Losers: The Art of Self-Image Modification* (New York: David McKay, 1974), p. 25.
62. Greenwald, op. cit., p. 26.
63. Fritz Perls, M.D., Ph.D., and John O. Stevens, *Gestalt Therapy Verbatim* (Lafayette, California: Real People Press, 1969), p. 4.
64. Robert J. Ringer, *Winning Through Intimidation* (Los Angeles: Los Angeles Book Publishers, 1974), p. 96.
65. Baer, op. cit., p. 208.
66. Newberger and Lee, op. cit., p. 192.
67. Ibid., p. xiv.
68. Greenwald, op. cit., p. 10.

69. Mildred Newman and Bernard Berkowitz with Jean Owen, *How to Be Your Own Best Friend* (New York: Ballantine Books, 1971), p. 74.

70. Ibid., p. 88.

71. Lynn Z. Bloom, Karen Coburn, and Joan Pearlman, *The New Assertive Woman* (New York: Dell, 1976), p. 11.

72. Brothers, op. cit., p. 136.

73. Bloom et al., op. cit., pp. 24–25.

74. Quoted in Elayn Bernay, "Growing Up to Be Chairperson of the Board," *Ms.*, June 1977, p. 80.

75. Bloom et al., op. cit., pp. 16–17.

76. Baer, op. cit., p. 173.

77. Newman, Berkowitz, and Owen, op. cit., p. 34.

78. Newberger and Lee, op. cit., p. 198.

Index